Apron Strings

Also by Jan Wong

Red China Blues: My Long March from Mao to Now

Jan Wong's China: Reports from a Not-So-Foreign Correspondent

Lunch with Jan Wong: Sweet and Sour Celebrity Interviews

Beijing Confidential: A Tale of Comrades Lost and Found

Out of the Blue: A Memoir of Workplace Depression, Recovery, Redemption and, Yes, Happiness

Apron Strings

Navigating Food and Family in France, Italy, and China

JAN WONG

GOOSE LANE

Edited by Jill Ainsley.
Cover and page design by Jaye Haworth and Julie Scriver.
Printed in Canada.
10 9 8 7 6 5 4 3 2 1

Library and Archives Canada Cataloguing in Publication

Wong, Jan, author
Apron strings : navigating food and family in France,
Italy, and China / Jan Wong.

Includes index.
Issued in print and electronic formats.
ISBN 978-0-86492-961-7 (softcover).--ISBN 978-0-86492-950-1 (EPUB).--
ISBN 978-0-86492-951-8 (Kindle)

1. Wong, Jan--Travel. 2. Food--Social aspects. 3. International cooking.
4. Globalization. 5. Families. I. Title.

GT2850.W66 2017   394.1'2   C2017-902815-4
                                          C2017-902816-2

We acknowledge the generous support of the Government of Canada,
the Canada Council for the Arts, and the Government of New Brunswick.

Goose Lane Editions
500 Beaverbrook Court, Suite 330
Fredericton, New Brunswick
CANADA E3B 5X4

www.gooselane.com

For Sam

Contents

CHINA

A Note on Names

I have used the standard Pinyin system for spelling Chinese names, occasionally including the characters should you want to buy the ingredients. All names in France and Italy are real. In China, I changed many personal names or rendered them in poetic translation to avoid unwanted scrutiny from Chinese authorities. In some cases, I also altered minor identifying details, such as where someone attended university. In all three countries, all the events happened as described. All the quotations are real. None of the characters are composites.

Principal Characters

IN ALLEX, FRANCE

Marie-Catherine Jeanselme, 62, retired nurse
François Jeanselme, 68, her husband, retired headmaster
Pierre-Marie, 24, their son
Philomène, 21, their daughter
Mamie, 93, Marie-Catherine's mother
Bernadette Seguin, 67, their housekeeper
The Georgian refugees
  Rüska, 25
  Davit, 28, her husband
  Andrie, 20 months, their son
  Kéti, their newborn daughter

IN REPERGO, ITALY

Maria Rosa Beccaris, 48, nurse
Fiorenzo Cavagnino, 57, her husband, highway authority employee
Chiara, 17, their daughter
Nonno, 80, Maria Rosa's father, Guiseppe
Papa Franco Cavagnino, 86, Fiorenzo's father (in Montegrosso)
Mirella Massasso, 48, Maria Rosa's cousin, vineyard owner
Beppe Massasso, 57, her husband, vineyard owner
Alessandro, 29, their older son
Luigina, 78, Mirella's mother

Rocca d'Arazzo (fifteen kilometres away)
  Federica Battilla, 46, nurse
  Luigi Campini, 47, her husband, town hall messenger/handyman
  Eleonora, 14, their daughter
  Maria, 81, her mother

Asti (thirteen kilometres away)
    Antonella Bossotto, 59, hospital secretary
    Luigi Epifani, 64, her husband, manager of radiology department
    Matteo, 30, their younger son
    Beatrice, 3, their granddaughter

    Maria Stella Puddu, 57, hospital accountant
    Bruno Colaianni, 59, her husband, owner of autobody shop
    Cristina, 18, their daughter
    Matteo, 28, their son
    Giulia, 27, his partner
    Maria Lucia, 58, Giulia's mother, vineyard owner
    Beppe, 61, Giulia's father, vineyard owner

IN SHANGHAI, CHINA

First home
    Hilly, 47, housewife
    Allan, 47, her husband, executive for a foreign manufacturer
    Dickie, 12, their son
    Peace, 37, their live-in maid

Second home
    Anthea, 51, housewife
    Joy, 12, her daughter
    Orchid, 47, her live-in maid

Third home
    Peony, 49, businesswoman
    Paul, 50, her British husband, executive for a British company
    Suzy, 9, their daughter
    Pete, 11, their son
    Little Chen, 32, their live-out maid

Fourth home
    Plum, 47, housewife
    Building-the-Army, 48, her husband, CEO of firm managing foreign
        country's real estate holdings
    Amanda, 18, their daughter
    Fred, 13, their son
    Little Wang, 45, their live-out maid

"Stay With Us"

I couldn't believe my luck. As the sleek Eurostar train slid out of London's St. Pancras station on an overcast winter morning, I regarded my son with wonder. Somehow, I had managed to convince Sam, twenty-two, to join me on a journey to learn home cooking with complete strangers in my three favourite foodie countries—France, Italy, and China.

At first, my younger son had hesitated. "Um," he said, that summer when I first broached the idea, his face scruffy with honey-coloured day-old stubble, eyelids drooping with fatigue. He was in our kitchen in Toronto, gulping a glass of orange juice before he bicycled off to his job making salads and deep-frying mini-doughnuts at a neighbourhood BBQ joint. The endless hours with me were a concern. Would we get along? Would we have to live in the same room? Worse, would we have to share a bed?

After he left for work, I pondered the "um." It wasn't a *flat* rejection. But his body language had not been encouraging—shoulders hunched, eyes darting sideways, knees jiggling in that annoying way guys do when they feel trapped.

I am a journalist turned journalism professor. After I covered a school shooting in Quebec in 2006, hate mail inundated me. At the office, I received a package containing my books sawn in half with a power tool. Someone sent excrement. I received an all-caps death threat. The prime minister of Canada criticized me, and so did the premier of Quebec. My newspaper threw me under the bus, and I sank into a clinical depression that lasted two years. While I was sick, my newspaper ordered me back to work and then fired me. After I regained my health, I couldn't bear the thought of an editor assigning me to another school shooting. I took a job teaching journalism at a small liberal arts university in the Maritimes, dividing my time between Fredericton and Toronto, where my husband, Norman, lived and worked.

The colleagues I left behind in the trenches were initially pitying, then curious, and finally envious.

What? You teach three classes a week?

Me: Sometimes two.

What? You get sabbaticals?

Me: Yup.

My first six-month sabbatical bestowed that biggest luxury of all for a journalist — time. Then my literary agent phoned. We hadn't spoken in some time. Any books in the works, he asked. Nah, I told him. But the moment I hung up, a glimmer of an idea popped into my head. Food. Travel. Maybe Sam?

I've always been a foodie. I'm the granddaughter and daughter of restaurateurs. In the 1930s, my maternal grandmother ran a Western-style restaurant in the small Ontario town of Woodstock. My father's flagship restaurant, Bill Wong's, was a Montreal landmark. Dad had opened the first Chinese restaurant outside the safe confines of Chinatown in what was then Canada's largest city. My Montreal-born father, an engineer by profession, couldn't cook to save his life — we had to hide the good pots from him so he wouldn't scorch them. But he was a savvy businessman who hired the best Chinese chef he could find from our ancestral village back in China and, crucially, made him a partner. Dad eventually opened five restaurants and made his first million before he was forty.

It seems quaint now, but his innovations included take-out menus and free delivery. His biggest culinary creation, however, was Montreal's — and perhaps the world's — first all-you-can-eat Chinese buffet, which he launched in the mid-sixties after dining at an all-you-can-eat roast beef restaurant in Toronto. When he proposed the concept to his four partners, they predicted Bill Wong's would go bankrupt. Dad prevailed. In addition to dozens of Chinese dishes, he served salads and, yes, roast beef. He scorned fortune cookies, which aren't even Chinese, and hired a French pastry chef to make strawberry tarts and Black Forest cake with real whipped cream. Lineups stretched out the door. Now you can find Chinese buffets everywhere from Helsinki to Beijing.

Unlike Dad, I loved to eat *and* cook. I enjoyed reading cookbooks. My idea of relaxing was inviting a couple of friends for dinner. I had a memory not for names or numbers but for meals, flavours, and ingredients. Starting back in 1972 when I was nineteen, I also became interested in the impact of politics and economics on food cultures. That year I became the first Canadian, and one of only two Westerners, to study at Peking University since the start of the Great Proletarian Cultural Revolution.

Our campus mess hall was a dimly lit, minimally heated warehouse-like structure of concrete floors and whitewashed walls. We students sat on sawhorse-style benches, hunched over bowls of shockingly execrable food. Meat was rationed. If we got any at all, it was a tiny piece of pork fat the size of a postage stamp, with skin and *hair* still attached. Rice, also rationed, was greyish, with broken grains. I learned to chew carefully to avoid chipping a tooth on bits of gravel. Those were the good meals. The bad meals consisted of *bangzi mian zhou* (cornmeal gruel) or baseball-sized lumps of unseasoned steamed cornmeal called *wotou*.

I remember, however, my aunt in the nearby city of Tianjin making me crisp spring rolls with her rationed cooking oil. I also remember the fiery kung pao chicken with crunchy peanuts at the Long March Restaurant across from campus. When I dropped a brick on my foot and broke a toe during the students' weekly stint of mandatory physical labour, Norman thoughtfully brought me dinner from the Long March (in an aluminum container; this was before China had Chinese take-out). My future husband, the only American draft dodger in China, couldn't cook, but he figured the way to a woman's heart—mine, at least—was through her stomach. He was right. Women's brains are "significantly more responsive to romantic [pictures] after a meal than prior to it," according to a neuroimaging study published in the journal *Appetite*. "Across cultures, food and romantic reward are closely intertwined."

For the record, Norman and I have been married for more than forty years.

After studying in China for most of the 1970s, I became a business reporter. In 1988, I became the Beijing bureau chief for a Canadian newspaper, in time to cover the 1989 massacre at Tiananmen Square. During my six years as a foreign correspondent, I travelled—and ate—in all twenty-three of China's provinces and five autonomous regions, including Xinjiang, Inner Mongolia, and Tibet. I even persuaded an editor to let me write a magazine piece about enrolling as the first student at a new cooking institute in Sichuan province. Impossible as it seems now, newspapers were so flush back then that one of my perks was a personal chef. Chef Mu's Chinese food was too salty and too oily. However, he had been trained by the French embassy and could make spinach soufflés, medium-rare filet mignon, and *tarte au citron*. A Chinese chef cooking French food was a harbinger of the globalization to come.

I pondered what shape the book should take and how to research it. I spoke French and Mandarin. I told myself I could take a crash course in Italian at my university (for free!). I considered cooking schools but quickly discarded the idea. The *cuisine* program at Cordon Bleu in Paris took nine months and cost $42,000. In contrast, in Tuscany, many courses lasted only four or five days, and seemed designed and priced for rich American tourists.

I wanted to learn *home* cooking. I wanted to know how ordinary folks made dinner, whether in this time-starved world they were still sitting down to dinner with their families. I wanted to know how the politics and economics of globalization had affected what they ate. Unlike cooking schools, you can't Google "ordinary family" and find someone who loves home cooking and is willing to take in a total stranger. So, like journalists everywhere, I worked my contacts. A Chinese friend, Hilly, who lived in Shanghai, said she could set me up with rich friends and I could cook with their maids. Ashley, a British friend who owned a country home in Italy, recommended his neighbour. That left France, where my only contact had inconveniently decamped for Washington, DC.

In the meantime, I focused on other logistics. This was going to be a long road trip. Norman couldn't abandon his job as a software developer, and, as I've said, he can't cook. I hoped Sam would be my companion. He was fluent in French. He had a working knowledge of Mandarin after spending his third year of university in Taiwan. More important, he was a fervent foodie. He didn't read cookbooks — that was *so* twentieth century — but he was addicted to YouTube cooking videos.

As a toddler, he liked hanging around the kitchen. As soon as he and his older brother, Ben, were out of strollers, Norman and I would take them on family trips to France and Italy, where the biggest tourist attraction was usually lunch. Aside from a summer job as a groundskeeper at a botanical garden, Sam had always worked in restaurants, from a hole-in-the-wall café to a French bistro to a private golf club, even in remote firefighting camps in northern Alberta. He could carve roasts, prep salads, slow-cook ribs, and make pizza. He could whip up a vat of asparagus risotto for a hundred wedding guests. He loved the rhythm of a professional kitchen, the pressure of incoming orders, the relief when the meal service ended without disaster. Now he was graduating from university with a degree in philosophy, quite sure he never wanted to spend another day in a classroom. Like so many millennials, he was moving home while he figured out his next step. Unlike so many millennials, who felt entitled to a well-paying, stress-free job, Sam wanted a low-paying, high-stress job. He wanted to be a cook.

To be honest, the real reason for the whole project, the cooking and the travelling, was so I could spend more time with Sam. When he was a toddler, he would literally jump for joy when I got home from work. As I watched him grow into an independent adult, I sensed our mother-son bond evolving, stretching, even thinning out. Each summer when he came home from university, I noticed he spent less and less time with me. He was currently unattached, without a job or romantic partner. Who knew how long that would last? Perhaps I was overwrought, but it seemed possible that this trip might be my last chance to cook with Sam, to ride next to him on planes, trains, and automobiles, to eat 267 consecutive meals together. The last time we travelled together, just the two of us, he was thirteen and his hockey team was playing in Finland and Sweden. I was clinically depressed. Let's just say it wasn't a dream vacation.

Sam's initial lack of enthusiasm for my latest proposal might have been grounded in that Scandinavian trip — or in his childhood memories of helping me report stories. For instance, I was assigned to write about an extramarital affair the premier of Ontario was having with a neighbour. Now, neither my newspaper nor I cared much about politicians' sex lives, but this particular one had refused to march in that year's Gay Pride parade in Toronto. He declared that his definition of marriage was between a man and a woman. A man and *two* women in his own marriage was news.

Sam was only six, but he had a child's sense of fairness and justice and understood the story's essence: cheating, and being mean to gays. I figured he could provide cover while I lurked in a suburban cul-de-sac to observe the houses of the premier and his paramour. A few months earlier, Sam had proudly shed his training wheels, but he agreed to pretend he was still learning to ride a bike. As he faked fall after fall, I got the details I needed for the story. Once I called the premier's office for comment, he issued a press release announcing he was separating from his wife of twenty-five years.

In 2003, when Sam was ten, SARS hit Toronto. I was officially quarantined after spending time in one of the infected hospitals while searching for the first patients, and my editor asked me to write a public-service column about what someone quarantined with kids and a partner should do: stop eating together; use separate bathrooms and bedrooms; wear a mask at all times. "Does this mean we don't have to go to school?" Ben, then thirteen, asked hopefully. When he saw me writing down his quote, he yelped, "That's off the record." (Some journalists have a self-imposed rule about not writing about their children. But, as Nora Ephron famously said, "Everything is copy." Of course, *she* avoided writing about her kids.)

When Sam was twelve, I was assigned to write about a minuscule hike in the provincial minimum wage. I decided the most vivid way to describe the thirty-cent hourly raise was to work undercover for a month as an agency maid and replicate the life of a single mother with two kids living below the poverty line. While Norman stayed happily at home, I persuaded Ben and Sam to move into a dingy basement apartment. I believe I billed it as a once-in-a-lifetime experience. My boys say I didn't give them a choice. Ben, then fifteen, refused to share a room with either Sam or me, relegating us to the double bed in the only other room. My editor asked each boy to write a first-person piece to accompany the series. In his, Sam told readers he was unused to having his own bed, anyway—a year earlier I had given his bunk bed away to a family of needy immigrants and hadn't gotten around to buying him a new bed. Although I stretched our food budget with beans and pasta, we were chronically hungry. When a parent at Ben's private school heard that he was living in a basement apartment, he opened the trunk of his Mercedes-Benz to offer some canned food.

Given this history, it's easy to understand why Sam hesitated to sign on for this trip. He agreed only after various friends, including our next-door neighbour, told him he was crazy to turn it down. Norman promised to visit us twice, in Bologna after we finished our Italy segment, and later in China after we left Shanghai.

Then something shocking happened. At least, it shocked me, and it accentuated how little time I might have left with Sam. While the book was still in the planning stage, Ben phoned to say he was thinking of getting married.

"To who?" I blurted, so shocked I momentarily misplaced my grammar.

Ben paused. He said he wanted to marry his girlfriend, Puck, a Dutch mathematician at the University of California, Los Angeles. I'd met her. She was very nice, very smart, and very beautiful, but I'd had no inkling she was the One. In fact, I had no idea Ben was even ready for the One. I stammered something about not rushing into anything. I asked, *What about the children?* Mixed marriages worried me. No, not *that* kind. His beloved is a gluten-intolerant vegan, and I am a vegan-intolerant omnivore. Ben said they weren't planning an absolute prohibition on meat for their offspring, at least, not *outside* the home.

If I'm honest with myself, the problem wasn't meatlessness; I was psychologically unprepared for mother-in-lawhood. What goes around, comes around. Forty years earlier, when I told *my* parents I was marrying a white guy from New York, *they* jumped on a plane to Beijing to try to stop me, asking, *What about the children?*

To calm down, I reminded myself that my goal as a mother had been to guide Ben into adulthood without him turning into a serial killer. He was twenty-five, a year older than I was when I married. And, as a fully funded doctoral student at UCLA, he was financially independent. I should be happy. But have I mentioned she's a *vegan?*

One day later, Ben phoned back. He informed me, nicely, that he had made up his mind. I did a pivot. I told him Norman and I would fly five thousand kilometres to be there, and when was the date? He replied that he and Puck were only signing paperwork. I told Ben I *loved* watching people sign paperwork. Then he told me he didn't want us showing up. Puck's mother couldn't make it from the Netherlands, and my presence would remind Puck of her own mother's absence, and she would feel sad. *Her? Sad? What about me?* In an instant, I realized I had just lost my ranking as Number One Female in the Life of My First-Born Son. Second place was a distant spot, somewhere so remote, so far back in the boonies that I barely registered on Ben's radar.

Of course, I *know* the definition of a healthy mother-son relationship is one in which the son goes on to a happy, productive life — and puts his romantic partner first. As the second-century satirical poet Juvenal wrote, "Domestic accord is impossible as long as the mother-in-law lives." I wasn't ready to volunteer for the ice floes, and certainly, no one wants a mama's boy. But what about the *mama?*

I was shocked by how bereft I felt. I had not anticipated being unceremoniously relegated to the sidelines. Who was to say Sam wouldn't meet someone tomorrow and tell me I wasn't invited to his paperwork? To unburden myself, I called him. Would *he* promise to invite me?

"Oops," he said. "I forgot to tell you — I got married last week."

That cheered me. In no time at all, Ben and Puck did the deed, dashing to Beverly Hills City Hall between lectures. Nora, their lovely and generous landlady, was official witness, photographer, and sole invitee. Norman was fine with that, but I found it very hard to be supplanted by a landlady.

Over the Christmas holidays, the newlyweds flew to Toronto for a celebratory dinner to which Ben restricted invitations to six guests (besides my sister's family, Norman, Sam, and me). Out of solidarity with his bride, the groom ordered a vegan meal, but I hardly noticed because I was fretting about my impending trip. I still hadn't found a family in France, and my sabbatical was about to start. Staring at Ben across the banquet table, inspiration flashed. Five years earlier, while studying in France at Université Lumière Lyon 2, he had stayed with a French family for one term. Maybe they would know someone who might teach cooking to Sam and me.

Ben was reluctant to impose, but I shamelessly leveraged my still-bruised feelings over paperwork deprivation. Ben then said he had been out of touch. He'd heard they'd left Lyon. He had no idea where they were. Well, thank goodness for Facebook. A day later, he'd found their email. As I lurked behind him, he wrote the Jeanselmes a polite, formal note in French explaining the book project and asking for their help in finding a family.

Forty minutes later, a reply arrived.

"*Cher Ben, Quelle belle surprise!*" Madame Jeanselme emailed back. She said she had retired from her nursing job and the family had moved from Lyon to southeast France. She was busy taking care of their two handicapped children and her bedridden ninety-three-year-old mother. Her husband had retired as headmaster of the *lycée* and was helping to rescue refugees from the Middle East.

"*Quant à ta maman et ton frère, soit avec nous, soit avec une famille qu'on trouvera, le projet est tout à fait realisable ... et sans chercher un hôtel.*"

And then she added the magic words: "*Ils pourront loger chez nous.*"

They can stay with us.

France

CHAPTER ONE

Allex

As we hurtled at two hundred kilometres an hour toward France, the clogged streets of London receded in a blur. Soon the wintry golden fields of southeastern England lapped at our windows. In no time, *le Train à Grande Vitesse,* the TGV, reached the Chunnel. Our destination was the tiny village of Allex (pop. 2,400), nearly six hundred kilometres southeast of Paris. As we wouldn't arrive at the family's home until the evening, I told Madame Jeanselme not to worry about our dinner. At St. Pancras station, we raided the Marks & Spencer gourmet store and bought crudités, prawns and avocado on whole wheat, chunky chicken salad on white bread, and five desserts: fresh fruit wedges, sherry trifle, *panna cotta* with raspberry sauce, rhubarb yogourt, and Victorian sponge cake. Just in case that wasn't enough, we had three hard-boiled eggs saved from our hotel breakfast buffet.

Other passengers ogled, first our picnic, and then us. My son and I don't look remotely related. Ben, who is slim and slight, with olive skin and dark brown wavy hair, at least seems half Asian. Sam looks like a standard-issue white guy, his genes apparently hijacked by Norman, a Jewish New Yorker with roots in czarist Russia. Sam has an aquiline nose, needle-straight chestnut brown hair, and eyebrows so thick they are practically a unibrow. When he was a toddler, other mothers at the sandbox often assumed I was his nanny. I joked he was adopted—someone had to redress the demographic imbalance of all those adopted Chinese girls. (Sam strenuously objects to this description. His eyebrows may be thick, he says, but they do not meet in the middle.)

After changing trains at Lille, it was pitch-black when we pulled into Valence, the closest TGV station to Allex. François Jeanselme was waiting for us on the brightly lit platform. At sixty-eight, he was a scholarly, balding man with black beetle brows and a warm smile. He embraced us and, in the Gallic manner, kissed us on both cheeks. We threw our bags into the trunk and piled into his ancient white Citroën.

Like all Frenchmen, he drove crazy fast, but apparently not crazy fast enough. Car after car swooped past us as we roared down the highway.

"We have a family from Georgia staying with us," said François, taking one hand off the steering wheel to gesture. I glanced back at Sam. "Not the *American* Georgia," François said, sensing my confusion. "They are illegals, *les réfugiés.*"

He said the Georgians had a little boy and a newborn girl. Until recently, the house had been very crowded with a lone Georgian man and an Iraqi family of six—a couple in their fifties, their three adult children, and one son's wife. I started counting on my fingers and got to seventeen people when François told me the Iraqis and the single Georgian had already left.

Allex was a half-hour drive from Valence. Tires crunching on gravel, François soon pulled into a walled courtyard. When he switched off the ignition, the silence was complete. I got out and looked up at the stars glittering like pinpoint halogens. Suddenly Madame Jeanselme burst out of the house to greet us. Their adopted children, Pierre-Marie, twenty-four, and Philomène, twenty-one, flanked her, hopping with excitement.

After we all hugged and double-kissed, we entered their home, a large nineteenth-century farmhouse of timber, stucco, and stone. Madame Jeanselme took us up a narrow, twisting, dark-wooden staircase to our room. The bedroom belonged to Philomène, who had Down syndrome and was thrilled for the chance to sleep with her mother again. It was big enough to sleep four or five people on two mismatched beds pushed together. "Or you can have your own space, Sam," said Madame Jeanselme. "But it's downstairs in the *salon.*"

He grinned with relief. We trooped back downstairs.

The *salon* had a massive stone fireplace, an upright piano, a carved oak armoire, nineteenth-century armchairs and French doors (called, no kidding, *les portes françaises*). Sam would sleep on a velvet-covered divan. When Madame Jeanselme announced dinner was ready, Sam and I exchanged looks. We had already stuffed ourselves on the train. I quickly learned that she didn't always read her emails, and we weren't late for dinner at all—French families dine at eight p.m. or later.

Our first home-cooked meal was disappointing. The main course— well, the *only* course—was a gigantic bowl of rice salad, dotted with mushy canned *petit pois* and a surfeit of mayonnaise. I had never encountered this dish before. The grains of the rice salad were unpleasantly hard, the mayonnaise overpowering. Although I love rice in most variations, I had a problem with ice-cold rice. Sam managed to consume an entire plate. I borrowed his childhood trick of minimizing what was left by smearing the remains over random parts of my plate. I stared glumly at the white and grey-green mess. If this was home cooking in France, Sam and I were making a big mistake.

The next morning, I slept late. Flinging open the ancient dark-wooden shutters, I drank in our new surroundings. Farm fields of winter garlic came right up to the edge of the house. We were in Drôme-Provençal, one of 101 *départements*, the mid-level of government between municipalities called *communes* and larger administrative regions such as Brittany, Normandy, and ours, the Auvergne-Rhône-Alpes. Provence was an hour by car to the south. The Drôme's cool winters and hot, sunny summers were the perfect climate for olives, black truffles, lavender, and grapes—and also some of France's greatest wines: Côtes du Rhône, Hermitage, Crozes-Hermitage, and sparkling dry Clairette de Die.

The farmhouse, on Route des Berengeres, was on a fertile nut-brown plain that bordered the Drôme River, a tributary of the mighty Rhône. A two-lane highway separated us from the actual village of Allex, which tumbled down a hillside so steep that stone steps had replaced some of its hairpin roads. Through the window, I could see the foothills of the rugged Vercors *massif*, the *Pré-alps* where the French Resistance established a base in World War II. The Jeanselmes' home had been an important parachute-drop site for the Resistance.

"Only one house in Allex was bombed in World War II, and it was ours," said Madame Jeanselme, whom we began calling Marie-Catherine.

In the kitchen, I found the Georgian family eating breakfast, or trying to. Andrie—pink cheeks, angelic blond curls, and aquamarine eyes—was screeching. As fast as Davit, his father, put bits of cereal on his high-chair tray, the twenty-month-old toddler flung them onto the floor. Davit was moodily handsome, a dark-haired six feet three. Ignoring the din, Rüska, who looked like a medieval Madonna, with clear white skin, flowing chestnut hair, and a figure still swollen from giving birth, was breastfeeding their two-week-old daughter, Kéti.

Neither Rüska, twenty-five, nor Davit, twenty-eight, spoke English. We managed to converse in fragmentary French. When I asked what language people spoke in Georgia, Davit replied, unsmilingly, "Georgian." Rüska, somewhat friendlier, told me she had made the previous night's rice salad. I should have realized it wasn't French food. *That's why Georgian cuisine hasn't taken the world by storm.* But I kept that thought to myself.

Instead, tempted by the sunshine pouring through the kitchen windows, I opened *les portes françaises* and stepped onto the terrace. It was a chilly 10°C. The walled garden still provided Swiss chard, cabbage, celery, rosemary, and thyme. An olive tree was heavy with last autumn's fruit even as the almond tree put forth its first pale pink blooms. On the far side of the yard, against the garden wall, a dozen chickens squawked and scurried around a coop. François raised them for eggs. Probably because he tossed them kitchen slops every morning, the chickens seemed hysterically happy to see me.

Back inside, I studied the long, narrow kitchen where Sam and I would work. Like Julia Child's test kitchen in nearby Provence, the Jeanselmes' was utilitarian. They had installed a double sink and a few cupboards when they bought the farmhouse a few years earlier, but the workspace was cramped. Appliances cluttered the counter, including a yogourt maker, a microwave, a Moulinex blender, and a scale to weigh food for Philomène, who had diabetes. A long rectangular table with a green Provençal tablecloth and ten narrow mismatched chairs dominated one end of the room. When extra guests arrived, the table could miraculously expand to accommodate fourteen or fifteen.

There were two refrigerators, both smaller than ours in North America. Only one had a freezer compartment, and it was tiny; the frost build-up was so thick it was virtually unusable. This suited the Jeanselmes, who shopped several times a week and rarely ate anything frozen. The four burners on the small gas cooktop couldn't easily accommodate four pots or pans. The built-in oven could hold only one large item, either a roast or a *gratin*, but not both. Surprisingly, they owned neither a toaster nor a coffee maker. At breakfast, everyone dunked arrowroot cookies, rusks, or day-old slabs of baguette into bowls of warm milk.

Beyond the kitchen was a laundry room, which doubled as cold storage for root vegetables, cartons of ultra-high-temperature milk, and toilet paper. A small window looked directly into another tiny room, panelled in unvarnished pine, furnished with a narrow bed, a small desk, and a shelf of books. This was François's retreat. A devout Catholic, he had once considered becoming a priest. Now retired, he was a key organizer in a refugee rescue network. Despite chronic back pain sometimes so severe he had trouble tying his shoes, François drove to meetings all over the region.

That first morning, with the Georgians still eating breakfast, Marie-Catherine pulled me into the formal dining room, which they never used except on major holidays. Like so many French women, she had an innate glamour. She was slim, with fair skin and short-cropped blond hair, and looked much younger than someone in her early sixties. She could pull an ordinary outfit together with élan, matching a bright cotton headband to a kerchief twisted around her neck. She had gotten up early to fetch two local treats from the village *pâtisserie* for me to try. *Pogne*, a crown-shaped brioche perfumed with essence of orange blossom, was a Drôme specialty — the nearby town of Bourg-de-Péage devoted an entire museum to it. The *Suisse*, a buttery cookie flavoured with rum and candied orange peel, was shaped like a soldier, inspired by the Swiss Guard who in 1799 accompanied a pope into exile in Valence. While I nibbled on *pogne* and *Suisse*, she gave me an impromptu lecture on the culinary history of the Drôme, using notes from her work as a nursing professor.

The Drôme had prospered from its dual position on the east-west cross-roads between Rome and Gaul and on the ancient north-south salt route. Each summer, shepherds transported salt and spices as they moved their flocks from the Mediterranean toward northern Europe. Up until the nineteenth century, the Drômoises had been involuntary vegetarians. The fertile plain produced celery, lettuce, eggplant, tomatoes, beets, cauliflower, cabbage, potatoes, leeks, pumpkins, and cardoons, an edible thistle resembling an albino celery. Potatoes, boosted by eggs, became the foundation of many dishes, including the *gratin*, derived from the word *grat*, for "scrapings" or leftovers. The pre-revolutionary name of the Drôme had been "Dauphiné," for the heir to the French throne, and the classic dish of potatoes baked with eggs, milk, and butter is still known as *gratin dauphinois*.

Another potato dish — *brandade de morue* — was a poor man's fish dish. A small piece of salt cod, the only available fish in landlocked Drôme, would be soaked, shredded, and used to flavour a large amount of mashed potatoes. Beef and lamb were expensive because almost all the meat went to the abbot and the *seigneur*. Marie-Catherine's mother, Mamie, loved guinea fowl braised with olives or mushrooms, a Drôme specialty. The first live *pintade* reputedly escaped from Hannibal's provisions as his elephants marched through the region circa 200 BCE.

Pork was the most important meat in the Drôme. In the depths of winter, farmers would kill a single pig in an all-day process called the *tuade*, which until the 1950s was a highlight of rural life. An itinerant *tueur* would arrive at family farms in the Drôme on a cold, dry winter day to ensure the meat would not spoil. He would slaughter the animal with minimal muss or fuss, but his real skill lay in preparing charcuterie. Fatty sausages known as *couenne* were air-dried from ceiling beams or conserved in oil-filled earthenware pots. Even lard, preserved with coarse salt, was used to flavour the vegetables. On the day of the *tuade*, children would be excused from school. "All the village helped," said Marie-Catherine. "And when you helped, they gave you a piece."

Until the 1950s, peasants would have only coffee before heading out to the fields. They returned home at mid-morning for bread, wine, and *tomme*, a goat cheese. Before returning to work, they would begin simmering a vegetable soup enriched with a hunk of salted fatback. At lunch, they would eat only the potatoes, onions, and leeks from the soup pot, filling up with bread and a bit more *tomme*. At night, they would finish the soup, including, finally, the piece of fatback, sopped up with more bread. Growing up in the Drôme, Marie-Catherine knew no one who ate dessert on a regular basis. Fruit was a luxury, eaten only in season. In summer, she noted, if you wanted to eat a peach, you would walk into the orchard and pick one. As a child, her only Christmas present was an orange from Spain.

The upheaval of the French Revolution and, later, the imperial ambitions of Napoleon delayed industrialization. Thus the traditions of rural life persisted longer in France than in England. In the Drôme, farmers began leaving the land in large numbers only in the waning years of the nineteenth century. They went to work in the silk, jewellery, and shoe factories of Ardèche and the Drôme, and when they did, they brought their rural habits with them. Unlike English factory workers, the French refused to eat standing beside their machines. Instead, they negotiated with employers for a proper sit-down lunch.

Even today, mealtimes in France are sacrosanct. Many shops and offices, including pharmacies, butchers', bakeries, and clothing stores, close for two hours or more at midday. "At 1:00 p.m., half the population is at table and at 8:15 p.m. this activity concerns more than a third of the population," wrote Thibaut de Saint Pol, a sociologist. "If you add the hours of domestic labour directly related to eating—cooking, washing up, and so on—this is one of the day's main activities." A 2014 story in the *Guardian* reported that lycée students from Toulouse heading for a homestay in the US were warned not to expect an evening meal. Instead they were advised the Americans would show them the refrigerator and microwave, and encourage them to help themselves.

For a large swath of the twentieth century, people ate locally and seasonally. Marie-Catherine remembered that her grandparents preserved *petit pois* in jars, churned their own butter, and steeped their own wine vinegar. An only child, she often played with the fourteen children, including two adopted ones, of the neighbouring family. The father was a poor tenant farmer, but Marie-Catherine remembered being welcomed to join them at the table for a simple lunch. "The father would open a drawer at the table and shave off a piece of *tomme* for each child. When we finished eating and had wiped our plate clean, we would flip it over. Then there would be two spoons of cherry jam for each child. I never had such delicious jam in my life."

In the 1950s, enormous changes swept post-war France. Social security was established. Public schools improved. With the building of railways, the paving of highways, and refrigeration, workers and bourgeoisie alike began to eat fresh meat regularly. In the 1960s, the Pill coincided with the proliferation of washing machines, simultaneously eliminating large families and an arduous chore. Abortions were more readily available. The Catholic Church lost its grip on the hearts and minds of the people. As unions formed, the influence of factory bosses likewise declined. With families shrinking and women working, people began shopping at *hypermarchés*. In village after village, the bakery, the butcher shop, and the *pâtisserie* closed. Families stopped living in multi-generation households. The implications for cuisine were inevitable. "There was no more transmission of *savoir-faire* in the kitchen," said Marie-Catherine. "No one knew how to make *flans* or *gâteaux*. You could buy it all in the *hypermarché*."

She promised to teach Sam and me a little *savoir-faire* while we were there, and maybe we could even help kill a pig.

CHAPTER TWO

Philomène and Pierre-Marie

The farmhouse was so sprawling that for the first few days I kept making wrong turns and getting lost. Previous owners had added rooms, like Russian nesting dolls. The thick ancient walls meant the Wi-Fi signal worked only in François's study. I noticed crucifixes and portraits of Jesus, Mary, and Joseph. A niche on the garage wall sheltered a tiny plaster saint. On the far side of the garage, François raised two white doves, symbols of the Holy Spirit. Later I learned that François attended Mass every day, and the rest of the family went once a week. Until I arrived at the Jeanselmes, I had never had much to do with religion. I attended Protestant churches as a child but stopped going as soon as I understood the sermons. Norman and I raised our boys in a firmly atheist home. Yet Marie-Catherine didn't seem to mind unbelievers like Sam and me. At mealtimes, we waited while the family said grace. Occasionally I even joined in when they ended by singing triple *hallelujahs*.

Marie-Catherine's deep faith was untainted by dogma or cant. For guidance, she looked to God. When their four healthy biological children — a daughter, a son, and fraternal twin girls — were seven to thirteen years old, she and François thought about adopting a disabled child. They discussed the matter with their children. "My children love those who are different. They were very tolerant," Marie-Catherine said. And that's how they found four-month-old Pierre-Marie, abandoned at birth with Down syndrome, called *Trisomie 21* in France, after the French discovery of the extra copy of the twenty-first chromosome that causes the condition. Five years later, Marie-Catherine began thinking about adopting another disabled child. This time, François objected. He was fifty, and Marie-Catherine was forty-four. She persuaded him to at least visit the orphanage. They met Philomène, then two years old; on the drive home, Marie-Catherine felt there was no turning back — they had seen the child, and she had seen them. François was too upset to speak. As they were driving past a religious shrine, she asked him to stop. She got out, and prayed to God for a sign. A week later, a cyst on her neck spontaneously healed. She told François that God had spoken.

After they adopted Philomène, they realized that the orphanage had failed to disclose the extent of her handicaps. In addition to Down syndrome, she was diabetic and autistic, and one of her eyes was diseased. She had never walked or talked. She couldn't even sit up. She hated to be touched, spoken to, or even looked at. The first months were nightmarish. Philo screamed and fought. She smeared her feces all over the walls and floors. But the entire family, including Pierre-Marie, tried to connect with her and, slowly, Philo bloomed. She learned to walk and talk. But even now, she preferred not to be touched, avoided eye contact, and was still easily distressed.

People often mistook Philo, now a young woman, for a child because she was only four feet tall. She had silky dark hair, skin as white as skim milk, and slanted cornflower blue eyes. She was sweet, joyful, and hyper-sensitive to the moods of others. A life-like prosthetic replaced her diseased eye, but she unfortunately kept rubbing her fake eye with dirty hands, so the socket would get inflamed and crusted, which only made her rub harder.

Five mornings a week, a school bus took Philo to a special-needs school where she attended classes in cooking and music. She brought her insulin kit with her but kept misplacing it, leaving it on the school bus or secreting it somewhere in the house. When anyone asked where it was, Philo shut down completely or stared dreamily into the distance. She would submit to a shower only if her mother got in with her. She hated changing her clothes. Marie-Catherine and Bernadette, the housekeeper, would conspire to hide whatever Philo had worn each day so they could launder it. Philo also got angry when Marie-Catherine told her to put on a winter coat. Later, however, her mother would sometimes hear her having a conversation with herself. "She'd say, 'Oh. It's actually a little cold out. All right. I guess I should put on my coat.' And then she would."

Pierre-Marie was as talkative as his sister was silent. He had pale blue eyes and light brown hair cropped very short, which emphasized his disproportionately small head. At school, he had been bullied and beaten. Painfully aware of his handicap, he would explode if anyone mistakenly assumed he was as handicapped as his little sister. His mental capacity was a seven- to nine-year-old's, whereas Philo's had been assessed at four or five years old.

Like her, Pierre-Marie resisted personal hygiene. He would wear the same shirt again and again. Every few days, his mother would shave his blond stubble, often over his objections. His narrow chest was concave. He had problems with his feet and ankles which made it hard for him to run or play sports. His lungs, ears, nose, palate, throat, and thorax were all malformed. His dysmorphic esophageal muscles meant he couldn't eat regular food, only mush. His parents puréed his meals in the Moulinex blender.

Whereas Philo was blind in one eye, Pierre-Marie was somewhat deaf. Mostly he spent his days with his earbuds stuffed in his ears, playing his favourite pop music at top volume. Or he sat alone at the computer, watching dubbed episodes of the Canadian television show *Heartland*. He believed it was real. He couldn't understand that the star, Amber Marshall, wasn't speaking French and wasn't actually living on an Alberta ranch. He dreamed of moving to Canada to be closer to her, and kept asking Sam to help him get there. Unless he donned his expensive hearing aids, he often was oblivious. Not that he listened to his parents anyway. Once François called for him to leave for an outing Pierre-Marie was eager to attend. When he didn't respond, François eventually drove off in disgust.

When Pierre-Marie wasn't in a snit, he could be excessively charming. He greeted guests like me with a courtly bow, one arm bent at his waist, a gesture he had evidently acquired from watching movies. He loved *The Mask of Zorro* and believed Zorro was real, too. Once Marie-Catherine came home to find him wrapped in a cape, about to leap off the roof.

"*Je ne regrette rien,*" said Marie-Catherine. "Philomène is very sensitive when I'm tired or sad. Also, Pierre-Marie."

As if two disabled children, an endless stream of refugees, and a Canadian mother-and-son cooking duo weren't enough of a burden, Marie-Catherine also cared for her elderly mother. By the time the family moved from Lyon to Allex, Mamie could no longer manage stairs. Marie-Catherine installed a hospital bed in the salon adjacent to Sam's. Mamie needed oxygen, diapers, and twice-daily visits from district nurses. Marie-Catherine was generous, but she was not a doormat. When we first arrived, Mamie was in the hospital for a week, not because she was sick, but because Marie-Catherine needed a respite. It was a free benefit provided by

France's national healthcare system, ranked by the World Health Organization as the best in the world. And when Jabba, the lone Georgian the Jeanselmes had sheltered, had gone on *two* benders during the recent Christmas holidays, Marie-Catherine asked him to leave. She had no idea where he ended up.

Every afternoon or evening, Marie-Catherine went to the hospital, or deputized François, to check up on Mamie and make sure she was eating. Pierre-Marie or Philomène or I went along, sometimes all three of us. Even though we were in rural France, the hospital was just fifteen minutes away, a modern facility with free parking and pleasant, efficient medical staff. The first time I went with Marie-Catherine, she kissed her mother on the forehead and tucked her knitted shawl around her shoulders. She told her that I was visiting, that I was Ben's mom, that we had met before. Mamie didn't seem to understand. She lay unhappily on her hospital bed. Her roommate in her semi-private room cheerfully confirmed that Mamie had eaten dinner and had taken her medication. Marie-Catherine fed her some pudding. She rearranged the bedsheets around Mamie's feet and kissed her again. Then we left.

I was lucky to have met Mamie five years earlier in Lyon. A slim, aristocratic woman with soft white hair twisted in a chignon, like all French women of a certain age, she wore only elegant dresses, never trousers, even at home. She made it her business to make sure Ben got up for his classes. She was then in her late eighties and already had trouble with stairs, so she would call his cellphone from hers at precisely eight a.m. He'd stumble downstairs where she'd have his breakfast waiting, a *pain au chocolat* and a warm bowl of *café au lait*. While he ate, she would regale him with stories. She grew up on a farm near Valence. At the outbreak of the war, she had immediately joined the Resistance. At seventeen, Mamie, a slim blond beauty with aquamarine eyes, bicycled around the villages, seemingly visiting friends, but, in fact, gathering intelligence and distributing food to refugees. Later in the war, she worked as a volunteer nurse, caring for the wounded and the tubercular. It was perilous work.

Left at home while the rest of us were at the hospital, Sam was unsure what to make for dinner. So he cooked a huge bowl of pasta, which he served with the remainder of Rüska's cold rice salad and a pot of *lentilles du Puy*. Everyone enjoyed it but, again, I was disappointed. Eating Sam's pasta was not home cooking *à la française*.

The next night was even more chaotic. At dinnertime, every able-bodied adult seemed preoccupied with saving refugees, visiting an ailing *grand-mère*, placating a hyperactive toddler, or nursing a screaming baby. "I think *we* should make dinner," said Sam.

In the *frigo* we found a perfect head of butter lettuce and some tiny ruby-red radishes. There was a sack of potatoes in the cold-storage room. But what about the main course? In the other *frigo*, we spied some cut-up pale pink meat on a yellow foam tray, a garnet-red liver lavishly displayed atop it, like a brooch on a lady's gown. "*Lapin à la moutarde!*" said Sam, his eyes lighting up. He tore off the plastic wrap. The butcher had already cut the rabbit into eight parts, not counting the head, which had wide-open, doll-like eyes. "Oh, good," said Sam, "I can make a broth with the head."

Online we found *lapin à la moutarde* by Alain Ducasse, a French chef with twenty-one Michelin stars to his credit. The recipe, auto-translated into English, required one "Farmer Bunny," olive oil, salt, pepper, shallots, onion, a *bouquet garni*, garlic, mustard, *crème fraîche*, white wine, and chicken stock. We were in France! So almost everything was on hand, including fresh thyme and rosemary from the herb garden for the *bouquet garni*.

Ducasse said to braise the rabbit stovetop, but we needed the burners for mashed potatoes, broth, and other dishes, so we ignored the great chef. We finished the rabbit in the oven, covered with aluminum foil, at 350°F. While Sam cooked, I prepped the salad and set the long kitchen table for nine. I had no idea how many would show up for dinner, an uncertainty that normally would have made me highly anxious. In France, I gave a Gallic shrug. *C'est la vie* and all that.

Marie-Catherine arrived home from the hospital and gave Philo an insulin injection. Then François returned from his refugee meeting. It was just after eight p.m., dinnertime across France. Davit joined us, but Rüska was dieting to regain her figure. We passed bowls of salad, leftover rice salad, lentils, and buttery mashed potatoes. The rabbit went surprisingly well with the rice salad. There was just enough rabbit to go around: each person, including Philo, who had exquisite manners, took one piece only.

"This is good," said François, sounding pleasantly surprised. "Where did you get the recipe?"

"Alain Ducasse," I said.

"*Mais oui,*" he said, beaming. "*Un chef français.*"

CHAPTER THREE

Bernadette

Cooking online with Alain Ducasse was fun, but our goal was to learn home cooking from an ordinary French family. Instead we were cooking *for* an ordinary French family. Marie-Catherine promised salvation would arrive the next morning. Bernadette Seguin was the family's *femme de ménage,* but she was more than a cleaning lady. She was the Jeanselmes' anchor. "She's our Mary Poppins," said Marie-Catherine.

Four mornings a week, Bernadette drove twenty-five minutes to Allex from Bésayes, a village on the outskirts of Valence. The Jeanselmes normally wouldn't have been able to afford a housekeeper, but government support payments to Mamie and the two handicapped children covered her wages. Bernadette, sixty-seven, was barely five feet tall and ample-figured, with dark eyes and dyed auburn hair. Like Mary Poppins, she brooked no nonsense. And like Mary Poppins, she was warm and loving, one of the rare people from whom Philomène would accept a hug. She often invited Pierre-Marie to stay over at her home on the weekend, a treasured and exciting change in his daily routine.

In a household perpetually on the brink of chaos, Bernadette got the mountains of laundry done, swept the crumbs off the floors, and gathered the still-warm eggs from the chickens. She zealously swabbed the spills on the stove, restocked the toilet paper, kept the household's two bathrooms in sparkling shape, and washed the never-ending accumulation of dirty dishes. She also was the first to acknowledge her obsessive-compulsive fixation. "*Maniaque,*" she said, pointing to herself with an apologetic shrug, as she folded Philomène's laundry with military precision.

Years earlier Bernadette had worked as an accountant. Her first marriage, which ended in divorce, had been to a manager at a designer-shoe factory in nearby Romans-sur-Isère. She quit working when she married her second husband, a socially prominent doctor who was mayor of Bésayes. An inveterate smoker, he died of lung cancer, ten years ago now. That's when

Bernadette discovered he had left behind a mountain of debt. A notary advised the grieving and shocked widow to renounce all claims to her late husband's estate or face the burden of paying off his obligations. She renounced her claim. Now all she had left was their beautiful home, which her adult children were trying to sell out from under her.

Bernadette was forced to go out to clean houses. At the Jeanselmes' she also whipped up many of the meals. An accomplished cook, she had raised a culinary dynasty—three of her four children were professional chefs. Valérie owned her own restaurant in nearby Haute-Loire, Marie was a sushi chef in Martinique, and Julien had worked at the triple Michelin-starred Fat Duck in the UK, at the luxury *pâtisserie* Ladurée on Rue Royale in Paris, and at restaurants in Istanbul, Moscow, Taipei, and Morocco. He had also cooked for Elton John and, as part of a team, for Queen Elizabeth at Buckingham Palace. Only Fleur had followed in her mother's professional footsteps and become an accountant.

That morning, after Bernadette started a load of laundry, she came into the kitchen and briskly announced she was ready to teach Sam and me. We were going to make cauliflower and then *gâteau de foie* (it sounds elegant in French; in English, it means, yuck, "liver cake"). She would also show us five classic sauces: vinaigrette, mayonnaise, and three warm sauces for the cauliflower—tomato, *béchamel*, and *mousseline*.

The cauliflower was a flawlessly fresh dome as big as a beach ball (which was why we were making three sauces for it). Sam rinsed it in the sink and began chopping it into big, even-sized florets. Bernadette plunged the pieces into a pot of cold salted water with lemon juice "to keep it white," she said, adding that you could serve *chou-fleur* cold, warm, or hot. It could be dressed with vinaigrette, roasted with olive oil, or baked *au gratin* with *béchamel* sauce and sprinkled with grated Emmenthal cheese. Bernadette herself preferred firm cauliflower, but François liked his extremely soft. So for him, we cooked the cauliflower at a rolling boil for twenty minutes.

Bernadette grew up in the shadow of a mountain in the Drôme. Her father herded goats, and they were so poor she had no shoes to wear to school, only wooden clogs. When she was a child, olive oil was a luxury. Her family would use a few drops to dress a salad, never for frying or cooking. Although the Drôme was adjacent to Provence, a generation earlier olive trees had not flourished here. "Olive oil was very expensive so we used only butter and cream," Bernadette said. "Now with global warming, we have olive trees this far north. Today everyone uses extra-virgin olive oil." She glanced through the kitchen windows at the olive trees the Jeanselmes planted after they moved to Allex a few years earlier. "*C'est incroyable.* It feels like March."

Béchamel, a classic French sauce, tasted of cream. Magically, it was made only from milk, butter, and flour. "Heat the milk first to avoid lumps," Bernadette instructed. She melted a fist-sized lump of unsalted butter in a saucepan and, as it let off a heavenly smell, whisked in some flour. "Don't let it brown," she cautioned. Before the white paste could change colour, she whisked in the hot milk. Once the sauce thickened, she added two generous pinches of ordinary table salt and pre-ground, extra-fine white pepper.

BERNADETTE'S BÉCHAMEL SAUCE
Makes 1 cup.

1 cup	milk
4 oz.	unsalted butter (salted butter is okay, but then add only a pinch of salt later)
2 tbsp.	flour
½ tsp.	salt
½ tsp.	ground white pepper

Heat milk. In a separate saucepan, melt butter over low heat, then whisk in the flour. Whisk in the hot milk. Stir 2–3 minutes until sauce thickens, then add salt and white pepper.

The *béchamel* could be used on anything from crepes to vegetables to pasta, but she needed it for making *gâteau de foie*. The baked chicken liver mousse was Bernadette's specialty. She preheated the oven to the equivalent of 350°F and dashed out to the garden to fetch half a dozen eggs and all the available parsley. "*Pas beaucoup en hiver,*" she said glumly, coming back with only a few sprigs. While Sam chopped the parsley, Bernadette squeezed a clove of garlic through a garlic press. Marie-Catherine had bought eight plump chicken livers from the supermarket. Bernadette sautéed the minced garlic in butter until it turned light gold, then added six of the eight livers, whole, the parsley, a generous pinch of salt, and three or four twists of black pepper from the grinder.

Seven minutes later, the chicken livers were caramelized and slightly firm when we prodded them with a fork. Bernadette set them aside to cool. She beat three eggs, pouring in a bit of warm *béchamel* to temper them. Then she stirred the tempered egg mixture into the pot of *béchamel*. She whizzed the semi-cooked chicken livers briefly through a blender, stirred the liver mash into the *béchamel*-egg mixture, and poured the batter into a square Pyrex dish. Thirty minutes later, *voilà*!

BERNADETTE'S GÂTEAU DE FOIE

2 oz.	unsalted butter
1 clove	garlic, minced
1 tsp.	minced parsley
½ tsp.	salt
½ tsp.	black pepper
6	whole chicken livers (about ½ lb.)
3	eggs
1 cup	*béchamel* sauce (see recipe, page 36), still warm

Preheat oven to 350°F.

Melt butter over low heat, then add garlic. When garlic turns light gold, raise heat to medium-high, add the chicken livers, and sauté with parsley, salt, and pepper. When the livers are slightly firm and caramelized – this should take about 7 minutes – set aside to cool.

Beat the eggs in a small bowl. Temper the eggs by pouring a bit of warm *béchamel* into them, then add the egg mixture to the pot of *béchamel*. Whiz the semi-cooked chicken livers briefly through a blender and stir into the pot of *béchamel* and egg mixture. Pour into a square Pyrex dish. Bake for 30 minutes at 350°F.

Serve warm, cold, or at room temperature, cut in squares like brownies. Accompany with toast or a green salad dressed with a vinaigrette.

Despite her later affluence as a doctor's wife, Bernadette never wasted anything. She combined the lone rabbit liver we'd saved from the night before with two chicken livers she had held back from the *gâteau de foie*. Sautéed, they would make a simple appetizer at lunch. The rabbit liver was glossy, dark red, and surprisingly large — the size of a medium bar of soap. Holding a fork and paring knife as if dining at a table, Bernadette cut the rabbit liver in chunks, removing a few tough stringy parts. She seared the liver chunks in hot, sputtering butter, flipping them with a fork until they were slightly firm to the touch. Then she cooked the chicken livers to the same degree of doneness.

Sam couldn't believe Bernadette cooked with a *dinner fork*. As we would see on our journey through three nations, kitchen equipment was surprisingly crappy. For centuries, people with the greatest cuisines in the world had been turning out meals with a fork or a pair of chopsticks. Kitchenware shops in France and Italy were few and far between and shockingly expensive — perhaps because they rarely deigned to stock anything made in China. As for China, they prepared everything with a cleaver, a chopping board, and chopsticks.

The Jeanselmes had no tongs. Our main tool was a thick, charred wooden spatula. Their non-stick pans were scarred and dented. Pots were missing lids, and sometimes even handles. The chef knives were dull. The can opener was an old-fashioned stab-push type that left a can of tomato paste mangled.

France, the nation that invented canned food, neglected for nearly a century to invent a decent can opener. "An army marches on its stomach," Napoleon famously said. In 1795, to supply its far-flung military operations, France offered 12,000 francs ($330,000 in today's dollars) to anyone who could invent a method for preserving food. Nicolas-François Appert, a Paris confectioner from the Champagne region, took up the challenge. Surmising preservation might be connected to airtight glass bottles of bubbly, he began stuffing vegetables, fruit, beef, fowl, and fish into champagne bottles and sealing them with cork and wax. Later he also boiled the bottles in water — half a century before his compatriot, Louis Pasteur, discovered that heat killed bacteria and sterilized food. We still talk about "pasteurization," but *"appertisation"* has vanished in the mists of history.)

Appert soon moved on to wide-necked containers — what we would call jars. Once he managed to, um, ram an entire sheep into a huge glass bottle. The French navy took some of his products out for sea trials, but the glass shattered on pitching ships. In 1804, he made the technological leap to metal, tin-plated steel cans, and, later, cast-iron ones, which he soldered shut. Any that didn't swell he deemed safe for consumption. Appert didn't worry about details like can openers. Starving French soldiers stabbed the cans through with bayonets, the ancestors of the stab-push can opener in the Jeanselme kitchen.

Their gadgets, or lack thereof, taught me that you didn't need *stuff* to prepare a good meal. It was something Sam already knew from his experience cooking in those firefighters' camps in northern Alberta, where he helped feed an army of three hundred from a trailer with insufficient oven space and dull knives. At the Jeanselmes' our plates didn't match, but family dinners were always lively and fun. We were perennially short a couple of water glasses, in part because we kept breaking them. Sam and I were clumsy in an unfamiliar kitchen and, as I've mentioned, there was a dearth of counter space. As our supply of water glasses steadily diminished, I had to set the table with tiny two-ounce glasses. No one except Sam seemed to mind. The French (and Italians and Chinese) historically eschewed glugging quantities of H_2O because water had to be sterilized, which consumed scarce firewood. Instead, they sipped wine or drank tea with meals. Alas, Sam and I were used to North American–style "hydrating." In our first few days in Allex, we felt perpetually thirsty. Eventually, Sam got his 32-ounce green Nalgene water bottle out of his backpack and plunked it on the table at dinner. Pierre-Marie and Philo thought he was hilarious.

"I cook for pleasure only, not for a job. I don't want to cook for money," said Bernadette, as she demonstrated variations on the classic *béchamel*. She added tomato paste to the *roux* instead of hot milk to make a *sauce aux tomates*, which could be used for blanched cauliflower, baked pasta, or roasted meat.

At home, a partial can of tomato paste invariably went mouldy before I could use it. I'd tried spooning the leftover paste into an ice-cube tray, but that was messy and time-consuming. Half the time I forgot about the second step: pop out the frozen cubes twenty-four hours later and store in a Ziploc bag. I often ended up with freezer-burned tomato paste and a red-stained ice-cube tray. Bernadette had a clever *truc* that echoed the technique for *confit de canard*. Slam the can on the counter to level the paste. Pour on a film of neutral-tasting oil, such as canola, and refrigerate. Pour off the oil before use.

Rüska wandered into the kitchen. I was so impressed by the oil-film trick that Bernadette tried to show her, too. "*Je sais*," she said nonchalantly, sampling a chunk of freshly sautéed chicken liver. "*Délicieux!*" she said, helping herself to several pieces more. Sam and I exchanged hungry glances and began gobbling morsels of chicken liver, too. They were smooth and creamy. The rabbit liver was granular and intensely flavoured, like a meaty version of Parmesan cheese. By the time Rüska, Sam, and I had finished grazing, only a couple of pieces of chicken liver remained.

Bernadette kept the Jeanselme family supplied with homemade vinaigrette and mayonnaise, which everyone consumed with astonishing speed. "*Il y a mille et une façons de faire une vinaigrette*," she said, pulling out bottles of sunflower and olive oils, red wine vinegar, and jars of salt and Dijon mustard. Her *truc* was to use a neutral oil as the base and olive oil only as flavouring. "Otherwise, it's much too heavy," she said. She whisked together mustard, vinegar, and salt, drizzling in sunflower oil, drop by drop. Sam held the jar steady for her, but Bernadette didn't need any assistance. Once the vinaigrette began to thicken, she poured the oil in a small, steady stream, still whisking briskly. At the end, she whisked in a bit of cold-pressed virgin olive oil. "The slower you add the oil, the longer it stays emulsified," Bernadette said.

BERNADETTE'S VINAIGRETTE
Makes 24 servings. Keeps in the fridge at least 3 weeks.

5–6 tbsp.	Dijon mustard
¼ cup	red wine vinegar
1	scant tsp. salt
¾ cup	canola or sunflower oil
¼ cup	extra-virgin cold-pressed olive oil

Whisk together mustard, vinegar, and salt. Drizzle in the first oil, whisking steadily until each drop emulsifies. Finally, whisk in olive oil.

To make mayonnaise, Bernadette separated the deep orange yolks from two of the eggs she had just gathered from the coop. She put the whites in the *frigo* and cautioned that we had to use them within one day. (That evening, Sam would thicken a chocolate sauce with a froth of beaten egg whites.) "*Sauce mousseline* is just mayonnaise with beaten egg whites," she said, as an aside. For fresh mayonnaise, she beat a generous spoonful of mustard into the egg yolks, added a shower of salt, and whisked in a steady stream of sunflower oil. "*Pas de poivre*," she cautioned. "*C'est pas joli.*" In less than five minutes of brisk whisking, the mixture turned pale gold and thickened to the consistency of Greek yogourt. "*Voilà! La mayonnaise!*"

BERNADETTE'S MAYONNAISE
Makes 1 cup. Keeps in the fridge 1 week.

2	egg yolks
2 tsp.	Dijon mustard
½ tsp.	salt
¾ cup	neutral-tasting oil such as canola or sunflower (olive oil is too strong)

Whisk mustard into egg yolks, add salt, and whisk in oil drop by drop so that it thickens.

We did *all* this — *gâteau de foie*, boiled cauliflower, *béchamel*, sautéed chicken and rabbit livers, mayonnaise, and vinaigrette — in an hour. At one point, Marie-Catherine wandered into the kitchen. She wanted Bernadette's opinion on organizing a meal for us for Sunday lunch. But deep down, I could tell, she was hoping her housekeeper would come through with an invitation.

"I welcome you with all my heart," said Bernadette, her eyes bright, her smile wide.

"Can you make a *flan* on the weekend?" Marie-Catherine asked hopefully.

They began discussing the *menu*. "We'll make *une bonne salade*," said Marie-Catherine, clapping her hands.

"We'll make a chicken broth for *ravioles*," said Bernadette. "*Une Poule au pot Henri IV!*"

"A slab of *caillette!*"

"*Fromage de chèvre!*"

CHAPTER FOUR

Rôti de Pigeons

MAMIE WAS MIFFED about her week of exile. From her point of view, the hospital stay had been totally unnecessary. Once she returned home, nurses dropped by twice a day.

Unlike six years earlier when I had visited the family in Lyon, Mamie no longer joined us at the dinner table. In fact, she ate very little, usually some cream of wheat or porridge and her favourite pomegranate juice, which Pierre-Marie diluted with a bit of water. Marie-Catherine turned on her television only once while we were there, so Mamie could be pushed over in her wheelchair to watch the Pope's visit to Mexico. Despite the nurses' and Marie-Catherine's best attempts to get Mamie up and about, she slept all day. Consequently, she was up all night. Marie-Catherine kept a baby monitor on in Mamie's room, with predictable results. Every night, Marie-Catherine was unable to sleep as Mamie called her repeatedly. And when Mamie finally stopped calling, the wheeze of the oxygen machine kept Marie-Catherine awake. It was why she was close to a breakdown and, I suppose, why François had retreated to his private cabin behind the laundry room.

Caring for Mamie had sapped her last bit of strength. On the advice of her doctor, Marie-Catherine had booked a spa day for the first time in her life, in Romans-sur-Isère, forty-five minutes north of Allex in the Rhône valley: a Saturday morning exercise class, an afternoon spa treatment. Despite her exhaustion, she still took the time to work out a plan for Sam and me. While she exercised, we would explore Romans. Later we would meet up for lunch. Then while she went to the spa, we would spend the afternoon shopping with Bernadette for Sunday's big lunch.

We parted ways with Marie-Catherine on the banks of the Isère River. Sam and I wandered through the twisting cobblestoned streets, running headlong into the infamous *mistral*, the winter-into-spring gale that roared down the Rhône valley at speeds of up to one hundred kilometres an hour.

The *mistral* tore at our jackets and flung grit in our faces. Normally it would bring the famous clear blue skies of Provence, but this was a *mistral noir*, which brought clouds and storms. Heavy rain was forecast for the next day, but for the moment, at least, it was dry.

Romans-sur-Isère, as its name indicated, was originally a Roman settlement on the Isère, another tributary of the Rhône River. In medieval times, the town had prospered due to its dual position on the north-south salt route from the Mediterranean ports to Lyon, Belgium, and the Netherlands, and on the east-west land bridge between the Alps and the *Massif Central*. Romans's sister town, on the other side of a graceful stone bridge, was Bourg-de-Péage, or Toll Town, named for the tariffs it collected from every traveller and shipment of goods.

In the eighteenth century, Romans-sur-Isère's population was five thousand, a significant size for that era. Today, it had thirty thousand people and was a town in decline. Unemployment was massive, and anyone who could leave had left. A full circle on foot of the deserted town centre, once famous for its fashionable shoe boutiques, took just ten minutes. I saw only a couple of shops selling handmade hippie-style sandals.

Sam and I spotted a billboard advertising the museum in Bourg-de-Péage devoted to *pogne*, the crown-shaped brioche scented with orange blossoms. We were about to cross the stone bridge when I saw a sign to the International Shoe Museum. Citing the history of industrialization in Romans, I persuaded Sam that shoes were more interesting than *pogne*. I'm kidding. I told him I wanted to see the shoe museum, and he didn't protest.

In the Middle Ages, France's first tanneries and silk factories opened here to take advantage of hydropower generated by the fast-flowing Isère. Shoemaking naturally followed. During the industrial revolution, factories sprang up, the constraining medieval wall was demolished, and docks were built to ship out the product. Romans-sur-Isère became the shoe-design capital of France. By the early twentieth century, the industry employed about five thousand men and women. Two of Marie-Catherine's cousins ran shoe factories here. In the 1920s Charles Jourdan founded his eponymous luxury shoe company here. Sales boomed after he figured out how to curve the sole of stilettos to make them marginally less painful. Wealthy women, including Edith Piaf and Marlene Dietrich, came from Paris, Geneva, and Berlin to select the latest styles.

In World War II, the Germans bombed the ancient stone bridge linking the two banks of the Isère. After the war, Romans-sur-Isère and Bourg-de-Péage rebuilt the bridge, and the shoe industry was revived. The Jourdan factory began manufacturing shoes for couturiers such as Dior, Chanel, Yves Saint Laurent, and Pierre Cardin, and trunk-maker Louis Vuitton. Its customers included Marilyn Monroe, Sophia Loren, Jackie Kennedy, Imelda Marcos, and Her Royal Highness Diana, Princess of Wales. Then globalization arrived. By 2000, China was wiping out shoemakers around the world. One by one, every shoe factory in Romans-sur-Isère shut down. In 2007 the manager of the Jourdan factory, the last survivor, shuttered its doors. (The manager was Bernadette's first husband, whom she had already divorced.)

The International Shoe Museum, founded partly by Marie-Catherine's two cousins, was housed in an elegant seventeenth-century hillside convent. The imposing U-shaped granite edifice, with arched porticos, crushed limestone footpaths, and ornamental garden of manicured boxwood, befitted a palace rather than a convent and epitomized Catholicism's once-powerful grip. Nearly 90 percent of people in France identified as Catholic, but only 5 percent regularly attended Mass. The average age of a priest was seventy-five.

One moribund industry — Catholicism — provided a memorial to another — shoe manufacturing — that was already dead. The three clerks at the ticket booth outnumbered Sam and me, the only visitors. We wandered past displays of ancient shoemaking techniques and vitrines of thousands of shoes: a single boot of Napoleon's, tiny three-inch embroidered slippers for Chinese women with bound feet, and an Indian fakir's flip-flop that was a literal tiny bed of nails. Sam didn't complain about spending an hour staring at old shoes. But he put his foot down at the section where visitors could try on designer stilettos. *I* thought it was fun, but that is why mothers and sons don't travel well together.

The museum was mute about how cheap Chinese exports had annihilated France's shoe industry. Yet deep inside we stumbled upon a four-room *Musée de la Résistance en Drôme et de la Déportation*. Suddenly we had a context for Mamie's stories. We saw on the map that the Jeanselme farmhouse was adjacent to the parachute-drop site and understood why the Nazis had bombed it. The Museum of the Resistance was inside the shoe museum because factory workers joined the Resistance in droves, basing themselves in the Vercors *massif*, twenty kilometres away. They had been easy to organize because, well, they were already organized into trade unions.

Afterward, Sam and I climbed further up the hill until we reached a plateau overlooking the city. The only stores, a kebab outlet and a pizzeria, were closed. At a bank, Sam stood watch while I withdrew cash from an ATM. A few toughs a block away stared hard at us. "Let's go," I said nervously, shoving the euros deep inside my jacket. In the medieval centre, the streets were still deserted at midday. When we met up with Marie-Catherine and I mentioned how creepy it had felt withdrawing money, she warned me that Romans-sur-Isère was especially dangerous at night because of so much unemployment. But it was midday, the sun was shining, I hadn't been mugged, and we were all starving. We peered into restaurant windows and decided to try Au Petit Maxime, a family-run bistro facing Place Maurice Faure, named after a Resistance hero. Half the tables were occupied, and the rest were rapidly filling up. Marie-Catherine ordered a carafe of local Crozes-Hermitage, from Syrah grapes, and urged us each to order a *salade aux Romans*, a main course, *and* a dessert. She said she was treating us, and we obeyed because Sam and I had a pre-arranged scheme for ensuring *we* paid. (It involved me distracting her with a flurry of questions at the end of the meal, while Sam pretended to go to the bathroom but instead quietly settled the bill at the bar.)

The *salade aux Romans*, easily a main course, was a mountain of crisp, dark-green lettuce, ripe tomato wedges, cured olives, a generous slice of Brie, *and* a slab of *caillette*, a kind of large meatball that was a specialty of the Drôme. Scattered on top were tiny chartreuse-green pillows of … well, I had no idea.

"*Les ravioles*," said Marie-Catherine.

They were the size of postage stamps, greaseless, crisp, and feathery light. Tinted green with spinach, the tiny pasta pillows were stuffed with parsley, *fromage blanc*, and Comté, an unpasteurized cow's milk cheese. As Sam was swooning with excitement over the *ravioles*, the *patron* came over to explain they had been flash-fried from frozen. They could also be eaten poached in chicken broth, Marie-Catherine added.

In the Drôme, *les ravioles* was a quintessential French dish with Italian origins. The globalization of food culture started centuries earlier. As farmhands from Piemonte and Liguria crossed the Alps looking for work, they brought with them the knowledge of *ravioles* and beef *daube* with polenta. *Lasagne*, the traditional harvest dish of the French Alps and Isère region, crept into the French language as a phrase for a job well done: "You have earned your *lasagne*."

The first written record of *les ravioles du Dauphiné* was 1228. Originally stuffed only with vegetables such as kale, meat and cheese were added as the standard of living improved. By the nineteenth and early twentieth centuries, women known as *les ravioleuses* would go house to house in the Drôme preparing the tiny dumplings. In 1953, a ravioli-making machine at a fair in Romans-sur-Isère astounded everyone. Today, no one made *les ravioles* at home, which was pretty well the case in Italy, too. But everyone in the Drôme ate them, buying them frozen from supermarkets and eating them in restaurants, like Au Petit Maxime, that also bought them frozen.

After finishing an enormous *salade aux Romans*, Marie-Catherine demolished her *brandade de morue*, the dish of creamy mashed potatoes studded with bits of salt cod. I was so full from the salad I doubted I could put a dent in my main course, *cuisses de grenouilles à la meunière*, sautéed with garlic, parsley, and butter, and served with crunchy roast potatoes and buttery puréed spinach. After the shoe museum, it seemed rude to rub it in so I kept silent, but I suspected I was eating Asian frog legs. The French enthusiastically consumed three to four thousand tons a year of *cuisses de grenouilles*, the most in the world. In 1980, it had designated frogs a protected species and now imported the bulk of its supply from Indonesia and China.

Sam ordered tripe stew with boiled potatoes. He loved guts, but once upon a time, he was just another fussy toddler. (And so was Ben.) Norman and I never coaxed them to eat. We refused to bargain: *broccoli, then dessert.* Instead, at the slightest expression of hesitation, Norman and I would snatch the morsel off their high-chair trays. "More for us!" we'd yelp, as our toddlers, eyes round as saucers, studied us chewing and smacking our lips.

To be sure, different cultures revile different foods for religious, philosophical, mystical, health, or a combination of reasons. Depending on who is doing the counting—herbivores or omnivores—between 5 and 19 percent of Americans are either vegetarians or sort-of-when-I-feel-like-it vegetarians. Between 2 and 9 percent are vegans.

I adore vegetables, deplore vegetarians, and despise vegans (my new daughter-in-law excluded, of course!). Nothing makes me happier than linguine with pesto or spaghetti drenched in raw, sweet cherry tomatoes. I adore Spanish black-bean soup. I'm a fan of Indian daal. I love stir-fried Chinese greens. But I don't understand exclusionary, holier-than-thou vegetarians who spend their entire meal talking about why they eat plants.

Still, I'm an equal-opportunity scorner—for instance, meat-eaters who waste the skin—ice of their duck confit. *Why else would you eat duck?*

At the restaurant in Romans-sur-Isère, Sam, who can usually stuff down enormous quantities of food, could not finish his huge casserole of tripe, which had come with enough steamed potatoes to feed a family of four. He asked the restaurant to pack up his leftovers, once a no-no in France. A poll found that 70 percent of French diners had never asked for a doggy bag for fear of looking rude, tacky, or poor. To reduce food waste, however, a new French law required restaurants to provide containers, which they called *le gourmet bag*.

Marie-Catherine insisted we order the *coupe archédoise* for dessert, another Drômoise specialty. She would not hear of us sharing one. Out came two gigantic sundaes, each big enough to feed a Chinese family of six, with generous scoops of vanilla ice cream and chestnut ice cream, covered in a cream of puréed chestnuts, and topped with clouds of whipped cream. I thought I would pass out. But I ate it, and I didn't.

After lunch, Marie-Catherine drove to nearby Bésayes (pop. 996), where Bernadette awaited us with her shopping list. (At Marie-Catherine's suggestion, I had already given her enough euros to cover the groceries.) Unlike me, Bernadette's makeup was perfect, her hair was coiffed, and she had dressed in a chic outfit for our Saturday afternoon expedition to the butcher's. As we piled into her SUV, she apologized for how dirty it was—the *mistral* had been kicking up dust all day.

Bernadette was an even crazier driver than François—no one passed *her*. At top speed, she tailgated whoever was in front of us, scaring even Sam. As she zoomed past a field of grazing cows, I mentioned the time we'd taken Ben and Sam to France when they were ten and seven and hadn't let them eat hamburgers because of an outbreak of mad cow disease. Bernadette snorted. In her view, the entire crisis had been an international conspiracy: chicken farmers trying to undermine cattle farmers. "It's one sector trying to bring down another sector. It's the same with H1N1," she said darkly, referring to swine flu.

Her favourite stores for meat and cheese were not in Bésayes, which had lost its last butcher and *fromagerie* some years earlier. She liked Laiterie Gérentes, twelve kilometres away in Chabeuil, in a bland-looking cluster of stores off the highway. An award-winning chain of cheese shops across the Drôme that had been in business for three generations, it boasted of using only milk from cows that grazed six hundred metres above sea level on the volcanic plateau of the Haute-Loire and the Ardèche. Together we perused the dazzling array of butters, yogourts, cream, and ice cream, even *foie gras* ice cream.

"I buy *seulement* French products," Bernadette said, grabbing a couple of packages of frozen cheese-and-parsley *ravioles*. Then we got in the long line to choose four cheeses for the cheese course.

Her favourite butcher, Comptoir Drômois des Viandes, was next door. It was as antiseptic as a surgical outpatient clinic, with clerks who wore spotless white coats and serious expressions. The displays were breathtaking: charcuterie, merguez and sausages, lamb tongues and brains, veal sweetbreads, rabbits (whole or legs only), pheasants and guinea fowl, legs of lamb, goat ribs and chops, cuts of pork and beef, even horse, elegantly called *chevaline*. For *blanquette de veau*, Bernadette chose a kilo of pale milk-fed veal, already expertly cubed. She said we would also make a *Drômois* specialty, *rôti de pigeons*, which required four thick slices of bacon, rind on, and, of course, pigeons. The butcher wrapped the bacon neatly in sturdy brown paper.

"*Plus de pigeon,*" he said, looking sad. He instead proffered a slab of artisanal pigeon pâté.

"Mine's better," said Bernadette, with a sniff. Besides, we needed pigeons, not pâté. She turned to Sam and me. "We'll have to go to the pigeon farm."

Outside, squinting against the grit whipped up by the *mistral*, we threw our parcels of cheese, *ravioles*, and veal into the back of the SUV. As she sped back down twisting country roads, Bernadette suddenly turned into a long narrow driveway leading to a farm. "*Entreprise Pigeonneaux Chabert. Spécialité: La Rôtie de Pigeons,*" declared a hand-painted sign decorated with a drawing of a pigeon. According to the address, we were in the *Quartier Mistral*, which would explain why, as Bernadette flung open her car door, the gale nearly slammed it shut on her leg.

"Oh, my hair!" she cried, more concerned about her locks than her limbs. She was even more upset to find the shop's metal shutters shut tight. She pushed the buzzer anyway. She waited a few seconds then hit the buzzer again. And again. Eventually a man with curly blond hair emerged from the adjacent barn. He was wearing denim overalls and knee-high rubber work boots.

"*Bonjour,*" he said formally.

"*Bonjour,*" said Bernadette.

Bonjour is the most important word in the French language. It's not a casual greeting like "Hi there," but the key to all civilized encounters. Without first saying "bonjour," you might as well go home. On that previous mad-cow trip to France, we were standing outside a Parisian café one night when Ben suddenly needed to pee. I sent my ten-year-old in alone because he spoke French (he attended a bilingual school) and I figured his chances of charming the bartender were better that way.

"*Non, non, non!*" the bartender admonished him. "First you must say *bonjour.*"

"*Bonjour,*" Ben said. The bartender replied, "*Bonjour.*" And then he pointed the way to the washroom.

Jean-Louis Chabert was the owner and operator of Entreprise Pigeonneaux Chabert, a seventy-hectare farm that had been in his family for generations.

"I was just at Comptoir Drômois des Viandes and they don't have any pigeon," Bernadette told him. "Do you have pigeon?"

"*Of course,* the Comptoir doesn't have pigeon," said Chabert, looking us up and down. "They sell only *pigeonneau.* I know this because *we* are the supplier."

"Well, I'm looking for pigeon," Bernadette repeated. "I just went to the Comptoir. I always buy my pigeon from them, and they didn't have any left."

"We have none left at this moment," said Chabert. "We won't have any *pigeonneau* until next week. We only slaughter on Tuesdays." He added that his store opened a few mornings a week, and right then, in the middle of a Saturday afternoon, it was most definitely closed.

"Oh dear, they're from Canada," said Bernadette, gesturing to Sam and me. "I wanted to make them *rôti de pigeons.*"

"*Rôti de pigeons?*" said Chabert. "For that, you must use pigeon, not *pigeonneau.*"

Bernadette looked surprised. Chabert repeated himself. "We supply the butcher with *pigeonneau. Pigeonneau* is smaller and more expensive. What you want to make *rôti de pigeons* with is pigeon, not *pigeonneau.*"

"Oh, I didn't know there was a difference," said Bernadette, confused. "The butcher always sold it as pigeon."

"No, we've always sold them *pigeonneau*. We *never* sell them pigeon," said Chabert.

"I've bought pigeon from them for years," Bernadette insisted.

Seeing her bewilderment, Chabert patiently explained. "The difference between *pigeonneau* and pigeon is like the difference between *veau* and *vâche*." Sam grasped that, but Bernadette didn't. She was fixated on all the pigeon she'd bought over the years from the Comptoir.

Meanwhile the savage *mistral* lashed us. The impassioned rapid-fire conversation about pigeon and *pigeonneau* made me cross-eyed. In essence, *pigeonneau* was baby pigeon, the way veal was baby cow. And like veal, *pigeonneau* had to be slaughtered at one month. But all the back and forth was confusing everyone. Chabert was growing impatient because no matter what he said, Bernadette kept resisting.

Chabert decided to speak her language. "Making a *rôti de pigeons* with *pigeonneau*," he told her, "is like making *blanquette de veau* with a veal chop." Well, Bernadette understood *that* because in fact our other dish was *blanquette de veau*. She also understood the principle of not wasting an expensive ingredient when a cheaper one could substitute. The problem was she didn't realize *pigeonneau* cost twice as much as pigeon. Then Chabert made the fatal mistake of repeating himself: "I only slaughter on Tuesdays."

"But we need them now," said Bernadette, sighing dramatically.

Chabert sighed, too. Then he said, not in a rude way, "I'm not going to explain it anymore."

"Okay, I didn't know that," said Bernadette, sighing again. "Too bad I can't make *rôti de pigeons*."

By now it was clear to Chabert that he was *never* going to get rid of us unless he bent to Bernadette's version of reality.

"Wait, do you want *pigeon*?" he said, as if the preceding conversation had never taken place. "Because I *have* pigeon. I have it in the back. How many do you want?"

Bernadette's face lit up. She, too, acted as though they were just starting to talk. She said she wanted two pigeons. When told the price, she beamed.

"It's half the price of the butcher. I'm coming here *all the time*!" she whispered happily.

As the farmer disappeared into the barn, I thought I should have reinforced that these were pigeon, not *pigeonneau*, and ... oh, never mind. After puzzling over my notes later and a long discussion with Sam, I disentangled the problem. Chabert sold *both* pigeon and *pigeonneau*. He slaughtered the *pigeonneau* only on Tuesdays. And he sold only *pigeonneau* to Comptoir Drômois des Viandes. For years, Bernadette had wastefully used baby squab to make *rôti de pigeons* when she could have been using cheaper mature birds.

We were still standing outside in the gale when Monsieur Chabert returned with two pigeons, neatly wrapped in butcher paper. He beckoned us inside to pay, telling us to be quiet. In the middle of his shop, an infant slept peacefully in a carriage. I inspected the shelves and grabbed a few jars of preserved apricots and some pigeon pâté. Or maybe it was *pigeonneau* pâté.

The baby slumbered on.

The pigeon farm was four minutes from Bernadette's home. She parked in her long gravel driveway that ran the entire length of her deep rectangular garden. Even in February, it was in bloom with yellow daffodils and pink almond trees. With the sure eye of an Impressionist painter, she had planted contrasting trees — glossy laurel, Japanese red maple, flowering cherry, dusky olive, and a dozen varieties of evergreens and golden junipers. Lavender bushes and papyrus encircled a free-form goldfish pond. Clematis and grapevines climbed a trellis. The lavender bushes were leafless shrubs now, but in midsummer they would blossom into stunning purple domes, a famous Drôme export for perfumes, oils, and meditative pillows.

We rushed, head down, through the *mistral*, laden with groceries. Bernadette's house was the home of a prosperous doctor. She had renovated it extensively, completing the work just before her husband died. She retained the original heavy nineteenth-century beams and three-feet-thick stone walls but added skylights, knocked down some inner walls, and installed high-quality sliding glass doors to the garden. Everywhere were signs of her past affluence — a Roche Bobois designer lamp in her light-filled living room, bottles of French perfume in her bathroom, and, on a counter, a Christian Dior purse, a genuine one, not a knock-off.

As she showed us around her immaculate home, she told me it was her last tangible tie to her late husband. The pièce de résistance was her modern open-concept kitchen. It had blond wood cupboards, deep sliding drawers for pots, granite countertops, and excellent task lighting. She owned beautiful pans of solid copper, Le Creuset, and cast iron. And despite her ability to cook with just a paring knife and fork at the Jeanselmes' home, she had every imaginable kitchen tool, including three wire whisks, tongs, spatulas, graters, blenders, and scales. Her appliances were top-of-the-line. She had no freezer. "I cook everything fresh, nothing frozen, nothing with preservatives," she explained.

In the kitchen, four pristine towels hung from a rack. None matched, and a warning bell went off in my head. Was there a special use for each? *Mais oui!* Bernadette was delighted I asked. The first one, a *matelassé*, a woven quilted pattern, was for drying hands. The second one, a Provençal cloth, was for drying pots and pans. The third one, pure linen, was for drying glasses. The fourth one ... I've forgotten. I gave Sam a look, meaning, *Watch out!* He nodded. To start preparing the food, he washed his hands in the kitchen sink, intending to show that he knew he should wipe his hands on the *matelassé*. Bernadette freaked out before he could turn off the tap. "*Normalement,*" she explained, trying to regain her equilibrium, "when I first come into the house from outside, I wash my hands in the *laundry room*. Only once I'm already cooking, I wash my hands in the kitchen sink."

She showed us the adjacent laundry room, which was spotless, the cleaning products lined up like a platoon of soldiers. Later, when Sam asked to use the toilet, Bernadette uttered a small shriek and dashed ahead of him to give the already spotless powder room an emergency touch-up. "*Maniaque,*" Bernadette conceded when she emerged, breathless, from the powder room. She *was* a maniac, which of course made her a fabulous housekeeper. But I'm sure it was traumatic for her to deal with the chaos at the Jeanselme household.

Donning a red gingham apron, Bernadette hauled out a heavy cookbook. It was bound in beige cloth, well-used, but without a single food stain. *Maniaque.* "This is my bible. It's the base of all good cooking," she said. "I have always had the same cookbook. I got it when I got married." Her copy of *Je sais cuisiner* (I Know How to Cook) by Ginette Mathiot was 773 pages long. Its defiant title was perhaps a reaction to France's male-dominated chef culture and the author's own experience of being shunted into home economics after expressing a desire to study medicine. Intended

for the family cook, the recipes were frugal while still covering the gastronomic canon. Mathiot, then twenty-five, wrote it in 1932, in the depths
of the Depression. By the time she died at age ninety-one in 1998, it had
sold five million copies—including one to Bernadette and one to Marie-
Catherine.

I flipped through the cookbook while Bernadette unwrapped the veal.
Among its two thousand recipes were a hundred and twenty-six for sauces
alone, everything from *sauce à l'abricot* to *sauce Zingara*, and even "*ketchup
à la crème*." Each of the hundred veal recipes were only a single paragraph,
even for *blanquette de veau*. Julia Child's nearly four-page recipe for
blanquette de veau à l'ancienne made me want to lie down in a darkened
room with a damp towel over my forehead. Child's 684-page tome,
Mastering the Art of French Cooking, Volume I, would discourage all but the
most enthusiastic novices. In contrast, Mathiot's was encouraging. Who
couldn't follow *one* paragraph of instructions? At other homes in France
and Italy, I discovered similarly minimalist cookbooks. They presumed a
level of technical competency that everyone had learned at their
grandmother's knee. Recipes didn't explain *how* to make a roux. They didn't
even provide the correct proportions of flour and fat. They merely said,
"Make a roux."

Bernadette put her cookbook on a table six feet away from the stove,
safely beyond the spatter zone. After scanning the single-graph recipe, she
dumped the cubed veal into a sturdy pot, covered the meat with cold water
and brought it to a simmer. After five minutes, she drained the water and
added fresh cold water. "It's necessary to *blanchir* the meat to get rid of the
scum," she said.

For the *bouquet garni*, Bernadette dashed into the *mistral* to pluck a
fresh bay leaf from her laurel tree and a few stems of fresh thyme. By the
time she had rinsed the herbs and tied them in a bundle with cooking
twine, the second rinse was simmering. She added a carrot, an onion, two
cloves of garlic, and a leek. "My grandmother always added a leek," she
said, throwing in three pinches of coarse salt and reducing the heat.

"Is the cuisine of France the best in the world?" she asked as she began
making a blond *roux*. I hesitated. French cuisine was *one* of the best, I told
her, one of the top three in the world, along with Italy's and China's. I
added that Japanese and Indian food were great, too. Although her children
roamed the world, Bernadette herself stayed strictly local. She was not

interested in sushi. And her impression of English food came from her son's frequent phone calls seeking her culinary advice. She noted with distaste that he'd had to adjust to local preferences. "*Les anglais* like their meat *bien cuit* but their vegetables *croquante*."

Bernadette's talent in the kitchen was restricted to cooking, not baking, so she left several phone messages for Fleur, her youngest, who knew how to make a *tarte aux pralines*. Except for simple cakes, *flans*, or brownies (which they call *les brownies*), real French people didn't bake at home. They bought their croissants and baguettes at the *boulangerie*, and no one even tried to compete with a professional *pâtissier*.

Bernadette made sure the butter didn't brown as she made the blond *roux*. The word *blanquette* derived from *blanc* and meant a stew of milk-fed pale meat in a white sauce. If you wanted a brown stew, she explained, you would brown the veal, add flour to create a roux, half a bottle of white wine, and some water. "Or a whole bottle and no water," she said, shrugging. With home cooking, the recipe was merely a guide. After adding the blond roux to the cubed veal, she let it simmer, half-covered, with the *bouquet garni* for ninety minutes.

Both Mathiot's and Child's recipes specified exactly twenty-four mushrooms, but Bernadette didn't bother to count them. Like any home cook, she just used the whole package. She cut the larger mushrooms in half and left the smaller ones whole. Then she soaked them in water spiked with lemon juice to keep them white. What she did next was interesting. After draining the mushrooms and patting them dry, she dry-seared them—without butter or oil—in a non-stick pan until they were golden brown. "This method gets rid of the moisture," she told Sam. Only then she added a chunk of unsalted butter. On Sunday, she would add the cooked mushrooms at the last minute.

"Everything will keep until tomorrow," Bernadette explained. "We will thicken it with egg yolks and cream just before we eat it."

MY EASY VERSION OF
BERNADETTE'S BLANQUETTE DE VEAU

Serves 6. Serve with rice, short pasta, or steamed potatoes.

2½ lbs.	cubed veal shoulder or breast
1	carrot, peeled and cut in half
1	leek, trimmed of root and dark-green top
8	cloves
1	onion, peeled and studded with the cloves
1	bouquet garni of parsley, bay leaves, and thyme (or improvise with 2 bay leaves, 10 parsley stems, ½ tsp. dried thyme)
24	pearl onions, peeled (or substitute 2 yellow onions, quartered)
½	bottle white wine (or water)
24	button mushrooms (or an 8-oz. box; halve or quarter the biggest ones, aiming for a uniform size)
2 tbsp.	butter

FOR THE ROUX:

5 tbsp.	butter
5 tbsp.	flour
½ cup	white wine
1½ cups	stock or water
1 or 2	egg yolks (optional; can be omitted entirely)
½ cup	cream (whipping or half and half)
salt to taste	
3 tbsp.	minced parsley

In a large pot, cover meat in cold water. Bring to a boil, then reduce to a simmer. Skim surface foam (or don't bother. I also skipped Bernadette's step of draining and rinsing the meat, adding fresh cold water, and bringing it to a boil again. Why waste good broth?). Add carrot, leek, cloved onion, and bouquet garni. Simmer, covered, for 75 minutes. Remove carrot, leek, onion, and bouquet garni and discard. Set aside the pot of meat and broth.

Peel the pearl onions, a finicky task, which can be eased by blanching the onions in a small pot of boiling water and then shocking them in cold water. You can substitute quartered yellow onions if you wish, but they aren't as good. Once peeled, simmer the pearl onions (or yellow onions) in half a cup of the veal stock for 15 minutes; any longer and they'll fall apart. Then add to the big pot of meat and broth.

Dry-cook mushrooms over medium heat in a non-stick pan. Once mushrooms are lightly browned, add the 2 tbsp. butter. At this point, the mushrooms can be refrigerated for several days, as can the pot of meat, broth, and onions.

To serve, reheat the pot of veal, broth, and onions. Salt to taste.

In another large pot that will eventually hold the entire dish, make a blond roux by melting butter over low heat. Whisk in the flour. Do not let it brown. When paste is smooth, add wine and stock, whisk well, and stir until thickened.

In a bowl, mix 1 or 2 eggs yolks with cream. Temper the mixture by slowly adding a ladleful of hot stock and mixing thoroughly. Repeat 3 more times. Add tempered egg-cream mixture to thickened roux. Stir well. If you omit yolks, then add cream gradually to the hot roux, stirring constantly. Add mushrooms, and then all veal, broth, and onions. Stir. Heat, but do not let it boil. Adjust for salt. Garnish with minced parsley.

Serve piping hot with rice, plain noodles, or steamed potatoes.

As the *blanquette de veau* simmered, we tackled the pigeon dish. Bernadette dropped a knob of cold butter into a well-worn Le Creuset casserole, turned on her gas stove to medium, and unwrapped the package from Pigeonneaux Chabert. The two pigeons were russet coloured and cleanly plucked, heads and claws removed. Bernadette wrapped strips of thick-cut bacon around them, trussed them with twine, and put them down to sizzle. "I cook with my eyes" — she pointed to her nose — "and the fragrance."

Once the birds were evenly browned and the bacon was golden and crisp, she added five cloves of garlic, sea salt, and freshly ground pepper. She splashed in a half cup of water, adding more every time the casserole was about to dry out. The birds should braise, not boil, she explained to Sam. French restaurants often serve *pigeonneau* medium rare, with the breast meat still rosy. But older *pigeons*—the kind we'd bought from Monsieur Chabert—were tough and needed an hour of braising. When the birds cooled, Sam and I stripped off the meat. It was a finicky task because, unlike chicken, the pigeon meat clung stubbornly to the tiny bones, but we needed every morsel to make enough of an appetizer for seven. Our reward: we got to suck on the minuscule flesh-free wings while we worked. Pigeon tasted richer than chicken, leaner, greaseless, and finely textured.

Bernadette whirred the shredded pigeon meat, bacon, and softened garlic cloves in her Moulinex blender for ten seconds. So far, *rôti de pigeons* tasted like a gamey liver-giblet pâté, yet I couldn't suppress the apostate thought: this was way too much trouble. Why not just eat roast squab?

Thank goodness Bernadette had scratched *Poule au pot Henri IV*, an even more complicated dish, named after a sixteenth-century king who ruled in an era when the dishes of the aristocracy sacrificed flavour for showiness. *Poule au pot Henri IV* involved stuffing a chicken with milk-soaked stale bread, minced shallots, parsley, garlic, an egg, chopped Bayonne ham, crumbled sausage meat, minced chicken liver, *and* two livers from other kinds of fowl. After sewing the chicken shut, you had to poach it for ninety minutes—with carrots, baby turnips, leeks, celery, garlic, a *bouquet garni*, and an onion studded with two cloves. Then you served it with a risotto made with the broth and mushrooms sautéed in chopped onion and butter. Phew!

In 2013, Bill Buford, a *New Yorker* writer, and Daniel Boulud, a French chef with twenty restaurants in three countries, recreated several nineteenth-century aristocratic dishes. To make one called *Chartreuse*, they stuffed pigeons and partridges with cabbage sautéed in pork belly, duck fat, and *foie gras*. Then they encased the stuffed birds in a mould of root vegetables. After three arduous days of work, Boulud tasted the *Chartreuse*. "*Pas mal*," he said.

Rôti de pigeons didn't take three days of work, but Bernadette was far from finished. She returned the ground-up pigeon to the still-warm pot and added freshly ground pepper and two tablespoons of Dijon mustard. "You could add cognac, too, but I don't like that," she said. She was about to add an eighth of a cup of red wine vinegar when Fleur, her youngest daughter, walked in, her boyfriend and their young son in tow. Bernadette spoke to all her children by phone almost daily. Each morning she arrived at the Jeanselmes', beaming, and couldn't wait to show me the latest family photos on her cellphone. But beneath the surface, relations were deteriorating. It had to do with money, inheritance, property, and everyday family dysfunction.

Intergenerational relations in France were changing, for the worse. French law forced parents, regardless of how badly they had been treated, to leave their estates to their children. People over sixty-five accounted for one-third of suicides in France; in contrast, the suicide rate for seniors in Canada was lower than the average. A decade earlier, after fifteen thousand people died in a summer heat wave, and some bodies lay unclaimed for weeks because the rest of the family was on holiday, France had made elder neglect a crime.

When we had pulled into the driveway that afternoon after our shopping trip, Bernadette explained why she always parked almost at the end of her garden. "My nephew lives there," she said, pointing to the house edging the other side of her driveway. She said he hated her so much he used to toss rotting vegetables from his kitchen window onto her car. That would upset anyone, but for a *maniaque* who cared about order and cleanliness, it was unendurable.

The nephew's mother — Bernadette's sister — lived in another house on the far side of the backyard. She piled garbage hard up against the boundary line with Bernadette's garden. Her sister and nephew were plotting to drive her out, Bernadette told us, so they could take over her home. I was skeptical until Marie-Catherine filled me in. When Bernadette was still grieving for her husband and under pressure to renounce any inheritance, her four children banded together and asked their mother to sign over the house to them. Bernadette did. Now they were trying to sell it out from under her — to their cousin, the hated nephew next door. The deal had fallen through only because the bank denied him a mortgage. Meanwhile Bernadette's children were urging her to move into government-subsidized senior housing, but she was resisting. At sixty-eight, she was in excellent health. She cleaned houses for a living, after all. It was conceivable she could live, like Mamie, into her nineties. The children could not be disinherited, but apparently they didn't want to wait.

Marie-Catherine said that although Fleur made decent money as an accountant, she frequently showed up at Bernadette's home at dinnertime, expecting to be fed or at least treated to a fast-food meal. And indeed, that night, in order not to pillage our Sunday menu, Bernadette would take Fleur, her boyfriend, and their child to McDonald's, her grandson's favourite. Bernadette paid.

She originally worked four and a half days a week at the Jeanselmes', where Marie-Catherine paid her a rate almost 30 percent higher than the minimum wage. She also worked as a personal-care worker half a day a week for an invalid in her village. Then Fleur asked Bernadette to babysit one day a week, for free. Knowing Bernadette couldn't refuse her daughter and knowing that the housekeeper needed the money, Marie-Catherine didn't dock any pay. She continued to pay Bernadette as if she still worked four and a half days a week at the Jeanselmes'.

Bernadette's love for her children was unconditional, total, and blind. I understood. For instance, it seemed unthinkable to me that my boys would ever plot against me. Then again, I never expected Ben to persona non grata me from his matrimonial paperwork.

Fleur, twenty-nine, peered into the pot of *rôti de pigeons*. Sniffing it, she disagreed about adding the wine vinegar just yet. Bernadette ignored her daughter and dumped it in. "I cook it well so the flavours blend," Bernadette told Sam and me, stirring the mixture over low heat. "Tomorrow I only need to warm it up." Rebuffed, Fleur focused on the *tarte*. She had arrived with all the ingredients for the *tarte aux pralines*. Carefully explaining each step to Sam, she got out her portable scale and weighed the flour, sugar, and butter ("must be at room temperature"). Meanwhile she asked Sam and me to smash the pralines, sugar-coated almonds a lurid shade of pink that were a specialty of Lyon, a hundred kilometres to the north. I remember seeing them in the *pâtisserie* windows when I visited Ben, but the unnatural colour had disconcerted me, and I'd never tried them. In France, regional cuisines were so distinctive that food tastes changed every fifty kilometres, a reflection of the furthest a person might travel from home in the pre-industrialized era. In Canada, although it took fifteen hours to drive from Toronto to Thunder Bay, everyone ate the identical feedlot hamburgers, the same boxes of cornflakes, the uniformly tasteless broccoli shipped from mega-farms in California.

It seemed a pity to smash the candied almonds to smithereens, but I soon stopped feeling sorry for them. The pralines were like stones. We tried pulverizing them with a mortar and pestle, but they bounced out of the mortar. We used a rolling pin, but when we clubbed them, they flew all over Bernadette's spotless tiled floor. Sam finally put the almonds in a thick plastic bag and pounded them into oblivion.

Fleur, the only one of Bernadette's four children who wasn't a professional chef, told me she loved to cook. She was methodical and organized. She preheated the oven to the equivalent of 350°F. As she mixed the flour, butter, and sugar with her bare hands, she debated aloud whether to add an egg now or later. She added the egg. "This is *pâte sablée*," she explained. "It must end up like sand or the pastry will crack when you bake it." She formed the dough into a ball, wrapped it in plastic, and stuck it in the fridge. Later she would roll out the chilled dough and bake the crust. Once it cooled, she would fill it with a mixture of crushed pralines and *crème fraîche*. But we couldn't hang around and watch the baking. Marie-Catherine arrived, looking relaxed and refreshed.

It was time to head home.

CHAPTER FIVE

Sunday Lunch

The *mistral* brought heavy rains overnight. A steady downpour lulled everyone to sleep in except François. He rose before dawn and quietly made himself a simple breakfast. Then he slipped out to Mass at the church in Allex. He planned to spend the rest of the day helping Davit pour a new cement floor for an apartment the Jeanselmes were paying him to build in the garage for his family. François had borrowed a cement mixer from a neighbour, who needed it back the next day.

Marie-Catherine and the children planned to attend Sunday Mass in Romans-sur-Isère while Sam and I explored the Sunday market in the municipal square. The rain meant the outdoor market would be closed. However, we needed to go to Bernadette's right after church, so for logistical convenience Sam and I needed to attend Mass, too.

Marie-Catherine quickly roused Pierre-Marie and Philomène while I hauled Sam out of his daybed. He was sleep-deprived because Mamie's room was in an adjoining *salon*, originally connected through an archway that was now plugged only with a bookcase. Back from the hospital, she muttered to herself all night, which was good for Sam's French comprehension but not his sleep patterns. Eventually the old lady would drift off to sleep, and so would Sam. Then early each morning the baby's crying would awaken her toddler brother, who would stomp and clatter around their upstairs room, which just happened to be directly above Sam's *salon*.

I buttered six rusks and warmed some milk for Philo, who came into the kitchen sleepily rubbing both her good eye and her prosthetic one. Marie-Catherine hurriedly packed a lunch for her because, as a diabetic, Philo couldn't eat the lunch we would later have at Bernadette's.

"*Dix centimètres*," said Marie-Catherine as she drove as fast as she could through the downpour. By the time we arrived in Romans-sur-Isère, Mass had already started. Marie-Catherine dropped us off while she went in search of a parking space.

Inside, the cathedral of Notre Dame de Lourdes was packed. People recognized Philo and Pierre-Marie and made room for them. Sam and I squeezed into what should have been a single spot at the end of the very back row, next to a woman with three young children. I don't know how Sam felt, but I was happy. As the late *New York Times* media columnist David Carr wrote in his searing memoir about his crack addiction, he would go to church just "to sit next to them," his kids.

Biology determines that dads can never experience the same physical intimacy as mothers, so a mom's separations and milestones are more bittersweet. We start with the womb, where we feel the kicks and later the powerful contractions, and finally the stupendous spasm down the birth canal. And when our breasts swell with milk, we experience a physicality that cannot be replicated by anything else. I breastfed Ben for eleven months and Sam for ten. Sam latched on so well I could *hear* my breast milk gushing down his tiny throat. I feared the torrent would choke him, but he never coughed once. His turbo-feedings lasted an astonishing fifteen seconds, so I also fretted he wasn't getting enough to eat. Surprising new research found that mothers produce higher-quality milk, with greater calories and lipids, for sons than for daughters. Scientists theorize this has something to do with evolutionary biology. At any rate, Sam grew fatter and fatter until I could insert dimes into the folds of his thighs. (Don't worry—I restrained the impulse.)

Once he started walking, and inevitably tired himself out, he would clamour to be carried. When he turned three or four and became too heavy to lug around, he still occasionally raised his arms in the air. "Carry me," he'd say. Norman would respond like a normal parent: "You're too big now." But I heard something different—less a request for transportation, more a plea for affirmation. So I would swoop him up in my arms, whispering, "Sam, I'll *always* carry you." At the same time, I would warn him I might get tired. In other words, *he* was not the problem for continuing to grow; *I* was just not strong enough. I'd stagger with him in my arms for half a minute and set him down, and he contentedly went on his way.

As a kid, Sam gave me endless hugs and kisses, but that stopped as he neared puberty—the Oedipus complex and all that. Now in the cathedral in Romans-sur-Isère, I closed my eyes and soaked in the warmth of my son. Even if I had to sit through a Mass, the chance to be so close to Sam, even involuntarily on his part, was bliss.

The church in this economically depressed town seemed to provide spiritual sustenance. The turnout was large. The congregation — young, middle-aged, and very old —was casually dressed in jeans, stretch pants, and bomber jackets. No one looked prosperous. Early industrialization had created a strong labour movement, but the unions had been destroyed along with the factories. Despite massive unemployment, or perhaps because of it, Romans retained its proletarian leanings. The town continued to elect left-wingers and socialists to the *Assemblée Nationale*.

The neo-Gothic outline of the pink stucco cathedral dominated the modest skyline of Romans. Built in 1937 in the heyday of the shoe industry, a seven-metre statue of Our Lady of Lourdes topped its sharply pointed bell tower. Frescoes depicting the stations of the cross, by Jacques Martin-Ferrieres, a French impressionist painter and local Resistance fighter, decorated the main V-shaped auditorium. Toward the top of its soaring ceilings, modern stained-glass windows allowed in soft pearly light from the rainstorm.

I counted about three hundred people, all white except for three black kids in the pew in front of me. I was the only Asian. The heating was minimal. Everyone, the choir included, kept their overcoats on throughout. At the back, a few babies crawled on the freezing concrete. Half a dozen parents rhythmically pushed strollers in vain attempts to silence their infants. At the front, a priest paced confidently back and forth like a talk-show host. Microphone in hand, he preached about God and love and St. Paul. The choirmaster, a hefty thirtysomething in a leather jacket, looked like a truck driver, but conducted the choir with impeccable musicality and sang the tenor solos like an angel. The parishioners knew the rituals and melodic responses without consulting the hymnbook. They sang with gusto, especially the *hallelujahs* and *amens*.

A procession of choirboys of wildly varying heights carried fat white candles, lit, as they circled the pews. When it was time for communion, I spotted Bernadette in line for a wafer. When Marie-Catherine urged Sam and me to join the queue, I feared she had forgotten we were heathens. "When you reach the priest, fold your arms into a cross," she whispered. "Then you will get a blessing but no wafer."

As I reached the priest, he put the palm of his hand on my forehead.

"*Benédiction*," he said.

I suddenly felt at peace.

After Mass, Pierre-Marie found Bernadette and kissed her on both cheeks. He was in a particularly good mood because he would sleep at her house, a welcome change from his routine of watching endless videos.

By the time we reached Bernadette's house, the skies were cottony and grey, but the rain had finally stopped. Overnight the *mistral* had knocked over several flowerpots and had even uprooted her outsized canvas patio umbrella. Sam quickly set things right. "What about wiping down Bernadette's car?" I whispered to Sam. My son, who had helped me wash our family van maybe a total of *once* in his life, immediately agreed. It was the least we could do to repay her, an act of kindness for a *maniaque*.

By the time we finished swabbing down her car and returned to the kitchen, Bernadette was warming the *rôti de pigeons* on the stovetop. Sam and Philomène spread the warm grainy dark pâté onto slices of fresh baguette. The pigeon was good but not *that* good considering the trouble we'd taken—buying good bacon, hunting down a pigeon farmer, trussing the tiny birds with the bacon, pan-braising them with garlic, pulling off all the meat, and then grinding it all up and mixing it with vinegar. Speaking of which, I couldn't detect a trace of acid, despite the eighth of a cup she had added.

Bernadette, who owned many fine things, brought out hand-painted flutes from Perrier-Jouët, the champagne maker. Into each glass, she poured a slug of *crème de cassis*, topped with two inches of Bourgogne Chardonnay, to make *kir*, the classic French *apéritif*. The *apéro* was named after Félix Kir, the post-war mayor of nearby Dijon, who tirelessly promoted the cocktail because it used two local products.

Somehow Bernadette had found the time to prepare a second appetizer: tiny glass ramekins of garnet-red chilled beet mousse, topped with a dollop of *crème fraîche*, an *amuse-bouche* that wouldn't have been out of place at the three-star l'Atelier de Joël Robuchon. We scraped our glasses clean and licked our spoons. As we stood around her kitchen island, the women began discussing the best way to skin a goat. "You slit a hole in the leg, and pump it full of air," said Marie-Catherine. They moved on to the traditional Drôme pig slaughter. Marie-Catherine grabbed my notebook and sketched a cartoon of a boy and a girl tugging at a pig from opposite directions, one pulling the nose, the other yanking the tail. Her caption: "C'mon, big beast.

Don't be afraid. You're going to enter a good house!" She showed it to Bernadette, who laughed uproariously.

They decided Sam and I needed to witness a pig slaughter to truly understand the *cuisine du terroir* of the Drôme. The *abattage fermier traditionnel du cochon*, or *la tuade* in the vernacular, was a key event in rural life. Itinerant butchers went farm to farm in winter to slaughter pigs and make snout-to-tail charcuterie on-site. Using every part of the pig—blood, stomach, snout, ears, brains, and trotters—they produced *boudin noir*, hams, *lardons*, sausages, headcheese, and *caillette*. Marie-Catherine and Bernadette promised to put out the word. Sam looked hopeful.

The heavy oak table in the formal dining room was set with dark-green charger plates, Bernadette's grandmother's antique porcelain and silver, crystal wineglasses, and pressed linen napkins. We drank Badoit mineral water, flat and sparkling, and a bottle of a light red Crozes-Hermitage from the northern Rhône region. For our first course, Bernadette served two versions of *caillette*, the local meatball of ground pig parts. A large *caillette de Chabeuil* she'd bought the day before from Comptoir Drômois des Viandes was served cold. A smaller *caillette de Grimaud*, the size of a softball, had been warmed in the oven. We cut the richness of the *caillette* with a salad of butter lettuce dressed, of course, with Bernadette's own vinaigrette. She mixed the dressing right in the salad bowl—salt, freshly ground pepper, splash of red wine vinegar, ¼ cup of sunflower oil, and a dash of olive oil. She normally would have added a clove of crushed garlic, but Marie-Catherine, who was classically French in every other way, hated garlic.

Bernadette had left the lettuce leaves whole. I watched everyone, including Pierre-Marie and Philomène, use their knives to neatly fold each leaf into layers onto their forks so the lettuce wouldn't slap them wetly on the cheek as they ate. Curious, I asked Bernadette why she hadn't torn the lettuce into bite-sized bits or why no one cut their lettuce into smaller pieces. Was it because cooks wanted to inflict the least violence on the delicate lettuce? She shrugged. Marie-Catherine suggested the custom stemmed from medieval times when cutting lettuce would have corroded the iron blades of knives. No one knew the answer (and neither did Google). That was the way it always was done, Bernadette finally said.

Sam and I returned to the kitchen to watch her prepare the broth for the *ravioles*. She put on a pot of water to boil and tossed in two chicken-flavoured bouillon cubes. When I expressed shock, she shrugged. "With a family, you make whatever you have on hand." As we cooked our way through France and Italy, I would discover that many home cooks relied on bouillon cubes and gels, but *not*, surprisingly, in China.

We polished off the miniature pillows of pasta stuffed with cheese and herbs, served in shallow soup plates. Next Bernadette warmed the *blanquette de veau*, stirring in ½ cup of full-fat cream from Normandy and the mushrooms she had prepared the day before. Her cookbook called for a last-minute dash of lemon juice and two egg yolks to thicken the cream sauce. "*Pas necessaire,*" Bernadette said, blithely skipping both steps. And she was right. The *blanquette de veau* was rich enough without yolks, although frankly shoe leather would have tasted fine in that cream sauce.

By 3:25 p.m., I slipped into a food coma (*un coma alimentaire*). We'd been eating and drinking for two and a half hours. I was also red in the face from drinking, first the *kir*, and then a glass of Crozes-Hermitage. I had taken a risk by mixing wines because I've been known to pass out after a shockingly tiny amount of booze. Sam and I (but not Ben) suffer from something called "Asian Flush Syndrome." One-third to one-half of Asians, including Japanese, Koreans, Vietnamese, and Filipinos, lack acetaldehyde dehydrogenase, an enzyme that metabolizes alcohol. Not only do Sam and I get uncomfortably red in the face if we drink, we have an increased risk of esophageal cancer. Thanks to Asian Flush, half a glass of wine turns me bright red, including my eyelids, neck, forehead, chin, and nose. It feels like I'm simultaneously having an allergy attack and cardiac arrhythmia. I start sneezing. My fingertips vibrate with my pulse. Very occasionally, the room spins, and I might throw up. The advantage is I'm a very cheap drunk.

Bernadette brought out the cheese course from Laiterie Gérentes, artfully displayed on a crystal platter: a crumbly blue, a velvety soft disc of floral *brebis* from ewe's milk, a mild Saint-Félicien from cows grazed in the Ardèche, and its famous little brother, a soft creamy Saint-Marcellin that came in its own glazed ceramic pot. Bernadette had added a tangy St. Môret, a cream cheese that shares zero DNA with that xanthan-gum-laced white brick known as Philadelphia Cream Cheese. By now my eyelids were fluttering. With a super-human effort, I kept them open. Fleur's *tarte aux pralines* had failed. It should have solidified, but instead it resembled a runny raspberry pie. I forced myself to taste a sliver. It was tooth-achingly sweet, indistinguishable from pecan pie (which I hate).

At five, as I was in imminent danger of toppling off my chair, Bernadette prepared an invigorating tisane of thyme fresh from her garden. Then she suggested we move to her sunken living room to watch old VHS wedding videos because, somewhere in them, was a glimpse of her late husband. I collapsed on her sofa and snoozed while Sam and the others dutifully watched the videos. At seven thirty, our six-and-a-half-hour lunch finally came to an end. As we kissed Pierre-Marie and Bernadette goodbye, she said, "We don't do lunch like this *every* day."

Back in Allex, we found François mixing cement under a dripping tarpaulin. Despite his bad back, he had been shovelling sand and powdered cement for hours while Davit poured a new floor. Sam urged François to go inside, but he wouldn't budge, so the three of them worked for several more hours in the dark. Eventually François retired to his private bunkhouse. When Davit and Sam finished around ten, Davit was starving and Sam, incredibly, was hungry again. He found his tripe from the previous day's lunch in Romans-sur-Isère. With some leftover mashed potatoes, there was enough to feed two. He and Davit wolfed the tripe down, splitting a bottle of beer between them.

CHAPTER SIX

The Georgians

The three-room apartment Davit was building in the garage for his young family wouldn't have a real kitchen — just a microwave and sink — but it would be bright and airy and, most important, a place they could call their own. Crucially, if Davit could show French authorities that the family had lived at a fixed address for several years, they would have a better chance at asylum.

The Jeanselmes covered all the Georgian family's living costs. They even gave Davit a second-hand grey Citroën they'd bought eight years earlier with eighty thousand kilometres on it *and* paid for the gasoline. Now he could pick up a weekly food basket from a refugee centre, take Rüska and their newborn daughter to the doctor, and get to appointments with the French bureaucracy all over the Drôme. The most generous people might have considered Davit's labour — building the garage apartment — a fair exchange. After all, he and his family were going to live in it once it was completed. But the Jeanselmes paid him the going rate for construction. "He should not work for free," Marie-Catherine said firmly. "It is very important that he be able to pay for things for his family — a haircut for Rüska, toys for his children. One day they will leave. I have no idea when. But then the apartment reverts to us, and that is why we pay him. They keep their dignity. The most important thing is they don't owe you anything."

Rüska had arrived in France first. In Georgia, she studied sports science, massage, and kinesiology at university, and had been a competitive fencer. In late 2013, she paid a smuggler to take her to France. That Christmas, Catholic nuns in Lyon found her shivering outside a church. She was three months pregnant. They placed her in a women's shelter but asked her to leave after Andrie was born. She had nowhere to go. Then someone remembered the Jeanselmes, who had recently left Lyon after François retired as headmaster of Lycée Don Bosco. The Jeanselmes took in Rüska and her baby. Davit arrived by plane a few months later, fully intending to overstay his tourist visa. He, too, moved into the farmhouse in Allex. A month later, Rüska was pregnant again, giving birth two weeks before Sam and I arrived. She and Davit named their second child "Kéti," a diminutive of *Katayoun*, or Catherine, in gratitude to the woman who had given them refuge.

By the time we showed up, Rüska and Andrie had been living at the Jeanselmes' for more than a year, and Davit for ten months. When Andrie had a tantrum, they couldn't discipline him in private. If Kéti cried, they tried to shush her. If the couple quarrelled (which they never seemed to) they had no privacy. Sam and I understood because as houseguests we, too, had to be on our best behaviour. When I developed a bad cough, I felt twice as bad because I worried about spreading it to Rüska, her newborn baby, Mamie, the handicapped children, or the whole household. Every time I coughed at night, I worried I was keeping Marie-Catherine awake. Like me, the Georgians tried not to make noise. And when the door to their separate wing was closed, I heard almost nothing. Only Sam heard them each morning when Andrie's feet clattered across the floor.

Davit was a good husband. Late one night when Rüska had a fever, he dosed her with a traditional Georgian tonic: a mug of boiling water mixed with half a jar of homemade raspberry preserves he found in the pantry. Miraculously, the excessive sugar didn't kill her; it cured her. The jam was a gift from François's eighty-nine-year-old mother, who had picked the berries from her own bushes. (Full disclosure: I had a spoonful, too, purely for investigative purposes. It was delicious.) The annoyance of having houseguests who helped themselves to your elderly mother's artisanal jam aside, covering the Georgians' expenses was not trivial.

Both François and Marie-Catherine were retired, with three dependents. The utility bills were high with so many people living together, taking showers, cooking, and doing their laundry. In France, a kilowatt-hour cost one-third more than in Canada. Sam observed that François worked in utter darkness at his computer late into the night. "Our expenses broke the sound barrier this year," said Marie-Catherine with a deep sigh. "It cost so much money to take care of the Iraqis. But that's how I expressed my faith in God. We saved one family." At least the Iraqis were gone. They had stayed five months. Jabba, the single Georgian, had stayed even less time. But the new Georgians had no foreseeable departure date. And now the Jeanselmes were trying to save more families. François was organizing the rescue of Iraqi Yazidis, who practise a syncretic religion influenced by Christianity, Zoroastrianism, and Islam.

I didn't enjoy houseguests who stayed longer than a week. I was still scarred from a friend's visit (a family of three) that had somehow stretched to more than five weeks. The previous summer, Marie-Catherine had had no room to put up her own adult children, so she'd booked a *gîte*, a holiday rental, in a nearby village. What with looking after Mamie, Jabba getting drunk, and her full-time teaching job at nursing school, she reached the breaking point.

"I finished the school year on my knees," said Marie-Catherine, who had just retired. How did she cope with the lack of privacy, with strangers, including me, cooking in her kitchen, breaking the crockery, and slowing down her Wi-Fi? "Taking care of friends and taking in refugees are different. With you, I make arrangements, I take you out," she said. "Now Rüska and Davit are my friends, but they are not like guests. You give them your roof. You help them with paperwork. They have a need. You tell them the rules. If they get drunk once, you tell them, 'No.' They leave. They can't give me their laundry. I don't cook for them."

Her sheltering of refugees was in the finest French tradition of *liberté, égalité, fraternité*. Yet she and François were doing this against a backdrop of far-right politicians who were promising to secure France's borders against migrants. "The fact that they have no status or papers—it's an honour for me to meet people like that. I have no idea if Iraqis or Syrians are coming next. When I hear the parable of Jesus, how God says, 'I was hungry and you fed me, I was thirsty and you gave me drink,' I know that love is the most powerful force. You find the beauty in someone. All the love of God is found in people. For us, faith is radical."

Marie-Catherine grew up with a violent and abusive father. At thirteen, she had an epiphany when a priest came to her school to speak about rescuing the poor of Calcutta. "I felt he was talking directly to me. I understood that faith was not babbling, *blah, blah, blah*." Her faith was reinforced after her father subsequently underwent a religious conversion and became gentle and loving. She and François did not impose their religion on others. For instance, they never uttered a critical word about Rüska and Davit living in unwedded bliss, but they were pleased the couple was planning to get married as soon as certified translations of their birth certificates arrived from Georgia; it also helped that one of the Jeanselme daughters was a single parent.

Rüska and Davit were Eastern Orthodox Christians for whom the Catholic Pope was a mere bishop. The Iraqis refugees had also been Christian. Wealthy elites who had trouble adjusting to sleepy Allex, they had suddenly decamped for Lyon without a word, stealing some of the Jeanselmes' household items as they left. François's refugee organization continued to help them, putting down a deposit for a Lyon apartment. The family didn't like that, either, and disappeared for a second time. Perhaps the Iraqis had endured unspeakable trauma, or perhaps they were jerks. Despite their thievery and ingratitude, Marie-Catherine still spoke fondly of them. She even laughed at herself for committing a faux pas — she once tried to serve them port-soaked melon with Bayonne ham, not realizing that Iraqi Christians had adopted the majority Muslim culture's prohibition on pork and alcohol.

Unlike the Iraqis, Davit and Rüska were less cavalier, more cautious. As an undocumented migrant in France, he couldn't get a driver's licence. For a year now, he had been illegally driving the Jeanselmes' gift, always staying within the speed limit. He also fished illegally in the Drôme, not to amuse himself but to feed his family. (He had carefully doctored Pierre-Marie's recreational permit with his own photo in case the cops stopped him.) By this point, Sam and I decided I should use pseudonyms in my book to avoid causing legal trouble for the Jeanselmes and the refugees.

Then François explained it was no longer a crime for a French citizen to harbour an undocumented migrant if the citizen was acting for humanitarian reasons, a result of recent rulings by the European Court of Justice. Organizations such as Secours Catholique and the French Red Cross openly provided food, showers, and shelter to the *sans-papiers* who gathered near Calais, waiting for a chance to cross the Chunnel to the UK, which didn't require ID cards for work. Indeed, the Georgians were known to French authorities in myriad ways. Under the French social system, refugees' medical expenses were covered. Rüska had given birth, twice, in French hospitals, using her own name, and had been treated like any other mother. Davit went regularly to a refugee centre for help with his refugee file. He and Rüska were applying to the government for permanent residency, under their real names. Each week, the local food bank prepared a basket for them—not the packages of cheap pasta and peanut butter we foist on the needy in Canada but unblemished apples, tangerines, a dozen kiwis, a giant cauliflower, a sack of potatoes, containers of yogourt, individually wrapped wedges of real Camembert, jars of duck *confit* and *cassoulet*, slices of *tarte Tatin*, hot dogs (the good French kind), slabs of smoked bacon, and diapers in two sizes for his children.

Still, the Georgians, without papers, lived in a kind of limbo. Far-right politicians were trying to end the basic right to free education for all children in France, a law that dated to 1881. Their presence in Allex was a poorly kept secret. At any time, a neighbour or a shopkeeper could snitch to the authorities, and Davit and Rüska could be deported. But the neighbours were on board. "They said, 'If *les flics* show up, send the Georgians over to my place to hide,'" Marie-Catherine said, using the slang for cops. Some neighbours hired Davit to do odd jobs for them, paying him the going rate. And when there wasn't enough room at the Jeanselme farmhouse to shelter the Georgians *and* the Iraqis, an elderly neighbour two doors over stepped up. "I can have some of them stay with me," she said.

During the past century, France has experienced waves of immigration. After World War II, Vietnamese, Moroccans, and Algerians arrived from the French colonies. In the 1980s, migration continued from Africa, Asia, and Eastern Europe. Following the financial crisis of 2008, the number of migrants from Spain, Portugal, and Italy doubled. Each year thousands of undocumented workers obtained residency permits in France—including more than twenty thousand in 2009—some on humanitarian grounds. That gave Davit and Rüska hope. At the very least, their children would automatically attain citizenship at age eighteen because they had been born on French soil.

Estimates of *les sans-papiers* in France, including the traditionally nomadic Roma, ranged from two hundred thousand to four hundred thousand. In 2011, France expelled twenty-eight thousand undocumented migrants and said its goal was to deport thirty-five thousand annually. The ongoing economic crisis, coupled with Britain's Brexit vote to leave the European Union, intensified pressure on France. Today nearly one in five residents hail from elsewhere or have at least one immigrant parent, many of them Arabs, Berbers, sub-Saharan Africans, or Turks. High unemployment rates for citizens and immigrants alike have created pools of alienated youths. Then came the attacks, some by French-born terrorists.

The first was at the satirical magazine *Charlie Hebdo* and a kosher super-market (17 dead, 22 injured); then at the Bataclan theatre (130 dead, 352 injured); finally, the truck mowing down pedestrians on Bastille Day on the Promenade des Anglais in Nice (84 dead, 434 injured).

I was sympathetic to migrants. My grandfather arrived from China in 1880 to help build the Canadian Pacific Railway. My three other grand-parents, who came from China at the turn of the twentieth century, paid a discriminatory head tax. François was sympathetic, too, but he said that fifteen years earlier his country had made a mistake in ending universal conscription as a condition of citizenship. The shared experience of mil-itary training had been the cultural glue that held people together, he said. But instead of imbuing young men with common values, official govern-ment policy encouraged immigrants to retain their ethnic traditions. Canada did that, yet as a third-generation Montrealer, I was the only one among my siblings to speak Chinese, and only because I studied it at uni-versity. By the time Sam and I visited France, the authorities were so anxious about undocumented migrants that the country was threatening to withdraw from the Schengen Agreement, the landmark 1985 treaty abolishing border checks among European signatories. The Jeanselmes told me that France set impossibly high hurdles for undocumented migrants. Davit had only eight days to claim asylum once he landed in France. He had been too nervous to reveal himself to authorities and let the deadline pass. Now we watched him struggle with another deadline: twenty-one days to complete an application file. He missed that deadline, too, because several critical documents he needed were in Georgia, requiring certified translations, and hadn't arrived in time. "*C'est impossible*," said Marie-Catherine. "The authorities want to discourage people." While she and François offered advice and encouragement, they believed that Davit and Rüska had to sort out their status themselves.

Davit became our default guide whenever Marie-Catherine was busy. I felt bad about draining his gas tank. Gasoline cost more than in econo-mically straitened Georgia, 50 percent more than in Canada, and 200 percent more than in the US. I offered several times to fill up his tank, but Davit always declined and continued to drive us around. He was tall and athletic—his father had played professional basketball—and I had to trot beside him to keep up with his long stride when he took us for a walk along the Drôme River.

As we hiked along the river bank, it became apparent that he knew a lot about many things. When we passed some men in white suits huddled around large raised boxes in an empty field, Davit explained that they were beekeepers — he'd kept his own bees back in Georgia. Sam had never met anyone like Davit, a miracle man who could lay bricks, pour cement, and repair an old Citroën. He'd fermented his own wine in huge oak casks in his cellar back home. He understood the local geology, too. He explained why the water level of the Drôme was so low, the type of drainage system engineers had employed, and the kinds of fish that swam there — trout, grayling, and carp.

At night, sitting around the kitchen table, Sam and Davit would companionably split a single beer — never more — mindful of the sensitivities of our hosts. Davit told us he had been shocked that the Iraqi family staying with the Jeanselmes had no idea where Georgia was, even though only Turkey separated their respective countries. "We're almost neighbours," Davit said in frustration. He turned to Sam. "Do *you* know where Georgia is?" One day earlier, Sam had been curious enough to Google Georgia — he now knew it was a country of 4.5 million people at the intersection of Europe and Asia, located between the Black and the Caspian Seas. Davit was pleased. After graduating in engineering and economics, he worked as an economist at the Ministry of Population in Tbilisi, the capital. Unfortunately, Georgia was in a precipitous economic decline following the collapse of the Soviet Union. One day the government stopped paying him. Davit became a statistic, one of 65 million refugees and migrants, the largest number in history, roaming the world in search of a stable home. In Allex, whenever he amassed 600 euros from construction jobs, he sent 500 home. He and Rüska used the Jeanselmes' computer to Skype their parents. Each online visit was emotionally wrenching. "Their parents go to a neighbour's home to borrow a computer," said Marie-Catherine. "Everyone is wearing coats indoors because there's no heat. They have nothing to eat."

Occasionally when preparing meals, we helped ourselves to the Georgians' food supplies, guiltily at first. Then I realized nobody in the Jeanselme household seemed to care who ate what, including François's mother's raspberry jam. It was like living in a 1960s hippie commune. Given that I seemed to be the only adult with a steady paycheck, I bought groceries whenever I could. I leaned on Davit to take me shopping, usually with Andrie in tow. Sam sat in front with Davit. I sat in back with the toddler. I had to watch him closely because the ancient Citroën had no child-safety locks, and Andrie loved to fling his door open while his dad was speeding down the highway.

I was surprised the first time Davit took us to a mall. I had expected a picturesque farmers' market, where I could wander from stall to stall, wicker basket under my arm. But those outdoor markets are largely a travel writer's cliché. Commercial vacancies in French towns exceed 10 percent, with many of the surviving stores selling clothing, not groceries. Modern French families tend to buy nearly half their food at *hypermarchés*, which, unlike farmers' markets, are open seven days a week, accept plastic, and don't yell at you if squeeze the tomatoes. With the highest density of malls in Europe, French chains that combine groceries with general merchandise, such as Carrefour and Monoprix, compete ferociously. Back in 1961, when Julia Child wrote *Mastering the Art of French Cooking*, she altered her recipes to suit American supermarkets because in that era, the French shopped daily at local markets. But as families moved to the suburbs and daily commutes took longer, there was less time for shopping and for making dinner. Nowadays the French increasingly buy groceries online, picking up their orders from drive-through kiosks on the way home from work.

Yet France remained France. The typical *hypermarché* had everything the outdoor markets once had, but more conveniently. In North America, our closest equivalent was Whole Foods, the sticker-shock emporium derided as "Whole Paycheck." The French *hypermarché* was aimed not at Gwyneth Paltrow wannabes, but everyday folks. Eating organic or local were givens. Produce was labelled not only as French but also with the specific *région* and *département*. Bright-green leeks came in several varieties, unlike in our supermarkets, which offered only one kind. There were gleaming eggplants, emerald-green Swiss chard, fat white onions, and many varieties of potatoes. We spotted a dewy *frisée* the size of an extra-large pizza, its delicate fronds creamy white in the centre, deepening to chartreuse and dark green toward the outer leaves. Sam and I instantly had the same thought: *frisée aux lardons*.

The butcher section was manned by professionals who knew how to cut *and* cook meat. You could confer with them about a recipe. When I inquired about fresh *foie gras*, a butcher told me I was a couple of months too late; he sold whole lobes of raw goose livers only in November and December. They had locally made sausages and pâtés, and a dozen different varieties of ham, including several on the bone; every imaginable cut of pork, beef, duck, rabbit, chicken, goat, and kid. The counter offered four kinds of liver: pork, beef, rabbit, and calf—and each animal's kidneys, sweetbreads, and brains. In the aisles of pre-packaged meats, Sam and I spotted half a *cabri* (kid) cut up in pieces and ready for the roasting pan. We consulted Davit. Was he interested? He nodded happily.

At the cheese counter, you could buy plastic-wrapped cheese, or ask the *fromager* to cut a slice of Bleu d'Auvergne, Brie de Meaux, Roquefort, Camembert, or Époisses. *Brebis* made from ewe's milk was packaged in golden straw; small rounds of *tomme* came in terracotta ramekins. The deli counter sold everything you could order in a French bistro: *céleri remoulade*, grated carrots lightly dressed with oil and lemon, *boeuf bourguignon*, and *coq au vin*. Being a big box store, the *hypermarché* also sold detergents, table linens, electronics, budget clothing, shoes, and convenience foods such as frozen pizzas and chicken-flavoured potato chips. The wine ranged from plonk-in-a-box to pricey whites like Pouilly-Fuissé and Pouilly-Fumé.

I found *crème brûlée* in little glass ramekins; two dozen types of butter, including the best Breton variety with crunchy crystals of sea salt; and jars of *pâté de foie gras*, sealed with a thick layer of luscious yellow goose fat. In the dairy section, I found individual containers of unsweetened full-fat yogourt and gently sweetened yogourt flavoured with violets, salted caramel, pistachio, rhubarb, or pink grapefruit. Individual portions of fresh *fromage blanc* came in little recyclable glass containers. I normally skip the cake section at supermarkets back home because I'm not a fan of petroleum-by-product icing. Here, everything was made with real butter and whole eggs. I hesitated between *madeleines* and pastel-coloured *macarons*, but succumbed instead to a huge tart of fresh apricots, secure in the knowledge that our family of eleven would polish it off in one meal. Many products were made with full-on animal fats, yet obesity rates—10 percent in France—were among the lowest in Europe, compared to 66 percent in Canada. It turned out that North Americans and French view food very differently. When researchers asked subjects to free-associate words like "chocolate cake," North Americans thought "guilt," and the French thought "birthdays." Her spa day aside, I never saw Marie-Catherine exercise at all.

Davit reminded me that we needed bread. The *hypermarché* baguettes were mediocre, but I bought them anyway because they were not inferior to the village *boulangerie*. Throughout our time in France, no matter how picturesque or rustic the bakery, no matter how pretty the loaves, the *boules* and *baguettes* were often dry and flavourless, tasting more of cardboard than crust, with insipid interiors. Before you feel sad about the decline of this linchpin of Gallic cuisine, understand that the French have complained about baguettes since the reign of Louis XVI. Abbé Jacquin, an eighteenth-century writer, grumbled that the bread in his town was "a pitiful thing."

Until the 1950s, rural folk baked their bread in communal village ovens to save fuel. By 1982, almost no one was baking their own bread, but 75 percent of consumers were complaining about the quality of store-bought bread, according to a poll conducted by the governing body of the bakery trade (yes, France had one). At the same time, the price of a baguette soared by nearly 60 percent from 1990 to 2011. The baker blamed the farmer, and they both blamed consumers, who insisted on cheap bread.

When Sam and I first arrived at the Jeanselmes', I noticed a huge, restaurant-sized, brown paper sack of more than a dozen *baguettes* on the floor in a corner of the kitchen. A good Samaritan had helpfully dropped off the stale loaves to help the family feed all the extra mouths, but no one would eat any of it. Day after day, the bag got in the way, propped up, as it was, against the kitchen waste bin. After the bread had been left untouched for a week, I suggested to François that perhaps I should feed it to the chickens. He laughed.

"The chickens eat everything, but they won't eat those *baguettes*."

That night the house was in chaos again. After her hospital stay, Mamie seemed more helpless than ever. Philomène required her pre-dinner insulin shot, but couldn't or wouldn't say where she'd left her insulin kit. Pierre-Marie was feeling emotionally needy, literally hanging off Rüska as she was trying to cook a vat of buckwheat for him and a pot of fusilli for Philomène. Although she often helped us cook dinner, Rüska never ate anything after lunch. I know *I* was perpetually famished when I breastfed Ben and Sam so I don't know how she stuck to her strict post-partum diet while breastfeeding Kéti. But within a few weeks, she had dramatically slimmed down.

It was almost eight, the time when France stopped en masse for dinner.

Obviously, Sam and I would have to supplement Rüska's pasta and buckwheat. We pulled all the leftovers out of the fridge. We found gherkins, salad, and cheese. We also had the groceries from the *hypermarché*, including a container of *céleri remoulade* and that package of cut-up *cabri*. We ran to François's office to check the internet. We found a simple French recipe for roast kid—salt, pepper, and a slick of olive oil. In no time at all, Sam and I had made dinner for everyone.

The *cabri* was tender, golden, and succulent. I worried that only a few ounces of meat per person wouldn't be enough. Yet as we passed the platter of roast kid around, everyone, including Philo and Pierre-Marie, knew enough to take just one piece. Like in China, a French meal was a communal experience. It was not merely a chance to refuel but a convivial time to discuss sports, politics, culture, or food itself, all glorious meals past and future. François was impressed with the *cabri*. He asked where we got the recipe. "The internet," Sam said. Suddenly Philo choked on something. François pounded her on the back. Then Pierre-Marie gagged on a lump in the mush. I began choking because the gherkins were so sour. By then, I was fitting right in.

Most weekday mornings, the house was quiet. François usually left early for Mass and then headed to a meeting somewhere in the region about Iraqi refugees. A school bus picked up Philomène. Pierre-Marie would watch *Heartland* on the computer. Once they had had breakfast, the Georgians usually kept to their quarters. Sam would sleep in. And Marie-Catherine was often bedridden with a migraine.

At breakfast, I often found myself alone. I would make myself a steaming mug of English tea—I'd carried my favourite King Cole teabags from the Maritimes, where the tea is always strong, and the people are strong *and* nice. I would transform a slice of stale baguette with a smear of sweet butter and a spoonful of homemade apricot jam. We always ate day-old bread in the morning at the Jeanselmes' house because no one could be bothered to drive to the *boulangerie*. The yogourt, however, was fresh. Every night Marie-Catherine made a batch in small glass containers by heating whole milk, adding starter yogourt, and warming it for twelve hours in a small machine. The homemade yogourt was ambrosial with the preserved apricots I'd bought from the pigeon farmer's shop.

Sometimes, before breakfast, I would go outside to toss a pail of kitchen slops at the chickens. They scurried over excitedly, pecking at orange peels, *lentilles du Puy*, cheese rinds, bones from the roast kid. The chickens weren't garden-variety omnivores — they were *cannibals*. One night after we'd had roast chicken, I asked François if I should put the bones in the slop pail. He looked a little embarrassed and nodded. The next day when I threw the scraps at the chickens, I watched in horrified fascination as three hens fought over a thighbone. The laying hens mainly ate a special feed grain. The slops were dessert, a diversionary tactic to lure away brooding chickens so I could gather eggs without getting hen-pecked. One morning I found six eggs in shades of sienna, tan, and russet, still warm and covered with poop, straw, and feathers. Davit said that in summer, the chickens easily laid a dozen eggs a day. At the kitchen sink, I scrubbed the eggs with soap and water. Sometimes I put one on to boil and, while I waited, tackled the sink full of dirty dishes. When my egg was ready, I sat down all alone at the long table, lopped off the top, and sprinkled on sea salt and freshly ground black pepper. The yolk, the colour of a ripe persimmon, was so rich it tasted like butter.

Living in the countryside amid bucolic fields seemed a wholesome way of life. But Marie-Catherine pointed out that the traditional French farm was dying. Instead of raising a few pigs, sheep, cows, and chickens, and planting a variety of vegetables and grains, many farmers had been pushed into more profitable monoculture. The fields surrounding the Jeanselmes had been planted only with garlic, sprayed with industrial-strength pesticides that killed everything else. Some pesticide ended up splashed on the Jeanselmes' windows. Concerned, Marie-Catherine had written to the farmer to inquire what chemical he was using, explaining that she had two disabled children in fragile health. The man had written back a nasty letter. "And that was the end of that," she said.

So much for bucolic.

CHAPTER SEVEN

Odette's Flan

When we first arrived, Marie-Catherine had been close to a breakdown from sleep deprivation. The baby monitor in Mamie's salon was so sensitive Marie-Catherine could hear her mother's oxygen machine wheezing, *shssss, shssss, shssss*, all through the night. And because Mamie knew her daughter was listening, she made frequent and voluble demands — she wanted to get out of bed; she complained she was thirsty. Exhausted, but also worried that she wouldn't be able to teach us enough French cooking, Marie-Catherine had dropped notes in neighbours' mailboxes up and down the Route des Berengeres, explaining that a mother and son were arriving from Canada to learn home cooking. Could anyone help?

Nathalie, a neighbour across the road, offered to let us watch her husband prepare a dinner party. But wires got crossed, and we missed it. Then the same husband offered to teach us brioche, but by then we were so busy, we sent regrets. Another neighbour, Odette Cleysac, volunteered to teach us a classic French dessert. But in the excitement of her first-ever spa appointment, Marie-Catherine forgot to tell us. When Odette dropped by that Saturday to fetch us, Sam and I were in Romans-sur-Isère at the shoe museum. Odette came by *again* the next morning. Again Marie-Catherine forgot to tell us. We went to Mass and then lunch at Bernadette's. Twelve hours too late, Marie-Catherine slapped her forehead and confessed we'd once again stood Odette up. I figured we'd burned our bridges, but I looked on the bright side. Monday would be our first slow day. I was brushing my teeth around ten a.m. when Marie-Catherine pounded on the bathroom door.

"Can you go over to Odette's in half an hour?"

I roused Sam, who groaned and rolled over. Ten minutes later, I called him again, to no avail. Marie-Catherine arrived as reinforcement. "What are you doing here?" she said, barging into Sam's darkened room. "You're supposed to be *there*." She pointed vaguely in the direction of the kitchen. Sam sprang out of bed and pulled on his clothes. We raced out of the house … in the general direction of *there*.

Standing on the Route des Berengeres, my son and I looked at one another. Where exactly was *there*? I was still having trouble orienting myself *inside* the house, never mind outside. Sam thought *I* knew where Odette lived. I thought *he* had understood Marie-Catherine's finger pointing. We hustled blindly down the road, worried we were late, conscious we had twice stood Odette up, arguing about which side of the road Marie-Catherine meant. We hesitated in front of a creamy stucco house with pale green shutters, three small chimneys, and a terracotta-tiled roof. Might this be Odette's home? Gingerly we rang the doorbell.

Someone inside shouted that the door was unlocked. We opened it a crack.

"*Est-ce qu'Odette demeure ici?*" I called out.

"*Oui, oui! Je suis Odette. Allez, allez!*"

We climbed the stairs to the second floor. A woman with pure white hair waited at the top. Without so much as a handshake, she led us into her spotless utilitarian kitchen. Odette, I realized, was the neighbour who had sheltered the young Iraqi couple in her ground-floor apartment. Compared to handling refugee overflow, perhaps our double no-shows were only a minor annoyance in her life. She brushed off our apologies. "*Pas de problème,*" she said briskly, donning an apron.

At eighty, Odette was as rotund as the Michelin tire man, but in a grandmotherly, huggable way. Even though she was at home and about to impart a cooking lesson, like Mamie, she was dressed formally in a dark wool burgundy skirt that fell below her knees, a flowered blouse, thick hose, and low-heeled leather shoes. Her kitchen was simple but cozy. Lace curtains covered windows overlooking the same garlic fields. Her stove was an ancient electric model. Her toaster, obviously rarely used, was on the floor, relegated to a corner next to her iron. A mid-century green Formica table in the centre of the room doubled as a worktable.

"We're going to make a *flan* today. It's very simple." Formally called *crème renversée au caramel*, it was such a classic dessert that it had been on Julia Child's final exam at Le Cordon Bleu in 1950. Like *crème brûlée*, it was always eaten chilled. Despite its name, it used no cream—only sugar, eggs, and milk, baked slowly until silky smooth. Odette, a farmer's daughter, said that it was a dish from her childhood. "On the farm, everything was available," she said. "And our region, the Drôme, is full of delicious things."

Odette bent down, opened a low cupboard, and pulled out an ancient aluminum ring mould with scalloped edges. Setting it on her stove, she tossed in ten sugar cubes, splashed in some tap water and turned on the flame. "Do *not* stir it," she cautioned, or the sugar would crystallize around the spoon and create a mess. She carefully swirled the liquid around until it turned a deep amber, then shut off the heat and tilted the mould to coat the sides.

Odette abruptly decided to double the recipe. She melted more sugar in another saucepan, then poured the caramel into individual ramekins, swirling each to coat the sides. In another pot, she heated a litre of milk, dissolving ten more sugar cubes. As an afterthought, she added two tiny envelopes of vanilla-scented sugar. While the milk heated, she whisked six eggs from Marie-Catherine and beat in a cup of sugar.

"I got this cookbook when I got married, sixty years ago," she said, pulling out a tattered tome. She knew the recipe for *crème renversée* by heart but wanted Sam and me to read it. Unlike Bernadette's cookbook, which was well-used but pristine, Odette's was yellowed and stained. "It's all busted up because I use it so much," she said, shrugging. Like Bernadette's, it had hundreds of brief recipes. The one for *crème renversée* was a single paragraph and suggested that the oven be "hot, but not too hot." Odette added the hot milk to the egg-and-sugar mixture, ladle by ladle. "She's tempering the mixture," Sam explained to me. "Otherwise, she'll end up with scrambled eggs." As she boiled some water to prepare a *bain-marie*, she asked Sam, "What do you call it in English?" Sam said, "A *bain-marie*." Odette laughed.

Her legs were thick and swollen, and she had trouble walking. Still, Odette stood during our entire cooking lesson. She exercised with a daily swim at the community pool. Each year, Marie-Catherine told me, Odette went away to a fat farm to lose weight, but always returned, her face gaunt, her figure as rotund as ever. Widowed in 1967 when her husband was killed in a farming accident, she raised her two young boys alone, earning money by babysitting other children. One son was now a priest in Prague. The other lived two kilometres away, so she often had lunch or dinner with him and her grandchildren.

I said it was so good of Odette to shelter the Iraqis. She told us she admired the Jeanselmes. "They're a remarkable family, so generous, so kind. Marie-Catherine is a nurse. She comes by to take my blood pressure, to see what's wrong with me. She helps all the neighbours."

She slipped the *bain-marie* into the oven. How long should the *crème renversée* bake? "Maybe twenty minutes. It depends." And how hot? "When you make it often, you don't worry about the exact temperature," she said, batting my question away with her hands.

Another neighbour suddenly appeared in the kitchen. She had come upstairs without knocking. "I'm so sorry I'm late," she said breathlessly. "I was picking up all the branches in my garden after yesterday's terrible wind." Her name was Madeleine, and she lived next door. She was eighty-three, and, like Odette, she was dressed formally in a skirt with a silk scarf artfully twisted around her neck. Later, I heard from the Jeanselmes that Madeleine rarely helped others. But just as Marie-Catherine and François had tolerated the Iraqis with Christian forbearance, they put up with Madeleine. The latter always asked François to help her change the cylinder of propane gas she used for heating. She frequently prevailed upon Marie-Catherine to take her blood pressure. But she wouldn't teach Davit French, and she had dismissed Marie-Catherine's request to show us a dish.

"I can't teach you anything. I do not know how to cook," Madeleine declared airily as she settled into a kitchen chair. She had shown up at Odette's ostensibly to translate (even though we needed no help). It became clear that *she* wanted a chance to practise her English, which was charmingly accented but disconcertingly blunt. More than half a century earlier, she told us proudly, she had won a six-month scholarship to study in Cleveland and had sailed across the Atlantic. Later she returned to France and became a social worker. She handled, as she put it, "delinquents and murderers."

The cleanup was simple — just two pots and a mixing bowl. "Don't wash it," Odette said, pointing to the pot sticky with crystallized sugar. "Just boil it with lots of water, and pour it down the drain."

ODETTE'S CRÈME RENVERSÉE
Serves 8.

1 litre	whole milk
6	eggs
2 cups	sugar, divided
2 tsp.	vanilla extract

Preheat oven to 325°F.

Melt 1 cup of sugar with 3 tablespoons of water in a saucepan over medium heat. Watch attentively – sugar burns fast. When golden, pour molten sugar into eight ovenproof ramekins or one medium-sized metal mould. Tilt so the caramel covers the sides.

Mix milk with ½ cup sugar and heat until steam rises; set aside.

Whisk eggs and remaining ½ cup sugar until pale and thick. Add vanilla extract. Temper egg-sugar mixture with warm milk, ladle by ladle, while whisking constantly, until the temperature of the egg-sugar mixture itself becomes warm. Then add it to remaining warm milk. Pour into the ramekins or mould.

Put ramekins or mould into a *bain-marie* (a baking pan filled halfway up with hot water) and bake at 325°F for 20 minutes or until the flan moves slightly when you shake the pan. If it trembles like unset Jell-O, it needs another 5–10 minutes.

ODETTE'S TIP: To clean the pot in which you caramelized sugar: fill it half full of water and bring to a boil. Swirl. Once the caramel dissolves, dump it down the drain.

Our work finished, Odette finally sat down. She mentioned she'd read online about the sad case of Benoît Violier, a Michelin-starred chef who had just committed suicide. The articles said he'd lost a fortune on fraudulent wine and had probably been headed for bankruptcy. They must have been desperate for money, she added, because two days after his burial, his restaurant had reopened. "I don't have internet," Madeleine replied dismissively. "I like to look at my birds."

They had been next-door neighbours for forty years. Like an old married couple, they argued over everything, including whether Sam and I should witness a pig slaughter. Marie-Catherine had been working on the problem for several days now and solicited their advice on how to find a traditional winter *tuade*. Madeleine, I was learning, was not very helpful, whether with translation or pig slaughters.

"It's forbidden to kill a pig," she said flatly.

"No, you can kill a pig," said Odette. "*Mais c'est fini en février.*"

"*Non, non.* You need a permit," said Madeleine, suggesting we ask the village butcher if we could work with him.

"The butcher won't let you watch," said Odette. "He wants to keep the recipes a secret." She got up heavily from the table to check the *flans*. When she shook the *bain-marie*, the *flan* in the mould still jiggled, but the smaller ones were perfect. The cookbook had helpfully said to bake the *flan* until "it is ready." Odette pulled out the entire batch.

That evening, despite her bad legs, she carried over all the *flans* to the Jeanselmes'. Her *crème renversée* was smooth as satin. Technically, you're supposed to unmould the *flan*, but we didn't bother. So when you hit the golden sugar at the bottom, just call it "Caramel Surprise."

CHAPTER EIGHT

Le Tuade

Until the 1950s, the itinerant *tueur* would arrive very early on a cold winter's day. At sunrise on the big day of the pig slaughter, the family put cauldrons of water to boil over open fires. With the pig suspended by a hind leg, the farmer and a farmhand braced the forelegs while the *tueur* plunged a knife, no bigger than a stiletto, into the carotid artery, bleeding out the pig into a bucket positioned beneath. Still working outdoors, several men would manoeuvre the carcass onto a wooden trestle table where they clipped and trimmed each trotter. The women poured pitchers of boiling water over the skin as the men scraped the bristles. The *tueur* neatly decapitated the pig, rinsed it, and hung it up to dry in the freezing air. Then he sliced off the haunches and legs, cut open the chest, and pulled out the viscera. Next, he removed the spine and tail. Lastly, he split the pig's head from cheek to cheek, separating the upper and lower jaws, and removed the snout, tongue, jowls, and brain. The most perishable part—the pig's blood—was made into blood pudding, or *boudin noir*.

When the *tuade* crew broke for lunch that day, the menu was always crusty bread, wine, and *boudin noir*. The finest parts—the filet, spareribs, and chops—were eaten fresh at a feast that night. Everything else was salted, smoked, or made into sausages and pâté. The lard and jowls became *caillette*, the most famous Drômoise charcuterie, which we had tasted in two versions at Bernadette's Sunday lunch. The trotters would be cooked and served with a parsley sauce. The head and cartilage would be transformed into *fromage de tête*, or headcheese. The only parts discarded were the eyeballs, spleen, and bladder, although sometimes the latter became a toy or a musical instrument. As Sam and I would find in Italy and China, too, people who knew their food enjoyed eating all the weird parts of the animal. Peasant-based cuisines wasted nothing.

"The saying goes, '*Tout est bon dans le cochon*,'" said Marie-Catherine. The farmhands lugged the meat into the kitchen for processing into charcuterie, a word derived from *chair* (flesh) and *cuit* (cooked). Women scraped the ears and snout and with darning needles sewed them into handy pockets, ready for stuffing. Men split the cleaned trotters lengthwise, pounding wooden mallets against the blunt back of axe heads. Massive hams were massaged with coarse grey sea salt and buried in crates filled with loose salt.

The tougher cuts were ground up with lard, stomach, liver, jowls, kidneys, and lungs. The farmer's wife spread the fresh mince onto a large table and scattered shocking amounts of salt on it. Younger men, who had not yet acquired precision knife skills, worked the seasoning into the ground meat with their bare hands. In the Drôme, this specific charcuterie was called *salaison*, derived from "sal" for salt, a nod to the region's strategic location on the salt route. Air-dried, *salaison* would keep for several years. Tougher cuts, like the *poitrine* (breast), were rubbed with salt then rolled like a miniature sleeping bag and hung from the rafters. Other pieces were brined in earthenware jars. The intestines were cleaned and rinsed with saline water. Then they were stuffed with ground meat to make *saucisses*, a process that required a team of three: one to crank the meat grinder, one to funnel the mince into the casing, and one to support and coil the sausage as it formed. The ground meat, mixed with chopped sturdy greens such as Swiss chard or escarole, was also moulded into savoury meatballs called *caillette*.

Marie-Catherine said it was essential that Sam and I see a *tuade de cochon*. She began calling everyone she knew, but the weather was already warming up. There would be no more *tuades* that year. She proposed the next best thing: a visit to an artisanal charcuterie. Again, she called around, only to encounter evasions, unreturned calls, and outright refusals. The friendly butcher in Col des Limouches didn't call back. Her favourite butcher, well, the *only* butcher, in Allex said he'd think it over. She called Pierre, the younger brother of François, who had inherited the family charcuterie factory in Tain-l'Hermitage, an hour's drive away. He begged off, saying he was retired and would have to ask his wife. "That means he doesn't want to divulge his secrets," said Marie-Catherine.

Finally, a nursing classmate said a charcuterie an hour away would allow Sam and me to watch them make *caillette*. The owner asked us to arrive before dawn. That night I slept fitfully, waking at two a.m., fearing I'd overslept. I finally got up at five a.m. or, as Sam put it, "as early as fuck." Not even the chickens were up when I trudged outside into the darkness and flung a pail of scraps at them. Instantly, they flew down from their roost and began pecking. I gathered eight warm eggs, rinsed them off, and cracked open three. The whites of the still-warm eggs were thick, the yolks deep orange. I fried them up for breakfast for François, Sam, and me.

Marie-Catherine had intended to drive us. Unfortunately, she was incapacitated with another migraine because Mamie had kept her awake throughout the night. Instead, she deputized François to drive us and left a note: "Entreprise Grimaud, Zone Artisanale, Marches." That was it: no more specific address, no phone number or directions or contact name. François insisted it was not an imposition to take us there because he had a morning meeting about Iraqi refugees in Valence, which apparently was close to Marches. (In fact, it *was* an imposition — his meeting was five hours after our charcuterie appointment. But we didn't realize that, and François was too obliging to mention it.)

Outside, it was pitch-black and freezing. The inky sky was studded with a million stars. Ice coated the windshield of François's battered Citroën. When he started chipping away with a scraper the size of a teaspoon, Sam took it from him and went to work. "*Expert canadien*," I told our host.

We set off down the deserted road, François driving crazy fast. I worried aloud about how we would find the charcuterie without an address. "Don't worry. It's a tiny place," said François, as he whipped around a curve. Ten minutes later he confessed to a slight problem. It turned out that Marches meant "the steps" — and there were several places with the same name. "It's what you call every village at the base of the mountain," he confessed.

Eventually he turned off the highway onto a bumpy country road. Suddenly we forded a stream. Or a river. Water was flying everywhere. We made it across. Sam, who was sitting in front, spotted a tiny sign: "Marches." We found a medieval dot of a village that was indeed at the base of a mountain. We drove up one twisting street with the post office and down another with the church. And that was the village. In fifteen seconds. But there was no charcuterie or, at that early hour, even anyone on the street to ask directions. With impeccable French logic, François reasoned, "The trucks must load and unload, so the charcuterie can't be in the village. It must be near the highway."

We roared out of town and found ourselves on a side road surrounded by farm fields. It was still as black as night. In the distance, we spied a light. Someone was up! As we sped down the road, we realized it was a car with headlights on. Perfect. *Oh, no! He was about to drive off.* Like a plainclothes *flic* on a drug raid, François gunned the engine and whipped into the driveway, neatly blocking the other car. Rolling down the window, he shouted, "Where is Entreprise Grimaud?" It must be normal to accost French people in their driveways before dawn to ask the way to the local charcuterie. "It's just down the road," the driver said calmly, pointing us in the right direction.

As François predicted, the *atelier* was just off the highway. In fact, a tractor-trailer honked at us because we were obstructing access to the loading dock. While François moved the car, Sam and I rang the doorbell. A middle-aged man with spectacles and a shaved head opened the door a crack. From his imperious gaze, I surmised he was the *patron* (boss). Fearing he was about to shut the door in our faces, I quickly pushed Sam inside and stepped in behind him.

"*Bonjour*, we are from Canada," Sam said in rapid French, smiling and nodding, as he sized up the precariousness of our situation. "We have been cooking in France. My mother is writing a book, which is why Marie-Catherine contacted you . . ." The *patron* looked dubious until Sam uttered three magic words: *rôti de pigeons*.

"With bacon?" he asked, beginning to smile. Sam nodded and launched into a detailed play-by-play of Bernadette's recipe.

"How did it taste?"

"*Délicieux!*" said Sam, searching for a more precise word.

"Like giblets?"

"*Oui! C'est ça!*" Sam said, nodding happily.

We suddenly had street cred. He was indeed the *patron*, and he ushered us into his office, where he pulled out two sets of disposable white coats and blue plastic hospital-style shoe covers. He gave me a white baseball cap, instructing me to tuck in every strand of hair. His name was Dominique Grimaud, and he told me his father, who died three years earlier, had been a *tueur* who went from farm to farm to make charcuterie. When Dominique was twenty-two he took out a bank loan to open Entreprise Grimaud. It operated under the brand name "Charcuterie de Charpey" and sold only to restaurants and specialty shops. At forty-seven, he was trim and athletic. He didn't look like someone who spent his workday elbow-deep in lard. He looked like the kind of guy who ran marathons. (And later, I found out that he did, to work off stress.)

"Have you had a chance to learn *pommes de terre dauphinois?*" he said over his shoulder as he led us into the workshop, referring to the classic also known as *gratin dauphinois*. "*Pas encore*," Sam said. Grimaud rattled off the recipe. "Cook sliced, peeled potatoes in milk and cream with garlic cloves. When it's almost cooked, put it in a shallow casserole, sprinkle with grated Gruyère, and bake in the oven. *Et voilà!*"

With a spring in his step, he showed us the loading dock where the tractor-trailer that had just honked at us was now unloading a shipment of freshly slaughtered pigs, halved lengthwise and suspended from hooks on a stainless-steel trolley. A white-garbed worker in white rubber boots rolled the trolley directly onto an industrial scale for weighing. Later he hosed down the receiving dock three times—a preliminary rinse, a vigorous scrubbing with detergent, and finally a thorough hosing down. It was such a contrast with what I remembered in China during the Cultural Revolution. Sides of fresh pork were dumped onto the dusty streets, which is why recipes in Chinese cookbooks invariably begin, "First wash the meat until it's clean."

Entreprise Grimaud was famous for its sausages, pâtés, and *caillette*. Pronounced kye-YET, the meatball of pork and greens dated to the sixteenth century. Like all famous foods in France, the specifications were regulated and precise. A *caillette* had to start as 320 grams of raw mince that, once baked, weighed 250 grams—a little over half a pound. It should measure twelve centimetres in diameter and must always be shaped by hand. The Drômois took their *caillette* seriously. In 2003, Grimaud had been inducted into the *Confrérie des Chevaliers du Taste-Caillette de Chabeuil*. Each year on the first Saturday in October, the members donned medieval hats and green velvet capes to feast on hot and cold *caillette* washed down with red wine. Despite the camaraderie, the competition was fierce. Entreprise Grimaud jealously guarded its techniques and recipes. No competitors could see the workshop, which employed nine workers, none of them immigrants. They had been with Grimaud on average ten to fifteen years, including the mother of his two children. Each week, the company produced four and a half tons of charcuterie, including more than a ton of *caillette*. Luckily for us, it was *caillette* day.

The *patron* led us inside the brightly lit, white-tiled workshop, chilled to 8°C. Percussive rock music blared. He introduced us to his team—four men and two women, all dressed in white caps, white rubber boots, and white plastic ankle-length aprons. Grimaud told them we were permitted to watch and could ask any questions. Then he left. The employees glanced up only long enough to smile and nod a greeting. A worker dumped plastic bins of blanched lettuce into a coarse chopper. "You can use Swiss chard or escarole if you like," he said, introducing himself as Jerôme. He assembled stainless-steel hoppers of pig's skin, ears, liver, kidneys, lard, brick-sized chunks of fatty pork, snouts, and, unsettlingly, nipples. A hydraulic lift dumped the contents into a stainless-steel chopper to mix with the lettuce. Jerôme tossed in handfuls of salt and a secret four-spice mix. Sam and I sniffed it. We guessed it was Chinese five-spice mix—cinnamon, cloves, fennel seed, and star anise—minus the Sichuan peppercorns. Jerôme dumped the minced meat and lettuce into another gigantic machine for a second, finer processing. I was somewhat embarrassed that my mouth watered at the scent of the raw meat.

There was no assembly line. As the finely minced meat poured out of the second grinder, Alain, the foreman, instinctively grabbed the right amount—320 grams—and in one graceful motion, hurled the raw lump fifteen feet down a long worktable to a precise spot in front of a worker, who instantly patted it into a softball-sized orb. Like a baseball pitcher on the mound, Alain expertly whipped handfuls of minced meat every two seconds—I timed it—keeping two workers fully occupied. *Splat! Splat!* The workers grabbed the flying mounds, shaped them into orbs, and placed them neatly in tight rows in an industrial-sized baking pan. A third worker, a woman, snipped a small square from a mantilla-sized sheet of lacy *crépinette*, laying the caul fat over each meatball. "It's what tears when you have a hernia," one worker helpfully explained. That was quintessentially French—no squeamishness about body parts, even the white membrane that cradled the intestines and abdominal cavity of pigs. In the old days, caul enrobed the entire meatball. Now merely aesthetic, it was a Proustian remembrance of things past.

In an adjacent room, slabs of pig's skin, head, rib tips, and stomach bubbled in an industrial-sized stainless-steel cooker. Alain said the broth was seasoned with garlic, white wine, bay leaves, and salt and pepper. The meat would take three hours to tenderize, and then everything would be finely ground and stuffed into intestines for *andouillete*, a slender tripe sausage. In poorer times, the farmers skimmed off the liquid fat and saved it for cooking. In modern times, no one wanted it. Alain said the *atelier* threw it out.

On *boudin noir* days, the workers simmered the blood sausages as gently as possible because a rolling boil burst the casings. Once the sausages floated to the surface, a worker tested doneness by pricking one with a knife. If no blood seeped out, the *boudin* was ready for the chill room. On another day, the workers made *saucisse d'herbes* by grinding lard, fresh ham, pigskin, and herbs, or they made tripe terrines, pâtés, and a long thin sausage made from pork, veal, and kidney fat called *godiveau*.

The workers had been at it since four thirty. At 8:05 a.m., it was time for *casse-croûte*, literally "breaking the crust." They invited us to join them around a small table. Someone sat on an overturned plastic barrel, another worker took the only chair, and the rest of us stood. One of the women laid out a slice of creamy Bleu de Bresse. Some fresh *fromage blanc* went well with a glossy side of gravlax that an apprentice had cured earlier in the week. Another woman, who snacked on yogourt, shared a bar of dark chocolate and some mandarin oranges. One of the men passed around steaming cups of espresso.

Suddenly I understood why my mouth had been watering all morning. I hadn't been salivating over raw pork—the fragrance filling the *atelier* had been the scent of sausages, ribs, and *poitrine* simmering for the workers' snack. Jerôme sliced the steaming meat into chunks, which he laid on a sheet of butcher paper. He cut slabs of an air-dried sausage, too. We ate with our fingers, passing around a baguette from which each person tore off a piece. The fresh sausage was hot and juicy. The tough breast meat had been transformed into succulent tenderness. I hesitated, however, over the air-dried sausage. The casing looked mouldy, coated with a kind of grey-green silvery dust. I carefully watched the others. They chewed and swallowed the sausage with gusto, mould and all. When they didn't drop dead on the spot, I tried a small piece. The mould gave the garlicky sausage a funky, ammonia-like edge, like a stinky cheese.

Grimaud reappeared. He wanted to show us his sausage chamber, a climate-controlled windowless room where hundreds of sausages, coated with the same silvery green mould, were hanging from wooden racks at a constant 12°C and 80 percent humidity. It turned out that the mould, or *fleur*, which coated the wooden racks as well, was prized for the special funk it imparted to the sausages. Like probiotic yogourt, he said, the mould was excellent for the immune system. "It has taken thirty years to achieve this *fleur*. We never wash the wooden racks, ever. If we did, it would be a *désastre*."

Grimaud, who put in twelve-hour days, wouldn't finish until five p.m. (which is partly why he ran marathons). His daughter, Faustine, twenty, was studying business in Barcelona. His son, Simone, fifteen, was in high school in Marches. Neither was interested in making *caillette*. Their mother, Cecile, worked in the packaging department, although she and Grimaud had separated.

"And you wonder why the kids don't want the business," said Sam.

CHAPTER NINE

Michelin Stars

When François picked us up, Grimaud gave him a gift bag of *caillette* and several links of mouldy sausages. As we drove off I noticed a charcoal smear on François's forehead. "Are you okay?" I asked. It was Ash Wednesday, he explained. After he had dropped us off at six thirty a.m., he'd gone to the only place open that early—a church—and attended Mass. He estimated his impending meeting, in nearby Valence, would take several hours.

"Why don't you visit Anne-Sophie Pic?" he said, referring to one of only a handful of female chefs to earn three Michelin stars. He didn't mean visit *her*. He meant we should check out her empire, which in Valence alone included a restaurant/hotel, a gourmet shop, a bistro, a cooking school, and a *pâtisserie-café*. (She also had restaurants in Paris, London, and Lausanne.) "Talk your way in," said François, as he dropped us off at Scook, her coyly named cooking school. "It helps that you look Asian. They will talk to you."

Only after I embarked on this adventure did I realize I was committing a kind of reverse cultural appropriation. White people write about Asian cuisine all the time. Someone who looks like me rarely does the opposite. But now my Chinese-ness could be advantageous.

Through the huge windows, I could see the cooking school was deserted except for one employee, a slim black-clad young woman with glasses and a pointy nose. Uncharacteristically self-conscious, I hung back, so Sam took charge. Buoyed by his success at the charcuterie, he walked in and explained that I, his mother, was writing a book about home cooking. The young woman stared at us like we were insects.

"This is not an actual *school*," she said frostily. "It's *pour s'amuser*."

Scook was designed to let non-cooks dabble, for a price. Most sessions lasted ninety minutes. A day-long session cost $372, a child's birthday party, $60 per kid. Emboldened by Sam, I refused to be shooed away. I stubbornly perused the $10 chocolate bars, $35 linen dishtowels, and $100 butter knives. *Mademoiselle* trailed us, step by step, making me feel like a shoplifter, or at least someone who was ruining the ambience. We had dressed for the charcuterie: running shoes, winter jackets, and, in my case, polyester athletic pants. My hair was a mess after stuffing it in the baseball cap. Sam (who didn't care what she thought) possibly looked worse; he hadn't shaved the entire time we were in France.

Losing patience, the young woman told us the "school" was booked for a private event later that morning and she was about to lock the doors. "Talk to the publicist at the hotel," she said, hustling us out. The hotel, which also housed Maison Pic, Anne-Sophie Pic's three-star restaurant, was just down the street. The cheapest room was $360 a night, a suite $1,440, neither of which included breakfast; that cost an extra $100 for two. As we walked through the lobby, I couldn't help noticing that only two people were sharing that $100 breakfast in the lobby. I felt cowed anew, but Sam was undeterred.

At the front desk, he again explained about the book. And this time, he uttered the magic word — journalist. "*Mais oui!*" said Marie Beatrice Mignot, a senior manager, her face wreathed in smiles, emerging from behind the counter in very high heels. Before I could stop myself, I blurted out a question about her shoes: how she could possibly survive the day? "I usually sit down," she deadpanned.

As she gave us a tour, she told us she had worked for Pic for twenty-seven years. With practised eloquence, she recounted the story. The Pic dynasty began in 1889 with a family inn in the Ardèche region, on the far side of the Rhône. In 1934, André Pic, Anne-Sophie's grandfather, opened Maison Pic in Valence. It soon won three Michelin stars. Eventually he and two other chefs with three Michelin stars, Fernand Point and Alexandre Dumaine, were crowned as the founding triumvirate of France's *nouvelle cuisine*. At that point, Mignot's narrative leapfrogged sixty-plus years. I knew, but she didn't know I knew, that the next twist in the Pic dynasty's saga was not so happy. In 1946, André lost a star, and then another in 1950. Many places would have been thrilled with a single star, but for Maison Pic it signalled a death spiral.

André's son, Jacques, was just three when his father opened Maison Pic and seven by the time the restaurant won three Michelin stars. He had had a front-row seat to the stress of running a three-star restaurant and decided he'd rather become a car mechanic. But after Maison Pic fell to a single star, Jacques, then eighteen, knew his father needed help. He didn't want to train with his dad, but he couldn't persuade either of his father's rivals, Point or Dumaine, to accept him as an apprentice. Like *charcutiers*, chefs considered their techniques and recipes top secret.

So Jacques moved from restaurant to restaurant, learning the classic three-course repertoire. In 1957, he returned to Valence where he stunned the gastronomic world with an eight-course tasting menu that included a truffled tart with *foie gras* and exotic flavours of cumin, caraway, and coriander from Algeria, where he had spent his mandatory French military service. In 1959, he won back his father's second Michelin star. In 1973, he won back the third star. And in 1992, he dropped dead of a heart attack at his stove. He was fifty-nine. Jacques's son, Alain, took over Maison Pic. Three years later, it again lost one of its stars. This time, Alain's younger sister, Anne-Sophie, swiftly stepped in, while Alain left to open a restaurant in nearby Montbonnot-Saint-Martin. (It later closed.) By 2007, Anne-Sophie had regained the third Michelin star.

Odette had already told us about the suicide of Benoît Violier, a three-star Michelin chef. His death at forty-four, by a self-inflicted gunshot wound, echoed the suicide of Bernard Loiseau, another three-star Michelin chef, who shot himself in his kitchen in 2003 after media rumours spread that Michelin was about to downgrade his restaurant. And here was the direct link back to André Pic: Loiseau was the successor thrice-removed to Alexandre Dumaine, one member of the *nouvelle-cuisine* triumvirate, who had refused to train André's son, Jacques. Loiseau's restaurant, La Côte d'Or, was posthumously downgraded to two stars. In its chef's memory, however, it was now called Le Relais Bernard Loiseau. Naturally, our polished guide mentioned nothing about the loss of the Pics' Michelin stars. Instead, Mignot noted the Pics were the first family to earn three stars in three generations. She pointed out the custom wallpaper that reproduced vintage menus from New Year's Eve and other festive dinners past; the sepia-tinted photographs of the Pic family peeling potatoes with other celebrity chefs, including Paul Bocuse and Pierre Troisgros; their black-and-white glossies with clientele such as Catherine Deneuve, Gérard Depardieu, and Mick Jagger.

Now Maison Pic offered only three *prix fixe* menus at dinner. Not including wine, "Discovery" cost $230 per person, "Harmony" $346, and "Essential" $460. At lunch, the *prix fixe* meal was $160. Mignot walked us through the pearl-grey and pink formal dining room, which seated sixty and had a view of a courtyard garden of palm trees, bamboo fronds, and a fish pond. Crystal chandeliers fell daringly to hip height. A waiter was steam-ironing damask tablecloths directly on the tables. They were set with those $100 butter knives, sold at Scook, cunningly designed to stand upright so you wouldn't run the terrible risk of smearing that damask tablecloth. Mignot said they were custom-made for Anne-Sophie Pic by Laguiole, the French artisanal knife maker.

We ventured a few steps into the glassed-in white kitchen where a team of chefs prepped for lunch. At the end of the tour, Mignot offered us coffee or fresh-squeezed orange juice, but Sam and I declined, with thanks. As we left, we peeked at the ongoing renovations in the hotel's second restaurant, a casual bistro. Anne-Sophie Pic was such a sharp businesswoman that, despite the freezing weather, she had moved the operation outdoors and called it "Pic Blanc," after nearby Mont Blanc. She installed an old ski-lift cabin where she encouraged customers to take selfies and pretend they were frolicking in the French Alps. "Smart," said Sam admiringly, as he looked at the unpainted rustic furniture. Fish and chips — no heat included — cost $26.

We headed for the Pic gourmet shop, a few blocks over. As we retraced our footsteps past Scook, the private event, a children's party, was in full swing. Like homeless folk, Sam and I stood on the sidewalk, gawking at the kids in aprons and little paper toques. Suddenly I spied Anne-Sophie Pic. I must have been still under the sway of Mignot's corporate personality-cult propaganda for I cried excitedly, "Sam, take a picture!" He dutifully whipped out his cellphone and took two shots of the celebrity chef, getting mostly window glare and the backs of kids' heads. I noticed a grandmother-type client shaking a warning finger. The snooty young woman we had met earlier was waving her hands and frowning. Suddenly she burst through the door. "I was nice to you," she snapped. "And I talked to you about giving us *space*."

She hadn't, but I was too shocked to respond. We weren't trespassing. We were standing on a public sidewalk, looking through plate-glass windows. "You do not have permission to put these photos on the internet!" she yelled as she marched back inside Scook.

I looked at Sam for a reality check. "It's like having an open kitchen, and then yelling at someone for looking at the chef," Sam said, shrugging. We trudged another block to "l'Épicerie Anne-Sophie Pic," which sold overpriced jams and spices, wine, chocolates, and prepared foods, much of it Pic-branded.

Our last stop was Daily Pic, a self-serve café where you grabbed a plastic shopping basket and chose from an array of refrigerated appetizers, mains, and desserts, all in mason jars. After you paid, a clerk zapped your jars in the microwave. Like Anne-Sophie Pic's concept of persuading clients to eat outdoors in winter because she was renovating her bistro, Daily Pic leveraged her three-star reputation to peddle self-served, microwaved food. But you can't fool the public all the time. Like every Pic enterprise we visited that day, it was deserted. By then I was tired and thirsty. I ordered a cappuccino and considered a *macaron*, which were only ten euro cents more expensive than the ones sold at the nearby McDonald's. In the end, I chose a Mont Blanc, a pretty dome of chestnut cream atop a crunchy base, surrounded by a citrus gelée, scattered with real gold leaf. Alas, it was all glam and no taste, perhaps because it came straight out of the refrigerator. In contrast my coffee was barely warm. The sulky counterwoman hadn't bothered to steam the milk.

When François picked us up, we recounted our adventures in Pic-land. He told us his parents had had their wedding dinner at the Pic restaurant because his grandmother, a restaurateur herself, knew the family. "The place wasn't so fancy then." I described my lukewarm cappuccino and ice-cold Mont Blanc. François laughed when I said that Entreprise Grimaud's coffee was better, as was Odette's *crème renversée*. I mentioned I'd bought a crusty *boule* from Daily Pic. "Probably she doesn't bake it herself. She buys it," he snorted.

Back at the farmhouse, for lunch for François, Sam decided to make *frisée aux lardons*, a Lyonnaise specialty. He got out the giant head of *frisée* and told me to wash enough lettuce for three. He fried up cubed bacon until it was crisp then swirled sharp red wine vinegar into the molten fat. He tossed the *frisée* in the warm dressing and topped each plated portion with a warm poached egg. "*Tu es Sam-Sophie Pic!*" joked François, who didn't even know how to poach an egg. We mopped up the runny yolk and rich dressing with the excellent bread from Pic (whoever had made it). Later Odette came by to retrieve her aluminum mould. François told her that her *crème renversée* was better than the Mont Blanc at Daily Pic. "Of course it is," said Odette without rancour. "*Mine* is homemade."

SAM'S FOOLPROOF POACHED EGGS

Can be made in advance.

Bring a shallow pan of water to a bare simmer. Crack a single egg into a small bowl. Try to use the freshest eggs, with thick whites. Supermarket eggs have a thick white surrounded by a thin, watery white, which is the part that creates the feathery mess when you poach.

Slide egg into barely simmering water. Turn off heat and cover the pot for 3 minutes. (This helps cook the top part of the egg white, while leaving the yolk runny.) Gently poke the yolk; if it jiggles, it's ready. Remove with a slotted spoon. With a paper towel, dab away excess water at base of spoon. Serve immediately.

To poach several eggs, turn off heat while you slide in all the eggs, then turn it back on. Lower heat as soon as bubbles reappear. Turn heat off entirely after 1 minute. Cover. After 3 minutes, check for doneness. Total cooking time will depend on original temperature and number of eggs.

For next-day use, refrigerate poached eggs in a bowl of water. Bring to room temperature an hour before you plan to eat. Just before serving, submerge eggs in a bowl of hot water for ½ a minute.

Before we knew it, Kéti had reached her one-month anniversary and would be christened. Like in China, where historically infant mortality rates were high, the Georgians celebrated this auspicious milestone. Davit got a haircut, as did Rüska, who looked svelte. Tiny Andrie got a new navy-blue suit and ruffled tuxedo shirt. To do my bit, I bought a *Paris-Brest* from the *pâtisserie* in the nearby town of Crest. The wheel-shaped confection was created for the 1910 Paris-Brest-Paris bicycle race, the precursor to the Tour de France. Unlike the lacklustre baguettes, the *Paris-Brest* was authentic — *pâte à choux* stuffed with hazelnut-flavoured cream and garnished with sliced almonds, spun sugar, and a single chartreuse *macaron*. I told Rüska that as Kéti's mother, she got the *macaron*. She happily scarfed it down, for once ignoring her diet.

Marie-Catherine had finally slept soundly. Newly energized, she organized a quintessentially French outing for us: combining an appointment with the bureaucracy and a visit to a chocolate factory. Philo's government cheques had dried up the previous summer. At twenty-one, her social benefits were being reduced, but they shouldn't have been zero.

"Every time she changes status, it's a mess," said Marie-Catherine. Clutching a thick green file, she led the way to the government office in Romans-sur-Isère. The tired and defeated souls you see waiting at government offices in any country packed the reception area of the *Caisse d'Allocations Familiales*. French and foreigners alike, they were asking about unemployment payouts, missing welfare cheques, and other benefits. "They don't work, but they know their rights," Marie-Catherine told us. "Many of the foreigners hate France. They have ten or twelve kids and live on *allocations*." If I didn't know she was sheltering undocumented migrants, I might have assumed she was a bigot. But she was merely describing reality.

With the confidence that comes with having an education, status, and economic security, Marie-Catherine strode to the front, slapped down a small card, and said with a polite smile, "*Bonjour*. I have an appointment."

"This card is no good. You should be in Valence," said the clerk, scowling.

Of all the problems Marie-Catherine had to deal with, the French bureaucracy was the last straw. "I've waited three *months* for this appointment," she cried. Another, more sympathetic, clerk took over. The message, however, was unchanged. "We can't take you. Your husband should have pointed out that your appointment *can't* be in Romans because *your* office is in *Valence*."

"It's not *my* fault," said Marie-Catherine. "*Your* clerk wrote down the wrong place." She stabbed the handwritten scribbled— "Romans"—on the card.

"Nevertheless, Madame, *this* is the wrong place." And to underline his point, the clerk took a pen and crossed out "Romans."

Marie-Catherine started waving her hands. To calm her, someone ushered us into a manager's office with a breathtaking view of an ancient stone bridge over the Isère River. As I enjoyed the view, I had trouble reconciling a culture that had designed such an aesthetically pleasing bridge with one that had invented the word *bureaucracy*. (China invented bureaucracy circa 221 BCE, but in the eighteenth century a French economist coined the Western term, originally satirical, from the words *bureau*, office or desk, and *kratos*, the Greek word for political power.)

Suddenly it all made sense. Marie-Catherine told me the bridge I was admiring was a replica of the original, which had been bombed in World War II. Change was impossible in a culture that replicated its past, stone by stone. We were in the wrong city. It had been a bureaucrat's mistake. But nothing, absolutely nothing, could be done here in Romans-sur-Isère to rectify the missing benefits for a young woman disabled with Down syndrome.

As we trudged back to the car, Marie-Catherine vented. "They always say: *you should call.* I always call. Then they always say: *the problem is solved.* But it never is. Next week, I will go in the afternoon and tell my story again: that Philomène's payments have been stopped, and she is still entitled to them. If I'm very, very lucky, it will work. Otherwise I must go to another office and start all over again." She consoled herself with the prospect of our afternoon visit to the chocolate factory in Tain-l'Hermitage, a short drive from Romans-sur-Isère. A true Frenchwoman, she could eat chocolate endlessly and did—in her car, at home, at any time of the day or night.

But first, of course, we had to eat lunch. Tain-l'Hermitage, on the left bank of the Rhône River, had six thousand inhabitants and an outsized reputation for wine. The region was famous for reds such as Hermitage, Crozes-Hermitage, and Côtes du Rhône. We found a small café called... Le Café. It had mismatched Formica tables, rickety chairs, and a zinc bar, and was packed with locals. "*Allons-y!*" said Marie-Catherine, whose approach to finding a good restaurant was not reading reviews or following Michelin stars but peering through a window to see if her compatriots were having a good time.

We got the last, least-desirable table, right beneath a staircase that led up to a tiny bookstore. "Only one *menu*, thirteen euros," said the server, a middle-aged woman in jeans, who came over to take our drink orders. But what was the *menu*? She pointed to the plate of someone at the adjacent table. "*Salade, boeuf avec légumes, et pour dessert, compote de pommes,*" she rattled off impatiently.

Marie-Catherine ordered a carafe of a peppery Crozes-Hermitage, dispensed without ceremony from a large UHT box. The waitress sliced up a crusty, yeasty loaf on demand. It was the best bread we had in France, even better than the loaf from Anne-Sophie Pic. When we wanted more, the waitress grabbed an unfinished basket of bread from another table and plopped it down on ours, a practice that would get you fined by health inspectors at home. The food was worth the brusqueness. If I lived in Tain-l'Hermitage, I would go to Le Café twice a week. Our first course (and everyone else's) was a salad of radicchio, baby lettuce, and mandolin-sliced radishes, tossed in a sheer vinaigrette. This was followed by two slabs of strip loin braised in Crozes-Hermitage, with a small heap of perfectly cooked buttery carrots, zucchini, parsnips, purple and yellow turnips, and barely wilted emerald-green spinach. The freshly made apple compote came with a homemade almond *tuile*.

Le Café was a husband-and-wife enterprise. Nathalie was the waitress and cashier. Boris, the chef, worked alone in a closet of a kitchen. The concept was brilliant: home cooking turned commercial, with no waste or orders to mix up. You ate whatever Mom, or in this case, Dad, felt like making or could find in the market. The prep area, a trestle table at the back that overflowed with apples, carrots, and cabbages, could, in a pinch, be cleared for a party of ten. Le Café opened early, and closed early. Nathalie and Boris took the weekend off. That's right, a successful restaurant that didn't open on Saturdays or Sundays. It seemed a perfect model for Sam, a way to cook creatively and not drop dead at the stove. Perhaps it wouldn't work in North America's individualistic culture. In France, no one asks what dressing you want on your salad—it comes with vinaigrette. French chefs don't care how you'd like your steak cooked—it comes medium rare. When I think back, no one we cooked with in France or Italy or China ever asked whether I disliked anything, whether I was a vegetarian, or whether I was allergic to nuts or gluten or dairy. You ate what was cooked. Those with special needs adapted, including Philomène and Pierre-Marie. At mealtimes, someone would administer Philomène's insulin shot, and someone else would select acceptable foods for her, weigh it, and plate it. Pierre-Marie chose what he wanted—potatoes or cauliflower or chicken or *ravioles*—and he, or someone else, whirred it in the blender. Like Philo, he ate everything on his plate. I never once saw anyone in the Jeanselme family eating junk food or snacking at mid-afternoon or late at night. We ate, only at meal times, as much cheese and butter and bread as we desired. No one was overweight, including Marie-Catherine, a chocoholic.

After a one-euro cup of espresso, we crossed the street to the Valrhona chocolate factory, named for *valley* of the Rhône. Because some top

Canadian restaurants featured Valrhona in their desserts, I assumed it was one of the best in the world. "*Non, non, non,*" said Nathalie, a neighbour who had dropped off some free tickets for us. "It's just one of many *chocolatiers* in France — nothing special."

The displays at Valrhona explained chocolate production from growing the cocoa nuts and harvesting the sun-dried pods, to processing them into pure chocolate. For unlimited samples, all we had to do was insert our bar-coded ticket into strategically placed dispensing machines, over and over again. We tasted milk chocolate, dark chocolate, a blond chocolate called "Dulcey," white chocolate, and single-origin chocolates from Madagascar, Peru, Ghana, Venezuela, Ecuador, and the Dominican Republic. Everywhere were overflowing bowls of chocolates, including in the shop, where Marie-Catherine giddily spent several hundred euros buying chocolates for herself and her friends.

Bernadette announced she would teach us *Tajine de poulet au citron confit.* This north African dish of the former French colonies was named for the conical earthenware pot in which it is cooked. Marie-Catherine had a brightly coloured one in her cupboard but had never used it. We already had preserved lemons — I'd purchased a jar from the artisanal *huilerie* in the next town over. Not trusting supplies at the Jeanselmes' kitchen, Bernadette had brought her own spices: turmeric, powdered ginger, and cumin, both ground and whole seeds. Now she sent Davit, Sam, and me out to buy chicken legs from the free-range poultry farm down the road and to the *hypermarché* for medium couscous, dried currants, onions, zucchini, fresh coriander, and olives. Bernadette's recipe book specified purple olives. "But you won't find purple ones anywhere," she said. "Just buy some ordinary olives."

In the *hypermarché*, Davit stopped me from buying a bunch of coriander. "*Je sais où,*" he said. On the way home from shopping, he stopped the old Citroën along the wrong side of a country road and, without shutting off the engine, flung the door open, leaned out, and grabbed a bunch of something green. "*Coriandre,*" he said, grinning and tossing it into Sam's lap. Of course the miracle man knew the secret spot where wild coriander grew.

Back in the farmhouse, we separated the legs and thighs, briefly marinating them in olive oil, salt, freshly ground white pepper, and the spices. I quartered three of the preserved lemons. I wanted to use more, but Bernadette was the boss. At her direction, I chopped five medium zucchinis into chunks the size of large marshmallows. Sam sliced the onions. He minced two cloves of garlic, sprinkled on some salt, and, pressing on the flat of the knife, turned the garlic into paste. Marie-Catherine notwithstanding, Bernadette was a fan of garlic, and — have I mentioned? — she was the boss.

We sautéed the onions in a bit of olive oil in a heavy Le Creuset casserole until they were translucent then added Sam's garlic paste and the marinated chicken. When the meat was lightly browned, Bernadette added half a cup of water and the preserved lemons. Meanwhile we poached the dried currants in a bit of water and softened the dried couscous with boiling water seasoned with salt and olive oil. After the *tajine* had simmered for twenty minutes, Bernadette added the pitted olives and, a few minutes later, the zucchini.

She couldn't stay for lunch — this was her half day at the Jeanselmes', and she had to leave to help the invalid in her village. She instructed me on how to serve it, showered with chopped fresh coriander, in Marie-Catherine's pottery *tajine*. After grinding up a portion of chicken and couscous for Pierre-Marie, we called everyone to the table. With the two Georgians, we added up to eight. Everyone knew to take just one piece of chicken. We filled up on couscous and zucchini, drenched in herbaceous, lemony sauce. François was full of praise. He pointed at Sam. "Hey, Sam-Sophie Pic. This is better than Anne-Sophie Pic!"

BERNADETTE'S CHICKEN TAJINE WITH PRESERVED LEMONS

Serves 4 Canadians (or 8 French people).
Serve with couscous (see below).

Total prep and cooking time: 45 minutes.

4	chicken legs
4	chicken thighs
½ tsp.	ground white pepper
½ tsp.	turmeric

½ tsp.	powdered ginger
½ tsp.	ground cumin
1 tbsp.	whole cumin seeds
	salt to taste – remember, the lemons and olives are salty
3	medium onions, finely sliced
2	cloves garlic, minced
4 tbsp.	olive oil (2 for marinating chicken, 2 for sautéing onions)
3	preserved lemons, quartered (see recipe, page 108)
½ cup	purple or green pitted olives
5	medium zucchini, cut in chunks
6	sprigs coriander, chopped

Briefly marinate chicken with half the oil and all the spices. Sauté sliced onions with remaining oil. When translucent, add garlic and chicken, browning lightly. Add ½ cup water and lemons. Cover and simmer for 20 minutes, until liquid is syrupy, adding more water as pot dries out. Add olives, and simmer five minutes. Add zucchini chunks and cook until bright green – another 5 minutes. Garnish with chopped coriander.

COUSCOUS
Total prep and cooking time: 10 minutes.

½ cup	dried currants (or substitute raisins)
2 cups	dried couscous
½ tsp.	salt
	knob of butter (approx. 2 tbsp.)

Soak dried currants or raisins in a bowl of hot water for 5 minutes. Boil 2 cups of water in a pot. Add the dried couscous, salt, and butter. Remove from heat, keep covered, and let stand for 5 minutes. Drain currants, add to couscous, fluff with a fork.

Preserved lemons have an intense flavour without the bitterness of fresh ones. You can buy them at Middle Eastern grocery stores or you can make your own (at least three weeks in advance). It's not as good but you can substitute fresh lemons, sliced thickly; add a tablespoon of sugar to mitigate the bitterness.

CONFIT DE CITRON

3	lemons
7 tsp.	salt, divided
1	clean medium jar

Boil 1 cup water and let cool. Wash lemons and trim nubby ends off. Partially quarter lemons, leaving them attached at base so they look like a budding flower, and remove seeds. Put a teaspoon of salt in the bottom of the sterile jar. Add another teaspoon of salt to centre of each lemon. Press the first lemon into the jar hard enough to release a lot of juice. Sprinkle another teaspoon of salt on top of it. Repeat the process with the next 2 lemons. Juice should reach halfway up the jar. Fill rest of jar with cooled boiled water. Let stand at room temperature for 3 days, giving it a shake now and then, or even better, flip it upside down on the second day, and right side up on the third. Refrigerate for at least 3 weeks. To use: rinse well to rid lemon of excess salt.

CHAPTER TEN

Provence

Provence was the *département* adjacent to the Drôme, an hour's leisurely drive south through the mountains. Marie-Catherine organized a day trip to buy Ben a Provençal tablecloth for a wedding present. She also wanted to show us an artisanal cold-press olive-oil mill, where she planned to process the olives from her own trees. Unfortunately, we had neglected to pick the olives in advance. The morning of our excursion, it was raining too hard. *"Peut-être une autre fois,"* Marie-Catherine said with a shrug as the ripe olives fell onto the soaking grass.

Her cousin, Danielle, who lived in a villa a few hillsides over, had agreed to go with us. As we pulled into her driveway, her husband, Pierre, came out to warn us the front steps were slippery. He was in his seventies, very tall and handsome, with piercing blue eyes and that old-school gallantry common among older Frenchmen. Once when I bumped into him at the farmers' market in Crest, I removed my winter glove to shake his hand. "A lady *never* de-gloves," he admonished me. "Only the *monsieur* removes his glove." And then he embraced me, hugging and kissing me on both cheeks.

Danielle and Pierre's home had an outdoor swimming pool and a vast terrace with breathtaking views of Les Trois Becs, a trio of mountain peaks that uncannily resembled a recumbent profile of General Charles de Gaulle's high forehead, prominent nose, and jutting chin. Their living room reflected long ties to France's Asian colonies — it was filled with Chinese armoires, lacquered tables, and silk scrolls from French Indochina. In the nineteenth century, her grandparents had been professors of French literature in Vientiane, the Laotian capital. She herself had been raised by an amah in south China. Pierre, too, had grown up in Asia. Their families knew one another, and they became childhood sweethearts. After marriage, they moved to Vietnam where Pierre worked for Michelin, the French tire company. (Yes, the same one that published the restaurant guide that bestowed one, two, or three stars, originally part of a corporate plot to get

French people to drive further for a good meal—and buy more tires.) Three of Danielle's nephews still worked in Taiwan, Thailand, and Shanghai, and she and Pierre considered Asia their true home. But the couple spoke only French. In that earlier era of globalization, neither Danielle nor Pierre had learned a word of Chinese, Vietnamese, or Laotian.

Danielle, a slim elegant blonde in her seventies, had striking deep blue, almost turquoise, eyes. When she got in Marie-Catherine's car, she enveloped us in a cloud of Lanvin perfume, *Le Trésor*. "A Christmas present from Pierre." There was a new highway, but Marie-Catherine preferred the scenic road that retraced the medieval salt route. It was easy to imagine shepherds with their flocks, transporting precious spices from Marseille through the mountain passes. In the downpour, the farm fields were a green blur, the mountains a pewter mist. We passed thick forests where black truffles were harvested every year. "The locations are top secret," Danielle said.

Our destination was the Provençal town of Nyons (pronounced Nee-onss). On the way home, if the weather broke, we would visit an astronomically expensive institution for handicapped young men and women. It was an organic farm, and Marie-Catherine thought it might be a long-term solution for Pierre-Marie and Philo. French parents of disabled children faced a terrible dilemma. I had assumed the country's vaunted social welfare system was generous—*liberté, égalité, fraternité*, and all that. In fact, as soon Pierre-Marie and Philo had turned twenty, the state began keeping a running tab of every euro spent on them. They didn't pay anything now, but the state would collect later—from their inheritance.

The children owned no assets, of course. At the same time, Marie-Catherine and François were not allowed to cut Pierre-Marie and Philo out of their wills. "French law says you can't disinherit a handicapped person." And not only would the government confiscate the two handicapped children's inheritance, it would also seize any outstanding balance from their four non-disabled siblings. "It's a loan that falls heavily on the next generation," said Marie-Catherine. "Our own children will be disinherited. They will be obligated to repay the state for every penny spent on Pierre-Marie and Philo after the age of twenty." With the average lifespan of those with Down syndrome now reaching sixty years, the Jeanselme family faced a potential bill of millions of euros for forty additional years of care—times two.

Sam, who had been dozing in the back seat, woke up. "It's like pretending you have medicare," he said, "but once you die, your kids are hit with the bills."

Danielle clucked her tongue in sympathy. Just as the authorities hadn't disclosed the severity and scope of Pierre-Marie's and Philo's handicaps, they had not mentioned this long-term liability. Marie-Catherine only learned about the financial time bomb when Pierre-Marie was ten and Philo was five, and another family revealed that they had been forced to sell their home to pay the bills for their adult child. "The government didn't explain anything to us when we adopted Pierre-Marie and Philomène. If I had had to explain this to *mes propres enfants*, I'm not sure what I would have done. My children have said, 'Never mind about the inheritance. You gave us all a good education.'"

Their four biological children were now adults, living elsewhere in France and Turkey. They were all gainfully employed and had nine children among them. Still, Marie-Catherine and François contemplated selling their only significant asset, the Allex farmhouse, and distributing the money in advance to their biological children. But the couple still needed a place to live, and as her handicapped children's legal guardian, Marie-Catherine needed a judge's permission for any move that would affect the disabled children's patrimony, including selling her own home. Now that she was sixty-two and François was sixty-eight, they were chronically concerned about their disabled children's futures. François still jumped up from the table to grind Pierre-Marie's dinner (although it was clear to Sam and me that the young man could do it for himself). And despite his bad back, François still acquiesced to Philomène's bedtime demand for a piggyback ride up the stairs.

The previous year, Pierre-Marie had aged out of his special school for handicapped children. Because he had taken courses in music and horseback riding, and had particularly enjoyed the latter, his parents had tried sending him to work in a stable. That hadn't lasted. Then they sent him to an *atelier* for disabled adults, an hour's drive from Allex. They hoped eventually Philo would follow him there because she, too, was aging out of her special school. Pierre-Marie's job at the *atelier* involved sweeping the cafeteria and bussing dirty dishes. To make his single room more enticing, his parents bought him a television set and his own computer, neither of which he had at home. But Pierre-Marie made no friends, partly because he hated being around other disabled people. He also suffered acute homesickness. Every night he phoned home, weeping and asking to be allowed back. "Do not abandon me," he begged. "You didn't adopt me only to leave me here to the end of my days." After six months of tearful pleas, his parents caved. "Pierre-Marie can't be with ordinary people, and he can't be with handicapped," said Marie-Catherine, with a deep sigh.

Pierre-Marie's experience with the world of work seemed to have scarred him. Sam noticed he was unwilling to tackle any chores, instead wandering through the farmhouse, earbuds in, listening to his favourite music at full blast. It was as if Pierre-Marie was forever locked into that deeply irritating phase of aggressively idle adolescence. And like many adolescents, he daydreamed about getting married. He declared that he was in love with a young woman named Lolita, who also had Down syndrome. They wanted to marry. "But each of them wants to live with their mothers," François told me, shaking his head.

Sam, whose lazy teenaged years were not that far in the past, was surprisingly censorious about Pierre-Marie. I was surprised to hear my son echoing my own pitiless parenting style. "He should be given a choice," Sam told me. "Go work outside or take over the chores at home. Like taking out the garbage, doing the dishes, and sweeping the floors. François shouldn't be doing the dishes."

The villages in Provence were a harmonious palette of cream, biscuit, and blush. As we neared Nyons, the skies suddenly cleared. The *mistral* had blown away the fog, turning the Provençal light luminous and the sky a deep azure. We were in a different microclimate, with Japanese cherry blossoms, yellow mimosa, and deep-pink rose bushes in full bloom. Marie-Catherine had called ahead to the *huilerie*, which organized an olive-oil tasting and allowed us to watch the cold-pressing of small batches of olives picked that day. The previous year a parasite ruined the harvest, but this year had been a bumper crop. A technician ground up the olives, pits and all, explaining that the pits released antioxidants that helped preserve the oil. The thick gritty paste was then spun in a centrifuge to separate the juice from the deep green oil. Later the *huilerie* infused the oil with fresh basil, rosemary, lemon, or arugula.

Afterward we looked for a place to eat lunch. Unfortunately, the *mistral* blew in another rainstorm. We ducked beneath a medieval stone arcade and wandered down the rain-slicked Rue des Déportés. Using Marie-Catherine's methodology, we peered into restaurants, most utterly deserted. Marie-Catherine spotted a pizzeria with exactly one customer inside. She could see a wood fire ablaze in the back, and we were chilled to the bone. She voted for it, Danielle concurred, and so we trooped inside. I tried to hide my disappointment. I'd come all the way to Provence to eat a *pizza*? In fact, pizza was as much a part of French cuisine as pâté. From the sixteenth to nineteenth centuries, the boundaries of France and Italy criss-crossed and shifted multiple times under the Savoy, one of the oldest ruling families in the world. The Italianization of French cuisine began in 1533, with the marriage of a fourteen-year-old Florentine girl to the future Henry II of France. Catherine de' Medici would become one of the most important figures of the Renaissance. Her mother was a French princess from d'Auvergne. Her father, Lorenzo II de' Medici, was de facto ruler of Florence and patron of Machiavelli. Born in 1519 and orphaned when she was a few weeks old, Catherine's fate was sealed when her uncle, Pope Clement VII, accepted an offer from King Francis of France to marry her to his second son. Starting in 1543, at age twenty-four, she gave birth in quick succession to ten children, of whom seven would survive. In 1547 Catherine became queen of France when her husband unexpectedly ascended to the throne. Twelve years later, he died in a jousting match. She was then forty and, for the next three decades, ruled as regent on behalf of three feeble sons—and, in the process, transformed the crude cuisine of her adopted country.

Catherine is credited with introducing the fork to France. Before her arrival, French aristocrats ate with their fingers. With her Florentine aesthetic, Catherine decorated her dining tables with flowers and sculptured sugar. Before the French ate everything in a jumble; she separated savoury and sweet courses. She substituted fine wines for the heavily spiced wine then in vogue in France. She introduced olive oil and the *macaron*. She brought the fine white beans later used to make *cassoulet*. Her entourage included distillers, confectioners, and chefs. They prepared duck à l'orange, sweetbreads, and devilled eggs. They created ices, aspics, cakes, custards, puff pastry, and *pâte à choux*. They introduced artichokes, peas, broccoli, lettuce, parsley, Savoy cabbage, and spinach. They brought pasta, Parmesan, and turkey. To win friends and influence people, she embarked on a remarkable two-year tour of France with an entourage of eight thousand, throwing lavish dinners.

Not all were impressed. In his 1754 *Encyclopédie*, Diderot complained that so-called haute cuisine had seeped into France from "that crowd of corrupt Italians who served at the court of Catherine de' Medici." Even today, some food critics express consternation about Italy's perceived influence, noting with disdain that many top French restaurants cooked with olive oil rather than butter. Critics aside, French people were voting with their Medici-inspired forks. A 2010 survey by *Madame Figaro* magazine found that 87 percent of French consumers cooked Italian food. (Forty percent cooked Chinese.)

L'Alicoque, the pizza restaurant in Nyons, offered a bargain twelve-euro set lunch that included a large salad, half a pizza, and dessert. We three women ordered it, and a moment later, I was full of regret. The only other diner's order arrived — and I swooned. It was *spaghetti carbonara*, and it came topped with a raw egg yolk, still in its half shell. The diner, a businessman, expertly tipped the yolk onto the piping hot pasta and tossed the strands to mix it.

Then our own food came, and my envy faded. The salad was sprightly and huge. My half-pizza was scattered with tiny Nyons olives, silvery anchovies, and thinly sliced ham. Sam skipped the bargain lunch and ordered a *foie gras* pizza. It was the ultimate globalization — sautéed chunks of *foie gras* and slices of *magret de canard fumé* (smoked duck breast) with *crème fraîche*, Emmenthal cheese, walnuts, and mushrooms. For dessert, Danielle and Marie-Catherine chose the chocolate mousse. I had *île flottante*, a cloud of lightly baked meringue, drizzled with caramel sauce, floating on a pool of *crème anglaise*. Like so many French desserts, it was visually stunning, and not too sweet.

On the way home, the rain stopped so Marie-Catherine detoured to Le Béal in Taulignan, the therapeutic organic farm where she hoped to place Pierre-Marie. It accepted only thirty-two mentally handicapped adults. Mentors (one for every five or six residents) and residents lived together in nineteenth-century buildings connected by gravel pathways. Permanent teaching staff also lived on-site.

We drove up a formal *allée* of plane trees with camouflage-spotted trunks until we reached two stone chateaux. Formerly a silk mill, Le Béal had been converted into a working farm, with cows, horses, donkeys, vegetables, herbs, and olive, apricot, and apple trees. In small *ateliers*, the residents processed the bounty into organic oils, juices, and jams. Each day they worked in teams, cooking and doing housework, laundry, and farm chores. But the work wasn't obligatory. Residents could do nothing if they so wished. Leisure activities included music, drama, painting, and crafts. Marie-Catherine thought Le Béal would be ideal for Pierre-Marie. And if it worked out, Philo, who loved art and music, would follow. The two siblings could grow old together. With the farm only one hour's drive from Allex, François and Marie-Catherine could visit often. But Le Béal came with a whopping price tag: $175,000 Canadian a year per resident. The government would cover the costs up front—until Pierre-Marie and Philo came into their inheritance. "If we put them in a place like this, the government will keep track of all the money they owe. And when we parents die, the government will take its money back," said Marie-Catherine. She sighed deeply. "The only other option is the psychiatric ward."

Pierre-Marie wanted to immigrate to Canada to be closer to Amber Marshall, the actress who starred in *Heartland*. Marie-Catherine asked Sam to talk sense into him. Several nights in a row, they hung out together until late into the night. In his salon-turned-bedroom, Sam explained that the show was not real. Pierre-Marie countered that on the internet he had found an actual Heartland sign. Sam told him that was fake. He explained the series was dubbed, and that Amber Marshall spoke in English, as did most Canadians. Sam also said that it would be hard, if not impossible, for Pierre-Marie to travel alone on a plane. Sam didn't explain that the Canadian immigration system would automatically reject a disabled applicant. He also told Pierre-Marie it was time to start doing the household chores or move out. When the subject of Le Béal was broached, Pierre-Marie grew agitated. He detested the idea of living among other handicapped people. "I'm not *that* disabled," he kept repeating. "I'm not like Philomène."

As he talked to Pierre-Marie about the hopelessness of immigrating, it occurred to Sam that the Georgian family might have a chance—if they applied to Quebec. After all, the family was learning French. Both Davit and Rüska were young, educated, and healthy. And, to be blunt, they had the desirable skin hue. As white people from the Caucasus, they were the original Caucasians. The next day, Sam volunteered to help Davit navigate the Quebec immigration website. That evening, they sat hunched over Sam's laptop, while he translated the website into everyday French or English that Davit could understand. For an hour, they laboriously filled out a worksheet and sample application form—Davit had a minimal level of French and minimal work experience. They hit "submit." Moments later, the answer popped up: *don't bother to apply; you won't succeed.* Sam was as crushed as Davit. But the next day, Sam had an idea: fill out the application with better answers. This way they would know exactly what Davit needed to accomplish. Sam reasoned that by the time any application was approved and a face-to-face interview scheduled, Davit and Rüska would have improved their language skills.

Davit was so discouraged he wasn't willing to absorb another rejection. Sam, however, wouldn't let up because, to him, Davit was the miracle man, exactly the kind of person Canada wanted. Under Sam's badgering, Davit agreed to try again. The website rejected a second attempt from the same computer, so they switched laptops. This time, Sam input a "medium level" of French. As for work experience, Sam typed in three years instead of one, calculating that Georgia was so chaotic, no one could dispute Davit's resumé. Sam hit "submit." A few seconds later came this reply: "*We welcome you to apply to immigrate to Quebec.*" Davit immediately vowed to concentrate on learning French. Marie-Catherine clapped her hands and promised to correct his conjugations every day. Madeleine wouldn't help, but perhaps Odette would coach him, too. For the first time, I saw Davit smile.

Sam had finally persuaded Marie-Catherine to switch off Mamie's baby monitor at night by promising to tend to Mamie himself. After all, she was in the adjacent room and he could hear everything anyway, including the oxygen machine. That night, when he heard her calling out, he scrambled out of bed. It was past three a.m., and she wanted to get up. "Mamie, it's nighttime," Sam told her politely. "You can't get out of bed." She asked again. He rebuffed her again. The baby monitor had trained her to expect attention all night. And since she slept all day, she was up all night. But Sam had some experience with old people, like my father. Each time Mamie asked to get up, Sam firmly repeated that wasn't possible. He stood beside her bed for more than an hour until she settled back to sleep.

The second night Mamie altered her technique—and so did Sam. At two a.m., when she called out and he arrived at her bedside, she asked for a drink of fresh-squeezed orange juice. Sam knew we didn't have oranges. Instead, he fixed her a glass of her favourite pomegranate juice, cut it with water, and helped her sip it. When she finished, he told her firmly that she had to go to sleep. At five a.m. Mamie awoke and asked to get out of bed. Again, Sam appeared beside her and told her that wasn't possible. But this time he only stood around for twenty minutes. Then he went back to his room and listened to her muttering for another ten minutes. "*Sors-moi du lit,*" she kept saying. *Get me out of bed.* To pass the time, Sam opened his laptop and watched a cooking video. When Mamie finally stopped talking, Sam went to sleep.

The third night, Mamie slept like a baby—and so did Sam. In the morning, she anxiously asked Marie-Catherine, "Is the *patron* gone?"

CHAPTER ELEVEN

Valentine's Day

Our last day in France — a Sunday — fell on Valentine's Day. Marie-Catherine organized a special farewell luncheon for us, and invited Odette, Madeleine, and her cousins, Pierre and Danielle. Odette, alas, couldn't make it.

The weather that morning was cloudy and cool, and the household was unusually silent. It was Bernadette's day off. François was at Mass. Marie-Catherine had dashed out to buy last-minute items. The Georgians were nowhere to be seen. Presumably they were upstairs, sleeping off the revelry of Kéti's christening the previous day.

It was eleven a.m., and the guests would be arriving in ninety minutes. Somehow, we had to throw together Sunday lunch for ten, possibly twelve if the Georgians joined us *à table*. *Désastre.* Sam stumbled into the kitchen and turned the oven on high. His motto: *whenever you're having a party, turn on the oven.* He opened the *frigo*, surveyed the contents, and got out a few items I'd picked up a day earlier: two *magrets de canard*, a *pintade* (the guinea fowl that Mamie loved so much), and an organic chicken from the poulterer down the road.

Marie-Catherine arrived home laden with baguettes, tomatoes, and a huge three-layer cake filled with orange-scented cream. She announced we were going to make the famous *gratin dauphinois*. Sam and I speed-peeled ten potatoes, which he cut into even slices a quarter-inch thick. Marie-Catherine instructed us to dot the bottom of a shallow casserole with eight pieces of butter. Then we layered the potatoes with salt, pepper, full-fat Normandy cream, and grated Gruyère cheese. "It's very *onctueux* (smooth). And it will taste even better the second day," she said. "You can use Comté or Emmenthal. They're both good cheeses, but Comté is better. You can smell the mountain flowers in the milk." She poured in milk three-quarters of the way to the top and suddenly cried, "We need more cream!" The closest place was the butcher in Allex. Unfortunately, she couldn't show her face there because, in yet another snafu, she had set up a date for us to watch him make sausage but forgot to tell us and took us to Provence instead.

Marie-Catherine dashed off to another village to buy Normandy cream. We had forty minutes left. Sam said the duck breasts would be easy to cook—a quick sear in a hot iron pan so the interiors stayed properly rosy. But how would we roast the guinea fowl *and* the chicken with a huge pan of *gratin dauphinois* hogging the *petite* French oven? Sam remembered Bernadette had "roasted" a whole chicken on top of the stove. We found a Le Creuset casserole and began browning the chicken, tossing in some salt and dried *herbes de Provence*. Sam rubbed olive oil on the *pintade*, put it in a smaller casserole, and tossed in some Nyons olives. Having never cooked guinea fowl before, we argued about how long it would take. Sam wanted to start cooking it immediately. I persuaded him to wait a bit.

Rüska, who normally pitched in by making vats of pasta, was AWOL. Even Andrie, who was always underfoot screaming or pulling bowls down from the counter, was missing. Pierre-Marie wandered by, his earbuds blasting. I asked him to set the table for ten. He ignored me. By now Sam and I were both in a full-blown panic. What vegetables to serve? I found a red cabbage in the *frigo*, part of Davit's haul from the refugee food bank. Sam chopped it up and simmered it with some raisins, cider vinegar, and a couple of diced dried-out apples, also from Davit's supply.

Marie-Catherine arrived back from her second emergency shopping foray. "You haven't cooked the *pintade* yet?" she shouted. "Quick, in the oven. You must start *now!*"

"I wanted to, but Mom thought you would be mad," said Sam. I glared at him for ratting me out. Sam turned on our last available burner and began browning the guinea fowl over high heat. Marie-Catherine watched us carefully.

"You have to keep turning it," she said. Afraid it would scorch, I lowered the heat. "*Non,*" she snapped, cranking the heat back up. With tempers running high, Sam kicked me off stove duty. I sulked and turned to washing stupid organic lettuce. I say "stupid" because it was coated in black dirt, which required eight washes before the water ran clean. After that, I vowed to buy only chemically poisoned greens. Also feeling the strain, Marie-Catherine withdrew to François's study and began calmly painting powder-blue swirls on a hatbox that would eventually hold toys and clothing for her newest grandson, whose birth was expected the following month. A few minutes later, she popped back into the kitchen. "Have you turned the chicken?" she asked. Then she went back to painting her hatbox.

By noon, the sun was shining, the potatoes were browning nicely, and Sam had even managed to squeeze a tiny pan of *caillette* from Entreprise Grimaud into the oven. He removed the pot of simmering red cabbage and began grilling the duck breasts. Marie-Catherine returned to the kitchen and decreed the duck breasts and *caillette* would be the appetizers, along with olive crackers she had purchased during our trip to Nyons. Then she went back to painting.

Our guests arrived at exactly 12:30 pm. Madeleine looked *soignée* in a crisp yellow blouse and a mauve silk sweater. Danielle, in a cloud of perfume, wore a delicate amethyst wool sweater accessorized by a perfectly arranged aqua silk scarf that emphasized her turquoise eyes. Pierre gallantly brought two long-stem roses in honour of Valentine's Day. He meant them for Marie-Catherine and me, but Madeleine seized one of them for herself.

Danielle had brought her specialty, *couronne au saumon*, which had taken hours to prepare. She had macerated raw salmon with lemon juice, chopped it up, and mixed it with canned salmon, beaten eggs, and *crème fraîche*. She then poured it into a crown-shaped mould—hence its name, "crown of salmon"—and baked it in a *bain-marie* to create a *flan*. For the sauce, she combined a fresh tomato coulis with basil and a little curry. Finally, she unmoulded the flan—no mean feat—and set it on a bed of chopped raw Chinese Napa cabbage, piping on a fluted decoration of mayonnaise. I was exhausted just listening to her explain how she made it. The *couronne de saumon* was too rich, especially with the other heavy appetizers of warm *caillette* and duck breast. The duck was a bloody disaster, so rare that most of the guests recoiled. Oh, well. A crisp white burgundy, a 2015 Mâcon-Villages, helped.

Nine of us lined the long kitchen table. It turned out the Georgians had prudently stayed with friends in another town after drinking a lot at Kéti's christening. I was seated beside Pierre, who continued to tutor me in French gender etiquette. Whenever a heavy platter was passed to him, he gallantly refused to take a morsel until I had first helped myself. "This is how I was raised. *C'est mon éducation*," he said, his blue eyes twinkling. "It's impossible for me any other way."

The guests had brought presents for Sam. Pierre and Danielle gave him a cookbook of Drôme specialties. Madeleine gave him a hip flask of Marc

Vieux, a thirty-year-old *eau de vie* from Côtes du Rhône. She pointed out that Jacques Pic, father of Anne-Sophie, had selected it. Warming to the topic of Michelin-starred restaurants, she regaled us with the terrible meal she'd had that week at Allex's only bistro. "*Zéro, zéro,*" Madeleine declared, waving her hands in disgust. "*Zéro étoiles!*" (Zero stars.) She had ordered a terrine — "no good" — followed by salmon — "no taste" — accompanied by couscous — "inedible." The only thing that pleased her was that the server forgot to charge her for a glass of red wine. She said the owners were Vietnamese. I said I thought they were Chinese because I'd overheard them talking Mandarin while I was strolling through Allex. "*Chinois?*" said Madeleine, with a shrug. "Anyway, *Asiatique.*"

The conversation turned to immigrants and their French-born offspring. "Ending compulsory military service was a big mistake," said François, repeating his earlier theory. "In the past, it brought all the youth together equally — black, white, Asian. It gave them a national identity." No one asked when the Georgians were leaving. Everyone appeared to accept that next the Jeanselmes family might take in Iraqis or Yazidis or Muslims. It was just part of life in Allex, 587 kilometres from the terrorist attacks at *Charlie Hebdo* magazine and the Bataclan theatre.

I'd bought the guinea fowl especially for Mamie, but she was asleep in her *salon* and never got to taste her favourite dish. Although the *pintade* was small, Sam managed to carve it so that everyone got a rich, dark morsel to taste. The skin was mahogany-coloured, the meat lean and ruby red. Pierre told us that one of his friends raised free-range *pintade*. Only in France would you be lunching on guinea fowl and someone at the table would know someone who raised them. We could have gone to see the farm, Pierre said, but unfortunately his friend had broken his arm and was incapacitated.

The chicken was moist. After Sam browned it on all sides, he splashed in some white wine and fresh rosemary and covered it. For the salad, we had run out of Bernadette's magnificent vinaigrette, so I filled a charming earthenware pitcher with store-bought dressing and no one noticed. Marie-Catherine's *gratin dauphinois* was indeed creamy and rich. It went perfectly with the guinea fowl and the roast chicken. Madeleine, who had earlier told us she couldn't cook and therefore couldn't teach us, recited her own recipe for *gratin dauphinois*. "Just rub the casserole with garlic. Add two bay leaves. And put in an egg to thicken the sauce."

François, who had donned a tie for the occasion, cut some chicken into tiny pieces for Pierre-Marie, who managed to swallow it without choking. I watched Philo expertly dissect a wing with her knife and fork. It occurred to me that the French *never* eat with their fingers. Thanks to Catherine de' Medici, they even ate pizza with a fork. I tried to copy Philo and eat my wing with my cutlery, but failed. When I confessed as much and, defeated, picked up the wing with my fingers, she glanced up and grinned.

"You're grounded!" Pierre-Marie shouted in delight.

"We'll close our eyes," said François, in mock horror.

Marie-Catherine brought out the huge torte, which was big enough to feed twenty. Everyone accepted a large slice, except for Sam and me—we hadn't paced ourselves. To take the edge off its sweetness, I brought out a bottle of the sparkling Clairette I'd bought a few days earlier.

The conversation turned to mothers and sons. I mentioned my impression that a mother was demoted the instant her son married. "Generally speaking, it's over," said Marie-Catherine, nodding. "Daughters confide in you. Daughters complain about their husbands. But a son doesn't complain about his wife. With sons, it's finished."

Pierre disagreed. He felt his feelings for his mother did not diminish after he married. "*J'adore my femme*, but my mother is my *mother*. My mother was a hero."

At three thirty, someone made coffee. By five, the lunch guests were gone. Only then did I realize I had forgotten to serve the braised red cabbage. François, Sam, and I tackled the dirty dishes. François tried to push us away. "If you don't let me do the dishes," he joked, "I'm going to forget *complètement* how to do it." He added that he'd never eaten so well in his life. "I'm going to hold you hostage à la ISIS so you can't leave tomorrow." ISIS was very much on his mind because he was planning a five-day mission to Iraq within the week. With four other volunteers, François was going to a refugee camp in Erbil, the capital of Iraqi Kurdistan. His goal: to rescue some Christians and Yazidis and bring them to France.

That evening the farmhouse was preternaturally quiet. The Georgians were still away. Philo and Pierre-Marie had left for a special religious dinner in Valence for mentally handicapped people. François or Marie-Catherine would have to drive there to administer Philo's insulin shot before she could eat. They argued over who would go, but not the way Norman and I argued.

"I will go," said François.

"You're too exhausted. I will go," said Marie-Catherine.

François overruled her.

He was driving us the next morning, very early, to the TGV station for our train to Italy. Sam and I were so stuffed we couldn't even think of eating dinner, but it seemed like our hosts could eat a bit. We decided to make them a special Valentine's dinner, just for the two of them, even though they didn't celebrate the date because it wasn't a religious holiday. "Other couples measure their relationship by what kind of gift they get, or the value of the dinner," said Marie-Catherine. "We don't do that." Good thing, because we were throwing together leftovers. I began simmering the remnant chicken bones for soup and tossed in a handful of rice. There were a few wedges of leftover supermarket pizza. I found some pickled beets, which I added to what was left of the stupid organic green salad. There was still a slice of the *Paris-Brest* pastry from Kéti's one-month celebration.

The secret sauce was that, for once, François and Marie-Catherine would be alone. We would cook and serve this fine couple who done had so much for everyone else, including us, that they scarcely ever had time for themselves. We shook out the crumbs from the Provençal tablecloth. I put the remaining long-stem rose from Pierre in a bud vase, set it on the table, and lit a couple of candles.

Perhaps he was just being polite, but François expressed astonishment and delight at the chicken-rice soup. "I never had this before! *C'est délicieux*," he said. Marie-Catherine praised it lavishly, too. She remembered her grandmother would make it for her, but she hadn't had it in ages. From his years as a university student, Sam had a *truc* for reheating pizza. "Don't put it in the oven," he told me. "That dries it up. Grill it in a dry frying pan, covered with a lid on top to melt the cheese."

With François's impending trip on our minds, we talked about refugees, immigrants, honour killings, and arranged marriages. When he was headmaster of the *lycée* in Lyon, female students had sometimes asked him to help them obtain asylum because their parents were planning to marry them off.

"To men who already have so many wives," said François.

"To men so *old*," said Marie-Catherine. "Really old and disgusting." She shuddered and pointed to her husband. "Like François."

Sam and I looked at the chagrined expression on François's face, and burst out laughing.

"*Merci*," François said to his wife, with excessive courtesy. "That's very kind of you, Catherine. This couldn't be understood without an actual example."

"I'm sorry," Marie-Catherine started to say but began laughing so hard she started choking. Soon we were all laughing so hard we cried.

François quickly finished his meal and kissed her on the top of her head *and* on her hand. Despite her continued protests that she would take care of Philo's insulin injection, he hurried out to drive the hour-long return trip to Valence.

MARIE-CATHERINE'S GRATIN DAUPHINOIS (SCALLOPED POTATOES)
Serves 4 to 6.

Use shallow casserole for maximum surface to get a golden crust.

6	medium potatoes
1 cup	milk
½ cup	full-fat cream
½	stick of butter, diced
1	clove garlic*
1 cup	grated Gruyère, Comté, or Emmenthal cheese
	salt and pepper to taste

Preheat oven to 425°F.

Rub cut garlic clove on the bottom and sides of your casserole. Dot bottom of casserole with half the butter. Peel potatoes and cut into ¼-inch-thick slices. Layer potatoes, adding salt, pepper, and cheese to taste. Heat milk and pour over potatoes, then pour cold cream on top. Scatter on remaining butter and cheese. Bake for 30 to 40 minutes, or until potatoes are tender to the fork and milk is mostly absorbed. If top isn't golden, raise temperature to 450°F briefly.

*Marie-Catherine hates garlic, but traditional gratin calls for it.

Italy

CHAPTER TWELVE

Repergo

As the crow flies, the Drôme was right beside Piemonte, our destination. But getting there required a change of trains in Lyon and a five-hour journey through the Alps. At least this gave us time to reset our brains. I pulled out my Italian vocabulary lists and reviewed my file cards of verb conjugations from the beginner's Italian course I took at my university.

I am not a natural linguist. My Canadian-born parents spoke English at home. In high school, I learned stilted French. When I studied Mandarin at McGill University, I found it hard to distinguish among the four tones, which is partly why, when I went to China on my summer vacation in the midst of the Cultural Revolution, I talked my way into staying on to learn the language. I don't know why I thought I could pick up a fourth language at the age of sixty-four. Italian is the language of music, however, which meant that as an amateur flautist I already knew a few words. *Piccolo*, the smallest of the flutes, meant "little." *Piano* meant "soft," *forte* meant "loud." *Ritardo* meant "slow down." *Scherzo* — "playful" in musical terms, meant a "joke." And *ma non troppo* was "but not too much," in music, as well as in cooking.

My Italian class met three times a week. With more than thirty students enrolled, we had scant opportunity to speak. I never learned to roll the r's in *burro*, which means "butter," not a pack animal. Instead I learned alternative facts. The professor incorrectly informed us that, because coffee was a national birthright, Italian law forbade bars from charging more than one euro for espresso. He also said *colazione* could mean breakfast or lunch. My tittering Italian friends informed me it meant *only* breakfast, at least, in Piemonte. By the end of the term, I still hadn't learned words like "now" or "toilet." (I did know the names of every month, which turned out to be quite useless for anyone staying less than a year.)

Sam was supposed to take beginner's Italian during his final term at university, but only advanced Italian was offered that fall. He said he would wing it, relying on his fluent French and high school Spanish, and practise en route. On the train, however, he fell promptly asleep, exhausted from all the cooking, washing, and Mamie-watching. I poked him awake because he was missing a breathtaking view of Alps. "Nice," he grunted, opening one eye and glancing out the window. Then he went back to sleep.

I didn't mind. I was happy just to be beside him. When you raise your children, you hope they become independent. Paradoxically, when they do, you feel abandoned. Daughters, however, stay close even after they leave home. They come back to hang out with you at the mall or sit around the table and yak. They call or text frequently, perhaps daily, even as they secretly dread growing up to become your clone. At the same time, mothers and daughters negotiate constant friction, an unspoken rivalry, a one-upmanship about the best way, say, to bake a cake or soothe a baby.

Sons rarely become rivals because they are too different from their moms. Our XX and their XY chromosomes mean we are not and never can be the same. If all goes well, we bond not as competitors but as mutually sustaining allies. Comedy writers milk the trope that men don't understand women. If a woman tells her husband, "Sure, go ahead and watch that three-hour football game on TV," every woman knows she means just the opposite. When comedy writers joke about clueless men, they are talking about husbands and boyfriends, not sons. Unlike Norman, for instance, Sam and Ben always knew exactly what I was thinking or feeling. Sons — Pierre was a case in point — are exquisitely attuned to their mothers.

If a mother is lucky, she will have a lifelong romance with her son. Call it a "Momance." It starts from birth, from the moment she first holds her newborn boy. Consider the Chinese character for "good" — 好. It is a pictograph of a woman 女 nuzzling her son 子. When my boys were toddlers and I would get home after a long day in the newsroom, they would scamper to the door like puppies, yelping and demanding to be hugged. Once, when Sam was eighteen months old, he was upstairs when he heard the front door open, raced to the stairs, lost his footing, and tumbled down head over heels.

Head-over-heels love. That's how it starts. But every step that you teach them to be self-reliant is a step away from you. The parenting relationship is the only love affair where the final goal is separation. When the son finds a new love — Pierre being the exception that proves the rule — his mother is eclipsed. The mother experiences the darkness, like a total solar eclipse.

Her sadness is, of course, mixed with happiness that her son has found a mate and is starting the next phase in his life. But why is there no ritual at weddings for the mother of the groom? The father of the bride gives his daughter away. Why does the mother not give away her son?

In Allex, Sam often went out to kick a soccer ball around an empty farm field. He needed a break not only from being on his best behaviour at the Jeanselmes' but also from me. It was bittersweet because I still remembered how impatient I was when he was a toddler, how I yearned for that distant point in the future when I could go out without him, without the hassle and expense of hiring a babysitter. When did everything flip inside out?

I poked Sam again. He opened one eye and then the other. I passed him my Italian grammar book. He read it, or pretended to, for ten minutes. Then he fell asleep again.

In Turin, we wandered inside and all around the train station, hunting for the car-rental agency. Everything, including the police post, had shut down tight for lunch. Down a deserted side street, we spotted an Italian flag. It was a neighbourhood police station. When I approached the sentry, dragging my battered pink plastic suitcase behind me, he did not smile. *"Parli italiano?"* he snapped. I could tell he was thinking: *Of course you don't, you stupid tourists.*

My musical Italian surfaced. *"Un poco,"* I said.

Suddenly he smiled and rattled off the directions. *A destra, a sinistra.* Thanks to high-school Latin, I understood! To the right, to the left.

At the rental agency, we chose a Smart Car. When the clerk unilaterally cut the daily charge for GPS, we took it, a wise move because we had to find our way from downtown Turin, a city of 4.4 million people, to Repergo, a dot of a hamlet that wasn't on the free rental-car map. Whenever Sam drove at home, I was that annoying critic, complaining he drove too fast, turned too sharply, or steered with only one hand. In Italy, the tables were turned. I was scared. Hesitantly I asked Sam if he would drive, and he jumped at the chance. Suddenly I understood the evolutionary urge to procreate. I'd had a son twenty-two years earlier so he would take the wheel in downtown Turin.

Repergo was an hour's drive south on the autoroute, but we weren't supposed to arrive at our rental farmhouse until later in the afternoon. I proposed we use the extra time and take the scenic route. We could stop for lunch at some quaint *trattoria* along the way. Sam pulled out of the rental-car garage and was instantly engulfed in a sea of traffic. The traffic lights were confounding. I yelled a couple of times. Sam yelled back. But after a few wrong turns, he found the old road out of Turin.

The sky was a brilliant blue. The old highway passed through town after town. Finally, at three p.m., we stopped at a roadside pizzeria just as it was shutting down. So was every other place in sight. We had just missed the national one to three p.m. Italian lunch "hour," which was as strict and unbending as in France.

"We'd better stop for groceries," Sam said, thinking ahead, in a parent-child role reversal. "There might not be any place to eat in Repergo."

He pulled into a *supermercato* off the highway that looked ordinary from the outside but was the anti-Costco and better than the fanciest gourmet shop in New York. Most of the food came in small packages, hinting at the size of Italian kitchens to come. Eggs were sold by the tens, not the dozen. Flour came in one-kilo paper sacks. Coke came in four-packs, and the cans were half the size of those at home. The supermarket sold a dozen kinds of artisanal butter, five varieties of artichokes, and about thirty types of olives. I chose a small block of butter wrapped in parchment paper and sealed with metal grommets. We bought the original baloney, genuine mortadella from Bologna. Intensely yellow lemons, from the Amalfi coast, came with shiny green leaves intact. At the deli counter, Sam chose pickled red onions and marinated eel from Naples. We selected a bunch of dewy fresh *puntarelle*, a kind of overgrown arugula. We stocked up on wine, spicy *antipasti*, crusty bread, heritage tomatoes, dried spaghetti, and a jar of *passata,* the strained raw tomatoes that are the base of so many pasta sauces. And in case the farmhouse kitchen wasn't properly supplied, we bought a couple of kitchen knives.

Piemonte, pronounced Pee-MONT-ay, on the frilly top left of the Italian boot, was the springboard for Italy's unification in the nineteenth century. After Sicily, it was the second largest of Italy's twenty-three distinct regions. Famous for its white truffles and bold red wines, such as Barolo, Barbaresco, and Barbera, the region was also the epicentre of Italy's famed Slow Food movement. Launched in the late 1980s, its avowed mission was to preserve traditional cuisine, a call to arms sparked by the opening of Italy's first McDonald's. Later, a Piemonte entrepreneur in Turin opened Eataly, a play on the Italian pronunciation of Italy, which combined a Slow Food restaurant, bar, and bakery with a Whole Foods–style supermarket.

There were now more than a dozen Eataly emporiums across Italy and many more around the world, including in Dubai, Istanbul, Seoul, Tokyo, Hong Kong, Paris, London, and New York.

In Piemonte, Maria Rosa Beccaris, the neighbour of my British friend Ashley, at first had flatly refused his suggestion that she teach Sam and me to cook. Aside from the understandable bother, she worried that she wasn't a good enough cook. Ashley, a former diplomat, was relentless, and Maria Rosa eventually caved. That afternoon, with the help of the GPS, Sam drove confidently through the steep, twisting hills of Piemonte to Maria Rosa's village of Repergo.

"This is just like a video game," he enthused, as he whipped around a hairpin turn. "Do you know what they call this?" I didn't. "God's racetrack." I closed my eyes. Then I opened them because I didn't want to miss the scenery —the famous vineyards of Nebbiolo grapes. The twisting roads ended abruptly as we descended into a gentle valley and drove past farm fields and more vineyards. At four p.m. the GPS brought us to Vigneti Brichet, the winery owned and operated by Maria Rosa's cousin Mirella. She and her husband, Beppe Massasso, were renting us a farmhouse.

I rang the bell outside a tall wrought-iron fence. After a moment, the electronic gate swung open. We drove into an empty parking lot big enough for twenty cars. A slim young man with a shock of dark hair invited us into the fermentation workshop and offered us espresso, which we gratefully accepted. He was Alessandro, Mirella's and Beppe's twenty-nine-year-old son. As we sipped our espresso, his aunt, Maria Rosa, appeared as if by magic. Although we'd met only over Skype, she gave Sam and me warm hugs and announced we would be cooking dinner at her house shortly.

But first Alessandro led us to the farmhouse, a one-minute walk down the road. In English, he explained the complicated thermostat, a series of concentric dials calibrated to a twenty-four-hour clock, which neither Sam nor I ever figured out. Alessandro lived on the main floor of the farmhouse. We had the entire top floor, with a separate entrance, our own living room and eat-in kitchen, and, most important, two bedrooms. From a small balcony, I could see medieval hillside villages. Below were gnarly leafless grapevines, dark as coal. To my right, I could touch an almond tree about to burst into bloom.

Maria Rosa lived a five-minute walk down a hilly road. Like Allex in the Drôme, the advent of superhighways and *supermercati* had drained the lifeblood of Repergo (pop. 201). Aside from Alessandro's family winery, the only business in the village was a butcher store. There was nowhere to buy milk or bread. There was no post office or pharmacy or espresso bar. The last pizzeria was gone (although it still showed up on Google Maps). The only remnant of a shuttered tobacco store was its tiny metal sign. The local elementary school had shut down twenty years earlier. Repergo exemplified Italy's declining birth rate, among the lowest in the world. One in ten Reperghese was a widow or widower.

Maria Rosa's father, Giuseppe, was one. A retired autoworker at the Fiat factory in Turin, he was seventy-nine and in poor health. Stoop-shouldered, short, and diabetic, he used a walker. While he seemed doddering, he was sharp as a tack, ever on the alert against burglars and thieves. In summer, he would sit on the warm terrace beside the garden. In winter, he sat in the bright sunlight by a window overlooking the garden. Everyone respectfully called him "Nonno" (grandfather). He owned the house, a large nineteenth-century yellow stucco building with a wrought-iron Juliet balcony, twelve rooms on three stories, and soft grey terrazzo floors. To me, the house was lovely, but Maria Rosa disliked it. She and her husband owned a modern apartment in Montegrosso, a town five minutes away. They had moved here with their daughter, Chiara, to care for Nonno after he broke his femur in a fall. Like Marie-Catherine, Maria Rosa refused to put her parent in an institution even though it meant Chiara, then eight, had to commute to elementary school.

How long ago was that? "Nine years," said Maria Rosa, sighing and looking heavenward. At forty-eight, she wore no makeup. Her luxuriant dark hair ended in a feathered cut at the nape of her neck. With rounded hips and soft arms, she dressed comfortably and casually in a puffy black jacket, V-neck sweater, and jeans. Nonno had cut his finger earlier that day while slicing some stale focaccia. "He was greedy," said Chiara, laughing. Nonno gave an exaggerated good-natured shrug. When Maria Rosa, a nurse, had gotten home from work that afternoon, she'd taken one look at his bleeding finger and called ahead to her colleagues in the emergency room. She drove right back to her hospital in Asti, twenty minutes away. Nonno had received three stitches and now waited patiently for dinner, his finger swathed in white gauze, in his customary chair by the window. He assured me it didn't hurt at all.

Like Marie-Catherine's home, Nonno's had an exterior alcove that sheltered a plaster saint. The fifteen-foot ceilings—even the main-floor bathroom had soaring vaulted brick ceilings—meant the house was comfortably cool during Italy's scorching summers. In winter, though, it was cold. To save on heating costs, Maria Rosa had closed off parts of the house, including half the second floor and the entire third floor. Nonno's house bordered Via Repergo, the main street, without even a strip of sidewalk to separate it from the occasional car. Decades ago, his father, a builder and a farmer, had taken advantage of the prime location to operate a small convenience store from the kitchen window. Passersby had only to shout, and someone in the family would fling open the dark brown wooden shutters, lean out, and sell a package of tobacco or some sugar. The kitchen itself was small and narrow, opening onto a large room that in Canada would have been a combination living and dining room. In Italy, it was solely dedicated to the art of eating. There was a sofa where no one sat. Instead, family and friends always gathered around a square table that sat six comfortably but could be expanded to accommodate twice that number by pushing together an assortment of old desks and smaller tables until they formed one giant rectangle.

Chiara, a willowy, dark-haired beauty who had just turned seventeen, studied English at school. She shyly insisted she could not speak a word—until she realized I'd had only one term of Italian, and Sam none at all. She plucked up her courage to speak occasional words and then whole phrases in English. Luckily Sam picked up new words at lightning speed. By the end of our first evening, we managed to communicate. Maria Rosa planned to teach us Piemonte's most famous dishes, including *bagna càuda*, *vitello tonnato*, and *carne cruda* (the French embraced it as steak tartare). But because she had worked all day and then took Nonno to get stitches, that first evening we prepared a less labour-intensive meal. As she explained the order of the courses, I realized that Italy was governed by food rules. Our first dinner would unfold in a traditional sequence: *antipasti*, a pasta, a *secondo* of meat (which was really the third course, if you counted the appetizer as a first), *dolce*, fresh fruit, and *caffè* (always espresso—and *not* decaf).

The *antipasti* would be cheese, olives, and *taralli pugliesi*, a doughnut-shaped bread from Puglia made with white wine, flour, olive oil, and salt.

The pasta would be *agnolotti di Calliano*, a Piemonte specialty of ravioli in a meat sauce. The *secondo* would be *involtini di coniglio*, a ham-stuffed roll of rabbit from the only butcher in Repergo and braised with white wine, carrots, onions, celery, rosemary, and a fresh bay leaf from the garden. What kind of meat was in the ravioli sauce? *"Asino,"* said Maria Rosa. I looked at Sam. He shrugged. *"Asino,"* Chiara repeated. When I still didn't understand, she and her mother began braying: *EE-oo! EE-oo!*

We were having donkey.

Ravioli with ass sauce didn't taste like chicken. It tasted like venison.

CHAPTER THIRTEEN

Italian Food Rules

The next morning Maria Rosa's husband took us to Montegrosso d'Asti (which everyone simply called "Montegrosso"), where they owned the flat. Fiorenzo Cavagnino had taken a week's holiday from his job at the phone bank at the highway authority in Turin to help us out. He was fifty-seven, of medium height, with a bald pate ringed by an avuncular fringe of white. He knew about a dozen words of English, but was determined to teach us Italian. As he drove down the highway, he pointed through the windshield at the fog and rain. "*Nebbia*," he said. I was stumped, but Sam grasped it immediately. "Hey, it's just like Spanish. *Niebla*. I can understand." A moment later, my Latin kicked in. *Nebbia, nebula, nebulous…fog*. My limited vocabulary never dampened Fiorenzo's enthusiasm. He launched into an intricate explanation of his favourite sport, *tamburello*, a sixteenth-century game like tennis invented in Piemonte, played with two teams, five to a side. He boasted he'd been a standout player in his youth. He constantly cracked jokes. If we understood at all, we laughed thirty seconds or two minutes late, which delighted him.

First, Fiorenzo explained, we would have coffee at his favourite hangout. Then we would visit the farmers' market. Pasticceria Gaetano was packed with locals who seemed to have all the time in the world to eat pastries on a weekday morning. Like most of the customers, we stood at the counter. Sitting at a table incurred higher prices for the same food and drink. At any rate, our snack took two minutes. Fiorenzo grabbed the bill before we could. Sam and I split an unmemorable marmalade croissant. Fiorenzo scarfed three tiny cookies. He and Sam had thimble-sized cups of espresso. I ordered a cappuccino, which was no more than three ounces, because I figured it was my one and only chance that day. Italy was a country of chaos — twenty-seven prime ministers and sixty-three governments in sixty-eight years — but paradoxically it was governed by strict culinary rules.

Italian Food Rule: *never drink cappuccino after eleven a.m.*

Another Italian Food Rule: *caffè, which comes in one-ounce servings, is always taken black (although sugar is encouraged).*

Across the road, the weekly market was limping along in the downpour with a butcher, a *salumi* maker, a cheese stall, two fishmongers, and a couple of glum vegetable sellers. Fiorenzo told me the merchants moved en masse, hitting different towns on specific days of the week. I quickly bought a cheap made-in-China umbrella and got in line at the busier fish stall. Ahead of me, an older woman spent seventy-five dollars on some octopus. Another woman dropped eighty dollars on halibut steaks. The fishmonger, a middle-aged redhead, meticulously carved the fish with a knife as sharp and long as a samurai sword. She removed unsightly red blotches with surgical precision before she weighed the fish. And just like the fish markets in Hong Kong, she slipped in a few sprigs of free parsley.

Slow Food, indeed. The line moved at glacial speed. The fishmonger chatted desultorily with her customers, as if the person she was serving was her only client. This of course artificially inflated the queue and made her stall seem very popular (which is why I had chosen it over the other stall). Chatting was great for customer relations, unless you were one of the wretches waiting in line, rain dripping onto your shoulders from a too-small Chinese umbrella. After twenty minutes, it was finally my turn. I bought half a kilo of tiny baby squid called *seppioline*. My most thrilling purchase was a big net bag of pasta clams, each as tiny as the fingernail on my little finger, a variety impossible to get back home. I envisioned *spaghetti alle vongole* that evening at Maria Rosa's.

Italian Food Rule: *never touch the produce in a market* (but it's fine in a *supermercato*). Sam admired outsized sweet yellow peppers, crates of sparkling red and green lettuces, walnuts in the shell, glistening white onions, fat yellow lemons, and pale green zucchini with their golden blossoms still attached. He bought a bag of Sicilian blood oranges and was surprised when the vendor tossed in two extra oranges instead of giving him change, a crafty way to sell more.

Suddenly Fiorenzo announced we should have been at Maria Rosa's cousin's house ten minutes ago. Apparently we were cooking with Cousin Mirella, but no one had told us. I had assumed we would cook exclusively with Maria Rosa. Only gradually I understood that, like Marie-Catherine, Maria Rosa couldn't manage us every day. She, too, deputized friends and family.

At the winery, I proudly thrust my bag of clams and baby squid at Mirella. She paused. She sighed. A beat later, I realized that she had already planned her dinner menu. *"Allora,"* she said, smiling broadly. *Well, then.* "Next time we'll make *pasta e fagioli.* Tonight: *spaghetti alle vongole e seppioline."* I felt a twinge. I loved *pasta e fagioli,* too, and had always wanted to learn how to make the thick noodle-and-bean soup. I apologized for rudely hijacking my host's menu, but Mirella said it was no problem. Like in France, I often had no idea what my Italian hosts were planning. For his part, Sam adapted much better to the surprises each day brought. His easygoing nature was a model for me. When did *that* role reversal happen?

Mirella handed her shopping list to her husband. Beppe Massasso was fifty-seven, the same age as Fiorenzo. He was a tall, lanky, sunburned man with fingers stained grape-purple. Unlike Fiorenzo, Beppe spoke no English at all, and motioned for us to get in his Mercedes SUV like we were hearing impaired. He drove like a maniac, worse than François, even worse than Bernadette. In Asti, coincidentally a sister city to Valence, he parked in Piazza Campo del Palio. *"Palio,"* he said, pointing to the ground. Then, in spite of himself, he began to tell us the history of Asti. The piazza was the site of an annual bareback horse race commemorating the town's medieval victory against its rival, Alba. The re-enactment of the *palio* took place every year on the third Sunday in September. It was Italy's oldest horse race, second only to Siena's in importance.

Beppe led the way to Asti's famous indoor food market, housed in a stately nineteenth-century building with walls the colour of honey-vanilla ice cream. He halted in front of his favourite butcher, owned by the Massano brothers, Marcello and Paolo. "This is the best *macelleria* in Asti," said Beppe. "It sells only Piemonte meat."

The word *macelleria* derived from the Latin word for butcher and slaughterhouse. Macelleria Oro Rosso sold rabbit, beef, free-range chicken, liver, beef tripe, *salumi,* fresh sausage, meatballs, and hand-shaped patties with herbs and cheese. For our lunch later, Sam and I bought two flower-shaped burgers draped with translucent slices of *lardo,* the famous Italian cured fatback that can be eaten raw. Like Bernadette's favourite butcher store in Chabeuil, the ones we encountered in Piemonte were sparklingly clean. But the Italian ones also hung engraved plaques and framed certificates of merit on their walls. Some displayed trophies in their windows for the prizes they'd won for their meat. "First prize for the fatted calf," crowed a red silk banner at a *macelleria* in Nizza Monferrato.

Beppe ordered a kilo of minced beef filet from Paolo Massano, who was festively dressed in a red hat and matching apron. He carefully trimmed the glistening silver skin, the shiny white membrane that doesn't break down when cooked, and then ground the filet by hand. Mirella was making *carne cruda*, a Piemonte specialty that in 1950 inspired Giuseppe Cipriani of Harry's Bar in Venice to create *carpaccio*, paper-thin slices of raw beef served with lemon, olive oil, shaved Parmesan and, sometimes, white truffles. Cipriani named the dish after the Venetian artist Vittore Carpaccio, famous for the blood-red hues in his Renaissance paintings.

Beppe herded us back to his SUV and drove at breakneck speed to a gigantic suburban *supermercato*. He parked, leaving the keys in his Mercedes. "Clearly there's no crime in Asti," Sam whispered. That was surprising, considering Beppe had just cautioned us against a day trip to Genoa, a mere hour away. "Very dangerous," he warned darkly in the simplest Italian syntax he could muster. "You cannot drive there. Don't take your car. Or money. Pickpockets. Criminals. Go to Torino instead." Italians were intensely parochial about everything from food to crime rates. Don't tell Beppe, but according to *Corriere della Sera*, the leading Italian daily, the crime rate in Turin, the capital of Piemonte, was double that of Genoa, the capital of Liguria. To put it in perspective, however, overall crime in Italy, especially the homicide rate, was among the lowest in Western Europe. That didn't stop Italians from pulling down metal shutters over their windows whenever they went out. In tiny Repergo, Beppe's winery was gated, surrounded by a high fence, monitored with security cameras, and guarded by an attack dog. Nonno always kept the front door locked, even as he sat watch at the front window.

Beppe raced through the supermarket the way he drove his SUV. We trailed in his wake, listening while he phoned Mirella at least three times to find out exactly which type of sweet peppers she wanted, what kind of flour, what size of capers. She also asked him to buy three tiny tins of tuna packed in olive oil, which were expensive, but significantly richer tasting than the water-packed stuff I usually ate at home. At the checkout, we tried to pay for the groceries. Beppe was adamant that we would not pay for them, but Sam, a hockey goalie, was quicker than him.

For lunch back at our apartment, Sam pan-seared the burgers so that the *lardo* melted, contributing a rich umami flavour. We steamed artichokes and made a green salad. When we finished eating and had washed the dishes, it was time to walk over in the rain to start cooking dinner with Mirella.

☼

Beppe's grandfather founded Vigneti Brichet di Massasso e Figli in 1920. It grew a dozen varieties of grapes, including Merlot, Cabernet, and Moscato, producing white, rosé, and ruby-red Barbera wines (pronounced bar-BARE-a). Beppe began working in the business when he was eighteen. At twenty-five, he married the girl next door, and they had two sons. Alessandro, the elder son, helped him harvest and ferment the grapes and bottle the wine. Stefano, the younger son, worked in Sydney as a sommelier and had an import licence to sell Massasso wines in Australia.

Mirella said that Stefano emailed her daily. "When I go to sleep, I say, '*Buona giornata*.' When he goes to sleep, he says, '*Buona giornata*.'" They Skyped once a week. "I want to look at his face. I ask him, 'Are you eating?'" she said.

I gave Sam, who *never* emails me, an accusatory look. He grinned sheepishly, and shrugged.

Mirella was a confident, ample woman of forty-eight, with nape-length dyed auburn hair. When she tied a big apron around her girth, she looked like an Italian *mamma*. But she could glam up, too, shaving a decade off her appearance by donning a miniskirt and makeup. She handled all the bookkeeping, shipping, and wine-tasting dinners. Decades earlier the winery had stopped selling to the public and sold only to a private roster of customers. Beppe delivered cases of wine all over north Italy (which perhaps explained his crazed driving). Mirella couriered the rest to clients further afield, in central and south Italy. She also single-handedly cooked the ten-course wine-tasting dinners for fifty guests during the fall harvest and spring bottling seasons.

They lived above the shop in a large, well-appointed house with high ceilings and windows overlooking the vineyard. Beppe's parents had once lived here. When he took over the business, they swapped homes, and the parents now lived down the road. Mirella knocked down interior walls, repositioned the principal rooms, and built her dream kitchen, even though the winery below was equipped with a professional one. Hers was spotless and hyper-organized. On one shelf, she arranged by date her vast collection of *La Cucina Italiana*, a monthly magazine like *Cook's Illustrated*. Each copy was pristine, but Mirella seemed to know exactly which issue had which recipe. The kitchen's colour scheme reflected the Italian flag — red Brescia granite counters and green-stained trim on her custom cupboards. As in France, the appliances were compact. The Italian-made, built-in SMEG convection wall oven was gunmetal-grey with gold dials and a pretty oval window. Her built-in refrigerator was mounted eighteen inches off the ground, which meant less bending over and cleverly left a dark niche underneath for stashing potatoes and onions. The best design trick was the generous depth of her counters, 40 percent deeper than the North American standard of twenty-five inches, which meant Mirella had ample room to work. The back of her deep double sink, for instance, had enough space for a dirty pot or dripping colander of lettuce. The sink also had a built-in drain board, carved from the same red granite as her counters.

Sam had instant gadget envy when he saw Mirella's professional meat slicer. Hers was also the only home we worked in that had an espresso machine (Lavazza brand). Everywhere else we went, people used the two-piece stovetop coffeepot called *la moka*. Households had multiple versions — one cup, two cups, four cups, six cups, and ten cups — because the *moka* worked by forcing steam through the coffee grounds. You had to have exactly the right size for the amount you were brewing.

"Food is a concentrated messenger of a culture," noted Bill Buford in his book *Heat*. To me, kitchens reinforce that cultural message. The Italian kitchens we visited, no matter their size, always had two important pieces of furniture: a large central table and a comfy sofa. Although I rarely saw anyone sit on the sofa, it seemed essential because, just like in France, the kitchen was the place family and friends congregated. (Perhaps it was also a subconscious nod to ancient Rome, where the wealthy reclined to dine.) As for the table, it wasn't merely a place to eat but a key workspace. In the nineteenth and early twentieth centuries, Italian kitchens typically had a stove and, perhaps, a sink, but no counters. To roll out and cut fresh pasta, housewives placed a custom-made board on top of the table. When the meal was ready, they removed the board and everyone gathered around the table.

"The life of an Italian family is only at the table," Mirella said.

CHAPTER FOURTEEN

Cucina Povera

Italian cooking once had two distinctive schools. *Cucina alto-borghese*—what the French would call *haute cuisine*—was cosmopolitan, reflecting the globalized political influence of the Italian bourgeoisie ingratiating themselves with foreign occupiers such as the French in Piemonte and the Austrians in Lombardy and Tuscany. *Cucina povera*, "the cooking of the poor," was the food of peasants and workers who ate what they grew, fished, or hunted—the original locavore diet. Guess which one eclipsed the other?

After Catherine de' Medici began the transformation of French cuisine, the food of Italy and France went in opposite directions. French cuisine enjoyed a renaissance, developing intricate sauces, airy soufflés, and architecturally showy *pâtisserie*. The chef and restaurateur Auguste Escoffier summed up the art of *haute cuisine* in his seminal 1903 work, *Le guide culinaire*, aimed at professional chefs. Italy instead concentrated on home cooking. In his 1891 masterpiece, *Science in the Kitchen and the Art of Eating Well*, a wealthy businessman named Pellegrino Artusi devoted himself to gathering recipes from ordinary families. Unlike Escoffier, Artusi did not focus on how a grand hotel should make a hundred variations of a sauce. Instead he examined how mothers and grandmothers made *spaghetti con piselli* (with peas) or *panata*, a soup of stale bread, eggs, nutmeg, and a pinch of Parmesan cheese.

With abundant herbs and vegetables, the poorest Italian peasant could coax taste and nutrition from the most ordinary ingredients. Recipes were handed down not in writing but through generations cooking together. Often the meal would consist of a single dish. In the south, that meant pasta with tomato sauce or olive oil; in central Italy, polenta; in the north, rice seasoned with milk or broth. Always, bread accompanied the main starch. And to save fuel, bread was baked once a week, collectively, in the village oven, just as in rural Allex, which was why Italians had such inventive dishes for stale bread, like *panata* or *panzanella*, the latter a Tuscan salad of tomatoes, onions, basil, and stale bread revived with ice water.

After World War II, the upper classes could no longer afford the army of servants required to prepare and serve eight-course meals. *Cucina alto-borghese* went into decline. At the same time, refrigeration and improved roads expanded choices for the working class. As the standard of living improved, the old habit of eating bread *with* pasta ended. But across the nation, regardless of income or class, *cucina povera*, or the art of feeding a family on next to nothing, is the hallmark of Italian cuisine. That makes Italy different from France, where *haute cuisine* is still admired but hard to replicate at home. It also distinguishes Italy from China, where only professionals could pull off fussy dim sum or a lacquered Peking Duck. Ask a French or Chinese person the best place to eat, and they will likely name a restaurant. But if you ask an Italian, the answer will always be: *a casa della mamma*.

That evening, Mirella had planned a five-course menu: *carne cruda* with salad, *involtini di peperoni al forno ripieni con tonno, spaghetti alle vongole e seppioline, formaggio*, and *torta di nocciole* with warm *zabaglione*. By the time we arrived, she already had several dishes underway. She had soaked the clams in cool water and sea salt, changing the water three times over five hours. The salt water rid them of sand and kept them alive until the last minute. Mirella's method was much easier and more effective than scrubbing each clam with a stiff brush, as some cookbooks advise, or messily soaking them in water laced with cornmeal or black pepper.

Involtini di peperoni al forno ripieni con tonno was the quintessential Piemonte antipasto: roasted sweet red peppers rolled around a tuna sauce that tasted creamy but had no cream in it. Mirella had already charred the thick-fleshed peppers under her broiler and cooled them under a blanket of parchment paper. Sam's task was peeling away the tough burnt skin, seeding them, and slicing the succulent flesh into two-inch-wide strips. For the sauce, Mirella drained the olive oil from three small tins of Italian tuna. Then she put the tuna into a machine I'd never seen before, which looked like a cross between a coffee pot and a rice cooker. The Bimby was the Ferrari of kitchen mixers. German-designed (in 1961) and French-assembled today, it weighed, chopped, grated, stirred, mixed, whipped, melted, cooked, stir-fried, steamed, and simmered. The *Wall Street Journal* called it a "cooking robot." It took up only thirteen square inches of countertop real estate but could make pasta dough, polenta, focaccia, risotto, *fonduta* (melted cheese), and spaghetti sauce. It could also make sorbet, gelato, yogourt, cakes, cocktails, and baby food. It even cleaned itself (but apparently didn't iron).

Mirella had bought hers a decade earlier for 900 euros, more than the cost of a decent stove. I coveted one, but in Canada the machine costs $1,785, before taxes and shipping. Officially known as the Thermomix, the Bimby was sold through in-home demonstrations only. It was all the rage in Italy, France, and even recession-wracked Portugal, where the Bimby outsold high-end iPads and had more Facebook friends than the country's most popular rock band. In China, it was 40 percent more expensive than in Canada and was marketed as the "Goodness Food Multitasking Machine." It was said to make fishball soup from scratch in fifteen minutes.

To the tuna, Mirella added two teaspoons of brined capers, twelve green pitted olives, three peeled hard-boiled eggs, a third of a cup of lemon juice, and a spoonful of her own extra-virgin olive oil, cold-pressed from Leccino trees that she and Beppe had planted more than a quarter century earlier. She cooked everything in olive oil, which worked because she rarely cooked at high temperatures. "We have very limited quantities, usually just 150 litres," said Mirella. "In 2014, we had a drought and only made sixty bottles, but 2015 was great."

She let us taste the tuna mixture. It was as smooth as hummus, but tasted a bit flat.

"Needs more lemon?" asked Sam.

"Bravo," said Mirella, grinning. She splashed in more lemon juice.

"Boy, this would make the most awesome tuna sandwich," Sam whispered to me.

After dabbing the peppers dry with paper towels, he spooned a dollop of tuna atop each slice. Then Mirella donned latex gloves and carefully rolled the peppers around the tuna. Any time she handled something we would eat raw—salad or *carne cruda*—she grabbed a fresh pair of latex gloves, size medium, from a box in her cupboard. The slurs about Italian immigrants I'd overheard growing up in 1950s Montreal included the epithet "dirty," which just goes to show you the ignorance of racism. Italians were hyper-clean. In fact, they surpassed the famously fastidious Japanese. On an earlier cooking trip to Japan, I never saw a home cook don gloves to make sushi. But in Italy, gas stations offer free disposable gloves at the pump so you needn't soil your hands, and Italian supermarkets put out boxes of disposable gloves in the produce section so you never had to touch sticky fruit or wet lettuce. Italy also had a thriving chain that specialized in cleaning supplies: Acqua & Sapone (Water and Soap). A 2006 study by Procter & Gamble, the world's largest detergent company, found that Italian women spent twenty-one hours cleaning each week, compared to American women's four hours.

Mirella drizzled extra-virgin olive oil on top of the *involtini di peperoni* then pushed two hard-boiled eggs through a ricer to create a garnish called *mimosa*, after the fuzzy golden flowers of the mimosa tree. For the final touch, she retrieved a clear plastic bag containing something leafy and green from her freezer. "*Prezzemolo*," she explained. In winter, supermarket parsley had no flavour, so every summer Mirella rinsed bunches of fresh parsley and other herbs and froze them into bouquets. When she needed a garnish, she just shattered a few leaves straight over the pot or dish.

The next task for the Bimby was *torta di nocciole*. Washing the machine was as easy as putting on an electric kettle. Mirella rinsed it out, refilled it with water, brought it to a boil, and dumped out the dirty water. She weighed and melted two hundred grams of butter in the Bimby. Using a hand-held mixer and a separate bowl, she blended two eggs and two hundred grams of sugar, which she added to the Bimby, along with two hundred grams of crushed hazelnuts, two hundred grams of cake flour, a one-hundred-and-fifty-gram UHT box of 38-percent-butterfat Piemontese cream, a pinch of salt, and eight grams of baking powder. The Bimby instantly blended all the ingredients into smooth cake batter. It was like having a household slave but without the human rights implications.

Hazelnut torte was a local specialty because hazelnut trees were as abundant here as olive trees. The quality of the Piemontese hazelnut was so good—crisp with a delicate flavour—that they came with their own certified "IGP," *Indicazione Geografica Protetta*. Ferrero Rocher, head-quartered in nearby Alba, was famous, of course, for Nutella, its popular hazelnut-chocolate spread, and its gilt-wrapped chocolates encasing a whole hazelnut.

Mirella didn't butter and flour the round pan. Instead, she crumpled and dampened a square of parchment paper so that it fit compliantly. After she poured in the batter from the Bimby, she slammed the pan a couple of times on her granite countertop to flatten the batter. Half an hour in a

350°F oven and the *torta* was ready. She let the cake rest for five minutes, grabbed the edges of the parchment paper, and lifted it out of the pan. Like magic, the crumpled parchment released a perfect cake.

Watching her measure and weigh everything down to the gram, it occurred to me why I was such a deficient baker. Baking was chemistry, a subject I struggled with in high school. Baking also required obedience. As a journalist, I was predisposed to question authority. When a recipe decreed half a teaspoon of cream of tartar, I'd wonder: *would a teensy bit more kill you?* In contrast, cooking was improvisational and creative. You could deviate from recipes, drop or add ingredients. You didn't have to count out twenty-four mushrooms and could skip the egg-yolk thickener if you wished. You could take a detour, linger by the wayside to smell the roses. Want kale instead of carrots? Fine. Your pork roast will be different, but differently *good*. Cooking was expressive; baking was formulaic. When you cook, you rely on instincts and experience. When you bake, you measure. You had to sit up straight and pay attention. Thus, I have failed almost every time I attempted to bake a pie or a cake. Once, my cookies *stuck to Teflon*. I couldn't pry them loose even after I soaked the pan in the sink. The only solution was to throw out the tray, cookies and all.

MIRELLA'S BAKING TIP

Instead of greasing and flouring a cake pan, cut a square of parchment paper big enough to come up the sides of your pan. Crumple and dampen it under the tap, then line your pan with it. Pour in the cake batter and slam the pan on the counter so it settles well. Bake. Lift out the cake using the edges of the parchment, flip cake onto plate, and remove the parchment.

Next Mirella drafted the Bimby to make *zabaglione*, the boozy warm custard sauce that would accompany the hazelnut torte. "Eggs, sugar, and sweet wine, *not* Marsala," she said, wagging her finger. "That's what they use in *Sicily*. Here we use Moscato. Piemonte is the only place in the world that produces Moscato." She separated six eggs, letting the whites drip down the drain, and flung the yolks into the Bimby. Then she added six heaping tablespoons of sugar. She used the eggshells to measure an equivalent volume of Moscato from her own winery. The Bimby emulsified the yolk mixture in one minute. Then she set the temperature to 90°C (or 195°F) for eight minutes, and then 100°C (or 212°F) for one more minute, to pasteurize the eggs. The machine would keep the *zabaglione* warm until we were ready for dessert. In case the *zabaglione* wasn't enough, Mirella also whipped some 38 percent cream. I told her we only could buy 35 percent in Canada. Extra-high-fat cream wasn't available in Italian supermarkets either, she said, but she had her own supplier.

It was time to prepare the clams. I would finally unlock the secret of why, in Italy, *spaghetti alle vongole* tastes like the essence of the sea. Because I had also bought baby squid at the market, Mirella decided to add them to the *vongole* sauce. She rinsed the squid under running water and trimmed them, throwing out everything except the tender tentacles. Then she halved two cloves of garlic, removed the bitter green sprout in the centre, and sautéed them in extra-virgin olive oil in a... "What do you call this?" I asked with a shock of recognition. "*Un wok*," Mirella said. Globalization had arrived in the Italian kitchen. I would find Italian home cooks and restaurant chefs alike using Chinese carbon-steel woks, whose wide bottoms and wider openings were ideal for everything from clam sauce to risotto.

Once the halved garlic began sizzling, she lowered the heat before it could colour, and poured in a cup and a half of dry white wine. Then she dumped in the drained clams and tiny squid tentacles. We had been working nearly three hours, and Mirella had spent at least an hour in the kitchen before we arrived. It was time to prepare *il primo: carne cruda*.

Raw beef is said to have originated in the thirteenth century with the marauding Mongols, also known as Tatars (later called Tartars). Marco Polo, who served at the imperial court of Kublai Khan, the grandson of Genghis Khan, observed: "In case of great urgency they will ride ten days on end without lighting a fire or taking a meal. On such occasion, they will sustain themselves on the blood of their horses, opening a vein and letting the blood jet into their mouths." As these early globalizers swept across Asia and Europe, getting as far as present-day Hungary, they supposedly tenderized slabs of horsemeat beneath their saddles. Eventually the Mongols conquered all of China, which they ruled as the Yuan dynasty (1279-1368).

In France, steak tartare was boldly seasoned with mashed anchovies, capers, minced shallots, salt, pepper, Dijon mustard, and Tabasco, all modulated with a raw egg yolk. Steak tartare was often so spicy you couldn't taste the beef, but it stood up well to the *frites* that always accompanied it. In Italy, *carne cruda* was the polar opposite: chopped raw beef lightly dressed with fresh lemon juice, a touch of balsamic vinegar, sea salt, and a generous slug of olive oil. It was so delicate no one dreamed of serving it with fried potatoes.

The beef Beppe had bought from his favourite butcher was Piemontese Fassone. These purebred cattle, as silver-grey as glaciers, weighed half to three-quarters of a ton. Originally draught animals, they became prized for their meat as vineyards gobbled up farmland. Piemontese Fassone had a unique gene mutation called "double muscling," which resulted in less marbling, fewer connective tissues, and a higher lean-to-fat ratio. In winter, the cows were fed hay, cereals, and beans. In summer, the farmers transported the herd to the Alps where, two thousand metres up, they grazed on grass and wildflowers. Their milk made the famous floral-scented *toma Piemontese*, similar to the *tomme* made with goat cheese in the Drôme.

Mirella tore open a supermarket bag of pre-washed, locally grown lamb's lettuce and spread it over a serving platter. Unlike in Canada, where our lettuce often travels a thousand kilometres, each spoon-shaped leaf was in perfect condition with no slimy or yellowed bits. She whisked together the dressing of lemon juice, balsamic vinegar, salt, and olive oil. Donning a fresh pair of latex gloves, she hand-mixed half the dressing into the raw minced beef, which she mounded over the lamb's lettuce. Then she drizzled the remaining dressing on top and garnished the platter with half-moon slices of Sicilian lemon.

It was almost eight, dinnertime across Italy (as in France). Maria Rosa arrived, followed a few minutes later by Fiorenzo, Chiara, and Alessandro who, although he lived on his own, always ate *a casa della mamma*. Beppe, ruddy-faced from spending the day bottling wine in the unheated workshop, wandered into the kitchen looking for half a lemon with which to scrub his purple-stained hands. He returned a few minutes later, his fingers clean, bearing several bottles of his own wine.

At eight sharp we sat down in the formal dining room on high-backed leather chairs. Mirella had set the round table with a damask tablecloth, china, linen napkins, crystal wineglasses, and a single cream-coloured candle. *"Mangia, mangia,"* she said, lighting the candle.

Sam sneezed periodically. I swallowed an antihistamine but couldn't seem to stop coughing and sneezing. The Massassos had two cats. When they heard that both Sam and I were allergic, they threw their pets outside in the downpour. The poor cats kept darting back inside whenever someone opened the door. Each time, Beppe shooed them out, but it was obvious he hated to do that. Italians adored their cats. The government enacted laws to protect feral colonies. Civic groups mobilized to feed them and pay for veterinary care. Finally, I told Beppe not to worry, and the cats stayed in. In addition to a severe cat allergy, I was also coming down with a bad cold, so it was hard to say what was making me sneeze.

We passed around the platter of *cárne cruda*. Sam ate a mouthful and sighed. "It tastes like pure beef, but light, delicate, and refreshing."

In France, no one discussed the breed of cow while chewing steak tartare. In Italy, the *point* of the dish was the breed, and everyone wanted to talk about the superiority of Piemontese Fassone. Mirella's gossamer dressing enhanced its beefiness and married it to the nutty flavour of the lamb's lettuce. Beppe opened a bottle of his own Massasso Spumanti Brut Rosato, a sparkling dry rosé that he exported via his younger son to Australia. He grilled us on that morning's history lesson and looked pleased when we recited back the details of Asti's *palio*. Fiorenzo jumped in. "And what sport did I play thirty years ago?" I searched my aging brain. "*Tamburello!*" I crowed. Everyone applauded.

The truffle season had ended a month earlier. I didn't feel bad that Sam and I missed it. To me, the palate payoff for truffles was unworthy of the price. "Autumn rain," "burrowing earthworms," and "newly plowed soil," are how some food writers describe the flavour. "They might well be held in less esteem if they were available in quantity and cheap," wrote Jean Anthelme Brillat-Savarin, the eighteenth-century French gourmand, in his book *The Philosopher in the Kitchen*. Mirella said she thought black and white truffles tasted the same. Beppe flatly declared that Italy's white truffles were finer than France's black truffles. And the market agreed — white truffles from Piemonte commanded five times the price of the Drôme's black truffles. To meet demand in Asti, Mirella said, truffles were smuggled in from Romania and Yugoslavia and passed off as Italian. The government tried to prevent fraud, allowing only certified villages, such as Monferrato, to sell white truffles. For their fall wine-tasting dinners for tourists from Switzerland, France, and Germany, Mirella and Beppe feared being scammed, so they bought only from suppliers they personally knew. As the harvest of white truffles grew more and more scant and prices soared, the most visible buyers at Alba's famous fall truffle festival were rich Chinese and Russians, who nonchalantly bid thousands of euros a kilo at auction.

Like the Jeanselmes, everyone seemed to know instinctively how much *carne cruda* to take. The kilo easily served eight. The *involtini di peperoni al forno ripieni con tonno* was so rich that, had I not watched Mirella make it, I would have sworn it contained cream or mayonnaise. The olives and capers had seamlessly blended with the tuna to create a lip-smacking umami. Beppe decanted a bottle of 2012 Cinquestelle Barbera d'Asti into a silver-footed crystal carafe. An intense red wine aged in oak casks, it was one of his best wines, drunk only at important meals. Yet the price was stunningly low—eight euros (twelve dollars) a bottle—compared to our obscenely taxed wine in Canada. "It's the best grapes of the harvest," said Beppe. "We don't make it every year, only when the harvest is very good."

While the others relaxed at the table, Sam and I followed Mirella back into the kitchen to make the *spaghetti alle vongole*. A pot of pasta water with a built-in colander was boiling vigorously. She salted the water liberally. Then she *broke the spaghetti in half* so it would fit in the pot. At Mirella's and in other Italian homes I saw no cult of pasta. Boil water. Add salt. Break up the pasta if you felt like it. Done. So many cookbooks tell you to boil six litres of cold water. Nonsense. In Italy, the water can start at any temperature and in any quantity, so long as the pasta isn't so crowded it sticks together.

Al dente pasta requires noodles made with *triticum durum*, the hardest of all wheat varieties. Noodles made with ordinary cheap flour, sometimes called "farina," absorb too much water during cooking and can never end up *al dente*. Benito Mussolini famously made the trains run on time. It's less widely known that, in an effort at food self-sufficiency, he also ordered the planting of durum wheat in central and north Italy. Even today Italy produces only 70 percent of the durum wheat it needs. The rest is imported from Canada and the US.

With a thick sauce, such as tomato or cream, you cook the pasta until it is precisely *al dente*—"to the tooth." With a thin sauce, such as *alle vongole*, you undercook the pasta and finish it in the sauce. Mirella removed the spaghetti one minute before it was ready. When the noodles flopped over but still had backbone, she hoisted the colander from the pot and dumped its dripping contents directly into the bubbling wok.

As a kid in Montreal in the 1950s, I never tasted *al dente* pasta. Aside from Chinese and *haute* French, Italian was the only "foreign" cuisine available. Wearing a white paper hat, shaped like an upside-down rowboat, the "cook" would merely dunk pre-cooked spaghetti into hot water, plate the mushy, water-logged noodles, and ladle on a spoonful of insipid meat sauce. As a kid, I loved it. Then, in the late 1960s, my mother won a free plane ticket to Brussels in a department-store draw, and took me on a frugal tour of Europe. I will never forget my first plate of spaghetti, in Rome. It was tossed with cream, peas, and bits of ham, and it was a revelation: *al dente* pasta. I was a shy teenager, but I wanted to stand up at my table and scream: *Wowza!*

For years, the secret of *al dente* pasta eluded me at home. Some cookbooks suggested adding tablespoons of oil or even lemon juice to the pasta water. Don't. They suggested rinsing the pasta with cold water to halt the cooking. Definitely don't. When I worked as a reporter in Boston in the 1980s, a professional chef, a non-Italian, advised me to drain the cooked pasta, *then return it to the pot and turn up the heat to dry it.* His technique made a mess of the pot, at least for my husband, the designated dishwasher. The same chef told me I could also test a strand by throwing it at the wall to see if it stuck. The pasta still didn't turn out *al dente.* Worse, we had no designated wall washer.

On a subsequent vacation to Asiago, long before Norman and I had kids, I hung out with the mother-in-law of one of his Italian classmates at New York University. Every day I watched *Nonna* make pasta, and finally I understood. She did not dry her noodles in the pot. She did not throw it against the wall. She removed them when they were half a minute from *al dente.* In the few seconds that it took to briefly drain the pasta, the noodles finished cooking. She also taught me another important lesson. The pasta is the main event. The sauce plays a *supporting* role and should lightly coat the strands, not drown them ... unless it's *spaghetti alle vongole*, where the sauce is the star.

Another surprise: Mirella had brought the already cooked clams and squid to a rolling boil, a move Chinese chefs believe toughens the seafood. After thirty minutes, the clams and squid were meltingly tender. And a third surprise: during the final minutes of cooking, Mirella dumped a tiny tub of Knorr-brand seafood gel into the sauce. (Hmm—I always thought anchovies were the Italian MSG.) She brought the wok back to a boil, voluptuously impregnating the pasta with the briny essence of clam. After switching off the heat, she splashed in five glugs of extra-virgin olive oil and transferred the steaming pasta into a large serving casserole. She crumbled a bit of frozen parsley on top and marched in triumph back to the dining room.

Alessandro inhaled a mouthful and sighed. *"Magnifico!"* he said. The sauce tasted like the sea itself. I'd tried so many times at home to make a decent *spaghetti alle vongole*. Now I understood the whole sequence, from ridding the clams of grit to imbuing the noodles with the briny sauce. And it wasn't much work at all.

As we ate, everyone waxed enthusiastic about the Bimby, which apparently made fresh pasta, too. "Pasta, pizza dough. When I make pasta, I use thirty egg yolks for one kilo," said Mirella, kissing her bunched fingertips, Italian sign language for *extremely delicious*. "It's like you ate *nothing*," said Beppe, and he meant that in the nicest possible way.

We picked up the clam shells with our fingers to suck them clean. When I said that at home Sam and I always ate pasta with chopsticks, they laughed uproariously. But why didn't they use a spoon, the way North Americans did? In fact, the 1975 edition of Emily Post's *Etiquette* advised diners to place "the tips [of their fork] ... against the spoon" when eating spaghetti. The Massassos said they *never* twirled their pasta on a fork against a spoon.

Italian Food Rule: *don't use a spoon when you eat pasta.*

Sam didn't want to waste the last spoonfuls of *vongole* sauce. Hoping no one would notice, he used his dessert spoon to scoop up the clam broth from the bottom of his bowl. At our formally set table, Mirella had placed a chunk of bread at each place, right on the tablecloth, and Sam began mopping up the dregs with bread. Suddenly everyone started laughing at him, which is when we learned about another Italian Food Rule. "We *never* eat bread with pasta," said Alessandro. Sam reddened.

Fiorenzo quickly intervened. "Sam, I *always* eat pasta with bread," he said, ostentatiously picking up a chunk of bread and smearing it over his (clean) pasta bowl.

I countered: why did Italians put their bread *directly on the table*? Why no bread plate? The table fell silent at my question. When no one had an answer, Alessandro pulled out his smartphone and Googled it. He found nothing, which further embarrassed everyone. "We break the rules," he said lamely, as everyone laughed.

Real Italians (and French) by the way, never butter their bread, notwithstanding Anne-Sophie Pic's stand-up sculpted Laguiole butter knives. Nor did Italians ever dip their bread into saucers of olive oil and balsamic vinegar, an American abomination that has spread to Canada.

Mirella brought out the cheese course, a chalk-white rind-free *robiola di roccaverano*, made in Asti from raw goat's milk, and a square grassy *robiola bosina* with a bloomy rind, made locally from both goat's and cow's milk. She served them with two Piemonte condiments, an unusual white-pepper honey and a costly conserve of nuts, apples, pears, and figs called *mostarda*. Unlike other regions of Italy, which used mustard to spice the condiment, *mostarda d'Asti* was made from the *mosto* or must, the residue of seeds, skins, and stems of freshly pressed Barbera grapes.

At 9:55 p.m., I was ready to slump under the table. We still weren't finished. After the cheese course, Mirella served the *torta*. Worried that the ultra-high-fat whipped cream and *zabaglione* were inadequate, she also sifted an avalanche of icing sugar over the cake. She sliced the cake and pronounced it *friabile*—it had a good crumb. Beppe opened yet another bottle, his own Moscato, a dessert wine called Dulcis in Fundo. I could barely finish my slice of *torta* (because I'd had two helpings of *spaghetti alle vongole*).

Beppe had paired different wines with each dish — nine bottles for the eight of us.

Except for Maria Rosa, who was tipsy after one glass, no one was drunk. We drank for the taste, not for the buzz, so we hadn't finished the rosé, and we'd finished only one bottle of Barbera. Unfortunately, I was getting sicker. My cough had worsened, and I was losing my voice. So Beppe solicitously brought out *three* more bottles. "Just a drop," he said. "Purely medicinal." One was his own *grappa di Moscato*, an aged, eighty-proof brandy. Another was a sixty-proof grappa made with bitter herbs — *liquore d'Erbe di collina Amaro Repergheis*, also his own product. The third was a port of Barbera grapes, spiced with cinnamon, vanilla, and cloves.

I tried them all. At eleven thirty, Sam and I staggered two minutes down the road to our farmhouse. I wondered when Italians slept. The Massasso family would start work at the winery at seven thirty a.m. Maria Rosa's day would start an hour earlier, when she rose to prepare breakfast for the family. At seven fifteen she would drive to Asti, drop Chiara at school, and head to the early shift at the hospital.

MIRELLA'S SPAGHETTI ALLE VONGOLE
Serves 4 as a main course.

2 lbs.	fresh small clams
½ cup	extra-virgin cold-pressed olive oil, divided
3	cloves garlic (2 flattened with knife blade; 1 finely minced)
1 pkg	Knorr concentrated seafood gel (or substitute 1 bottle clam juice)
1 cup	dry white wine
1 lb.	imported Italian dried spaghetti
1 tbsp.	salt for pasta water
3 tbsp.	parsley, finely minced

Soak clams for several hours in salted water, changing the salt water three times, or until there's more no more sediment, to release grit. Rinse well.

In a wok or pot big enough to hold the final dish, gently heat ¼ cup of olive oil. Sauté the 2 flattened cloves of garlic until lightly golden. Remove garlic. (You can eat it later if you want.)

In the same wok, dissolve 1 small container of Knorr concentrated seafood gel into 1 cup warm water. (If not available, use a small bottle of clam juice.) Add dry white wine. Bring to a rolling boil.

Add clams and bring back to a boil. After 10 minutes, turn off heat. These can wait while you're having your first course.

Boil a large pot of water for pasta. Add salt. Cook dried spaghetti (spaghettini and linguine are fine, too, but don't use fresh pasta). Bring clam sauce back to a rolling boil. When pasta is a minute shy of *al dente*, drain and add directly into wok of boiling clam sauce.

Bring back to a boil and toss. Cook for 20 seconds. Turn off heat. Mirella doesn't do this, but I add 1 clove of finely minced raw garlic. The heat of the sauce will modulate the garlic, but it will still taste garlicky. Splash on remaining ¼ cup of olive oil. Toss well. Sprinkle with minced parsley and serve immediately – right out of the pot.

CHAPTER FIFTEEN

Maria Rosa's Two-Stir Risotto

After driving Chiara to school, Maria Rosa decided to take the day off to spend with us. None the worse for wear the morning after our gargantuan feast, she and Fiorenzo brought us to Repergo's one and only store — the butcher. We could have walked in three minutes, but Maria Rosa wanted to drive, which took thirty seconds.

Unlike Beppe, who swore by the butcher in Asti, Maria Rosa would buy beef only from L'Isola della Carne, literally "Island of the Flesh." She was going to teach us a classic Piemonte dish, *vitello tonnato*. Two-thirds of the veal and nearly half the beef sold in Italy was imported from other countries such as Poland, France, and Germany, so Maria Rosa wanted to be sure she got genuine Piemontese Fassone beef. The silver-grey cows grazed on a grassy slope, right behind the butcher shop. You could, and we did, wander into the barn for a peek. "See? They eat barley, corn, wheat, and fresh grass in winter," she said, with satisfaction. "Every spring and summer, they go to summer camp, on the slopes of the Apennine mountains." Never mind the hundred-mile diet, this was zero-kilometre cuisine. The cows were raised and sold here but slaughtered elsewhere because local zoning laws banned abattoirs in residential areas.

Italy had three famous varieties of cow. Besides Fassone from Piemonte, the other two were Tuscan breeds: Maremmana and Chianina. In Florence, restaurants charged $150 for *bistecca alla fiorentina*, a four-inch-thick, four-pound T-bone steak, grilled very rare over a wood fire and sprinkled with extra-virgin olive oil and salt. Many tourists had no idea that the beef was likely not Tuscan, or even Italian. For his book *Heat,* Bill Buford apprenticed with Dario Cecchini, a Dante-quoting, eighth-generation butcher in Panzano, a hillside town thirty-five kilometres from Florence. After waxing eloquently for many pages about the meat in Antica Macelleria Cecchini, Buford took some time to "come clean," as he put it. "Ever since I had made the discovery, I'd wondered how I'd convey its magnitude," he wrote on page 288 of a 315-page book. "Actually I don't know what to do except offer up the bare fact: the meat sold by Dario Cecchini — the most famous butcher in Italy, possibly the most famous living Tuscan — is Spanish." Buford said the beef was trucked in pre-dawn, before anyone in the village was up. Cecchini always sliced off any telltale stamps that said *Hecho en España*, he added. The butcher also kicked out nosy customers. A year after Buford published *Heat*, Anthony Bourdain did a segment on the famous butcher without ever disclosing that his Tuscan beef wasn't Tuscan. Cecchini, who remains a cult figure and has three restaurants in and around his butcher store, now notes on his menu that some of the meat he serves comes from Spain.

Like Fassone, Tuscan oxen were draught animals that once hauled goods to market and plowed the steeply sloping fields of Tuscany. When they died of old age, their hides were shipped down the road to Florence, where artisans made them into purses, shoes, and belts. But as vineyards became more profitable than agriculture, the Chianina, once some of the biggest cattle in the world, lost their raison d'être. The breed lingered for a few years as farmers tried to raise them for meat. But because they had lost their pasture land and were fed a diet of pellets and grain, connoisseurs said the meat tasted like mush. Sales fell, and farmers stopped raising Chianina. Buford connected the dots. The demise of Tuscan cows was also the death knell for Florence's famed leather trade. China dealt the mortal blow, exporting its own increasingly sophisticated leather goods *to* Italy. What no one predicted was that Chinese migrants themselves would eventually move to Italy to manufacture leather goods *in* Florence. Made in Italy, made by Chinese. Globalization had come full circle.

Antica Macelleria Cecchini passed out free wine, opened every day except Christmas, and offered $275 "butcher-for-a-day" workshops with lunch. In contrast, Repergo's L'Isola della Carne opened just two and a half days a week. On Wednesday morning it was normally closed, but the owner's daughter opened expressly for Maria Rosa. A young woman with cobalt-blue-rimmed glasses, her long brown hair tied back in a high ponytail and a red apron wrapped snugly around her slim waist, she looked like a TV food-show host, not someone who wrestled bloody meat for a living. She sliced a chicken breast into perfect cutlets and then picked out a ruby-red eye of round. She held it up for Maria Rosa's approval. When Maria Rosa nodded, the butcher trimmed it and expertly tied it up with string.

She wouldn't accept any money. "Next time," she said with a wave, jotting the sum down in her logbook.

We drove into Asti to pick up Chiara, who finished classes at one every day. Her school day lasted five hours, without a lunch break because no self-respecting Italian would eat before one. We were early so to kill time, we visited the twice-weekly farmers' market at Piazza Campo del Palio, which drew vendors from all over Piemonte. The piazza, where the traditional horse race took place, was now occupied with pop-up stalls. Arabs hawked pots, pans, and electronics. Chinese sold puffy coats, sturdy underwear, and cheap shoes. But only Italians sold food. Bewitched by chartreuse-green peaks resembling an avant-garde architect's take on a Thai temple, Sam bought a Romanesco cauliflower. Maria Rosa picked up some viciously spiked Sardinian artichokes that she promised could be thinly sliced and eaten raw. I bought jewel-like amethyst-hued onions, sweet enough to munch like apples. With another hour to kill, we went to a bar; in Italy, bars double as cafés. It was before lunch, so I knew I could order a latte without anyone laughing at me. And thanks to my Italian professor, I knew not to actually order a "latte."

Italian Food Rule: *If you order a latte at a coffee bar, you will be served a glass of milk.*

My *caffè macchiato* was an espresso topped with hot foamy milk. It was about three gulps worth, compared to a Starbucks twenty-ounce Venti (which means, yes, twenty in Italian). When Orlando Chiari, a Milan bar owner, attended a Lions Club International meeting in Denver, he and his seven friends would order a single cup of coffee each morning and divide it. "There was coffee enough for eight people," Chiari told Bloomberg news.

In the bar as in the *supermercato*, portion sizes were teensy — even water glasses were small. (Just like in France, everyone we met in Italy would be shocked by Sam's one-litre travel bottle.) In Italy, the one-ounce espresso, *un caffè*, was always downed in a single gulp. *Espresso*, get it? You could order a double espresso, *un caffè doppio*, but no one did. You ordered the second *caffè* when you were ready so you could swallow it hot, but not too hot, and not too cold. When Starbucks announced plans to open in Italy, one of Maria Rosa's friends told me she had scalded her mouth on one of their lidded coffees while vacationing in California. The chain's pending move into Italy was one case where globalization might fail. China's upper middle class embraced Starbucks, but it received a lukewarm reception in France. Like the French, Italians did not guzzle their liquids. In fact, the verb in Italian for coffee was not "drink," but "take," as in, "take a dose of drugs." Italians took their *caffè* standing at a bar. They never *carried* it as they walked down the street or, good heavens, drank it while they drove. Sometimes office workers would fetch take-out coffee, usually for their colleagues, too. The *caffè* was still served in tiny porcelain cups, on a waiter's tray; when everyone finished, someone in the office would return the cups to the bar. Unlike traditional Italian bars, Starbucks did have the advantage of opening every single day. One day when we were meeting a friend for coffee in Asti, Maria Rosa drove around the whole downtown core, twice, without finding a single place open for *caffè*. It was a Monday. Like museums, the coffee bars of Asti took Monday off.

Virtually all Italian teenagers attended specialized high schools. Some concentrated on science, others on the arts, business, engineering, even gastronomy. Chiara attended a *liceo classico* where she studied Latin, Greek, science, and English (*Hamlet* last year; John Donne this year). A top student, she dreamed of medical school, so Sam was stunned to learn her parents actively disapproved.

Fiorenzo and Maria Rosa explained that becoming a physician involved fourteen years of expensive training, with scant hope of a job at the end. Italy's state-funded medical care was practically bankrupt — only half of the ten thousand medical students graduating each year found residencies, the prerequisite for obtaining a medical licence. After that, many couldn't obtain staff positions. "A female doctor, who is thirty-four, was just hired on contract at my hospital — for three months. She can't get a permanent job anywhere. She moves from hospital to hospital. That is not a life," said Maria Rosa. Nurses, too, found only part-time contracts.

Italy's youth unemployment rate was nearing 40 percent. It also had Europe's fourth-highest dropout rate. One in five Italians never completed high school. Only 15 percent of Italians had post-secondary degrees, the lowest percentage among OECD member countries, compared to more than 50 percent of Canadians, the highest percentage. "In Italy, finishing high school is pretty good," said Mirella's son, Alessandro, who was impressed that Sam had graduated from university. In Canada, of course, no one was dazzled by Sam's degree, especially when he mentioned it was in philosophy. *What are you going to do with that? Flip burgers?* Alessandro held down *five* jobs. In addition to working at the family winery and managing visitors like us who rented their farmhouse, he also worked overnight as a front desk clerk at a hotel in Asti and as a bouncer at two nightclubs. Alessandro told Sam that a degree made it harder to find work in Italy because the most plentiful jobs were for baristas and waiters. After high school, he added, he worked as a tour guide in Egypt and later did odd jobs in Melbourne, Australia.

Sam, who until then thought himself industrious because he worked in restaurants during the school year and every summer, was shocked. Alessandro worked much longer and harder, six days a week, sometimes for twenty-two hours straight. He was at the family winery twelve hours a day, six days a week, fermenting grapes and making wine and bottling it. Wednesdays and Thursdays, when he worked overnight as a hotel clerk, he got only two hours' sleep. On Fridays and Saturdays, when he worked as a bouncer, he slept not at all, only crashing for a few hours on Sunday morning. The annual harvest was even more gruelling. For fifteen days every autumn, when the *Moscato bianco* grapes were ripe, Alessandro worked at his family's winery *and* hired out his expertise at making sparkling Moscato d'Asti to other vineyards. Unlike red grapes, which could sit a few days, white grapes had to be processed the same day.

"You need to put the juice into the cold cellar at −2°C to stop fermentation. You have to filter it at night because within a few hours the new grapes are coming in. We're always working all night. And when I finish there, I come home to work on *our* harvest."

To Sam's surprise, Alessandro's parents didn't pay him a salary. "It's family. If I need to buy something, I tell them." Of course, he lived rent-free in the farmhouse apartment, ate all his meals with his parents, and was building equity in the business. As the oldest son, he would likely inherit the winery, as had his father and grandfather. In the meantime, the part-time jobs provided spending money. But working over ninety hours a week meant Alessandro was perpetually exhausted, with no time for a girlfriend or a social life. Until recently he played soccer in a local league but quit because, he said, "I was so tired I kept injuring myself."

At one p.m. sharp, Chiara was waiting for us on the sidewalk outside her *liceo*. She suggested we have lunch at a favourite spot a few blocks away that specialized in freshly made pasta. Unlike the Chinese, who ate noodles in seven ways — stir-fried, deep-fried, steamed, boiled, braised, served in soup, or eaten cold — Italians used only three methods. *Pastasciutta* was tossed in a sauce, *pasta in brodo* was served in broth, and *pasta al forno* was baked. (They rarely ate pasta salad, an American aberration.)

Dietro l'Angolo, which means "around the corner," was indeed tucked inside an alleyway at No. 3 Via Carducci. On my own, I wouldn't have given the place a second glance. It had red-painted picnic tables on the sidewalk, sheltered from the wintry wind by a clear plastic barrier. Down a few steps was a cramped basement deli with counter service, a few barstools, and high tables. But the menu was more alluring than a top Italian restaurant in New York. There were local cheeses in peak condition, salads, *antipasti*, *vitello tonnato*, meatballs, and decent wines by the glass. A hand-scrawled list on a small blackboard offered half a dozen kinds of pasta or gnocchi to mix and match with various sauces. No matter what you chose, the pasta cost five euros ($7.50) including tax and service. There is no tipping in Italy (except in tourist traps).

It's hard to believe that, until a century ago, pasta was so expensive it was eaten only at religious festivals. In 1279, it was so valuable that a basket of dried pasta was listed in the inventory of the estate of a Genovese soldier. Centuries ago, Italians mostly ate *pasta fresca* because drying pasta was so difficult — too fast and it would crack, too slow and it became mouldy. The best dried pasta originated in Naples, with its sea breezes and sultry winds from Mount Vesuvius. Old black-and-white photographs show housewives hanging their pasta outside like laundry. Pasta could, however, take a whole week to dry using this method. Then in 1886 in central Italy, the De Cecco brothers discovered an industrial technique for drying pasta at low temperatures. Today the consumption of dried pasta surpasses fresh pasta. Italians average a pound each of fresh and dried pasta each week, but by weight dried pasta provides several more meals relative to the fresh. On this trip, for the first time I saw sidewalk automat machines, in Bologna, that dispensed packages of dried spaghetti and penne along with cat food, because who could predict a middle-of-the-night pasta emergency (or hungry cat)?

Until the 1950s, every Italian *mamma* made her own fresh pasta, which took at least sixty to ninety minutes of intensive work for something families would scarf down in five minutes. Mirella still made it for special occasions, but most Italians rarely went to the bother, just like few French women baked their own bread. Instead, busy families like Maria Rosa's got their fresh pasta fix in restaurants like Dietro l'Angolo.

I settled on fresh *tagliolini*, quarter-inch-wide noodles, from the verb *tagliare*, to cut. I chose a sauce of pesto, after extracting a promise from Sam that he would share his *tagliolini* with chunks of sautéed fresh porcini mushrooms. Chiara also chose *tagliolini* but with *sugo di arrosto*, a sauce made from roasted meat and its pan drippings. Fiorenzo had his favourite gnocchi with pesto, and Maria Rosa had *agnolotti*, a Piemonte ravioli, sauced with chopped hazelnuts. I preferred dried pasta. So did many Italians, notwithstanding the rapturous endorsements of cookbooks like Marcella Hazan's, whose fresh pasta recipe consumed six pages. In fact, Italians consider *pasta secca* more authentic than *pasta fresca* because the latter can never attain the apogee of *al dente*. Dried pasta, moreover, comes in any shape. It can adapt to the full repertoire of sauces — *vongole*, chunky sausage and eggplant, or *carbonara*. Fresh pasta takes only sheer, simple sauces such as cream, butter and cheese, thin tomato sauce, or a ragù. Incidentally, pasta was not sauced with tomatoes until the eighteenth century. The first mention of tomatoes, a New World fruit, was in the 1790 cookbook *L'Apicio*.

In the we-did-it-first global competition, Piemonte claims to have invented stuffed pastas, which is how the Drôme first obtained *ravioles* and which the Drômoises now considered a French dish. But who invented pasta itself, Italians or Chinese? Archaeological digs in present-day Qinghai province in northwest China prove the Chinese were eating noodles as early as 3000 BCE. They made noodles from many more kinds of flour than Italians, not just with wheat but also rice, mung beans, even sweet potatoes. Unlike the Italians, the Chinese preferred a tender noodle. Anything *ying* (hard) was bad, while anything *nen* (soft) was desirable. Piemonte's claim about ravioli aside, China was also the first to stuff pasta. Won tons, pot-stickers, and *jiaozi* date to the ninth-century Tang dynasty. Did that mean Marco Polo, who left Venice when he was seventeen and didn't return until he was forty-one, brought pasta back from China? Polo served at the court of Kublai Khan from 1266 to 1295. But Arab traders introduced long dried noodles to the Emirate of Sicily between the eighth and twelfth centuries, depending on which historian you believe. At any rate, that basket of "macaronis" in the estate inventory for the Genovese soldier was itemized sixteen years *before* Polo returned from China.

The China that Marco Polo visited in the thirteenth century was the world's richest and most civilized country. According to his memoir, dictated to his cellmate in a Genoa prison (an hour from Repergo): "The roof [of Kublai Khan's palace] is very lofty, and the walls of the palace are all covered with gold and silver. They are adorned with dragons, beasts and birds, knights and idols, and other such things. The Hall of the Palace is so large that six thousand people could easily dine there." Polo described many wonders then unknown in Europe: paper money, a postal service, coal, and, of course, steak tartare or, more properly, *carne cruda*. But he didn't mention pasta, a lapse that might be explained by his immersion in Mongol, not Chinese, culture. The horseback warriors who conquered China ate a diet of milk and meat, not noodles and rice. Polo, who spoke four languages, did not mention the unusual Chinese writing system, either. He did not describe foot binding, which the athletic, horseback-riding Mongolian women rejected. He was also silent about other striking aspects of China, including tea, chopsticks, and the Great Wall. The Mongols didn't drink steeped Chinese tea. Instead, they boiled tea leaves in salted, fermented mare's milk. They eschewed chopsticks, too, eating with their fingers and knives. And as invaders, why show Polo the wall built to keep them out?

At Dietro l'Angolo, we fetched our own brown paper placemats, plastic cutlery, and disposable cups, and sat in our winter coats at one of the outdoor picnic tables. Our orders emerged, one by one, piping hot, in paper bowls. Italian etiquette requires pasta to be eaten immediately, so whoever got a bowl first started eating. The pasta was silken and tender. I was surprised because, until that moment, I had always found fresh pasta leaden and gummy. But Beppe was right. Fresh pasta properly made *tasted like nothing*. It was as soft, insubstantial, and light as air. If I lived in Asti, I would eat lunch at Dietro l'Angolo twice a week. I wanted to order a second bowl for dessert, but resisted only because it offered pears poached in Barbera wine. Fiorenzo ordered dark-chocolate *budino,* a pudding as dense and addictive as ganache. Sam and I split a poached pear and a *panna cotta,* both of which were served in plastic containers. The pear, left intact with peel and core, was drenched in syrupy red wine spiced with cloves and cinnamon. The *panna cotta,* which means "cooked cream," came flecked with real vanilla bean. It was perfect, but my version is better.

JAN'S EASY PANNA COTTA

This dessert is almost as simple to make as Jell-O. I use less cream, which can taste greasy, and more skim milk. The gelatin firmly sets 2 cups of liquid. Use 3 cups of liquid to produce a less bouncy custard.

Serves 6.

2 cups plus 2 tbsp.	skim milk
1 cup	heavy cream
⅓ cup	white sugar
1 tsp.	vanilla
1	envelope unflavoured granulated gelatin (¼ oz.)

Sprinkle powdered gelatin to soften in 2 tbsp. of skim milk. Heat cream, rest of milk, and sugar in a pot, whisking until sugar dissolves and steam rises. Remove from heat. Add dissolved gelatin and vanilla to hot milk. Stir well. Pour into wineglasses or individual ramekins. When cooled to room temperature, cover with plastic wrap and refrigerate at least 3 hours before serving. Garnish with raspberries or, better yet, a slice or two of Poached Pears in Red Wine (see recipe, page 199).

At six we waddled over to Maria Rosa's house to start dinner. Chiara wanted to teach us an ingeniously simple yogourt cake, a specialty of her Great-Aunt Luigina who, at seventy-eight, was Nonno's baby sister. Chiara dumped the contents of a single-portion plain yogourt into a mixing bowl. Using the empty container as a unit measure ("only until the line of the yogourt"), she added stone-ground whole-wheat flour, sugar, and canola oil. She tossed in baking powder, vanilla, and half a cup of milk. "You can add more milk if you want. It makes it tender," she said, first in Italian, and then in English. She separated three eggs and beat in the yolks. In a separate bowl, she hand-whipped the egg whites — "We don't have a machine" — until soft peaks formed.

CHIARA'S GREAT-AUNT LUIGINA'S YOGOURT CAKE

1 individual-size container unsweetened plain yogourt
Using the empty container, measure to the fill line:

3 x	stone-ground whole-wheat flour
1½ x	granulated sugar
1 x	neutral-tasting oil such as canola or sunflower
3 tsp.	baking powder
1 tsp.	vanilla
½ cup	milk (more if you want a more tender cake)
3	eggs, separated

Preheat oven to 360°F.

Butter a 9-inch-diameter non-stick pan. Separate eggs. Mix all ingredients except egg whites in a bowl. In separate bowl, whip whites until soft peaks form. Fold into batter. Bake 30 minutes or until a toothpick inserted in the centre comes out clean. Let cool for 10 minutes, remove from pan.

Unlike her cousin Mirella, Maria Rosa had no fancy appliances like a Bimby. Her kitchen was also plainer — Formica counters instead of marble, and a utilitarian terrazzo floor. She owned a microwave, won in a supermarket contest but never used and still in its original box. Despite the vastness of the house, the galley kitchen was cramped. Most of its limited counter space was cluttered with jars of organic honey and bee pollen, bottles of extra-virgin olive oil and balsamic vinegars, an antique coffee grinder, even the original iron scale from the era when the family sold tobacco out the kitchen window. We made the cake at the only available work surface, the dining table.

Maria Rosa was making a heroic attempt to teach Sam and me as many Piemontese specialties in as short a time as possible. At this dinner, we were making *frittatine* (blini-sized miniature herb-and-cheese omelettes); *risotto al porro* (with fresh leeks), because Repergo was an hour from Vercelli, the centre of Italy's rice cultivation; *scaloppine di pollo carpione* (chicken cutlets with herbs and white wine); and sautéed zucchini. For the *frittatine*, Maria Rosa briefly sautéed half a kilo of fresh spinach until it was barely wilted then squeezed out the excess liquid. She pureed it in a blender with a handful of supermarket basil and mixed in four ounces of fresh goat ricotta and half a cup of Parmigiano-Reggiano, the best Parmesan cheese, which Fiorenzo had just hand-grated. We beat in six eggs. "Don't overblend it," Maria Rosa warned. She scrutinized the batter. "It needs another egg." She cooked the *frittatine* in extra-virgin olive oil in a large non-stick pan, flipping them, like Bernadette, with a dinner fork. It took twenty minutes to use up all the batter. By the time Maria Rosa was finished, the first *frittatine* were cold.

At 7:45 p.m., Fiorenzo's father arrived. Papa Franco was eighty-six, seven years older than Nonno, but looked and acted much younger. While Nonno hardly ever left the house, Papa Franco had driven himself in from Montegrosso. The two widowers ignored us and began chatting animatedly in Piemonte dialect.

Chiara started the risotto, which she promised would take only fifteen minutes. She wilted sliced leeks and celery in a pot slicked with olive oil, added half a cup of milk and brought it to a simmer. As the milk-leek mixture dried out, Maria Rosa stepped in. She added a second glug of extra-virgin olive oil, followed by some carnaroli rice which she hadn't washed because that would prematurely release its precious starches. We would be seven at the table tonight so she grabbed nine handfuls of carnaroli, which has a higher starch content and is costlier than arborio but is prized because it absorbs even more liquid while maintaining the *al dente* heart of each grain.

Maria Rosa stirred the rice until the grains were coated with oil, which would prevent the too-rapid absorption of liquid. The rice still looked a bit dry, so she added a knob of butter. In a separate pot, she heated two cups of water and — another shock like at Mirella's — threw in Knorr flavour concentrate gel. "I only use vegetable, never beef or chicken, because who knows what they put in it," she said, adding that she would get a bone from the butcher if she were making a meat-based risotto.

Cookbooks tiresomely insisted you stand over the pot, constantly stirring risotto, one reason I rarely made it. Restaurants back home made a fuss about risotto: they charged a fortune, forced you to order it for a minimum of two persons, and warned it would take forty-five minutes. In Italy, just as there was no cult of pasta, there was no cult of risotto. It was just *rice*. I watched Maria Rosa toss in half a cup of hot broth, give the rice a couple of stirs, cover the pot, and turn down the heat. *That was it.* Every now and then, she checked on the rice. When it dried out, she added more broth. She tasted the rice. "Another ten minutes," she said, turning the heat down even more.

CHIARA AND MARIA ROSA'S TWO-STIR RISOTTO AL PORRO
Serves 4 to 6.

3	large leeks
1	small stalk of celery
¼ cup	extra-virgin olive oil
3 tbsp.	milk
2 cups	carnaroli rice
3 tbsp.	butter
1	Knorr flavour concentrate gel (vegetable)
6 oz.	Castelmagno or Taleggio cheese, cut in chunks the size of gambling dice
grated Parmesan for garnish	

Finely chop leeks into rings, discarding tough dark-green sections; wash thoroughly. Wash and finely chop celery. On medium-low heat, sauté leeks and celery in a wok using half the olive oil. Do not brown. Once vegetables are translucent, add milk. When pot is almost dry, add remaining olive oil and stir in rice, coating each grain. Add butter. In a separate pot, heat 6 cups of water and dissolve Knorr gel. Expect a ratio of 1 cup of rice to 3 cups of broth. Keep broth on a bare simmer. Add ½ cup of broth to rice. Keep on medium-low heat. Whenever rice dries out, add another ½ cup of broth.

Stir once or twice. After 12–15 minutes, when the rice is cooked but still *al dente*, stir in cubed cheese. Plate and serve immediately. Pass a bowl of grated Parmesan.

If Maria Rosa made risotto with only a couple of stirs, what did professional cooks do? After we left Repergo, Sam and I lunched at a tiny trattoria in Florence near the Mercato Centrale, the city's famous market. La Capannina Bistrot was a narrow eatery at 49 Via Sant'Antonino which, fortuitously, had an open galley kitchen. It was possible to stand right in front of the stove and watch Antonio, the cook — provided you tucked in your hips so his wife, the waitress, could squeeze by. A harried middle-aged man, Antonio worked like a demon, grilling chicken, steak, and pork chops, pressing panini sandwiches, boiling spaghetti and *agnolotti*, even frying eggs and sausages, while his wife spun around the dining room, serving food and taking payment. To make an order of risotto with zucchini and *scamorza* cheese, Antonio put a wok — yes, a wok — on a burner over *very high heat*. So much for Maria Rosa's warning that the heat should be low.

La Capannina Bistrot made Slow Food, fast. Antonio splashed in olive oil and a big handful of raw rice. *He didn't stir it.* Instead, he shook the pan so that oil coated each grain. Hmm, shaken, not stirred. Then he poured in a cup of hot broth. With another decisive jerk of his wrist, he flipped the contents again. Meanwhile, he also made four pasta orders and a steak. Every now and then he glanced at the wok. Each time the broth dried out, he threw in more liquid, but *he still didn't stir the pot.* I hovered, convinced the rice was going to scorch. I urged Sam to stand beside me and watch — another Italian cooking lesson! — but he stayed at the table, pretending he didn't know me. How annoying to be with a mom who had trouble realizing that *not every single experience was a teachable moment.* It might just be lunch.

After ten minutes, Antonio threw in a dozen coins of pre-sautéed zucchini. Each time the wok went dry, he somehow noticed and tossed in a splash of broth. The tension was intolerable (for me; Antonio was fine). In the final two minutes, he added minced parsley and garlic, a bit of tomato paste, and salt. Even as the moisture evaporated for the final time, he *kept the heat on high.* He tore up three or four paper-thin slices of *scamorza*, a cow's milk cheese made by pulling curds so the cheese stretches when melted (mozzarella is made the same way). He dropped the rags of cheese into the risotto and, *finally*, stirred it for the first time. Then he shut off the burner. It was perfectly creamy, with grains of rice still firm in the centre.

What a lesson! One-stir risotto. Too bad Sam wasn't paying attention.

CHAPTER SIXTEEN

Cutting Against the Thumb

To make the chicken cutlets, Maria Rosa sautéed half a thinly sliced onion in her best olive oil, a fruity, cold-pressed, hand-harvested IGP batch from Taggiasca, Liguria, where the Italian Alps tumble into the sea. Unlike Cousin Mirella, Maria Rosa cut everything by hand, and I mean, *by hand.* Neither she nor Chiara used a chopping board. With a paring knife, they sliced potatoes, carrots, and fennel directly into a pot or bowl. "Cutting against the thumb," it was called.

Sam, who prided himself on his knife skills, watched in disbelief. "Cutting against the thumb" was clumsy and slow, not to mention dangerous. He thought he could convert Maria Rosa and Chiara to a board if he showed them how efficiently he could chop. With missionary-like zeal, he whizzed through a pound of zucchini. They smiled and praised him — and continued to cut in their way.

Maria Rosa sautéed the zucchini Sam had showily chopped up, then let it stew gently in its own juices. After a tactful interval, I asked why no one in Italy used a chopping board except for meat. Chiara and Maria Rosa both shrugged. "Habit," said Maria Rosa. It reminded me of the opening song in *Fiddler on the Roof*: "Tradition!" Examining sepia-tinted photos of nineteenth-century Italian kitchens, I realized that the technique evolved from necessity. The kitchens lacked counters (and almost everything else) so when the *mamma* was preparing vegetables, she sat on a low stool. Cutting against the thumb meant the pieces fell directly into the pot on the floor in front of her. Even bread was sliced by cradling the loaf in one arm and pulling the knife inward, toward one's chest.

Sam noticed other kitchen quirks. Maria Rosa kept sharp knives pointed up, in the same container as spoons and forks. No one got bloodied, and when we asked, she again shrugged. Maria Rosa and others also discarded the box that plastic wrap came in. The roll took less space in the drawer, and they easily ripped off pieces by starting the cut with a paring knife or poking it through with a finger.

Just before the onions browned, Maria Rosa added minced garlic, Beppe's sparkling white wine, and white wine vinegar. She tasted the sauce and added an extra splash of white wine and salt. Chiara stepped out to the huge walled garden to pick a branch of rosemary and some sage, which she snipped directly into the pan. Like Marie-Catherine and Bernadette, Maria Rosa grew all her own herbs and vegetables: oregano, marjoram, thyme, rosemary, basil, mint, lettuces, tomatoes, peas, beans, fennel, celery, cardoons, artichokes, broccoli, radicchio, spinach, zucchini, and onions. Peppers were about the only vegetable she didn't plant — they required pesticides, and she didn't want that in her garden. I now understood why Italians in Canada always had a vegetable patch, no matter how small their property. Maria Rosa's garden ran along the back of their home and up a small slope. She had a dozen trees — a laurel for fresh bay leaves, and peach, plum, and pear. She also cultivated her own lavender bushes, which made me feel stupid for bringing her a bottle of lavender cologne from Provence.

Maria Rosa washed the chicken cutlets under running water. Italians were indeed hygiene freaks — the only food item she wouldn't wash was the carnaroli rice (which was funny, because the Chinese *always* washed their rice). After patting the cutlets dry, she dredged them in flour, dipped them in beaten egg, and pressed them into a plate of breadcrumbs. Using her finest olive oil, she sautéed the cutlets in a separate pan until they were golden. She was using an expensive non-stick pan, but to Sam's horror, she flipped the cutlets using a fork. I didn't ask. I guessed the reason was ... tradition. *Mamma* had never used a silicone spatula.

MARIA ROSA'S SCALOPPINE DI POLLO CARPIONE
Serves 4 to 6.

FOR THE SAUCE:

½ cup	olive oil, divided
½	onion, sliced thin
1	clove garlic, minced

10 oz.	dry white wine
5 oz.	white wine vinegar
½ tsp.	salt (or to taste)
20	sage leaves, snipped
1	sprig rosemary, left whole

FOR THE CHICKEN:

2 lbs.	chicken breast, cut into cutlets
½ cup	flour
2	eggs, beaten
½ cup	breadcrumbs

To make the sauce, sauté onion in 2 tbsp. of olive oil in a saucepan over medium heat until translucent. Add garlic, wine, vinegar, salt, sage, and rosemary. Simmer and reduce by half. Turn off heat.

Dredge the chicken cutlets into flour, then dip in egg and press into plate of breadcrumbs. Fry in remaining olive oil in a non-stick pan. Stack cutlets in a small 2-inch-deep serving dish. As you get through frying half the batch, pour half the sauce over it, and then pour the remaining sauce over the rest so that the cutlets are more or less equally drenched. Serve warm or at room temperature.

At eight p.m. we sat down at the table. Maria Rosa and her family were Catholic but, unlike the Jeanselmes, no one said grace. The only condiment was a giant pickle jar filled with ordinary salt. As *antipasti*, we ate Nonno's favourite *grissini* (breadsticks), a loaf of crusty bread, a chunk of Parmigiano-Reggiano, and a platter of IGP prosciutto from Parma, which was two hours away by car. "Don't buy prosciutto in a supermarket," Fiorenzo cautioned. "It's too dry." The Parma ham was melt-in-the-mouth tender—sweet, salty, and porky all at once. The Parmesan cheese, also from Parma, was nutty and rich.

Italy's tap water had been safe to drink for years, yet Italians consumed more bottled water per capita than anywhere else in the world. Maria Rosa's family continued to drink only mineral water, hundreds of bottles a year.

"It's expensive," she said, with a sigh.

"And there's the problem of drinking from plastic all the time," said

Fiorenzo, who was concerned about carcinogens after a bout with brain cancer. At least they recycled. Fiorenzo loved to sneak up behind Maria Rosa or me to crush an empty plastic bottle, an explosive crack that always made us shriek. When I said that Sam and I had been drinking tap water, Papa Franco was shocked. He never touched the stuff. At dinner, the family put out still and sparkling mineral water, both at room temperature. Italian Food Rule: *never chill your drinking water (and don't even dream of putting ice in it).*

Chiara politely served both grandfathers first, who beamed at her display of filial piety. Sam and I had brought a bottle of Barolo from a gourmet shop in Montegrosso. Papa Franco said that at 14 percent alcohol, it would overpower the food. "We will drink it after," he ruled.

Maria Rosa served the *frittatine.* The miniature omelettes would have been perfect at brunch, but I found them too filling (and too much trouble to make) at a multi-course meal. Also, they were cold. No one else seemed to mind because food was often eaten at room temperature, another aspect of the Slow Food culture. While we were still eating the *frittatine*, Maria Rosa finished the risotto. During the final minutes on very low heat, the rice became perfectly *al dente.* The correct cheese for this risotto should be Castelmagno, a semi-hard cheese from Fassone cows, Maria Rosa said, but she was substituting Taleggio, a semi-soft raw-milk cheese from Lombardy because, well, that was what she had on hand. She had already removed the washed rind and cut it into chunks the size of matchbooks. Now she stirred the cheese into the hot rice where it melted into invisibility. She tasted it, corrected for salt, and served it straight from the pot. We passed a bowl of grated Parmesan. For the next ten minutes, the only sound was scraping forks. The creamy risotto was laced with pale green strands of tender leeks. Each grain was satisfyingly firm. All the men had seconds (and so did I).

Papa Franco broke the silence. Like many who lived alone, he became loquacious with an audience. He had owned a successful construction company and had become one of the richest men in Montegrosso. A serious collector of African and European art, he had never attended college but was an autodidact who loved world history. Impressed that Sam had studied philosophy at university, Papa Franco looked up from his second plate of risotto and asked, "Whom do you prefer, Plato or Aristotle?" Sam looked as though he were back at school, facing a multiple-choice exam question. "Aristotle?" he said, hesitantly. Papa Franco said he preferred Plato. And then they were off, somehow managing to conduct a conversation in Italian about Greek philosophers.

Papa Franco also wanted to talk about China. He'd recently watched a documentary on the Long March, the epic 1934 military retreat that nearly wiped out the Communist forces. Somehow, I managed that in Italian, too.

I thought we should have eaten the *scaloppine di pollo carpione* when they were hot and crispy, as soon as Maria Rosa forked them out of the frying pan. But what did I know? Like espresso and *frittatine*, the *scaloppine di pollo* was Slow Food for a warm climate, meant to be savoured, not burn your tongue. We could enjoy each mouthful, and talk. *Carpione* meant "marinated" or "soused." At room temperature, the golden crust around the chicken had softened and absorbed the wine and herbs. "This was the lunch that grape-pickers would take to the fields in the summer," Maria Rosa said. "The wine and vinegar would preserve the meat. In summer, the main herb would be fresh basil, not rosemary and sage."

I couldn't eat another mouthful, but I did when Chiara served the yogourt cake, a golden circle of sponge, with whipped cream and strawberries. Franco decreed it was finally time to drink the Barolo. Fiorenzo poured us each an ounce, leaving more than half the bottle for another day, another meal.

We were going to stagger up the hill to our apartment, but Fiorenzo insisted on driving us on the one-minute journey. Before we left, Papa Franco pulled out a shopping bag. He had brought two small sculptures from his collection. One was a buff-coloured stone lion with a chipped muzzle from Central Asia. He said it was several centuries old. The other was an eight-inch stoneware figure of an African pygmy with tattooed forehead, bulging cheeks, and rings around her neck, waist, and ankles. It was from Gabon, circa sixteenth to eighteenth century. "Which one do you want?" he said.

Sam and I were stunned. We said we could not accept. Papa Franco insisted, twice. Everyone else nodded. I looked at Sam. We chose the African statue. Papa Franco invited us to visit his house in Montegrosso the next day and see the rest of his collection.

I awoke with a bad cough. *Tosse,* according to my pocket dictionary. I suggested to Maria Rosa that it was a bad idea for me to visit Papa Franco. She and Fiorenzo shrugged. On the way to his house, they first stopped at a drug store on the highway. The shelves were mostly empty and it kept most of its inventory behind the counter. With the help of my dictionary and Chiara, who had the day off from school, I described my symptoms to the pharmacist: no phlegm, no sneezing, uncontrollable dry cough. He prescribed an Italian herbal powder that I had to swallow, dry, several times a day.

When Papa Franco, in a thick sweater and a black baseball cap, made to kiss me on both cheeks, I stuck out an elbow. "*Tosse,*" I explained, pointing at my throat. He looked puzzled but gamely bumped elbows. He lived alone in a large stucco house, which he'd built on a hillside in 1978 in the style of a medieval palazzo. It had fifteen rooms and an expansive terrace where he could look down and see Montegrosso's modern cathedral, which his company had also built. Maria Rosa, Fiorenzo, Chiara, Sam, and I trailed Papa Franco around the house, our footsteps echoing. The house was so big I could understand someone getting lost. Still, I was puzzled when Chiara asked where the powder room was.

Papa Franco pointed out the immense oak beams in the ceiling—"five hundred years old"—the grey stone quarried in nearby Langhe, and the red bricks from a demolished castle. Repurposing princely detritus wasn't as difficult as it sounded. Piemonte, home to the Savoy royal family, was littered with abandoned castles. His home resembled a museum in any small European city. Hundreds of works of art and artifacts, each properly lighted and meticulously labelled, were displayed on every surface and wall except in the kitchen. His collection included paintings, parchment maps, bronzes, carved sixteenth-century doors with their original iron hinges, ancient scales for weighing gold, Coptic Christian crucifixes of malachite and ivory, seventeenth-century Delft tiles, iron spears, and African masks that had inspired Cubism. He first became interested in African art because his father had worked in Italy's colonies there, mainly Libya. Papa Franco subsequently bought more items in Africa and at auctions in Europe, including at least one piece that cost half a million euros. He acquired works from Gabon, Côte d'Ivoire, Cameroon, Ethiopia, and Somalia. He also owned random European pieces: an eighteenth-century Italian sewing machine, a mirrored door from a sixteenth-century palace inhabited by the Savoy royal family, and a century-old radio that Franco's family had used to tune in to Mussolini's broadcasts. It still worked.

The entrance to the dungeon-like vaulted basement was secured with an eighteenth-century prison gate. Here, he kept his valuable wine collection, organized by region, his most prized Barolos displayed on a dusty side table. The cellar was packed with artifacts: a stone manger for cattle, from a Savoy palace; an old plow; sets of ancient iron keys; trophies from Papa Franco's *bocce* league; a nineteenth-century baby carriage; and a painting by Mussolini's son next to old Michigan licence plates. At eighty-six, he was trying to downsize. He had already sold one hundred and fifty pieces. When he was younger and his wife was still alive, he held dinner parties for thirteen friends at a massive table carved from a single oak tree. A built-in stone wall oven was a thousand years old. The giant stone fireplace was big enough to roast a sheep.

It was lunchtime, but Papa Franco didn't seem to have plans. It seemed natural that we would share a meal with him, but Maria Rosa said we would return to her house for spaghetti. She didn't invite him. Back in Repergo, as we cooked our lunch, she revealed the true state of their relationship with Papa Franco. What she told us shattered the stereotype of the tightknit happy Italian family. At Papa Franco's, Sam had shot me a meaningful look when Chiara didn't know the location of the guest bathroom. Now we learned that she hadn't been to the house since she was a child. While Papa Franco often came to Repergo for dinner, his invitation to Sam and me that morning was the first time in years that the family had visited his house.

Maria Rosa said we had left because Fiorenzo's sister was about to show up. They weren't on speaking terms, and of course it had to do with money. The sister, who was married, went to Papa Franco's house every day to eat lunch and dinner with him, which seemed astonishingly solicitous to me. But according to Maria Rosa, who had moved her whole family into Nonno's home nine years earlier to care for him, that was shockingly inadequate. She said she would worry less if only she could take care of Papa Franco herself. She added that the sister, who had never had a job and spent her days shopping in the fancy stores in Turin, was trying to get the old man to move out — and sell his house and art collection.

Like France, Italy had a law that barred parents from disinheriting their children. But if the sister liquidated the major assets—the house and the art—*and* took possession of the money *before* Papa Franco died, it would not be considered part of the inheritance, and she wouldn't have to share any of it with her brother. Maria Rosa blamed Papa Franco for not putting his foot down. Her expressive blue eyes brimmed with tears. Of course, this was estrangement, Italian style. She and Fiorenzo still invited Papa Franco over for lunch or dinner, and he always came. He just never invited them over to *his* house. And he apparently looked down on Fiorenzo as a failure, for having an ordinary job at the highway authority, instead of following in his footsteps as a builder and becoming rich. The most painful period of all was when Fiorenzo was diagnosed with brain cancer seven years earlier and underwent an operation. His sister never called, not once. Sam and I felt terrible as Maria Rosa cried and Chiara and Fiorenzo stood by, looking sad.

I assured them that every family had problems. To cheer them up, I pulled out my cellphone and showed them photos of an attack on our home in Toronto, two months earlier, on Christmas Eve. Red paint dripped like fresh blood over our front entrance, as though the Mafia had executed a hit on my doorstep. (I avoided using the word *Mafia* out of deference to Maria Rosa, who earlier had told me one of the neighbours *was* Mafioso.) The vandalism looked so shocking and violent that passing cars slowed down. Some people even snapped photos. "We think it's my brother," I said. And yes, it was over stuff. He usurped a commercial building that my sister and I owned in Montreal, and the mess had ended in a protracted lawsuit that he ultimately lost. After he lost, again, on appeal, someone had hurled a brick through my dining-room window late at night the Halloween before the red-paint attack. After the Chrismas Eve incident Toronto police advised us to install security cameras. My sibling horror story worked. Maria Rosa stopped crying. We went back to making lunch.

Our antipasto was *carciofi spinosi di Sardegna*, those prickly Sardinian artichokes she had told us we could eat raw. These artichokes were so distinctive they merited their own DOP, designation of origin protection, which was even more coveted than IGP. They had elongated, conical heads, and were olive green with violet undertones. Memorably, each curved outer leaf was tipped with a talon-like yellow thorn. After gingerly washing and trimming them, we sliced them paper-thin—quite a feat without a chopping board. And because Italians were hygiene freaks, we washed the slices once again before tossing them with extra-virgin olive oil, balsamic vinegar, salt, and wafer-thin slices of Parmesan cheese.

Maria Rosa had bought *burrata*, an umami bomb of fresh mozzarella and cream encased in a tender pouch of mozzarella. We ate it drizzled with extra-virgin olive oil and sprinkled with sea salt. We warmed some crusty bread and leftover chicken cutlets in the oven. Chiara put on a pot of water for pasta. Italians ate the same brands we ate in Canada—Molinari, Barilla, and De Cecco (the company that figured out an industrial way to dry pasta). Just as there was no cult of pasta, there was no cult of sauce. Maria Rosa opened a small jar of Parma-made Mutti brand tomato sauce with basil. A few tablespoons of sauce per serving was just right. Without heating it, she dumped it straight from the jar onto the hot pasta. The result was toothsome spaghetti at the perfect temperature.

For dessert, we passed a bowl of Piemonte kiwi and Sicilian oranges. Just as the Drômoises believed *les ravioles* were French, the Piemontese considered kiwi an Italian, not New Zealand fruit, because they have been cultivated in Emilia-Romagna, Lazio, and Piemonte since 1970.

After our four-course lunch, which Maria Rosa considered the bare minimum for a meal, she dosed me with her traditional cough remedy: a tablespoon of organic honey stuck into a jar of bee pollen. It tasted floral. "It's from Mondovi, where the best honey comes from. It's a natural antibiotic. Eat a spoonful every morning," she said, pressing gifts of honey and bee pollen on me. We cleaned up the kitchen. Then we set straight to work on dinner.

In Italy, as in France, no one thought it strange that we would shop, cook, eat, cook, and eat again without a break. In fact, by the time we finished lunch, we were a little behind schedule for dinner. Although it was winter, Maria Rosa wanted to teach us a Piemonte summer classic, *vitello tonnato*, cold sliced veal topped with a creamy tuna sauce. This dish required several hours, but you could prepare it the day before, so it was the perfect dish for low-stress entertaining—except you needed a meat slicer.

Unfortunately, we were making it with very little time. First, we had to braise it. Then we had to chill it thoroughly so it wouldn't crumble when sliced. And finally, we had to bring it to room temperature to serve. We began by searing the Piemontese Fassone veal bought the day before from L'Isola della Carne. The cut—eye of round—was deep red, indistinguishable in appearance from beef. Unlike the white veal prized in Canada, Italian calves were not fed a milk-formula supplement. They ate grain and grass and were slaughtered later, when they reached 300 kilos, compared to 200 kilos in Canada.

Chiara harvested a stalk of celery, a sprig of rosemary, and a few bay leaves from the garden. Cutting against the thumb, straight into the pot, Maria Rosa diced a carrot, an onion, and the celery. She added Chiara's fresh herbs, two cloves of garlic, and some dried oregano. The goal was to cook the beef stovetop so it stayed rosy but would be fall-apart tender. Before World War II, most Italian kitchens lacked proper ovens. Housewives sent their kids with a pan of lasagne to be baked at the local *panetteria*. As a result, Italians learned to pan roast meat on the stove, the way Bernadette roasted her chickens and pigeons in France. The chopped vegetables created a flavour base and a little liquid as the veal browned. Maria Rosa also added three-quarters of a cup of dry white wine, brought it to a boil, then lowered the heat and covered the pot. The veal would "roast" slowly in almost no liquid for an hour. When it was done, Sam noted happily that instead of washing the pot, Maria Rosa scraped the intense *fond* to make a ragù for the pasta course, using a bottle of tomato *passata*.

Unlike Mirella, Maria Rosa didn't have a professional slicing machine. L'Isola della Carne offered that service, but we needed to bring the serving platter or the paper-thin slices would disintegrate when we transferred them from a package. Unfortunately, the platter was in the dishwasher, on an excruciatingly slow European cycle. (Washing machines in France and Italy typically took two hours to process a small load of laundry, and don't get me started on dryers.)

Veal with fish sauce sounded bizarre, but the bland meat was a delivery system for the assertive sauce. Surprisingly, it was not a lot of work. Into a blender, Maria Rosa tossed two teaspoons of commercial mayonnaise; four tablespoons of salt-packed capers, rinsed; two egg yolks; three tablespoons of plain yogourt; and a small jar of good-quality tuna packed in oil, drained. She whirred it through the blender for one minute until the yolks emulsified.

For our antipasto, Maria Rosa made *bagna càuda*. A Piemonte winter classic, it meant "hot bath," and was a warm dip of anchovies, garlic, and olive oil. This time the delivery system was cut-up vegetables, raw or cooked. Every family had its own *bagna càuda* recipe. Maria Rosa's called for simmering ten cloves of garlic in milk. As the garlic softened and dissolved, she added dollops of thick cream and ten anchovy fillets, drained. "Some people include the anchovy oil, but it's too strong," she said, tasting the sauce. She opened another jar of anchovies, and added five more fillets—fifteen anchovies in a bit of garlic cream apparently *wasn't* too strong. With a final splash of extra-virgin olive oil, the *bagna càuda* was ready.

We would serve it with roasted yellow peppers, steamed Jerusalem artichokes, and cooked beets, the latter bought pre-baked from the market, just like in France. Jerusalem artichokes were tubers that looked a bit like ginger root but tasted like an insipid potato, and were unrelated to either Jerusalem or artichokes. The English name was probably a bastardization of *girasole*, Italian for "sunflower," because of the plant's yellow flowers. In Italian, they were called *topinambur*. They were expensive, but a co-worker of Fiorenzo's had given him a sackful from his garden. Maria Rosa donned disposable plastic gloves to scrub them. Then Chiara, Sam, and I began tediously peeling the precious knobby tubers.

For dessert, Chiara was teaching us *salame dolce*, a specialty of Fiorenzo's evil sister. He brewed a six-cup pot of espresso while Chiara separated three eggs (shocking Sam by discarding the whites). She creamed the bright orange yolks, called *il rosso* ("the red"), with three-quarters of a cup of sugar. Then she added a chunk of butter, unsweetened cocoa powder, and the now-lukewarm espresso. Meanwhile, Sam smashed a package of butter cookies, which were a lot easier than pulverizing the hot-pink pralines at Bernadette's. Chiara mixed the broken cookies into the batter. Using plastic wrap, she tried to shape the batter into a salami, but the mixture was too soggy. As Nonno dozed in his chair, Sam hammered another package of butter cookies, and another, until the roll firmed up. "*Cemento*," said Fiorenzo, approvingly. We put it in the freezer for an hour.

One of our six courses would be *zuppa di cavolo*, cabbage soup. Maria Rosa discarded the tough ribs from the leaves of a dewy fresh Savoy cabbage. Naturally, she triple-washed the leaves. Then she slivered the cabbage leaves with a small paring knife, cutting against the thumb onto a plate. Sam sliced an onion, which Maria Rosa *rinsed under the tap*. Chiara ran out to the garden for another stalk of celery. Maria Rosa washed the celery in *hot* water, and cut it against the thumb over the pot. She also diced a potato against the thumb straight into the pot. Sam kept throwing me looks, as if to say, *Can you believe this?*

Suddenly Maria Rosa glanced at her watch and gasped. We had to get to L'Isola della Carne before it closed. We fished the hot platter from the dishwasher and plunked the cooked veal in it. To calm Maria Rosa, I suggested that, in the worst-case scenario, we could always slice it by hand. That would be a travesty for such a sublime dish, she replied, in adrenalized Italian (or something to that effect). We jumped into her old Multipla, an anti-Ferrari that was a short, stout box on wheels. Maria Rosa had a love-hate relationship with the rattling, sixteen-year-old car, which could hit a top speed of 105 kilometres an hour. She adored its roominess—the front seat comfortably sat three. She also despised it because she was never sure when she left home whether she'd make it back.

I had to cradle the platter with the slippery piece of cooked veal on my lap. Luckily, we only had to drive a minute up the hill to the butcher. "*Magnifico!*" said the young butcher, as we burst through the door. Today she was wearing a red jacket, a lacy beige scarf artfully wrapped around her throat, and a red-checked apron that matched the fabric decorating the lids on jams and preserves on nearby shelves. As she reverently sliced the meat, letting each slice hit the platter *just so*, Maria Rosa explained to her that Sam and I were in Repergo to learn Italian home cooking. She beamed, stopped slicing, and reached into her glass display case. She plucked a chunk of raw meat from a bright red serpentine coil of sausage. "Taste this!" she said enthusiastically.

It was Piemontese *salsiccia*, made with veal, pork, and bacon. Italians ate it either cooked or *cruda*. An enterprising nineteenth-century *salumi* maker originally created it from only beef and veal to sell to the Jews in Piemonte. We'd never eaten raw pork before. Sam looked goggle-eyed. I pretended not to notice him. As Maria Rosa urged us to try it, we gamely chewed a mouthful. It tasted like cold steak, with hints of thyme, nutmeg, and garlic. Italians occasionally ate pancetta, rolled pork belly, without cooking it, although technically it was cured and was not actually raw. *Lardo*, pure white fatback, was also cured and could be eaten raw. We suffered no deleterious effects from eating uncooked sausage.

By the time we got home, the cabbage soup smelled heavenly. We tore stale bread into large croutons to toast in the oven. Chiara added a spoonful of butter, a Knorr vegetable-flavoured gel pack, and several cups of water to the pot. To thicken the soup, she dropped in three unbeaten raw eggs, stirring vigorously until they disappeared, leaving only a golden hue. Italian egg-drop soup!

The *bagna càuda* was overwhelmingly rich, even though I love anchovies and garlic *and* was starving. Raw vegetables might have cut the heaviness, but the winter version called for cooked vegetables. (Sam, for his part, thought the balance between the garlic, anchovies, and unseasoned vegetables worked well; later, when we had "true" *bagna càuda* made with olive oil, not milk, he found that too strong, rich, and salty.)

The platter of *vitello tonnato* looked and tasted like cold rare roast beef, and was the perfect foil for the piquant tuna sauce. The piece of veal shrank considerably after a one-hour braise but, like French diners, Italians instinctively calculated their share and served themselves accordingly. Even after twice passing around the *vitello tonnato*, leftovers remained. The secret to staying slim on a diet of butter, olive oil, and egg yolks is to eat for taste, not volume, and talk a lot to everyone else at the table. No one with whom we cooked and dined was fat on the scale of, say, Mario Batali. In fact, obesity rates in Italy (and France) were among the lowest in the European Union, well below that of England and Spain, according to the OECD.

Maria Rosa ladled out the steaming *zuppa di cavolo*. As a garnish, we passed a bowl of diced fontina cheese, which softened in the hot soup. All talking stopped. This was authentic *cucina povera*. Had I not seen it with my own eyes, I would not have believed a soup could be so scrumptious from cheap ingredients like cabbage, onions, and potatoes. Our fourth course, also in the spirit of *cucina povera,* was fettuccine, tossed in the ragù made from the scrapings of the veal pot. Chiara cut the *salame dolce,* which had hardened nicely in the freezer, into thick slices. I gave mine to Sam, who groaned. Maria Rosa passed a bowl of fruit. We each peeled our own blood oranges, which were in season. By 10:10, we were finished. Sam did the math: six courses in seventy minutes.

"Holy crap," he said, "we ate fast."

CHAPTER SEVENTEEN

Federica's Polenta and Pasta

We awoke to our first cloudless day. The fog had lifted and the rain had finally stopped. Piemonte meant "foot of the mountains," but I was nevertheless amazed to see that the green hills of Repergo were indeed the foothills of the snow-capped Alps.

Tiny Repergo was so empty, so quiet, you could hear your shoes scuff the asphalt. One morning I was out for a stroll when I happened to cough. (Yes, I was *still* sick.) My hack reverberated in the silence. The only other person in sight, an elderly woman a hundred metres in front of me, halted, turned slowly around, and peered at me for a long minute. The occasion of bumping into another Reperghese was so rare that it required a gesture of some sort. She figured she had to know me, except she didn't. I restrained myself from waving and kept on walking. Eventually she went on her way.

That evening, Maria Rosa had arranged for us to cook dinner with a nursing colleague. Showing up at the homes of strangers was an extraordinary privilege. It was also stressful. Sam and I had to be on our best behaviour. We couldn't quarrel. We couldn't be late. The language barrier notwithstanding, we needed to understand what we were seeing and absorb recipes and techniques, even if we sometimes were clueless about the local etiquette. Our hosts were under similar pressure — self-imposed, of course — to teach us. They felt obligated not to forget a step or omit an ingredient. Entertaining was by nature stressful. This was worse — they felt their national pride was at stake.

My secret weapon was Sam. Alone, I was a nosy journalist who never put down her notebook, who spouted endless questions, and who, on top of everything else, had a contagious cough. Sam was good with languages.

He was also unfailingly polite (I had told him he had to be). He never stood around *asking* what he could do. He spotted a task and did it, washed every dirty dish he saw, made people laugh, and knew his way around a kitchen. Aside from Chiara, a standout exception, the younger generation we encountered was generally uninterested in cooking. The home cooks we met in Italy, who all had teenaged or adult children, were intrigued that a reasonably well-adjusted young man had agreed to spend a near-eternity cooking with his mother. Who did that? Daughters, maybe, but not sons. I sensed the people we met were trying to sniff out the secret ingredient in our mother-son relationship. And frankly, so was I.

Why *was* Sam hanging out with me?

Federica Battilla lived along a zigzaggy road in a mountain village called Rocca d'Arazzo (pop. 946). Both she and Maria Rosa worried Sam and I would never find it, so Maria Rosa drove ahead of us in her Multipla while we tailed her in our car. In a deserted church parking lot in Montegrosso, we were handed off, like a drug deal. Federica formally shook hands then jumped in her car and roared off. Sam struggled mightily to keep up, chasing her around hairpin turns, swerving to avoid head-on collisions, trying not to veer off a cliff. Eventually Federica realized she had left us in the dust and slowed down.

She and her husband, Luigi Campini, lived in a modern duplex with a sweeping view of Piemonte's valleys and hills on one side, and a white-domed church on the other. His parents had built the house in 1967. They planned, as they aged and their son married and had a family of his own, to swap flats, just as Mirella and Beppe had switched homes with his parents. Federica and Luigi had now taken the top floor, with the stairs, while her husband's parents had moved into the ground floor. Each family had its own entrance, yet could see one another every day if they wished: Italian family planning at its best. That evening, Federica's in-laws were dining in Asti because they had taken her daughter, Eleonora, fourteen, to a figure-skating class.

At forty-six, Federica was slender and vivacious, with a mass of curly blond hair pushed back with a black headband. Like Mirella and Maria Rosa, she had designed a typical Piemontese menu and had already bought all the ingredients we were going to use. She spoke almost no English but had carefully prepared a handwritten vocabulary list of all the English words she might need. She told me she was petrified that the dishes she was going to show us would flop. "Even if you're a confident cook, it's hard because you are writing a book," she said. Sam smiled at her in his friendliest way. I tried to look less scary.

First, she gave us a tour of her garden. In season, it produced all the vegetables and fruits they ate. She and Luigi grew parsley, three kinds each of rosemary and sage, and a dozen types of vegetables, including several varieties of tomatoes. They cultivated blackberry bushes, grapevines, and fruit trees—peach, plum, apricot, cherry, mulberry, almonds, pomegranates, and figs (both big brown ones and small white ones that dripped sugar).

Right off the garden, next to their in-laws' apartment, was a traditional *cantina*, the culinary heart of an Italian home. Devoted solely to food preparation, it was a serious kitchen for al fresco dining in summer and processing the harvest in the fall. The *cantina* had a deep sink, a stove, an oven, a wide prep table, and a cold-storage section. It was devoid of decoration, except for some jars of honey from friends' own hives and a wicker basket filled with ripe kiwis. "They were grown one kilometre from here, by a friend of my grandfather," Federica said.

She and Luigi made their own wine in the *cantina*, and processed everything from their own salt-cured prosciutto to *passata*. The uncooked tomato purée, strained of seeds and skin, was stored in jars and sterilized, the base for the tomato sauces she would use all winter. She also cooked vats of ripe peaches, apricots, pears, figs, and plums. She pickled the fat yellow peppers of Piemonte in a sugar-and-vinegar marinade called *agrodolce*. She also made apple-onion chutney to go with meats, pear and lemon compotes for dessert, and an orange parsley salsa to eat with aged *toma* cheese. She was famous for her *mostarda*, a dying art among city dwellers because no ordinary stove could manage a sixty-gallon pot. Each September, before the winemaking started, she and Luigi would haul a huge gas burner outdoors and, for twelve hours, slow-cook hazelnuts from her father's garden, their own walnuts, plus cloves, grapes, pumpkins, pears, and apples. It took fifteen kilos of grapes and thirty litres of wine to make three kilos of *mostarda*.

Their flat was probably one thousand square feet, but it felt expansive because of the clean lines and lack of clutter. They had a large living room, two bedrooms, and one bathroom, but no formal dining room. A high-efficiency pellet-burning stove kept their home toasty warm at a cost equivalent to three cappuccinos a day. Their modern eat-in kitchen was twelve feet wide by twenty feet long, with wood floors and granite counter-tops. The table extended to accommodate eight diners. Like Maria Rosa and Mirella, Federica used the table as her main prep area. Her compact refrigerator contained only milk, ricotta, cheese, carrots, and cabbage. For lack of space, she stashed her good china in the living room and kept her pasta board and polenta maker in a storage closet.

That evening, we would make *bagna càuda* (again); *baccalà* (salt cod) with polenta; *stufato di vitello* (veal stew), also with polenta; and a classic Piemontese winter dessert, *bunet monferrino*.

In the thirteenth century, *bunet*, a complicated version of Odette's beautifully simple *crème renversée*, was served at noble banquets. The chocolate version came later, after the discovery of America — and cocoa. Nowadays, the recipe also included crushed *amaretti*, those crisp yet chewy, slightly bitter Italian macaroons made from apricot kernels, almonds, and egg whites. Federica preheated the oven to 400°F. In a large bowl, she whisked three organic eggs and added nine tablespoons of sugar, half a litre of milk, two tablespoons of unsweetened cocoa powder, twenty finely crushed *amaretti*, and two ounces of dark rum. Sam helped her zest a Sicilian lemon. "It has to be organic because you're using the skin," she warned.

Unlike Odette, Federica didn't make her own caramel base. She opened a little bottle of caramel sauce, coated a loaf pan with it, and poured in the batter. She set the pan inside a *bain-marie* (called a *bagnomaria*) and put it in the oven. When it had finished baking, she set it outside on her balcony to chill. In Canada, you'd never put something tasty outdoors for fear of marauding squirrels and raccoons. But with sixty million two-legged omnivores in an area one-fifth the size of Quebec, Italy had few remaining wild animals.

Luigi arrived home at 4:35 p.m. He was forty-seven and worked for the town hall as a messenger and handyman. An avid cyclist, he was tall and lean, with a black beard and black-rimmed glasses. After greeting us, he got on the phone to deal with that universal problem, rotten internet service. For the next thirty minutes, he paced around his living room, waving his arms and shouting at his internet provider. When he returned to the kitchen, he was calm and pleasant. Apparently, he had solved the problem. His kitchen expertise, however, was limited to sorting the garbage into recycling categories. "He doesn't know how to cook, just to eat," said Federica, with a loving smile. "I like to cook, and I like to eat. I learned cooking from my mother and Luigi's mother."

Uncertain what to bring as hostess gifts, Sam and I had gone to a gourmet shop in Montegrosso to buy a bottle of Barbera d'Asti and a bag of *amaretti*. "Ah, from Mombaruzzo, the home of the *amaretti*," said Federica approvingly. She said Luigi loved bicycling all the way there, a sixty-kilometre round trip. "He always has three *amaretti* with an espresso." She, too, was an avid cyclist, once cycling with Luigi all the way to Rome. Last year they rode to Provence. Next year they were planning a bike trip to Vienna. "It's only nine hundred kilometres," said Luigi.

Federica said her mother-in-law cooked *bagna càuda* the traditional way, in a terracotta pot over a wood fire. Unlike Maria Rosa, she didn't use milk, but she did use an entire jar of anchovies. "The oil, it's no good," Federica said, draining the anchovies. She peeled an entire head of garlic, "from the garden of my father," and mashed it over medium heat in a quarter cup of olive oil. "Garlic lowers blood pressure, but it's hard to digest." Unlike Maria Rosa, who passed around the *bagna càuda* as a dip, Federica spooned the sauce over two huge platters of roasted yellow peppers like a marinade.

"Now *maize porridge*," Federica said in English, reading the translation off her vocabulary list. She looked inquiringly at Sam. "We just call it polenta," he said.

Federica got her polenta maker from the storage closet. Made of solid copper, it looked like an upside-down bell and was, in effect, an ultra-slow electric eggbeater with a bowl attached, which went on top of a burner on a regular stove. She filled the bowl with three litres of water. As it heated, she whisked in a handful of coarse Sicilian sea salt and tasted the water for saltiness. Then she gradually whisked in six hundred grams of cornmeal. She knew she was making way too much, but she planned to eat the leftovers the next day. "We fry it with sage, speck, and smoked cheese," she said. "During World War II, all the poor people in the country ate polenta." Luigi added, "Polenta is part of the history of Piemonte. This was a poor area. We only ate potatoes and polenta. Many years ago, we cooked it with milk."

"Only stone-ground organic cornmeal," Federica said, noting it would take forty-five minutes to cook and needed constant stirring, hence the usefulness of the electric beater attachment. But did polenta really need all that stirring? Bill Buford discovered that it didn't, and Mario Batali recommends using, horrors, instant polenta or, as he puts it, the "quick-cooking" type. When Federica's back was turned, Sam whispered to me, "You can microwave polenta." And he was right. Cooking polenta in the microwave takes five minutes. But we didn't tell Federica that.

Nor did I tell her that I hated polenta. It was the only dish of *cucina povera* I disliked. Polenta was made from coarse corn, the kind livestock ate. But if all you had was dreary barley mush until Christopher Columbus brought corn back from the New World, polenta would be a step up. As I've said, I'd eaten lots of polenta or, as the Chinese call it, *bangzi mian zhou*. During the Cultural Revolution when food was rationed, unseasoned cornmeal mush was a mainstay at Peking University, along with *wotou*, the same cornmeal steamed into leaden lumps. Today, it's fed to prisoners in Chinese jails.

Federica said you could add as much water as you liked to polenta. If you liked it solid, you added less water; if you liked it soupier, you added more. "Years ago, my grandfather cooked polenta and cut it with a string." That sparked another unhappy food memory. In the 1980s, Norman and I were dining *al fresco* in Asiago with the family of a graduate-school classmate from New York University. They served grilled sausages, polenta, and the famous Asiago cheese. The polenta, served on traditional planks of beech wood, was also cut with a string — and it was thick, rubbery, and painfully salty. But maybe Federica's polenta would be magical.

In the seventeenth century, Italian farmhands who crossed the Alps to find work in the Drôme celebrated the harvest with a pot of *daube*, or meat stew. In Italy, the same dish, called *stufato*, was served with polenta. For *stufato*, Federica browned cubes of veal in a large, heavy-bottomed pan. Like Mirella and Maria Rosa, she used the best olive oil she could obtain — cold-pressed extra-virgin from Tuscany. She added white wine, half a dozen fat sausages, and half a jar of her own homemade *passata*. Then she pulled a small cube of something green from her freezer.

"*Cubetti di gusti per il soffritto*," she said, tossing it into the pot. Each summer she made a fine dice of onions, carrots, celery, and parsley that she sautéed gently in olive oil.

"Oh, it's a *mirepoix*," said Sam, comprehending. He told her the French used the same holy trinity of onions, carrots, and celery. *Soffritto*, which meant "fried," was the flavour base of soups and sauces. In summer, Federica's father made his own mix of sage, rosemary, and bay leaves.

She started on the *baccalà*, one of the original Slow Foods. For three days, she had soaked the salt cod in numerous changes of water. Surprisingly, she didn't cut against the thumb. She whizzed a large onion through a tiny electric Moulinex. But because the blender chewed up parsley, she minced the herb with a curved, two-handed knife blade.

"This is a *mezzaluna*," she said. "What do you call this in English?"

"A mezzaluna," Sam replied. Federica grinned.

After sweating the diced onions, she laid the milky white *baccalà* atop, added white wine, and tossed in some Knorr vegetable powder. She sniffed the pot. "*Boom bam bon*," she said, Piemontese dialect for "delicious." In the sixteenth and seventeenth centuries, when the region fell under French rule, Piemonte absorbed many foreign words. *Bon* (or *bun*) meant good, the same as in French. "Artichoke" was *articiocc*, pronounced the same as in English, but *carciofo* in Italian. "House" in dialect was *mison* from the French *maison*, while the Italian word was *casa*. Dialect for "apple" was *pom* from the French *pomme*, while the Italian was *mela*. "Then the Spanish came and burned everything," said Federica. "My grandparents only spoke Piemontese. They defended Asti with guns." Luigi, whose family had lived in Rocca d'Arazzo for seven generations, was related to the family who had defended the town, which was later named in their honour.

We had been standing and cooking for four hours. I was faint with hunger, and my back was killing me. The veal had to simmer another hour. The polenta wasn't ready either. We watched the machine stir it, round and round, bubbles breaking the surface every now and then, like volcanic mud. Finally, at 7:57 p.m., a timer went off. Luigi tipped the pot of polenta onto a serving platter. Federica plunked the other pots and pans directly onto the table, just as Maria Rosa had done. At exactly eight p.m., we sat down. The antipasto of roasted yellow peppers with *bagna càuda* was sprightly. "It's good," Luigi said to Federica, who beamed. This polenta was a creamy, hot backdrop to *stufato di vitello*. It also paired well with the salt cod, which flaked on the fork and was not at all salty. Luigi opened the bottle of wine we'd brought. "We don't usually drink wine," he said.

"A normal meal for us is pasta with olive oil and Parmesan cheese,"

Federica added, "or rice and peas. We don't know what to do with leftovers."

As health-conscious athletes, they ate meat only once or twice a week. His favourite was *coniglio*. I knew what it was, but Luigi was determined to say the word in English. Suddenly his face lit up. "Roger Rabbit!" he cried. He ran to his desk and returned with a massive Italian-English dictionary. Every time he wanted to say something, he flipped through it, searching for the right word. When I wanted to respond, I did the same. Between his enthusiasm, my introductory Italian, and Federica's vocabulary list, we managed.

Smacking his lips, Luigi said his mother specialized in fresh pasta. She stuffed it with herbs and ricotta, baked casseroles of pasta, and rolled her own linguine. Sam and I were hopeful, but Federica said *her* mother might agree to teach us next time. And her specialty was … *insalata russa*. Ungrateful wretch that I am, my heart sank. Russian salad was bafflingly popular in Italy. To me, it was potato salad ruined by cooked carrots, canned peas, and a surfeit of mayonnaise. I prayed we'd get the Pasta Nonna to teach us, instead of Insalata Nonna.

As we neared the final two courses of our gargantuan meal, Federica set out a huge slab of Gorgonzola *dolce*. "We eat no butter or cream, except Gorgonzola cheese," she said. A specialty of Piemonte, *dolce* was aged only a month or two, a toothsome version of the sharp, crumbly blue-veined cow's milk cheese we get at home. Federica served it with her own *mostarda*, which looked scary, like black nail polish, and tasted of raisins, walnuts, and deep essence of fruit. She spooned some onto her polenta. Sam helped himself to a tiny taste. "No, you have to put more," Federica said.

"You don't eat the rind of the Gorgonzola," Luigi cautioned, explaining that *dolce* was the version of the cheese used to make a sauce for gnocchi. His mother made "fantastic" gnocchi with red and yellow potatoes, he added, looking heavenward. "It melts in your mouth." Again, I crossed my fingers that we'd get *his* mother to teach us pasta *and* gnocchi.

The *bunet monferrino* hadn't set properly because the temperature had been too mild. Federica was distraught. "We almost never make dessert," she said, apologetically. In truth, no one could eat another mouthful. We exchanged hugs and kisses at their front door. Across the road, the gleaming white-domed church was dramatically floodlit. I gave it a long look because it would be our landmark when we returned. "How old is the church?" I asked.

"Since the Second Crusade," Luigi said nonchalantly. "A thousand years."

The next time we arrived an inexcusable forty minutes late. Sam and I had gone exploring and lost track of the time. Whenever my Italian friends in Canada were late, they joked about being on "Italian time." But in Italy itself, almost everyone we met prized punctuality. We had less than four hours to make dinner if we wanted to start eating at the proper time of eight. Federica, a perfectionist, looked frazzled. Adding to the pressure, her elderly mother, Maria, the Insalata Nonna, would cook with us.

Federica, in skinny jeans, a violet fleece, and a frilly white apron, announced our menu. Our main course would be *brasato al Barbera*, pot roast simmered in local red wine. Our pasta course would be fresh egg noodles with *sugo di arrosto,* literally "the juice of meat," made with a few slices of meat and the scrapings from the *brasato.* This was the same sauce Chiara had ordered at Dietro l'Angolo.

But first, we were going to make, sigh, Insalata Nonna's signature dish. Maria, who was turning eighty-one that weekend, had waited for us to demonstrate that *insalata russa* required cooked diced carrots and potatoes. She cut the carrots against the thumb directly into a steaming pot of boiling water. The potatoes she peeled and cooked whole. When they cooled, she hand-diced them against the thumb into a salad bowl. She had a serious mien, smooth skin, and freshly coiffed silver-grey hair. Like all Italian women we had met, she had dressed up, in a chic grey sweater. Her spotless powder-blue apron was embroidered with pink and yellow flowers. She was less than five feet tall, but strong. With a sharp twist of her wrist, she opened a jar of cooked peas, drained them, and dumped the contents into the salad bowl. Then she added four ounces each of Dijon mustard and commercial mayonnaise. She splashed in olive oil and mixed it thoroughly. Sam and I watched in horror as she decided it needed more mayonnaise and then proceeded to dump in *the entire jar.* Federica tasted the salad and said, "It needs more salt." Maria nodded, shook in more salt, and mounded it all on a pretty oval platter, almost to the rim. Then she iced it with a thick layer of *more* mayonnaise. As garnish, she sliced several hard-boiled eggs and popped open a jar of small green olives with her mighty hands. "It's *insalata russa,* but it's *Italian,* you understand," said Federica.

The Italian origin myth held that a chef in Piemonte invented this salad to please visiting Russian aristocrats. The French, who also offered it on restaurant menus, called it *salade piemontaise*. I tasted the real McCoy on a reporting trip to Moscow, and it was abominable even there. The Russians, who loved the concoction, called it "Olivier salad," after Lucien Olivier, a nineteenth-century restaurateur who ran a French bistro in Moscow. Always be suspicious of a dish that no one claims as their own.

For the *brasato*, Federica dredged a top-sirloin cut of Piemontese veal in flour and browned it in extra-virgin olive oil in a deep casserole. She added half a bottle of Barbera d'Asti, a cube of her frozen homemade *soffritto* and some dried rosemary, sage, and bay leaves. While the *brasato* was simmering, we started a *torta di mele*, a traditional apple cake. Sam cut up four yellow apples, quartering two and dicing two. "It's also good with pears," said Federica, who used a scale to measure the ingredients. Occasionally she consulted her cookbook, *Ricetto Italiano*; it reminded me of Bernadette's and Odette's massive cookbooks. Its 1,700 very brief recipes were also conveyed in culinary shorthand. Sam laughed aloud when he read the *torta* instructions: "Cook the cake in a hot oven for about 45 minutes."

Like Bernadette's cookbook, Federica's was pristine. She kept hers away from the work area, next to her unused microwave. And, like all Italians, she was fanatically clean, scrubbing a lemon with *steel wool*. "It gets rid of the impurities on the skin," she said. I zested the lemon peel and squeezed the juice onto the diced apples, adding sugar. She separated three eggs and whisked the yolks with sugar and melted butter. "No margarine," she said, wagging her finger forbiddingly.

Then Federica sieved in baking powder, a small packet of vanilla-scented sugar and two hundred grams of "00" flour. *Doppio zero* was the white flour as fine as baby powder, used for cakes, pasta, and pizza dough. "If it's too thick, you can add milk," she instructed. Using an electric mixer, Sam beat the egg whites with a pinch of salt, and Federica folded them into the cake batter. She buttered the non-stick spring-form pan with her fingers, floured it, and poured in the cake batter. We arranged the quartered apples in concentric circles and put the cake pan in a *bagnomaria*. Her interpretation of her cookbook's "hot oven" was 385°F.

It was time to make pasta. From her storage closet Federica hauled out a huge wooden board so big it covered most of the kitchen table. It was made of beech, the same type of wood polenta was served on. "My father made this for me because he was in the wood business," she said, caressing it with her fingertips.

Every Italian cook had a dedicated pasta board, big enough so each strand of pasta could dry without touching another strand. The surface was always left unvarnished so the natural wood grain would impart a texture to which sauces could cling. Federica's had a floury residue from pastas past. Italians obsessively washed everything except their pasta boards, which they merely scraped clean and never used for anything else, for fear of polluting it with other flavours.

She measured out four hundred grams of 00 flour, one and a half teaspoons of salt, fifty millilitres of water, and the yolks of four brown-shelled eggs. "*A l'aperto*," she said. *Free-range*. Piemonte pasta used an abundance of egg yolks, typically one yolk to every hundred grams of flour. But there was no hard rule—Mirella's ratio of thirty yolks per kilo of flour was triple that. "If it's too soft, add flour," Federica said, adding three extra handfuls of flour. "If it's too wet, leave it to dry. The amount of water depends on the type of flour." With her bare hands, she mixed the ingredients in a bowl until loose clumps developed. She floured the pasta board, and began kneading the bright yellow dough with the heels of her hands. An anchor strip on the base of the board gripped the edge of the table, preventing it from slipping.

Her mother watched expressionlessly. There was no pressure on Federica, aside from the fact that I was taking detailed notes, Sam was photographing her, her husband adored *his* mother's pasta, and *her* mother was literally sitting in judgment.

"How long do you knead it?" I asked Insalata Nonna.

"Until it's good," she said. She did not smile.

Federica let us each take a turn. Once I touched the dough, I understood. But how to describe it? I looked at Sam, and the thought popped into my head: as soft as his bottom when he was a baby. (I kept that thought to myself.) Hot from her exertions, Federica held her floury hands in the air and allowed her mother to remove her violet fleece jacket. After cutting the dough into five chunks, Federica again kneaded the dough. In Maria's time, the pasta would have been arduously rolled by hand. Federica had an electric pasta machine. "It's too much work to roll it by hand. I use a rolling pin only for pizza," she said, glancing affectionately at her mother. "We're going to make pizza for her birthday tomorrow night."

Federica ran each sheet through the machine *five* times. Each time, she lowered the dial, until the sheets were almost transparent. When we had fifteen sheets, she switched the machine to the second-thinnest setting of all, and floured each slice.

"Flour the other side," Maria instructed. Federica obeyed.

Flipping a switch on the machine to start the cutter, Federica carefully fed in the silky sheets. As the cut pasta tumbled from the machine, she said, "*Tajarin*," Piemontese dialect for taglierini, which was like tagliatelle, but thinner. Sam and I dusted our hands with flour to receive each cascade of pale yellow strands. We quickly transferred each clump to a vacant spot on the pasta board, and gently teased the strands apart. We worked as fast as we could, with Maria scrutinizing our every misstep. It still took thirty minutes for three of us—one and a half people hours—to make enough pasta for six people. For one course. And we had a *machine*. No wonder Italians ate fresh pasta in restaurants.

By seven thirty, the kitchen smelled heavenly. Federica put the apple cake outside on the balcony to cool. She trimmed a thin layer of fat from the pot roast and, shockingly, threw it out. Then she sliced the meat and layered it back in the pan juices, holding back three slices for the pasta sauce. She hesitated. "Another slice," her mother decreed. Federica cut a fourth slice. She whirred them through a blender for a minute then added half a cup of the pan juices. "It's called *sugo di arrosto*. No tomatoes," she said.

At 7:55 p.m., Luigi arrived home with Eleonora. The sternness faded from Maria's face when she spied her granddaughter, who hugged her and kissed her on both cheeks. Eleonora had just finished her weekly ninety-minute figure-skating lesson in Asti. The fourteen-year-old was not interested in cooking. She left the kitchen to listen to rap music on her phone, returning only when it was time to eat.

As we passed around the huge platter of *insalata russa*, I noticed everyone took a tiny portion. Maria's masterpiece tasted too much like eating a jar of mayonnaise. The fresh pasta took a minute to cook. In a serving bowl, Federica mixed it with *sugo di arrosto*. Maria forked a taste-test mouthful. We held our collective breath. "It's good," she said, nodding. We all beamed. With the big Italian-English dictionary at Luigi's side, we discussed the newly passed gay-marriage law. Italy had been the last developed European country to legalize it, and Luigi said people were not pleased. "The Liberal Party is crashing in the polls," he said.

Sam asked if Italian law allowed people to rent surrogate wombs. He said no. Suddenly he revealed that Eleonora was adopted. I'd noticed she didn't look at all like her blond mother or her tall father, but then Sam didn't look like me, either. Luigi said that he and Federica had met on a train when she was seventeen and still in high school. He was eighteen. They tried to adopt in their thirties but the process had been gruelling. "Lots of investigation," he said, flipping through his dictionary. "Financial, work, psychology. The social workers asked me my hobbies. I like to paint. They asked me, 'Why?' I told them, 'Because.' They said my head's in the cloud." He and Federica all but gave up. Then out of the blue, they got a call. A preemie, weighing one kilogram, was in precarious health. Since Federica was a nurse, the social worker thought she and Luigi might be able to manage. "She fit into my hand," said Luigi. Eleonora grinned, as though she'd heard this story many times.

Federica served the *brasato* with a green salad. The sliced veal was tender and deeply flavoured from the Barbera wine, but unlike the veal Bernadette had cooked in France, it was not white. "Veal is always red," said Luigi, adding that his uncle raised cows on his farm. To my surprise, they told me they liked Chinese food. Federica said that her favourite restaurant in Asti was called Hai Ou. I wrote it down for future reference.

After the apple cake, Sam did all the dishes. Then it was time for coffee. "Cosa è *coffee?*" said Maria, repeating the English word. *What is coffee?*

"They have *caffè*, but they put a lot of water in it, and they add milk," Federica told her mother. Maria looked dubious.

I asked for a cup of herbal tea. And then I learned a new Italian word. To calm someone who is *agitato*, Luigi said, people wave their arms and shout, "*Camomilla!*" (chamomile, of course).

CHAPTER EIGHTEEN

Pizza and Poached Pears

On Saturday, we went with Fiorenzo, Maria Rosa, and Chiara to Alba. The entire town had shut down three days earlier to mourn the passing of Michele Ferrero, the eighty-nine-year-old founder of Nutella and Ferrero Rocher, and the wealthiest man in Italy. On the day of his funeral, schools closed. Four giant outdoor screens projected his funeral Mass. Mourners included the Italian prime minister, the CEO of Fiat Chrysler, and thousands of current and retired workers. "Everyone is sad. He gave a lot of money to causes and he created a lot of jobs," said Maria Rosa. As we wandered through the streets, inhaling the perfume of chocolate and toasted hazelnuts, we saw his photo in many shop windows: "Thank you, Michele. We are proud of you."

Ferrero's father was a *pasticceria* owner who shrewdly stretched wartime-rationed cocoa powder by mixing it with Piemonte's abundant hazelnuts. In 1964, Michele added vegetable oil to create a spread, which he dubbed with an internationally pronounceable name. A quintessential Italian, he never attended university and spoke only dialect. He didn't pay taxes—legally. (He lived in Monaco and helicoptered to Alba to work.) Ferraro shunned the media, declined honorary degrees, and stayed married to the same woman his whole life. He also made annual pilgrimages to Lourdes, France. In a country where labour strife was rife, his factories had never had a strike or layoff. He provided shuttle buses for rural employees and free medicine for all. Workers left their prescriptions at the front desk at the start of a shift, and picked up their pills at the end of the day. He built an on-site crèche for their babies and a social centre for when they retired. When employees died on the job from injury or illness, he paid their salaries to their grieving families for three years.

We had come to Alba to eat lunch at Eataly, the chain at the forefront of Italy's Slow Food movement. Beyond the enticing food aisles was a bar, an open kitchen, and a cavernous dining area. Aggressively unostentatious, the tables were covered with brown paper, the water cups were paper, and the cutlery stuffed in a plain white envelope. A waiter dropped off individual snack bags of crusty, yeasty bread, baked on-site in a wood-burning stone oven and immodestly billed as "the most delicious bread in the world." It *was* the best bread I'd tasted in Italy. (Naturally, there was no butter.)

We ordered and paid up front at the counter from a five-item menu. Fiorenzo urged me to try Afeltra-brand fusilli from Gragnano, Campania, which he said was the best in the world. Instead of being extruded through Teflon-coated dies, *la pasta di Gragnano* was pushed through bronze dies, whose rougher surface enabled sauces to better cling to noodles. My fusilli, sauced with cherry tomatoes and fresh ricotta, had a nutty taste and a voluptuous mouth feel. Sam, who couldn't get enough *carne cruda*, ordered a huge patty of raw veal from La Granda, a cooperative of sixty-five small Piemontese farms that followed strict and traceable breeding procedures.

After lunch, we drove past fortified villages with crumbling stone walls. The vineyards, precision rows of inky-black gnarly stumps, were surrounded by orchards of almond, hazelnut, and olive. Like Marie-Catherine, Maria Rosa remembered a time when Piemonte was too far north for olive trees. This winter was so warm the fruit trees were already in bloom. Our destination was the medieval village of Barolo (pop. 750), the eponymous epicentre of Italy's most famous red wine. By regulation, Nebbiolo grapes for the tannin-rich Barolo could only be grown on *sunny* hillsides, never on valley floors, humid plains, or northern exposures. The fermenting juice had to steep in their skins a minimum of three weeks, and the wine itself aged at least thirty-eight months.

Barolo was less than an hour's drive from Repergo, but Chiara had never been. We wandered together down cobblestone streets, past pricey wine shops and restaurants displaying signs in Chinese, Japanese, and Russian. In winter, the village was agreeably empty. Maria Rosa bought a package of handmade dried pasta with truffles from a shopkeeper who looked pleasantly shocked that she had made a sale in the off-season, and to an Italian no less.

That night Maria Rosa took us out for pizza with her friends in Asti. Italians rarely made pizza at home because no one had a wood-burning oven hot enough to properly blister the crust in five minutes. Around eight thirty, which I guessed was the fashionably late time for a Saturday night on the town, we squeezed into the last remaining seats at a long, skinny table cobbled together from ten small tables. We were twenty in all, including Maria Rosa's colleagues, spouses, and teenaged children. Cousin Mirella and Beppe were also there. But who were the others? We waved wordlessly across the table because of the din.

Half the restaurant was seated in parties like ours — birthday parties, family gatherings, groups of young people hanging out. The menu was as thick as a magazine, with pages and pages of pizzas, all individually sized. I wondered how the waiter would keep everyone's orders straight, and how we would sort it out when it was time to pay. The system, it turned out, was ingeniously simple. The cashier kept a running tally for each table: when you left, you reported your order and paid, and he crossed it out.

Using my restaurateur-daughter's eye, I calculated at least seventy-five orders ahead of us. Since I didn't relish the thought of making small talk in halting Italian over the roar, I wandered to the front to watch the pizza maker. Yes, *the* pizza maker. One man, in a sliver of workspace, was handling all the orders. He was even more impressive than the risotto maker in Florence — every two minutes, he managed to make a specific pizza *and* keep track of the five or six already in the oven, each of which cooked in less than five minutes.

Our pizzas arrived molten, with charred crusts, so big they flopped off the edges of the plates. I cut a wedge and, holding it with both hands, bit off a chunk. It was ambrosial. Then I noticed everyone else was using a knife and fork.

Italian Food Rule: *never eat pizza with your fingers.*

I hastily switched, hoping no one had noticed my faux pas. After dinner, Sam announced he was going to hang out with Chiara and another teen. We'd been joined at the hip for so many days, I felt a sudden panic, the way I'd felt when I left him at junior kindergarten on his first day of school. I blurted, "Where are you going?" Sam shrugged, and gave me a look that said: *Mom, don't bug me. I need a night off.*

The rest of us went back to the home of Antonella Bossotto for coffee and a *digestivo*. A striking silver-haired woman in a flowing black dress and dramatic chandelier earrings, she led us down cobblestoned streets to her home. As we crossed Asti's main square, every second or third passerby seemed to greet her by name. She lived in an eighteenth-century stone palazzo overlooking the quiet Piazza Medici, in an apartment tastefully decorated with sculptures, books, paintings, and silk carpets. As I sat down on her dark blue L-shaped sofa, I did a double-take. It was identical to the one in my apartment in Fredericton.

"IKEA!" I said, pointing at it. "*Io ho uno stesso!*" (I have the same one.)

"*Sì*, IKEA," said Antonella, beaming.

"*È un piccolo mondo,*" someone said. *It's a small world.*

"No," said Fiorenzo, in English. "It's a big IKEA."

The next morning, my cough was so bad I was losing my voice. Given how many people I was having pizza with and cooking with, there seemed a good chance I was going to become the Typhoid Mary of Piemonte. Brushing aside my misgivings, Maria Rosa invited us for Sunday lunch. "Come for spaghetti," she said warmly. The sun shone as we hurried down the road to her house. Papa Franco was joining us.

The tagliatelle with truffles she had bought the previous day in Barolo cooked in three minutes. We tossed the pasta — bright yellow from egg yolks — with good-quality butter and some grated Parmesan. It was tender but tasted only faintly of truffles. Sam and I brought a so-called "Barolo-cured" salami, which lacked any discernible flavour of the famous red wine. I should have been warned off by the vendor's Chinese sign translating "Barolo" into characters — 巴罗咯, pronounced *ba luo lo*.

As always, Maria Rosa meant so much more when she said "spaghetti." She also served a refreshing chicken salad made with minced celery, yogourt, olive oil, lemon, salt, and parsley. As we ate, Maria Rosa told us the best way to make rabbit-stuffed ravioli. "Cook the rabbit one day in advance. Then wash, chop, and cook some spinach, add an egg and . . ." She stopped herself. "I *never* make ravioli," she confessed. Everyone frowned. "Well, maybe occasionally," she conceded.

"It was better when women stayed home," said Fiorenzo, as his wife and daughter shot him dagger looks.

"Food was rationed then," Papa Franco chimed in, nostalgically.

Nonno reminisced about his childhood. "I used to go to Isola d'Asti across the valley to grind our grain at a mill powered by water. In the period of Fascism, I would go at midnight because if the Nazi police saw me, they would confiscate my grain." Nonno had never spoken at the table before.

When he saw that Sam and I were listening, he continued. "We hid a Jewish mother in the attic, right here," he said, pointing to the ceiling. "Otherwise she would have been killed."

In 1943, once the Germans occupied the north of Italy, many Italians risked their lives to protect their Jewish neighbours. Nonno's great-aunt, the village teacher, knew the woman, whose family owned a brick factory in Costigliole d'Asti, four kilometres from Repergo. Her husband, a gentile, and their daughter, who was not considered Jewish, were not in danger, at least in Repergo. But the woman, who was in her thirties, was in great peril. Nonno remembered her surname was Levi. As a seven-year-old boy, his task was to climb into the attic every day to bring her food and water.

If food was rationed, I asked, how did they have enough to share? Nonno waved his arm, a gesture that said: *don't worry*. "We lived in the countryside, so we had milk from our cows and eggs from our chickens. We had vegetables and rabbits. We shared our food with her." He said the woman stayed for a couple of months and then left. Nonno didn't know where she went or what happened to her in the end. The Italian census of 1938 counted forty-five thousand Jews. By 1939, Mussolini required Jewish owners of businesses to sell their assets to "Aryans" and barred Jewish children from attending school. Eight thousand Italian Jews died in Nazi camps and seven thousand more fled, but the majority—thirty thousand—survived.

Nonno's matter-of-factness, his utter lack of self-congratulation, reminded me of the quiet humanitarianism of Marie-Catherine and François. A family in France and a family in Italy saw desperate people in need, and each stepped forward to save them. Nonno's family risked their lives to hide a Jewish woman. The Jeanselmes risked police raids to shelter undocumented migrants. Nonno's family shared scarce food in wartime. The Jeanselmes covered all the expenses for the Georgian family—at a time when their dependent children's benefits were reduced.

Maria Rosa spoke of an uncle, a Resistance fighter who was captured toward the end of the war near Trentino, close to the border with Austria, and transferred to a German prisoner of war camp. "He came home, but was so destroyed that he died ten years later at the age of forty-five," she said. Papa Franco joined the partisans at fourteen, but lasted only a few days before his frantic parents yanked him home. Unlike Nonno, Papa Franco lived in town, without a farm to sustain his family. "We had no food. There were so many German troops around us—and all the food went to them. We suffered terrible hunger. All we had was the milk of one goat." His job was to make sure the goat survived. Each day he took it to the fields to graze. After the war, Papa Franco added, he and a chum found an unexploded shell in the same field. They began fooling around with it, and it exploded. Franco survived, but his friend was killed.

"We're always fighting," said Maria Rosa, sighing deeply. "It's terrible we can't learn anything from the past."

She had made four more courses: poached fresh porcini mushrooms; a sprightly salad of chicory, radicchio, and romaine; sliced tomatoes with *mozzarella di bufala fresca*; and an artichoke tart. We were washing the pots and pans when someone shouted, "Look!" Through the kitchen window, we saw Nonno's sister Luigina walking laboriously up the steep road, a cane in her left hand and a cake in her right. Chiara and Sam ran outside to take her arm and help her carry the cake.

Luigina kissed her brother and Papa Franco on both cheeks. She had brought dessert, her famous yogourt cake. "Her version is better than mine," said Chiara, graciously.

"The original recipe is from a nun," said Luigina, beaming. "It's better if you leave it one day. I made it yesterday."

And in case the cake, our seventh course, wasn't enough, Maria Rosa had also made pears poached in red wine.

MARIA ROSA'S POACHED PEARS IN RED WINE
Serves 4.

4 cups	dry red wine (Barbera if you want to splurge)
¼ cup	white sugar
1	cinnamon stick
8	cloves
1 inch	lemon or orange zest
4	pears (unripe is better)

Combine all ingredients except pears in a saucepan and bring to a boil. Peel pears, leaving stems intact. Reduce heat and add pears. Simmer, lid on, for 1 hour (or until pears are tender when pierced with a knife). Turn occasionally to ensure even colour. Remove pears. Reduce poaching liquid by two-thirds. Serve at room temperature in shallow bowls, with some syrupy liquid and, if you wish, a dollop of barely sweetened whipped cream.

Luigina was Mirella's mother, who lived one street away. At seventy-eight, she was two years younger than Nonno but looked much younger, partly because she wore dangly earrings and dyed her hair auburn. Like so many Italian women, she looked like she had just come from the hairdresser. She was in pressed pants and a multi-coloured sweater of mauve, grey, navy, and burgundy that she had knitted herself. She was so dressed up I thought she had come from church. She hadn't.

In fact, no one had gone to Sunday Mass. "They don't like the Catholic Church, but they believe in God," Chiara explained. Like the French, about 85 percent of Italians identified as Catholic. And, also like the French, many didn't bother attending church. Although the Vatican was in the heart of Rome, Italy was secular — its constitution explicitly prohibited state support for religious schools. It funded Church-selected teachers to provide optional religious classes in public schools, but the course material had to include content about other faiths.

It was six when our lunch finally ended. As we left, Maria Rosa said, "Come for dinner." I thought I misunderstood. We'd just finished a five-hour lunch. "We'll make *piadine*," she said. "You haven't had *piadine*. You must try it." Sam was laughing and nodding. I hesitated a nanosecond and then said, "Okay! *Piadine*."

We had just enough time to walk the few minutes to our farmhouse, brush our teeth, and have a post-prandial nap. When we returned at eight, Maria Rosa was busy preparing Monday lunch for both Nonno and Fiorenzo. She cooked a huge bowl of penne, the diagonally cut tubes of pasta named for quill pens, and tossed it in a silken tomato sauce flavoured with fresh basil. She grilled several hamburger patties to death, ironic considering the Piemontese loved *carne cruda*. She also made a pot of white rice and simmered whole baby zucchinis and whole white onions in extra-virgin olive oil. Nonno, who didn't know how to cook, could heat his lunch himself. Fiorenzo would take his food to the office. His lunch bag — no exaggeration — was the size of a small suitcase.

Sam and Chiara prepared the *piadine*, a pita-like flatbread from Emilia-Romagna, made with flour, olive oil, salt, and water. At Chiara's direction, Sam layered them with cheese and leftover chicken then folded them to bake briefly in a hot oven. I made a green salad. We set out a bottle of extra-virgin olive oil to dress it, a plastic bag of grated Parmesan cheese—real Parmigiano-Reggiano, of course—and Maria Rosa's ever-present jar of salt. We all bellied up to the table. No one was hungry, but we ate with gusto.

CHAPTER NINETEEN

Gigi's "Drooling" Gnocchi

Alessandro was getting ready to bottle Dolcetto d'Asti, a light, dry red. Fifteen hired hands, all from Eastern Europe, had just finished pruning the vines. Migrant workers, some with papers, others undocumented, came from Africa, Asia, and the poorer countries of Europe to pick Italy's grapes, potatoes, zucchini, and tomatoes.

On the highway to Asti, Fiorenzo once pointed out a few white women standing singly by the side of the road. "*Puttana*," he said. I understood, not because I'd learned the word for "whore" in my introductory Italian course, but because one of my favourite pastas was *spaghetti alla puttanesca*. "Spaghetti in the style of a whore" was an old standby, made by enlivening an ordinary tomato sauce with olives, capers, anchovies, and garlic. Its name supposedly derived from the quick sauce a prostitute could prepare between clients. In fact, *spaghetti alla puttanesca* was created by a nightclub owner in response to hungry customers who pleaded for a late-night plate of pasta. "*Facci una puttanata qualsiasi.*" (Make any old garbage.)

It took me several days to comprehend that the people at the Saturday night pizzeria were not a random collection of Maria Rosa's friends. All had agreed to take turns teaching Sam and me home cooking. Antonella Bossotto, the one with the identical blue IKEA sofa, had picked a night when her younger son, Matteo, was available to translate. But when we arrived, Matteo hadn't yet gotten home. Antonella was awaiting us, literally hanging out the second storey of her townhouse, smoking a cigarette. Most people doing that would look trashy. But no matter what she did, Antonella looked like a Vogue fashion model. At fifty-nine, she was tall and slim with high cheekbones and sculpted silver hair. She lived in the heart of Asti, a short walk from her favourite food shops, and so she shopped daily, unlike Mirella, Maria Rosa, and Federica, who drove to suburban *supermercati* with parking lots. She went everywhere on foot, probably one reason she was so slim.

At Fucci Formaggi, her favourite cheesemonger, she selected four cheeses for dinner after a lengthy, animated discussion with a stern-faced clerk in a white coat. The purchase came to half a day's pay. While Italians were historically big savers, they didn't skimp on food. As we crossed another piazza, Antonella pointed out a hulking concrete building. "*Fascista*," she said, spitting out the word. Built in the Mussolini era, grey and squat, it clashed with the adjacent eighteenth- and nineteenth-century palazzos. As I had noticed the night we had pizza, every second person we passed seemed to know her. Antonella explained that her family had once owned the biggest dry goods store in Asti—San Lorenzo Alessandro Tessuti—which sold fabrics and household linens. "Everybody bought from us, the Fascists, Germans."

The first record of Jews in Asti dates to the eighth century. By the fourteenth century, they had become a sizable community, swelled by French Jews expelled by Charles IV. In the fifteenth century Asti's ruler, the duke of Orléans, obliged Jews to wear a yellow badge of identification. In the sixteenth century, a Savoy duchess expelled the Jews from Asti, but they were permitted to return after her death. In the eighteenth century, the authorities established a ghetto and forced Jews to live within it. In World War II, when the government began arresting Jews and shipping them to internment camps, Antonella's great-grandfather began sheltering many of them in his home. "It was an old house with lots of passageways," she said. "There was the attic, the *cantina*, too. A lot of people, even Fascists, knew he was hiding Jews, but he was never arrested."

After the war, her grandfather inherited the shop and ran it until his death in 1974. Her grandmother kept the shop going, but had to cut the number of employees from eleven to four. Then she got cancer. "She closed the shop in June 1991, and two months later she died. I regret that I didn't take it over, but I couldn't," said Antonella, with a sigh. She was busy with her two boys, then six and thirteen. And she didn't want to risk quitting her job as secretary to the head of orthopedics at the hospital.

Her husband, the manager of the hospital's radiology unit, was waiting for us in the kitchen. Luigi Epifani (she called him by the diminutive Gigi), was sixty-four, a stereotypically dark, handsome Italian who had an effort-less, sweater-draped-around-his-shoulders, metrosexual style. "Cooking relaxes me," he said, as he tied a clean apron, emblazoned with the name of his favourite Italian soccer team, over his blue-striped Oxford cloth shirt and khaki trousers. Antonella confessed, "When I first married, I couldn't cook at all. I put pasta right into cold water." Sam winced, but was pleased because, for the first time in France and Italy, he would be cooking with a man.

Gigi grew up in nearby Emilia-Romagna, where school outings included visits to the local Parmigiano-Reggiano factory. He always liked to eat, but his passion for cooking had been ignited five or six years earlier—about the same time Sam began working in restaurants—by Gambero Rosso (red shrimp), Italy's first food network. Smitten, he invested in quality pots and pans. He also renovated the kitchen, installing a five-burner professional gas range and, "because everyone in the family is tall," raising the height of the granite counters. Their kitchen had a central table, soaring windows, and fourteen-foot-high ceilings. The counter, sink, and stove occupied one wall. The tiny refrigerator contained only milk and a Parmesan rind.

They stashed Antonella's heirloom china in an antique armoire. The dishtowels were from her family's store, eighty-year-old cloths of flax and linen, still thick and snowy white. Antonella told me she threw them in the washing machine but always ironed them. (A Procter & Gamble study found that Italian women iron socks, sheets, T-shirts, and even underwear.) A set of old-fashioned scales, an old coffee mill, and a dozen wall clocks grouped together, a half-finished design project of Antonella's, decorated their kitchen. On the wall was a china platter emblazoned with the name of her family's store. Framed menus from gala dinners past listed courses such as *bollito misto* and garlicky *bagna càuda*.

"It's impossible to kiss someone after you eat *bagna càuda*," said Gigi, beaming at us through fashionable rectangular glasses rimmed in royal blue and lime green. "The next day at the office, people say, 'Oh, you had *bagna càuda!*'"

Like all of Maria Rosa's friends, he and Antonella had carefully planned the menu to teach Sam and me as many Piemontese dishes as possible: *gnocchi alla bava, carne cruda*, artichoke salad, and *zabaglione*. To make the gnocchi, Gigi boiled a bit more than a kilo of potatoes. "New potatoes *non vanno bene*," he explained, wagging an admonitory finger. "You want *old* potatoes, which are drier. You cook the potatoes with the skin on so it doesn't absorb water. And you salt the water to draw the moisture out of the potatoes." Once the potatoes were tender, he riced them, skins and all, and added two hundred grams of flour and half a teaspoon of *sale di Cervia*, a premium salt used in the making of Parmigiano-Reggiano and Prosciutto di Parma. Harvested from Italy's last remaining artisanal flats in the Adriatic, *sale di Cervia* tasted mineral yet sweet and reminded me of Brittany's *fleur de sel*, but less metallic. When the potatoes cooled, Gigi tasted them, adjusted the salt, and added a beaten egg. Turning the dough onto the granite counter, he gently worked in another cup or so of flour. When it was soft and pliable, he broke off a lump the size of a clenched fist and rolled it between his palms to form a rope an inch thick. He then lopped off bite-sized cubes, gently pressing a fork into each cube, leaving an imprint that would help the gnocchi grab the sauce. "When my grandmother made gnocchi, we kids would eat it raw. It was so delicious," said Gigi.

Like Federica, he felt under pressure to make a perfect dish. He test-boiled a couple of gnocchi. When they bobbed to the surface a minute or two later, he fished them out. They tasted like toothsome potatoes whipped with hot air. "*È buono*," he said, looking relieved. As we worked, we nibbled on chunks of salami from nearby Monferrato, some tart marinated green olives, and squares of rosemary-scented *focaccia*. Gigi offered Sam a chilled bottle of lager from Menabrea, Italy's oldest brewery. Located in the foothills of the Alps, Menabrea lager was a product of eighteenth-century globalization — barley from France, hops from Bavaria, and yeast and brewer's maize from Italy.

In between cigarettes on the balcony, Antonella started the *zabaglione* for dessert. With a hand-held electric mixer, she combined six egg yolks, six heaping tablespoons of sugar, and one and a half teaspoons of flour. Using one of the half eggshells, she measured out a matching volume of *Marsala secco*, a dry red Sicilian wine (unlike Mirella, who used Piemontese *Moscato*). "My father was a very good chef," she said, stirring the custard. "He always made it over low heat, stirring it slowly, never using a *bagnomaria*. When you start to see bubbles, you turn it off." According to her father, the *zabaglione* was ready when it dripped slowly down the back of a spoon. Gigi came over for a sniff. "*Buonissima aroma*," he said, sighing like a man in love. Antonella beamed. She poured the sauce into a bowl, covered it, and set it on the radiator.

Italians are famous for gesticulating, even when talking on cellphones. Gigi showed us how to make the gesture for *buonissima* (marvellous, tasty, delicious): drill your index finger into the lower part of your cheek. The couple worked side by side, sharing the counter and the sink. Gigi made the gnocchi, while Antonella made the *fonduta* sauce. She melted 125 grams of butter and 250 grams of diced fontina, a cow's milk Alpine cheese, over a bowl of hot water, and kept it warm on the radiator. When it softened slightly, she whipped the cheese and butter with an immersion blender, thinning it with a bit of warm milk. Then she heated the sauce in a non-stick pan until molten.

"You can use this in sandwiches or omelettes," she said, drilling her finger into her cheek.

I asked about an old-fashioned concierge call bell on the shelf next to the stove.

"In the morning I tell her when her coffee is ready," said Luigi, slapping the bell with his palm.

"I'm so lucky," Antonella said, grinning.

They kept pre-ground coffee in a glass jar over the stove. She was shocked to hear that some coffee lovers in America grind their own beans. She said they *never* ground beans themselves. "We're very fussy about coffee," she said. "If you do it yourself, the heat of the blades wrecks the coffee. For fifty years, no one in Italy has ground their own coffee." To make sure I understood, she waved her hands in horror.

We had been managing in Italian quite well when their son, Matteo, returned home from his shift as a barista at a hotel bar. When I saw him, I remembered my iPhone charger had mysteriously stopped working earlier in the day. Stereotyping him, I figured young Matteo could help me. "No worries," he said. He called a friend with the same iPhone model, and twenty minutes later his pal dropped off a charger. Asti (pop. 75,000) was a place where everyone knew everyone or at least someone. Not only did Antonella know half the people she passed on the street, but Matteo's friend thought nothing of rushing over with a charger to help—let me get this straight—the brand-new acquaintance of the son of a friend of a friend of a friend.

Matteo, thirty, was slender with fashionably spiky brown hair. Unlike most young Italians, he had a university degree. He had studied agronomy and later drama at Sapienza-Università di Roma, one of Italy's best universities. "He went to the School of Unemployment," Antonella said, throwing her arms in the air in frustration. After graduation, he worked at menial jobs in Rome for nine years, living in substandard housing and splitting the rent with roommates. Later he taught French in Togo. Italy's staggering young-adult unemployment rate of 50 percent meant he was unlikely to ever find anything better than a barista. So, like an astonishing 60 to 80 percent of his generation, he lived with his parents. The older generation like his parents had decently paid, well-protected jobs. Matteo's generation found only precarious, low-paid work, if they could find work at all. Marriage and children were deferred. Matteo said he had no prospect of ever being able to afford a place of his own. His older brother, Nicolà, had been able to obtain a mortgage only because his wife worked at a bank. Despite the stability of their jobs, his parents weren't even eligible for a bank loan to renovate the ancient *cantina* in the cellar. Antonella cared for her grandfather in this house. She inherited the house from *her* father, whom she had also taken care of until his death. Perhaps in turn Matteo would care for his parents and eventually inherit the house — in the tradition of the happy multi-generational Italian family.

Matteo showed us his separate quarters on the third floor. His bedroom smelled faintly of weed. I didn't notice the half-smoked joints in the ashtray on the table. Sam did, and later told me he had sniffed pot as soon as we had entered the eighteenth-century stone stairwell. Matteo's room opened onto a larger terrace with a million-euro view of Asti's terracotta rooftops. That was where he hung out with friends, he said — and presumably smoked pot.

Downstairs in the kitchen, I idly inquired what year Gigi's father died. "In 2008 or 2009," he said hesitantly. Antonella couldn't remember, either. When they saw the surprised look on my face, Gigi explained that his father had deserted his mother. So much for the happy multi-generational Italian family. His father had dated Gigi's mother when he was a twenty-four-year-old medical student and she was a twenty-one-year-old elementary school teacher. When she became pregnant, Gigi's grandfather, who owned a profitable pharmacy, ruled she wasn't good enough for his son. She raised Gigi alone, and later married and had four more children. "They are all very nice," said Gigi, adding that his biological father also married and had four children: "All horrid people."

His biological father became a pediatrician, paid child support, and allowed Gigi to take his surname. But he refused to meet him until he was twenty-four — and then only once. But when Gigi and Antonella had Nicolà, their first son, the pediatrician got back in touch.

"*I* never met him," Matteo said.

"Yes, you did," Antonella corrected him. "You saw him once when you were five."

The father who abandoned his first-born son had the nerve to complain about what his daughter-in-law was feeding his first grandchild. "He would come into my house and check the pantry. He wanted to stop them"—she pointed to Matteo and his invisible brother—"from eating cakes and cookies. If he saw any, he would say, 'No, no!'" She waved her arms in fury. No wonder no one could remember what year he died.

Gigi turned his attention to making a salad of fennel and Sardinian prickly artichokes. He sliced some fennel, saving the feathery fronds for minestrone the next day. Then he washed and trimmed the artichokes and stripped the tough stringy parts off a stalk of celery. At first I thought the celery was going into the salad, but Gigi was doing what all home cooks do: multi-prepping, in this case, for minestrone the next day. "I'll cook the celery for two hours, and then purée it briefly, so the minestrone is still chunky." The Parmesan rind in his fridge would thicken the soup and give it that ineffable umami flavour. Gigi washed the artichoke slices again, prompting me to ask why Italians were clean freaks. I didn't know the Italian word for "freak." It turned out to be *maniaca*. Of course it was. Gigi said a friend of his had gotten very ill from food poisoning. "*Salmonella*," he said (which needed no translation).

At 7:45 p.m., Antonella reheated the *fonduta*. Gigi began cooking the gnocchi, gently plopping in two or three at a time to ensure the water temperature didn't plunge. He warned against draining them in a colander. "Too harsh," he said. Instead, he scooped them out with a spider, the same mesh ladle the Chinese use. At 7:55, we rushed to the table. No matter where we cooked or how long we slaved over a stove, dinner in Italy was always at eight. Because the home was several centuries old, the dining room was down a long hall, far from the kitchen. Antonella had set the table with an elegant grey polka-dot tablecloth, perfectly ironed. The cutlery—knife, fork, and cloth napkin—were all on the right side of the plate, Italian style. A silver *grissini* basket, which once belonged to Antonella's grandmother, was filled with skinny whole-wheat bread sticks. With our dinner, we drank a light red wine and tap water. They were the only family I encountered in Italy that didn't insist on drinking mineral water. "The tap water is very good," Antonella said.

Gigi's *gnocchi alla bava* were airy as clouds, Antonella's *fonduta* sauce pale velvety gold. *Alla bava* meant "drooling gnocchi" because the sauce supposedly looked like, yuck, saliva. It *was* mouth-wateringly good. Gigi and Antonella scarfed theirs in two minutes. Notebook poised, I impolitely wondered aloud why they ate so quickly. "It's because we have to eat in twenty minutes at the hospital," said Gigi, looking embarrassed. "*Brutta,*" said Antonella, shaking her head. She excused herself for a cigarette in the bathroom, where she blew the smoke out the window.

Gigi used a truffle shaver to shear off paper-thin slices of Parmigiano-Reggiano to garnish our *secondo, carne cruda.* He had deftly seasoned the minced raw veal with pink sea salt, fresh lemon juice, olive oil, fresh ground black pepper, Worcestershire sauce, and *senape*, a kind of mustard that also contained minced carrots, cabbage, capers, and anchovies. "*Poco, poco.*" A little bit, he meant, referring to the *senape*. The *carne cruda* was intensely beefy, without any of the stick-to-the-roof-of-your-mouth unpleasantness of raw animal fat. The cheese provided a salty counterpoint. "When Parmesan is one year old, you eat it fresh. When it's three years old, you grate it," Gigi said. The truffle shaver prompted a discussion of last year's truffle harvest, affected by drought. "Romanian truffles sold for the price of Alba truffles," he said. "Only the experts knew the difference."

Matteo wanted to talk about politics. "We have sixty million people and four different Mafia," he said, his voice rising in anger. "Each one has its own sector: guns, drugs, construction, or the ports. I go crazy when foreigners say, 'You're all Mafia.' I *know* Mafia. I *hate* the Mafia."

Italy's problems seemed intractable. The Mafia aside, other problems included cronyism, nepotism, crushing national debt, and high unemployment. The government couldn't even stimulate exports by devaluing the lira because when it adopted the euro in 1999, it abdicated monetary policy to the European Central Bank in Frankfurt. Tax evasion was rampant. Half of the GDP was hidden from tax authorities, according to researchers at the University of Milan and University of Pavia. In 2011, Reuters reported, "If official tax returns are believed, this nation of 60 million with some of the most expensive urban real estate in the world is home to only 394,000 people earning more than $135,000 a year. Newspapers in Rome and Milan are rife with stories of *evasione totale*—or entrepreneurs caught tooling around in Ferraris and Porsches despite declaring almost no income." Matteo said when he lived in Rome, landlords typically required him to sign a fake lease with an absurdly low nominal rent. He paid the real, much higher, rent in cash. The self-employed, such as dentists, were notorious tax evaders.

"In 2008, I had to have a lot of work done on my teeth," Antonella recalled. "I could only submit 19 percent of the bill to my insurance provider. My dentist said, 'If you want a receipt, the charge is 20,000 euros. But if you pay cash, it's 12,000 euros.'" Had Antonella submitted a receipt to her insurer, she would still have been on the hook for 16,200 euros. She paid 12,000 euros in cash.

The crooked culture started at the top. When he was prime minister, billionaire Silvio Berlusconi famously declared that evading high taxes was a "God-given right." In 2014, after two decades of desultory legal proceedings, he was sentenced to four years for tax fraud and kicked out of the Italian senate. His prison sentence was immediately commuted to a year of part-time community service because by then he was seventy-seven and deemed too elderly for jail. As hospital employees, Antonella and Gigi told me their income tax was deducted at source, at a marginal rate of 33 percent for anyone earning 30,000 to 55,000 euros ($45,000 to $82,000) a year.

"Ordinary people pay lots of tax," said Matteo. "Berlusconi paid less tax than my mother."

"There are only two hundred people in jail in Italy for financial crimes," Gigi added. "In Germany, there are two thousand."

It was a vicious cycle. With billions of euros in unpaid taxes, the Italian government had no money to pay teachers, or firemen, or doctors. And so parents like Maria Rosa and Fiorenzo discouraged their daughter from studying medicine. Yet people mourned the death of the founder of Nutella, who hadn't paid taxes.

We passed around the fennel-artichoke salad. I was horrified to see Matteo add soy sauce to the salad dressing. Chinese Food Rule: *never put soy sauce on your salad*. Antonella set out the platter of cheeses she'd purchased earlier: Parmigiano-Reggiano; Nerina ("little black cheese"), an ash-coated Piemontese *robiola*; Fontegidia, a straw-coloured *fontal*; and *robiola bosina*, a creamy cheese of cow's and sheep's milk. Like Federica, she served them with several condiments: *mostarda*; onion jam; an apple-chili compote "made by the mother of my brother's wife"; and honey "from the daughter of a friend of mine of thirty years."

Gigi said his sisters in Liguria made pesto by gathering special small-leaf basil from their gardens, which they ground in a mortar and pestle with pine nuts, garlic, and extra-virgin olive oil. Everywhere we cooked, people seemed to grow their own food, or have friends and colleagues, or an aunt or a grandfather or a cousin, a daughter or a nephew, who did. In France, Pierre had that friend who raised *pintade*. The uncle of Federica and Luigi raised cows. Fiorenzo's colleague gave him Jerusalem artichokes. Everyone consumed homegrown bounty—wine, *passata*, pickles, walnuts, kiwi, jams, preserves, or honey—artisanal food that wasn't merely made by an artisan, but made by an artisan they *knew*, or their aunt knew.

When it was time for dessert, I couldn't eat another bite, but of course I kept eating. The warm *zabaglione*, which the French call *sabayon*, was too rich and alcoholic for me. Sam, of course, loved it. As if that weren't enough, we had a second dessert of homemade *biscotti* and a fruit salad of bananas, pineapple, and local kiwi sprinkled with lemon juice and cinnamon. "I hate cinnamon on fruit," said Matteo, frowning. His mother shrugged. Matteo had a point, but I withheld my support. After all, what goes around comes around: he had desecrated the salad dressing with soy sauce.

As we left Antonella's home, she said, "You must come for *bollito*."

The next time Sam and I showed up, Gigi was in the kitchen, elbow-deep in a pile of bizarre animal parts. *Bollito misto*, or "boiled mix," was a snout-to-tail dish of the famed Piemonte Fassone cow. Like the *tuade* in France, it derived from *cucina povera*. "Italians are like Chinese," Sam said. "They eat every part of the animal, and they know how to cook it." *Bollito misto* was a poor cousin to France's *pot au feu*, the hearty winter dish of beef and chicken simmered with root vegetables. In France, they used tough cuts, but not weird animal parts; in Italy, people didn't even make a pretense of eating the vegetables.

Gigi had laid out an astonishing seven or eight kilos of meat on the counter. Matteo, our trusty translator, hadn't yet finished his barista shift, so Gigi tried to explain each piece of meat, somewhat unnervingly, by pointing to his own jaw, non-existent jowls, throat, tongue, thigh, and rump. One part, called *scaramella*, seemed to be the inside skirt or maybe the external muscle of the abdomen. Another part, *muscolo*, was, I think, the boneless foreshank muscle. Because every country broke down an animal differently, there sometimes were no common parts.

To keep different flavours separate, in the first pot Gigi boiled the jaw, tongue, and *testina*, a cut from the outside of the cow's head. In a second pot, he boiled the oxtail and other meats with two stalks of celery. Three times he skimmed off the scum. "No salt," he warned. "You can use carrots, but I think it would be too sweet. You can use onion, but after one day, the broth becomes too acidic." (As I said, the Italians weren't interested in *bollito* for the vegetables.)

Antonella, who somehow looked glam in black leggings and fuzzy lime-green slippers, demonstrated an apple-pear strudel. She had already cut up the apples and pears. Now she was caramelizing the fruit over medium heat in a knob of butter, the juice of half a blood orange, some cinnamon, two cloves, a handful of raisins and dried cranberries, half a cup of brown sugar, and some chestnut honey from a friend's daughter who kept bees in Castelnuovo near Nizza. Antonella unrolled some store-bought puff pastry called *sfogliata* (*mille feuille* in French and *phyllo* in Greek). When the fruit compote had cooled, Antonella spooned it onto the dough in a thick line down its length. She sprinkled on some chopped walnuts, rolled it into a log, pricked the pastry with a fork, and baked it at 350°F for twenty minutes. Midway through, she flipped it so it would brown evenly.

When Matteo arrived home, Sam and I went out with him to buy gelato — vanilla with lemon zest — to go with the strudel. By the time we returned, Gigi had started preparing the five sauces that traditionally accompany *bollito misto*: homemade mayonnaise, *salsa verde*, *mostarda di Cremona*, homemade ketchup, and chutney. "My grandfather would use only a fork," he said, taking out an electric mixer to make mayonnaise. He cracked two room-temperature eggs over the sink, saving only the yolks. With the beater on, he slowly drizzled in peanut oil until it emulsified. Then he added salt and the juice of half a lemon. For *salsa verde*, he used an immersion blender to pulse parsley, a bit of garlic, soft breadcrumbs, a splash of wine vinegar, two hard-boiled egg yolks, and an anchovy or two. "Don't let the blade get hot or it will cook the parsley, which is no good," he instructed.

Unlike Federica, Antonella bought *mostarda*. Fucci Formaggi, her favourite cheese store, sold *mostarda di Cremona* of candied cherries, pears, and apricots in a sharp mustard base. "It's very expensive, about twenty-five euros [thirty-seven dollars] a kilo, but it is way too much work to make," she said. "We only know of one lady who makes it herself. Even grape *mostarda* takes twenty-four hours. You need a huge pot and, in the end, you get five little jars."

Gigi had made homemade ketchup with ripe tomatoes the previous summer. The chutney was a gift from a friend named Laura. When I asked what was in the chutney, Antonella phoned Laura. The answer: "Usually dark purple plums, although this time she had used red peppers, along with red wine vinegar, sugar, cloves, and the smallest tomatoes without too many seeds or too much juice." Her friend had instructed, "Boil until thick, put in a jar, and sterilize." The phone rang. "Also, onions," said Antonella. "She forgot."

As we worked, we snacked on *grissini* and a wedge of mellow, nutty Parmesan. Sam happily accepted another Menabrea lager. Their daughter-in-law, who lived ten minutes away by foot, dropped off her two children for a few hours of free childcare. Antonella and Gigi's grandson, who was ten, watched cartoons in the living room. Their three-year-old granddaughter, Beatrice, wandered into the kitchen.

"What are we eating tonight?" she asked happily, pointing to a bright red vegetable peeler in Gigi's hand. Most grandparents would say, *No! Sharp!* and stow it away. Gigi handed her the peeler without hesitation. Scooping her up in his arms, he explained what it was for and pantomimed how to use it. "Whoosh, whoosh," he whispered in her ears. Beatrice giggled and imitated him. He held her over the hot stove, so she could inspect the bubbling pots of *bollito misto*. Grandparents normally boast about how smart their grandchild is. Gigi bragged about his tiny omnivore. "Beatrice eats *everything*—salad, pig's stomach," he said proudly. "She even likes *cachi* (persimmon)."

At 7:20 p.m., Gigi sharpened a large knife. He drained the jowl, head, and tongue, discarding the broth, which had an unpleasant animal flavour. After trimming a white membrane from the tongue, he sliced it into chunks and laid them on a huge platter. From the other pot, he tested the oxtail. Alas, it was still tough. They would eat it tomorrow. He forked out the *scaramella* and the *muscolo*, reserving the broth for our second course. He sliced those meats, too, arranging them on a separate platter. "If you don't use all the *scaramella*, you can make meatballs the next day," said Gigi. As his granddaughter beamed, he drilled his finger into his cheek and rattled off *his* grandparents' recipe. "Blend leftover meat with boiled potato, one raw egg, salt, Parmesan, parsley, and dry breadcrumbs. Mould into meatballs and fry. It's delicious. Beatrice loves these meatballs."

Unfortunately for his granddaughter, she didn't get to eat jowls with us. Just before eight, her mother showed up to take her and her brother home. On the dot, we sat down to dinner in the formal dining room. Just like at Maria Rosa's, there was no pretentiousness. The mustard was served directly out of the jar. The bread was in the paper bag it came in, the sides rolled down like cuffs on a pair of blue jeans. Antonella tied a paper napkin around the neck of the bottle of Barbera d'Asti, so the red wine didn't drip on her linen tablecloth. We drank water *and* wine out of sturdy IKEA tumblers, the same ones I had at home in Toronto.

With *bollito misto*, the meat is served first, followed by the broth. Some bits looked like gristle, others appeared as prickly as a cactus, but the mouth feel was luscious. A thick layer of gelatinous blubber from some part — the head? — tasted strangely comforting. The tongue was very tender, but I averted my eyes from the pinkish-grey, pimply texture, which looked just like a piece of someone's ... tongue. "This is a typical winter dish of Asti," said Antonella.

For our second course, Gigi had cooked tiny cheese-stuffed ravioli in the steaming, rich *bollito* broth. They were identical to the *ravioles* we'd eaten in the Drôme but here they were called *anolini* and made in Parma. "They take ten hours to make!" said Gigi, explaining why he had bought the ravioli instead of making it by hand. We sprinkled grated Parmesan over our bowls. I slurped up the broth, which was like liquid gold.

"*Fumare*," said Antonella, getting up from the table for a cigarette. The weather was too cold to open the living-room window, so she headed to the bathroom and closed the door. She returned with the still-warm strudel, which we ate with the lemon-zest gelato.

As we left, she gave us presents — for Sam, a jar of jelly made by her cousin; for me, a chic hat in turquoise and yellow she had crocheted herself. And then she gave me one of her antique linen dishtowels. It was hand-embroidered with a graceful *S* and *A*, after the name of her family's fabric shop, San Lorenzo Alessandro Tessuti.

CHAPTER TWENTY

Mirella's Pasta e Fagioli

The weather had suddenly turned warm. The almond tree beside our farmhouse balcony was in full bloom, creamy flowers bursting from stark brown branches. I was still coughing despite twice a day drinking warm milk mixed with the honey and bee pollen from Maria Rosa. Worse, I had passed my *tosse* to Federica and Mirella. They both blamed the weather, but they were being polite.

Cousin Mirella even invited us over to cook again, this time to teach us *pasta e fagioli*. When we arrived, Alessandro was in the winery, bottling Dolcetto, a light red wine made from one of the oldest strains of indigenous Piemonte black grapes. Upstairs, Mirella had organized ingredients as if she were the star of a television cooking show. The previous day she soaked dried red *cannellini* and *borlotti* (cranberry) beans. Overnight they had doubled in volume and she had already boiled them for twenty minutes. Sam diced an onion and pancetta, which Mirella sautéed in olive oil in a big soup pot. She added three cups of diced peeled potatoes, the drained beans, salt, freshly ground white pepper, a vegetable flavour concentrate, and *passata* that her mother, Luigina, had bottled the previous summer. Every ten minutes or so, Mirella added a ladleful of hot water to keep the soup from getting too thick.

For dessert, we were making a dark chocolate cake. Mirella rattled off the amounts of grated dark chocolate, sweetened cocoa powder, unsweetened cocoa powder, sugar, eggs, and butter. "It's the same proportions as the hazelnut cake," said Sam. "*Bravo!*" said Mirella, tossing everything into her Bimby.

Once the cake was finished, she ran the Bimby through a boil cycle, emptied it, and got to work on a spinach flan with *béchamel*, another Piemontese specialty, called *besciamella* in Italian. Squeezing out excess water from a mound of blanched spinach, she puréed it with salt, white pepper, five raw eggs, and a third of a cup of grated Parmesan. After a minute in the Bimby, it looked like a green milkshake. She poured the thick liquid into disposable aluminum cups, sprayed with aerosol olive oil, and set them in a *bagnomaria* to bake for half an hour. For the *béchamel*, she washed out the Bimby again then dumped in flour, butter, milk, and salt. She programmed the machine to cook for seven minutes at 90°C on a setting called "speed four." Then she added diced fontina and set it for twelve minutes at 80°C. Once the cheese melted, she poured in fresh cream and, finally, the yolks of two eggs. The Bimby would keep the sauce warm and smooth until it was time to serve the flan.

As we cooked, we talked about our favourite foods. Mirella and Sam bonded over tripe minestrone. We all loved calf's brains. Our recipes were identical (and classically French): poach brains in water sharpened with a bit of vinegar, pat dry, slice and dust with flour, and sauté in brown butter with capers. We were making cold, sliced, very rare veal, a close cousin of *carpaccio*. Mirella quickly browned the roast in butter and oil and finished it in a very hot oven for a scant five minutes to create an umami-rich crust. After chilling the meat for several hours, she used her professional meat slicer to slice it paper-thin. Wearing disposable plastic gloves, she arranged the ruby-red slices on a platter of arugula, chopped radicchio, and micro-greens.

Beppe was lighting a fire in the living room. The last time we were here, I'd assumed the fireplace was gas-fuelled and the artfully twisted logs were ceramic fakes. Now I realized he was using gnarled chunks of old vines. "What do you mean, 'Are these real?'" he said, laughing at me. "These are forty-five-year-old vines. They no longer produce grapes." Over the course of the evening, he would go through a bushel-sized basket of the sweet-smelling vines.

Mirella had invited Maria Rosa's family to dinner, too. Uncharacter-istically, Fiorenzo balked because he wanted to stay home to watch *calcio* (soccer). His favourite team, Juventus FC, was playing a key game against its fiercest rival, Torino FC. Both teams were from Turin because Italians were so passionate about the sport a single city could support two professional teams. The last thing Fiorenzo wanted on game day was a long and elaborate meal at his wife's cousin's house, especially as the wife's cousin's husband rooted for Torino FC. In the end, of course, Fiorenzo was dragooned into attending dinner. Beppe didn't have cable, so Alessandro hooked up a laptop, livestreaming the game from a sketchy website to the television screen in the living room. Occasionally the transmission froze in the middle of a crucial play, prompting wails and groans from the men.

In North America, the men would have filled their plates and eaten on the sofa. In Italy, that behaviour was unthinkable. There wasn't even an Italian equivalent for "couch potato." The closest insult was *teledipendente*, which had no undertone of eating. Seated at the formal dining table, Beppe and Fiorenzo ate their dark-green flans while darting agonized glances toward the living room. The *fontina-béchamel* sauce was so rich I had to stop eating after a few bites. Beppe poured us each a small glass of chilled Brichet Rosé Spumante Brut, a sparkling dry rosé made from Nebbiolo and Chardonnay grapes. When Mirella, Sam, and I headed back to the kitchen to finish the final steps for *pasta e fagioli*, Fiorenzo and Beppe took advantage of the lull to dash to the living room.

Mirella told us to cook the pasta for *pasta e fagioli* separately because boiling it in the soup risked scorching it. She used a tiny shell-shaped pasta called *gnocchetti sardi* made by Barilla, a privately held company in nearby Parma and the biggest pasta company in the world. I told Mirella we had that same brand in Canada. I didn't tell her I was boycotting it (along with many Italians) after the company's chairman, Guido Barilla, said he had "no respect for adoption by gay families because this concerns a person who is not able to choose." He later apologized, and the company has since scored a top rating on a list of LGBTQ-friendly employers.

To serve the soup, Mirella plunked the pot on the table and splashed on some of her own olive oil. Beppe and Fiorenzo reluctantly returned from the living room. We passed around a bowl of grated Parmesan as a garnish. *Pasta e fagioli* was creamy and thick, the beans tender and meaty, the pasta properly *al dente*, the tomato broth like a mouthful of summer. It was the perfect comfort food for my cough. I could have eaten two bowls, but several courses were still to come.

The men hurried back to the living room while we put the finishing touches on the cold sliced veal: fresh lemon juice, olive oil, balsamic vinegar, and salt. Beppe pried himself away from the game to pour a slightly chilled *Brichet Gioioso* (Joyful Hilltop), which he'd made a week earlier from blue-black Freisa grapes. He was happy because, with just fifty minutes left, the score was 1–0 for his team. Fiorenzo glumly ate a plate of veal, but I knew he hadn't tasted it. To change the topic, I asked Beppe if they always ate like this. "Always," he said, explaining to me the hallowed sequence of Italian fine dining. "*Sempre antipasto.*" Always antipasto. "Then pasta or soup. Then rabbit, turkey, roast pork, or fish. Then cheese. In the summer, we have a barbecue. We make steaks *alla fiorentina.*" He drilled his finger into his lower cheek. Mirella flamboyantly kissed her bunched fingertips.

"At lunch, there's not enough time, maybe only an hour, so maybe we don't have antipasto," Beppe continued. "We might have *pappardelle al sugo* or *polenta al formaggio.* We might have a big salad of oranges, anchovies from Abruzzo, artichokes, and onions. Then we might have salmon, or trout, or mussels, or *baccalà.*" Mirella said that in spring, when fresh sardines were available, she would stuff them with soft breadcrumbs and parsley, dip them in more breadcrumbs and bake them in the oven. Beppe and Fiorenzo returned to the living room while Mirella recited her recipe for *baccalà* from memory: soak the salt cod for three or four days; change the water frequently; drain and squeeze excess moisture; pan-fry with garlic, parsley, onions, tomatoes, and milk.

Fiorenzo returned to the table looking deeply upset. The soccer game had ended in a tie. Apparently, that was very bad news for Juventus. Chiara valiantly tried to explain it to me three times — something to do with jockeying for rankings, but I probably wouldn't have understood even in English. Apparently, a tie meant Torino FC moved up, which meant Beppe was happy and Fiorenzo was not.

The table was littered with wine bottles, but most were at least half full. Everyone had tasted the wine pairings, but no one had overdone it. For instance, although we were each served about two ounces of spumante, only Beppe and Fiorenzo finished theirs. Italians seemed to drink everything in moderation, even tisane. At the end of dinner, when Mirella made herbal tea, she served it, not in mugs or teacups, but in tiny shot glasses.

It was past ten. Chiara had school the next day. Beppe had to haul a load of nine hundred bottles to clients in Milan and Varese. Then he brought out another bottle, a Vigneti Brichet fortified red wine spiced with cardamom, vanilla, cinnamon, cloves, and the root of *calamo aromatico*, or sweet grass. "Good for your cough," said Beppe. "Sixteen percent alcohol."

I gulped down a shot and felt instantly better. Or drunk.

MIRELLA'S PASTA E FAGIOLI

Serves 6 as a soup, or 4 as a meal with cheese and crusty bread.

½ cup	dried white kidney beans, soaked overnight
½ cup	dried cranberry beans, soaked overnight
1	onion, diced
3-4 oz.	pancetta, diced
4 tbsp.	extra-virgin olive oil
3 cups	peeled potatoes, diced
1½ cups	*passata* (puréed/strained uncooked tomatoes)
1	Knorr flavour concentrate gel (optional)
½ tsp.	freshly ground white pepper
salt	to taste
1 cup	small-shell pasta

Soak beans overnight. Boil beans in unsalted water for 20 minutes. Drain. Set a pot of water to simmer on stove, replenishing as necessary. It should be large enough to cook a cup of shell pasta in at the end. In a larger pot, sauté onion and pancetta in 2 tbsp. olive oil over medium heat until onion is translucent. Add remaining ingredients, except for the pasta. Add 1 cup of boiling water. Keep soup on an energetic simmer for 45 minutes to 1 hour, adding a ladle of hot water whenever the soup gets too thick. Ten minutes before serving, salt the boiling water and cook the shell pasta. Drain, and add pasta to soup. Bring back to a rolling boil. Adjust for salt. Splash with remaining 2 tbsp. of olive oil.

Serve immediately with grated Parmesan and crusty bread.

CHAPTER TWENTY-ONE

Maria Stella's Spaghetti Carbonara

The generosity of strangers amazed me—people who only knew me as friends of friends of friends, like Maria Stella Puddu. She was an accountant at the hospital where Maria Rosa, Federica, Antonella, and Gigi worked. To teach us cooking, Maria Stella (pronounced Mari-stella) used two vacation days. She also pulled her daughter out of school to help translate. Why would she—or, for that matter, all the others—go to this trouble? Why would they let us invade their kitchens?

The answers were both simple and profound. Simply put, Italians were fiercely proud of their regional cuisine. This was a country where people still spoke in dialect and ate the food of their grandparents. But the more profound answer had to do with family. In atomized societies like Canada and the US, people moved from job to job, and from city to city. In Italy, people stayed close to home, literally. Antonella was living in her father's home, and so was Maria Rosa. Federica had swapped homes with her in-laws, and so had Mirella. In France and Italy, those who welcomed us into their homes all had children, sometimes adult children, with whom they ate dinner nightly. Everyone had kitchen tables that magically expanded to seat a dozen people. Social networks were robust. A friend of a friend was your friend, too, someone you would go out of your way to help.

Tourists experienced a different side of a country. Hospitality was in the cultural DNA of France and Italy, but tourism was, in the end, a flinty business. Tourists were a revenue stream and a nuisance, often simultaneously. When Sam and I subsequently went sightseeing in Bologna and Florence, we were bemused by the contrast. Waiters, taxi drivers, and ticket sellers at two museums all reflexively shortchanged us, or tried.

We'd met Maria Stella and her whole family when they came to dinner at Maria Rosa's. That was the night Maria Rosa had made the special *vitello tonnato*, and we'd made a mad dash in her Multipla to the butcher to have it professionally sliced. Maria Stella, a zaftig brunette, was fifty-seven, but she looked younger. She had dressed for the occasion with a flashy cocktail ring and a silk scarf. Her swarthy, lanky husband, Bruno Colaianni, who owned an autobody shop, was a man of few words, but very kind. One public holiday in August when absolutely no one worked, Bruno didn't hesitate to tow my British friend, Ashley, who was stranded on a flooded road.

The Puddu-Colaianni family lived on the upper floor of a modern duplex in suburban Asti. Like so many Italians, Maria Stella passionately loved cats. Her home was teeming with bric-a-brac, or rather, cat-a-brac — cat figurines, cat paintings, cat fridge magnets, cat calendars, and cat photographs. This rendered her incapable of understanding how anyone could be allergic to something so wonderful. When Sam and I started sneezing, she talked about shutting her pet cat in a bedroom but in the end simply couldn't bear to do it.

Likewise, equipment and food crammed her lime-green kitchen. When you opened a cupboard, items invariably fell out and crashed to the floor. (The brands were familiar: Illy coffee, De Cecco and Barilla pasta, and Kellogg's Corn Flakes.) Her Formica counters were cluttered with jars of flour and bottles of oil, spice racks, pots of salt and sugar, an unwieldy napkin holder, a giant crock for spatulas and spoons, and a huge earthen pot especially for minestrone. Three espresso pots of varying sizes occupied the rim of the sink's drain board. Despite the formal dining room, the family always ate in the kitchen, at a narrow table that could expand to seat ten. Maria Stella had installed in the cramped space the requisite sofa, where her daughter, Cristina, sat engrossed in her cellphone.

"*Gnocchi alla Romana*," Maria Stella proclaimed, getting out a bag of medium-coarse semolina. Gigi's version of gnocchi had been the familiar small dumplings made from potatoes. Maria Stella wanted to show us her mother's recipe, in which the gnocchi were large disks of semolina dough. Maria Stella was proudly from Sardinia, land of the prickly artichoke. Living in Piemonte, she was chronically homesick, and made trips whenever possible to the rocky, mountainous island in the Mediterranean next to Corsica. "There were only sheep. We were very poor."

When her back was turned, Sam whispered, "Everyone in Italy has the same name." We had met three Beppes and three Luigis (if you counted

Mirella's mother, Luigina). In France, we'd left behind Marie-Catherine and Pierre-Marie. Here, we were inundated with Marias. The full name of Maria Stella's daughter, Cristina, was Cristina Maria. And then there was, of course, the *bagnomaria* in every kitchen. I asked Maria Stella why every second female in Italy seemed to be named Maria. "For God's protection," she said.

For the first time, I had trouble communicating. Maria Stella spoke no English. Unlike the others, she refused, in the most good-natured way, to try to understand my rudimentary Italian. Before she even met us, she decided that the only solution was Cristina, who was learning English at her commerce-and-business *liceo*. But her awkward daughter was pathologically shy or sullen — it was hard to tell which. No matter how Maria Stella and I struggled, Cristina was as silent as a sphinx, her dark hair tumbling over her face like a protective shield. To prove we could manage, language-wise, I pointed to a brick of butter and said, *"Burro."* Maria Stella looked confused. *"Burro, burro,"* I repeated, pointing at the butter. Maria Stella wrinkled her forehead. She tilted her head sideways, as if that would help her hear me better. Baffled, she beseeched her daughter to help. Cristina ignored us. By now I was feeling like an idiot. *Burro* meant butter. What was the point of telling Maria Stella that butter was butter since it was *her* kitchen and *her* butter, *and* she already knew it was butter. I tried one more time. *Burro.* Comprehension lit up her face. "Aah, *bur-r-r-r-r-o*," she said, rolling her *r*'s like a manual lawnmower cutting grass. When she saw my embarrassment, she said kindly that she found English equally baffling. "Why does 'kitchen' sound like 'chicken'?" she asked (in Italian).

She heated some milk, added the *burro*, and when it melted, slowly mixed in semolina, spoonful by spoonful. When it thickened, she removed the pot from the heat and mixed in two egg yolks. Yes, she threw out the egg whites. Over the weeks of cooking in France and Italy, neither Sam nor I got used to how many egg whites were wasted. Maria Stella poured the thick batter onto parchment paper, smoothing it with the back of a wooden spoon until it was one inch thick. After it rested for ten minutes, she cut out circles with an oiled rim of a juice glass and layered the disks in overlapping slices in a baking pan, dotting each slice with butter. She finished with a thick shower of shredded fontina and grated *grana padano*. Once baked, the gnocchi looked like heavy, cheesy pancakes.

"*Finocchi gratinati,*" Maria Stella said, announcing our next dish. In fact, she was making two fennel dishes. In addition to fennel fritters for our dinner tonight, she was prepping fennel au gratin for our dinner the next day. Sam sliced up several pounds of fennel, which Maria Stella blanched, drained, and set to cool on her balcony, her backup refrigerator in winter because her kitchen space was so constricted. Sam then sliced up fat white leeks and rinsed the grit. (Leaving them whole made them impossible to clean, Maria Stella said.) She sautéed the leeks in olive oil and added ten cubes of bright-green frozen spinach. Apparently, that was also for the next day, when we would eat it two ways, in puff pastry and in calzone turnovers.

"*Ragù,*" she said. Traditional meat sauce. She set her huge earthenware minestrone pot over a diffuser on her gas stove and poured in a generous amount of extra-virgin olive oil, which she said was from "the uncle of a friend in Sicily." Next she added a single clove of garlic, two bay leaves, and half a pound of ground pork. "The trick is to cook it at low heat." Otherwise, she said, the minced meat would clump instead of blending smoothly into the sauce. She added a glug of red wine. "Nebbiolo, from the father of my son's girlfriend in Langhe." Finally, she added a tall jar of tomato *passata*—from Sardinia, of course—and a large pinch of salt. Meanwhile Cristina was still slouched on the couch, nose buried in her cellphone. Except for Chiara (and Gigi's unbearably cute granddaughter, Beatrice), neither Cristina nor any of the younger generation we met evinced the slightest interest in cooking.

"*Scaloppine di pollo al limone,*" said Maria Stella, announcing our fifth or sixth dish, chicken cutlets in lemon sauce. By now I'd lost track of how many courses we were eating that evening and what we were making for the next day. Home cooks everywhere multi-tasked multiple meals at a time. As one dish simmered, you prepared another. We floured pre-sliced chicken breasts from the supermarket and browned them in a bit of peanut oil, then splashed in white wine and an entire cup of fresh-squeezed lemon juice. The flour coating gradually thickened the sauce, to which she added salt. She simmered the cutlets about five minutes until the sauce had almost disappeared, leaving the essence of fresh lemon.

At 7:50 p.m., Bruno arrived home, and ducked his head into the kitchen. "*Buonasera,* good evening," he said formally before rushing off to wash the engine grease from his hands. They'd met after Maria Stella had moved to Asti, and they had two children, ten years apart. Matteo, twenty-eight, worked in Bruno's autobody shop and lived with his girlfriend in La Morra, half an hour away.

"*Frittelle di finocchi,*" she said, starting our next dish: fennel fritters. To make the batter, Maria Stella beat two yolks, tossing the whites down the drain. She was adding flour when Bruno suddenly reappeared. Startled, she accidentally dumped too much flour in the batter, threw her arms up in the air, and blamed him. She tried spooning out the excess flour. Then she tried thinning it with a bit of milk but added too much milk, so she added more flour. When the batter was as smooth and thick as whole-fat yogourt, she retrieved the blanched fennel from the porch. Dipping it in batter, she began frying small fritters in a non-stick pan.

"*Spaghetti carbonara,*" she said, announcing our next dish. I squealed. Maria Stella looked at me in alarm. I explained that it was one of my favourites, and now, finally, I was going to learn the secret. She beamed. Italians have written entire treatises on the origin of pasta with bacon and eggs, a dish invented no more than fifty years ago, but there was no consensus on who made it first, or how to make it. Whole eggs or yolks? I say whole, but that's only because I can't stand wasting the egg whites. (That pizzeria in Provence provided a yolk only.) Cream? No! Garlic? Yes! Just before we left Toronto, Sam and I had argued over whether to start *carbonara* with minced onions. Of course not, I said. Sam was equally adamant we should. (Being a loving and supportive mother, *I* prevailed.)

Now Maria Stella told Sam to chop two shallots. "I *told* you so," he said smugly. I pretended not to hear. She sautéed the shallots in olive oil in a wok, and when the onions were translucent, she added two-thirds of a pound of diced, salt-cured pancetta.

"Now you add garlic, right?" I said.

"No garlic!" she shouted.

I couldn't believe my ears. "Really? No garlic?"

"No garlic!" she repeated emphatically. "You only use garlic when you're making *aglio e olio*." That was another favourite of mine—spaghettini with garlic, olive oil, and crushed, dried chilies—the go-to dinner when my cupboard was bare. But I still couldn't believe she didn't use garlic in *carbonara*.

Maria Stella boiled a mid-sized pot of enthusiastically salted water. The spaghetti—De Cecco brand—didn't fit, so she pushed down errant strands with her fingers. Like everyone else, Maria Stella didn't worship at the cult of pasta. Why waste water, fuel, and time? Eight minutes later, she forked the dripping spaghetti directly into the wok of pancetta and onion. Pasta water was *carbonara*'s secret ingredient — the starch in the cooking liquid thinned the sauce, bound it to the pasta, and added flavour as well. At home I used to drain the pasta in a colander and always had to stick a measuring cup in the colander so I wouldn't absentmindedly toss out all the cooking water. Maria Stella's method was better. Somehow forking *al dente* pasta directly into the bacon resulted in exactly the right proportion of pasta water to pasta. And there was no colander or measuring cup to wash, either.

With the heat on very low, Maria Stella tossed the spaghetti in the bacon and onion. "No cream!" she said, wagging a finger at me. Okay, okay, we agreed on that one. *Carbonara*'s creamy taste was a sleight of hand, the magic alchemy of hot, starchy pasta water and raw eggs. In Italy, cream was expensive because cows required lots of land while chickens needed only a coop. In Italian restaurants in New York and Toronto, however, they scandalously dumped in cream, which to me (and Maria Stella) ruined the sauce.

"Now, one egg," she said. *One* egg? I was flabbergasted, horrified, shocked, and appalled. I always used about one egg per person. With seven of us, shouldn't we add half a dozen eggs? Maria Stella sighed. "Okay, *two* eggs." Sam chortled. She turned off the heat and mixed the hot pasta with two beaten eggs until each strand was coated. I asked, "Now cheese?"

"No cheese! No milk! No cream!" Maria Stella was practically shouting. For good measure, she repeated, "No garlic! No garlic!"

My head was spinning. My cookbooks at home, notably from renowned Italian chef Marcella Hazan, included lots of Romano *and* Parmesan cheeses. In fact, Hazan mixed the grated cheese in with the raw eggs before tossing it with the pasta. (Also, garlic. Just saying.)

Maria Stella ground black pepper over the pasta and scattered a few shards of frozen minced parsley. Like Mirella, she froze parsley the previous summer when the flavour was at its peak. Maria Stella gave the wok a final shake. *Carbonara* had to be eaten immediately because reheating would solidify the glistening sauce into unappetizing flecks of scrambled eggs. So now we were going to eat it, right? Wrong. We had to wait for Maria Stella's son and his girlfriend. Family came first in Italy, not *carbonara*. Perhaps I looked distraught. Sam shot me a look that said: *control yourself.* Bruno, sensing I was close to a meltdown, offered me an *aperitivo*: one small bottle of beer divided into three shot glasses for himself, Sam, and me.

Cristina had set the table, knives and forks to the right. Down the centre, directly on the tablecloth, she had piled little stacks of a crisp Sardinian flatbread called *carasau.* Also called *carta di musica* for its resemblance to the parchment paper upon which sacred music was written, it was made of olive oil, flour, and salt. *Carasau* was always baked twice; the second time, after it had been split into two separate sheets. Finally, Matteo and his partner, Giulia, arrived. We immediately sat down. The *carbonara* was still warm. It was the best I ever tasted in my life. Each strand was *al dente* and coated with the porky bacon and creamy egg. I inhaled my first bowl. I had seconds. I sighed with happiness. I didn't miss the garlic or cheese at all.

The lesson was not to be dogmatic in the kitchen. When I returned to Toronto, I repeated Maria Stella's recipe. Twice. It was not the same, and it was because of the ingredients. Her egg yolks were *il rosso* — mine were anemic. I bought vacuum packed, pre-diced pancetta (just as she had) but mine lacked porkiness. The second time, I bought a slab of "Pingue Sea Salt Preserved Air Dried" pancetta from an Italian grocery store. It was worse — tough and borderline rancid. I emailed Maria Stella and confessed my failures. She advised me to soak the pancetta in olive oil to soften it before cooking. In the meantime, I reverted to my own tried and true recipe. No onions! Yes garlic! One egg per person! Cheese! And here's *my* secret to working with pallid North American ingredients: half a clove of finely minced *raw garlic*. Toss it into the hot *carbonara* at the same time you add the beaten eggs. The residual heat will mute the sting of the garlic but leave its essential flavour.

Please don't tell Maria Stella.

SPAGHETTI CARBONARA ALLA MARIA STELLA
Serves 4.

2	shallots, minced
¼ cup	olive oil
⅓ lb.	pancetta, diced
1 lb.	dry spaghetti

1   egg, beaten
sea salt to taste, and for the pasta water
freshly ground black pepper
Optional garnish: ½ tsp. minced parsley

Sauté shallots in oil in a wok over low heat. Add pancetta. No garlic! Fry over medium heat. Boil spaghetti in a separate pot of salted water. Using pasta fork, transfer dripping spaghetti directly into wok. Turn heat to low. Add egg. Toss. Add sea salt to taste, freshly ground black pepper, and, if you wish, some minced parsley.

SPAGHETTI CARBONARA – JAN'S VERSION (WITH NORTH AMERICAN INGREDIENTS)
Serves 4.

⅓ lb.   pancetta, diced
¼ cup   olive oil
1   clove garlic, finely minced
1 lb.   dry spaghetti
3   eggs at room temperature, beaten
sea salt to taste, and for pasta water
½ cup   freshly grated Parmesan
½ cup   freshly grated Romano
freshly ground black pepper
optional: ½ tsp. minced parsley

Sauté pancetta in olive oil in a wok over medium heat. When the pancetta is almost crisp, add two-thirds of the minced garlic and turn off heat. Boil spaghetti in a separate pot of salted water. Using a pasta fork, transfer dripping *al dente* spaghetti into the warm pancetta. Turn heat under wok to very low. Toss with remaining minced garlic, salt, beaten eggs, and grated Parmesan and Romano. Garnish with freshly ground black pepper and, if you wish, minced parsley.

The next morning, Maria Stella (and Cristina) picked us up at the only place she was familiar with in Repergo, Maria Rosa's house. That should have clued us in. "GPS?" she asked. Nope, we shook our heads cheerfully. We'd left it back at the farmhouse. Why would we need it? After all, *she* was driving to the organic winery in La Morra where Giulia, Matteo's partner, worked. Maria Stella would know the way. At least, that's how we understood it. Maria Stella smiled. Meanwhile, Cristina was being her usual uncommunicative self.

La Morra was only a half hour away. The narrow highway from Repergo was clogged with trucks. A kerchiefed old woman laboriously pedalled her bicycle so slowly I thought she would tip over as five young spandex-clad cyclists whizzed past her. Maria Stella drove her Renault like a race-car driver; she slowed for no one, tailgating cars and trucks alike. On blind curves her sole safety measure was honking. Sam, I was gratified to see, was petrified. At home the way he drove had been a constant irritant in our relationship. Now watching his eyes widen and eyebrows lift, I understood that he was, after all, not *that* irresponsible a driver.

Eventually, I realized Maria Stella was lost. The clue came when she went around a traffic circle several times while begging the unresponsive Cristina to say which of the three exits to take. I glanced at the back seat where she was hunched over her cellphone. Was her map data streaming too slowly? Was she too busy texting friends? Or was she merely locked in her mute phase? *Maria Santa*, Maria Stella muttered. *Holy Mary.* That was the closest approximation to swearing a nice person like her could muster. Or perhaps she was praying for God's protection. On our third time around, she took a random exit, drove for a while, then turned around, and came right back to the same place. Many Italians, I realized, didn't travel far from home. Chiara, for instance, had never been to Barolo, one of Italy's most famous wine regions, only an hour from Repergo. I also realized that we were *such* a nuisance. Not only was gasoline twice as expensive as at home, not only had Maria Stella taken a second vacation day on our behalf, not only had she asked her daughter to skip another day of school to translate (even though she wouldn't), but now Maria Stella was trying to drive us to a winery she couldn't find. And I had been too dumb to understand we were supposed to bring our GPS.

Maria Stella roared through Bra, epicentre of the Slow Food movement.

In Alba, we passed *supermercato* after *supermercato*. Gradually I sussed out the day's program. First, we would visit the winery where Giulia worked. Then we would return to Asti in time to make lunch for Bruno and Matteo. In Italy, everyone who could possibly make it home for lunch went home to *casa della mamma*. Giulia, for instance, regularly ate lunch at her parents' home (and dinner at Maria Stella's). Those who couldn't make it home, like Fiorenzo, had their wives pack small suitcases with elaborate home-style meals to take to work.

Our first stop was Giulia's parents' home so her mother could show us the way to the winery. Gradually I understood that Maria Stella had been to Giulia's parents' home only once before, and couldn't quite remember the route. After nearly two hours of hard driving on a trip that should have taken thirty-five minutes, we barrelled up a steep hill and down a narrow winding road. With a sigh of relief, Maria Stella stopped outside a gated property and made a call on her cellphone. The remote-controlled iron gates swung slowly open.

As we got out of the car, she switched from flat driving shoes into very high heels. She had dressed beautifully for the visit — red lipstick, chic black pants with a flowing black sweater, a crisp white shirt, and a silver and black polka-dotted scarf artfully arranged around her neck. Like many Italian women, she took great care with her appearance. Her jewellery matched her outfits. She twisted her dark brown hair into an elegant chignon. She dieted.

Giulia's mother came out to greet us. She, too, was impeccably dressed in pressed grey trousers and a simple black sweater, her dark hair freshly coiffed. In the New World, people wore sweat pants and flip-flops at home. In the Old World, they dressed as if for a party. Of course her name was Maria, too. Maria Lucia hugged and kissed Maria Stella and Cristina Maria on both cheeks. With Sam and me, she formally shook hands.

"*Caffè?*" she inquired politely.

"No, thank you," said Sam.

I'd tried to teach my son to be polite, but at this moment I glared at him, poked his elbow, and said to Maria Lucia, "*Sì, un caffè, per favore.*" I knew Maria Stella could certainly use a coffee break. More to the point, I was dying to see the villa, which appeared to be more than a century old and was surrounded by lavender bushes and oleander trees. Maria Lucia showed us the grounds first. In a five-arched hayloft, she raised hens and, until 1988, dairy cattle. The loft housed a garage with four bays for vine-yard equipment. To one side was her large *cantina*. She gestured to a wicker basket of lemons on the counter. "Do you want some?" she asked. "They are our own."

She pointed out her salami press and pasta board. She had a huge red rolling machine for pasta and an industrial-sized dough mixer. She showed me her noodles drying in a wooden crate. When I oohed and aahed, she looked at me as though I were a little *pazza* (crazy). "We're in the *country-side*," she said. "Of course, we make our own pasta." A wood-fired stone oven looked medieval but had a modern temperature gauge. Maria Lucia told me she baked her own bread there, a dozen loaves at a time, which she would then freeze for use throughout the week.

The yellow and grey stucco villa was an imposing two storeys, with dark shutters and a roof of terracotta tiles. Just below the roofline, someone had painted garlands of flowers in ochre and dark grey that reminded me of ancient homes in the ruins of Pompeii. Maria Lucia led us up the stone steps, through a heavy wooden door, and past several rooms filled with heavy antique furniture. Electricity was only installed in 1955. The formal salon had a lacquered piano with built-in candle holders so the pianist could read the music at night. The house seemed to go on and on. She and her husband lived only on the main floor — they had shut down both the upper floor and lower level.

Maria Lucia told us that a wealthy family from Turin, connected to the Lancia automobile fortune, had built the villa as a summer estate for their three daughters in the early twentieth century. Her father-in-law and three of his brothers bought the property from the three sisters in 1967. The brothers started a winery, producing Barolo and Barbaresco vintages, two of Italy's greatest wines. UNESCO had recently designated the region's vineyard landscape a World Heritage Site, an honour that Beppe coveted because it pushed property values into the stratosphere. Chinese investors were buying up Italian (and French) vineyards. Cutthroat competition wasn't new, however. People in La Morra remembered a time when the penalties for illegally chopping down a Nebbiolo vine ranged from a fine to amputating a hand to hanging.

Maria Lucia led us into her large eat-in kitchen. A *flan* of Jerusalem artichokes was baking in her 1930s white-enamelled stove, fuelled by a blaze of hazelnut wood and Nebbiolo vine cuttings. On top of the stove simmered a red enamel pot of *vitello bollito*. Her other stove was a professional two-oven, six-burner, stainless-steel model. Her kitchen table could seat eight without even adding leaves. She had been expecting us for coffee. There were plates of homemade prune crostata and *dolci di carnevale*, deep-fried strips of dough sprinkled with icing sugar, traditionally eaten before Lent. We drank espresso and enjoyed the view of vineyards and soft green hills. Her floor-to-ceiling curtains of floral damask, tied back with matching yellow and pale blue braided silk, would not have been out of place in a formal living room. And yes, alongside the table was the requisite sofa.

With Maria Lucia as our guide, we headed to Erbaluna, the organic winery in La Morra where her daughter worked. Giulia had set up a tasting of Barolo, Dolcetto, Nebbiolo, and Barbera wines. She also showed us the cellar filled with gigantic oak casks twice as tall as we were. Teetering in her high heels, Maria Stella tripped on a step and crashed into a flimsy rack holding the stained, dusty bottles of the winery's best reserve Barolo. The rack held, she didn't twist an ankle, and we all breathed a sigh of relief, especially Sam (who dreaded having to drive back to Asti with Cristina as the non-navigator).

By then, it was nearly one, too late to get back to Asti to make lunch for Bruno and Matteo. "Have lunch here," said Maria Lucia. This time Sam knew not to demur. So how did a fifty-eight-year-old woman in rural Italy pull together a last-minute lunch for four extra visitors? It didn't hurt to bake your own bread, operate your own greenhouse, or own your own winery. The fire in the wood stove had died while we were out. Happily, Maria Lucia's husband had just returned home from the physiotherapist, where he'd been treated for a sore shoulder. He was impeccably dressed — crisp shirt and spotless dark-green corduroy trousers — as if he'd been expecting guests. Italian men, like Italian women, cared about *la bella figura* — "cutting a beautiful figure." In fact, he *wasn't* expecting guests. He looked surprised but obeyed in silence when his wife told him to relight the stove. Then he heard we were learning home cooking and brought out a loaf of her homemade bread. "Water, flour, salt, yeast," he said, adding in English, "stop."

Of course his name was Beppe. At sixty-one, he was handsome, with a fringe of grey hair and a strong profile like one of the marble busts of

Roman emperors in the Vatican Museum. And like Mirella's Beppe, his fingers were stained purple from winemaking. Next he set out two kinds of salami made by his brother, a farmer, who lived further up the hill. One was *crudo*, the other air-dried. "He uses only the best parts of the pig," said Beppe, as he sliced up the meats.

When Giulia arrived on her ninety-minute lunch break, we all sat down at the long table. We started with Maria Lucia's freshly baked *flan* of Jerusalem artichoke, served with a *fonduta* of fontina, high-fat whipping cream, and two yolks from her own eggs. (Yes, she threw out the egg whites.) Beppe opened a bottle of his own red wine, Dolcetto d'Alba 2015, which we drank from tumblers. He said it was so light he usually drank half a litre a day. For the pasta, we ate Maria Lucia's fresh homemade whole-wheat tagliatelle, which cooked in an instant. She served it dressed with butter, a splash of extra-virgin olive oil, and grated Parmesan. Everyone twirled the pasta neatly on forks. Beppe fed a few strands to his dog, Dina, short for *Dinamite* (Dynamite). "You should taste this with white truffles," he sighed. As we ate, Maria Lucia recited her recipe for pasta: "*Semolina dura*, 00 whole-wheat flour, egg yolks, salt."

For *il secondo*, in fact our third course (fourth if you counted the salami we had munched on at the start), Maria Lucia brought over the pot of *vitello bollito*—boiled veal—that had simmered all morning on the woodstove. For *contorno*, she served green beans from her garden, frozen from the previous summer. "We need ketchup," said Beppe. I shuddered, but he was talking about his *homemade* ketchup, stored in his cellar. Giulia got up to fetch it. Beppe opened the jar, tasted it, and nodded, "*È buono.*" And it *was* good, like a salsa that tasted of the sun. It went perfectly with the tender poached veal that, *naturalmente*, came from an uncle who bought sides of beef and butchered them himself.

Sam sopped up the *vitello bollito* with chunks of Maria Lucia's homemade bread. "*Scarpetta*," he said. Maria Lucia and Maria Stella both beamed. *Fare la scarpetta*—"making a little shoe"—meant using a small piece of bread to scoop up the last bit of sauce on your plate.

After the veal, we had a salad of lamb's lettuce and radicchio from Maria Lucia's greenhouse. Then we had two kinds of *tuma* (Piemontese dialect for *toma*), soft fresh cheeses that were a teenaged version of *pecorino* before salt was added and it was aged. Except for the cheeses, Beppe and his wife (and his brother and uncle) had made everything we ate and drank at lunch. He suddenly looked up. Speaking in Piemonte dialect, which I could sometimes understand because it was so close to French, he addressed his wife, "Who are these people and why are they eating lunch in my house?"

After an awkward pause, someone explained that Sam and I were friends of friends of friends of his daughter's not-yet mother-in-law. I added that I was writing a book about home cooking in France, Italy, and China, and that Sam wanted to be a cook. Beppe thought about that a moment and excused himself. He returned with a dusty bottle of Barolo from his winery. "For you," he said, smiling. I asked if he would autograph the bottle. He did. Maria Lucia gave us a loaf of her homemade bread.

As I sat there, fighting a food coma, I asked more questions about the house and surrounding property. As Beppe answered, it became clear that Giulia had never heard the story before. Beppe's father was one of the four brothers who had purchased the property from the Lancia sisters—and the only one of the brothers to have sons—namely Beppe and his brother.

As the oldest male in the next generation, Beppe eventually inherited the house and vineyard. His younger brother—the salami-making farmer—moved farther up the hill.

Beppe and Maria Lucia had two daughters and no sons. But times had changed. Giulia, twenty-seven, was learning the family business at someone else's winery. Their older daughter, Eleonora, thirty-three, was a chef. Beppe showed me photographs of her wedding; her bridal bouquet had consisted of red roses, fresh rosemary, sage, chili peppers, and glossy bay leaves. She and her husband worked at Bovio, a well-respected local restaurant with a thousand-bottle wine list. Eleonora's specialty was fresh pasta—her husband, also a chef, could cook everything else. The plan was obvious. One day the two sisters would inherit the villa, take over the winery, and transform the property into a hotel and Michelin-starred restaurant with a million-euro view. You heard it here first.

For dessert, Maria Lucia opened a big jar of her preserved peaches from their garden. We ate it with *amaretti* and chocolates. The phone rang. Giulia looked at her watch. It was three p.m. "Telemarketers," she said. "They always call right after lunch."

Giulia took the rest of the day off to show us another organic winery, which also distilled grappa. Originally the drink of poor farmers in Piemonte, the clear, 80- to 90-proof liquor was made from grape seeds, skins, and stems. Giulia had arranged a grappa tasting, which made me marvel that Italians could accomplish anything after a morning *caffè corretto*, espresso "corrected" with firewater. After a lot of grappa tasting, which Maria Stella, our designated driver, scrupulously avoided, we parted ways with Giulia and her folks.

After an uneventful thirty-five-minute drive back to Asti, we staggered up the stairs to Maria Stella's duplex. That's when the third part of our day's plan became clear. In less than one hour, we had to throw together a dinner party for ten. Giulia would attend with Matteo. Maria Rosa and her family were coming, too. I should have skipped the grappa.

Now I understood why Maria Stella had done so much cooking ahead of time. But the cluttered kitchen was a disaster. When we hadn't made it back to cook lunch, Bruno and Matteo had scrounged their own lunch, leaving dirty dishes and pots on the stove and in the sink. Worse, they ate half the spinach-leek mixture we'd made the day before. We no longer had enough to make the puffed pastry dish *and* the calzone. Sam began washing the dirty dishes. "*Esperto*," I told Maria Stella. *Expert.*

"*Girasole*," she said, naming our first dish, a torte of puff pastry stuffed with what remained of our pillaged spinach and leeks. It had nothing to with *girasole*—sunflowers—except that it *looked* like one, if we folded the phyllo just so. Instead of calzone, we would supplement the *girasole* with leftover fennel fritters from the previous day. To the ragù in the minestrone pot, she added fennel seeds, dried chilies, and a generous splash of extra-virgin olive oil. She set a pot of water to boil. When the guests came, she explained, we would cook three boxes of Barilla brand *gnocchetti sardi*, which originated from her home island of Sardinia. (They were the same tiny shells Mirella had used for *pasta e fagioli*.)

Sam, having washed all the dishes, began peeling and dicing potatoes at top speed. Our main course was Sardinian sausages and potatoes simmered in Nebbiolo and turmeric. Giulia arrived and immediately pitched in. Cristina, who had been sitting on the couch and texting friends, finally roused herself to set the table and put out extra chairs. She set out more *carta di musica* flatbread and the homemade bread we'd just received from Maria Lucia. Bruno and Matteo arrived home from the autobody shop at 7:50 p.m. Maria Rosa, Fiorenzo, and Chiara arrived promptly at eight.

We'd done it—a four-course dinner for ten in less than an hour. Bruno served tiny glasses of Sardinian red wine. Three men—Bruno, Matteo, and Sam—barely finished two little bottles of beer among them. For dessert,

I opened a jar of cherries in grappa I'd bought that afternoon from the distillery. Without ado, we passed around the jar and everyone dug in, once, with a clean spoon. Except for Matteo. He liked the grappa-soaked cherries so much he triple-dipped until Giulia glared at him, and Sam started laughing.

CHAPTER TWENTY-TWO

A Cultural Revolution

Chiara's teacher invited me to speak about China's Cultural Revolution. Asti's only high school occupied a yellow nineteenth-century edifice, close to the ruins of the medieval city wall. Liceo Classico Vittorio Alfieri had been designed in the imposing classical style, with soaring pilasters, a palazzo-style stone staircase, and sixteen-foot-high ceilings. But like so many public buildings in Italy, it was deteriorating because of a lack of funds. The building looked like it hadn't been renovated since it was built in 1840, when Piemonte spearheaded a nationalist revolt against Austrian rule.

The night before my talk, a torrential rain had flooded parts of the school. On the third and uppermost floor, the ceiling collapsed in the hallway and in at least one classroom. "There is no money for repairs," Chiara said. Or for janitors. The halls looked like they hadn't been swept in months. The cream paint was peeling. The classroom where I spoke lacked even a blackboard, unless you counted the dusty doormat-sized rectangle of slate on the wall. I found a crumb of chalk with which to scratch a few dates and names.

Tax evasion had destroyed public education. Like every state sector in Italy, schools were underfunded and teachers underpaid. With no revenue, the competitive examinations for new hires, normally held every three years, had been discontinued for thirteen years. When the tests finally resumed in 2012, more than 321,000 hopefuls applied for just 11,500 openings. The average age of candidates was thirty-eight.

The classics teacher who invited me to speak moonlighted as a DJ at a local radio station to make ends meet. Despite forty-three years of experience, he earned less than $30,000 a year, which was average for Italy. A short, harried chain-smoker, he introduced me to his class and promptly disappeared. I was a bit nervous presenting to a class that wasn't used to hearing English, but I got the students' attention when I told them their Chinese counterparts had shut down schools, beaten teachers, and flushed exam results down the toilet. During the Cultural Revolution, I explained, the personality cult of Chairman Mao later forced urban youth into the countryside to toil beside the peasants. I spoke slowly in English, repeated myself twice, and threw in any Italian vocabulary I could muster. When their eyes fogged over with incomprehension, I found a simpler way to express myself. Always, one or two students would understand and translate for the others.

After the *liceo*, I had originally planned to hit Dietro l'Angolo for a lunch of fresh pasta. Then I thought, just as Sam and I had sampled pizza in Provence, it might be fun to try French food in Italy. When I Googled "French restaurants in Asti," Trip Advisor replied, "Sorry, we couldn't find any restaurants that match your search." Instead, half a dozen Chinese restaurants popped up, including Federica's favourite, Hai Ou. When I first started travelling to Italy in the 1960s, the *only* restaurants were Italian. That monoculture persisted for the virtually the entire twentieth century, with the addition of kebab counters in major cities. Now, with globalization, Italy was becoming Sinicized. The influx of Chinese migrants has been described by Canadian journalist Suzanne Ma in her book *Meet Me in Venice: A Chinese Immigrant's Journey from the Far East to the Faraway West*. In spite of the Italian cult of *caffè*, Chinese migrants were finding work as baristas and, in the economic downturn of 2008, had even bought out struggling Italian bar owners. More than fifty thousand Chinese workers were toiling in five thousand Chinese-owned clothing factories in Prato, the largest concentration of Chinese factories in Europe. Less than a century earlier, this suburb of Florence processed the hides of Tuscan cows for Italy's famed leather trade. Now the workers and factory owners came from China, and their products—garments, handbags, and gloves—were truthfully labelled "Made in Italy."

Like the locals, many Chinese factory owners evaded tax authorities by opening, closing, and reopening their businesses under new names. Italian landlords who, like Matteo's in Rome, asked for rent in cash, aided and abetted them. Two-thirds of the migrant workers arrived on three-month tourist visas, toiling up to fourteen hours a day and leaving when they saved enough to start their own businesses back in China. Like sweatshops everywhere, there were fires and accidents, and workers died. There were riots and clashes, too, not against the Chinese bosses, but against Italian inspectors and police. Calling the situation "unacceptable," a municipal politician alleged that unpaid taxes amounted to one billion euros each year, a charge that failed to inflame sensibilities. After all, Italians weren't paying taxes either.

In Prato, a city of 195,000 people, one in four residents was Chinese. Sleepy Repergo, only four hours away by car, had not yet felt any impact. But Asti, the closest city to Repergo, was already experiencing a culinary change. Hai Ou, the restaurant Federica had recommended, was conveniently located one cobblestoned block from the *liceo,* not far from the *Torre Rossa,* an eleventh-century tower. After my talk, I invited Chiara, Cristina, and Maria Rosa for lunch. (Mirella, Federica, and Maria Stella had to work.) Hai Ou, which means "the seagull," occupied an airy, modern two-storey building. There were no red-and-gold lanterns, no one was using chopsticks, and everyone drank mineral water, not tea. I ordered nine dishes from the bilingual Italian-Chinese menu. Only two were duds, a botched kung pao chicken and a *fritti misti* (deep-fried seafood). The rest would have passed muster in China. The heat of the hot and sour soup correctly came from white pepper, not from bottled chili sauce; the sweet-and-sour pork was crisp and tart; the mung-bean vermicelli had been sautéed with a touch of soy sauce; the roast duck was greaseless; the jumbo shrimp had been braised with heads on (to demonstrate their freshness); the stir-fried Shanghai bok choy was bright green; the rice was properly long-grained jasmine. Then Cristina drenched her steamed rice with soy sauce. Chinese Food Rule: *never pour soy sauce on your rice. (In fact, never pour it on anything; it's an ingredient for cooking or, at most, dipping.)*

In Canada, I normally needed a Chinese fix once a week. But during our cook's tour of France and Italy, I now realized I hadn't missed Chinese food at all. When a nation's food is complex and varied, you don't grow tired of eating it. France took a century to absorb the ideas of Catherine de' Medici. Now, in a decade or less, Chinese migrants were transforming the restaurant scene in Italy. Come to think of it, that's how Chinese food came to Canada—with migrant gold miners and railroad workers trying to eke out a living.

When the bill came, I discovered the waitress had given me a 5-percent discount. "Because you're Chinese," she said. At the cash, I chatted in

Mandarin with the owner. She was in her early forties, slim and well-dressed, with a genuine Louis Vuitton designer bag stashed on the counter behind her. She said she was surnamed Zhu, and had arrived twenty years earlier from Qingtian, Zhejiang, the fountainhead for Chinese migration to Europe. She returned to China once a year. And what was her long-term plan? "I don't like China. I like Italy," she said. "I will stay here."

On our last Sunday in Repergo, I decided to check out Mass at the village church. The morning was overcast, with heavy gun-metal-grey clouds. In the distance, I could see a dusting of white on the hilltops. A rare snowfall had hit Alba overnight. I walked down the curved road, past a few houses where no one was stirring, past the long-defunct tobacco store. The little church was locked up tight. I knocked on a door. Silence. No sign indicated the hour for Sunday services.

Trudging back up the hill to our farmhouse, I noticed that the iron gates to L'Isola della Carne were wide open. I knew that Maria Rosa had ordered some veal for our Sunday lunch. Perhaps I could pick up the meat for her *and* ask what time was Mass. The store itself was closed, but as soon as I stepped into the parking lot, an elderly man came outside. He politely said the butcher shop was closed. I tried to explain I wanted to pick up Maria Rosa's meat order. He didn't understand. I tried again. And again. Then I gave up and asked, "What time is Mass at the church?" Now he looked thoroughly confused. Did I want meat or Mass? Finally he told me: Mass was at three p.m.

Sam and I arrived at Maria Rosa's shortly past noon. I had finally recovered from my *tosse*, but now she and Chiara were coughing, and Nonno's nose was running. When I abjectly apologized, they again blamed the weather. And then Maria Rosa gave me a box gorgeously wrapped with flowered paper and a wide orange grosgrain ribbon. Italians were preternaturally talented at creating beauty. In the land of Michelangelo, *la bella figura* indelibly shaped the psyche. Everyone dressed with care, all the women, including fishmongers, were elegantly coiffed, and no one casually tossed a present into a dollar-store gift bag with a pouf of matching tissue on top.

I opened the gift. It was a gleaming white-enamelled Bialetti *moka*, the best stovetop espresso maker in Italy. Maria Rosa said it was for Norman, a six-cup pot, because she had heard that North Americans drank vast amounts of coffee. She told me it would work on any stove—gas, electric, ceramic, even an induction cooktop. She pointed out its heat-proof silicone-coated handle. Her own *moka* pots were battered aluminum with handles that got dangerously hot.

Why *was* she so nice to us?

On this adventure, I had envisioned paying a lump sum to the families for their trouble, plus groceries, gas, and assorted expenses. Ben had told the Jeanselmes that Sam and I would stay in a nearby hotel and rent a car. Marie-Catherine insisted we stay with her. She said a car was unnecessary— we could borrow hers as needed. She tried to stop us from paying for anything at all, forcing Sam and me to carefully plot how to grab the bills in restaurants. We did manage to buy groceries, but only because she was so busy. Even Davit, an undocumented migrant with no steady income, steadfastly refused to let me fill up his car with gas. And when it came time to leave, Marie-Catherine and François refused to accept any payment. Ultimately, they allowed me to donate to their refugee cause, but then they loaded me down with gifts.

Like the Jeanselmes, Maria Rosa and Fiorenzo adamantly refused to accept any money. Mirella also refused, but at least I was renting her farmhouse. The most awkward situation was with Maria Rosa's hospital colleagues. Here, she was no help at all. She told me she wasn't getting involved and to settle directly with them. I chewed the problem over with Sam. It was as though strangers had invited me to a dinner party because I was a friend of a friend of a friend, and on the way out I had to figure out how much to pay, and how to hand the cash over without insulting them. In fact, it wasn't *like* that. It was *exactly* that.

Flummoxed, I emailed my friend, Ashley. As a former diplomat, I reasoned, he ought to have a solution. He figuratively threw his hands in the air and passed me onto his Italian-born wife, Silvia, who suggested I could buy Maria Rosa a trendy Italian-designed O bag, because Maria Rosa had once bought one for *Silvia*. That wasn't remotely adequate, yet the only way I even convinced Maria Rosa to accept an O bag at all was by saying it was for Chiara (a dirty trick because I lured them *both* to the purse store and, naturally, the seventeen-year-old instantly swooned). To convince Maria Rosa the bag was not expensive at all, I airily bought a second one for myself (which I never use). Of course, then Maria Rosa then went out and bought me *la moka*, saying it was for Norman.

As for Maria Rosa's friends, even Silvia had no idea what to do. So, stammering and perspiring and blushing, I asked each one—Federica, Antonella, and Maria Stella — to estimate what they had spent on groceries, and then I named an additional sum for their time and trouble. They always smiled and said nothing, so I can only hope the second amount was adequate. I told them I would leave the euros on their bedside tables, which, in hindsight, was a bit odd. But it worked, sort of. When we left, they, too, plied Sam and me with gifts of honey, preserves, wine, and liqueurs.

On our last day in Repergo, Maria Rosa invited eleven people for Sunday lunch. Papa Franco was coming, as was Maria Stella and her family. Nonno wanted to invite Luigina but got shot down because we were already too crowded. Sam and I were now familiar enough with Piemonte specialties that we could have prepared the lunch ourselves. For an antipasto of roasted peppers with *tonnato* sauce, the yellow peppers had already been roasted. Sam drained a can of tuna packed in olive oil, and threw it into a blender with parsley, two hard-boiled eggs, a heaping teaspoon of capers, and mayonnaise. Done. We sautéed *salsiccia*, the same sausage we had sampled raw at L'Isola della Carne. After browning it with onion, garlic, and rosemary, we added a jar of *passata*. Sam suggested adding some dried porcini, but Maria Rosa nixed that because Maria Stella disliked mushrooms. With the sausage, we were serving polenta. But because Bruno wasn't a fan of polenta, Maria Rosa was making a second *secondo*, *spezzatino di vitello*, veal stew with potatoes.

Her technique for making polenta was refreshingly unlike Federica's. "You just boil water and put in the cornmeal," Maria Rosa said, sounding confused when I asked her how she made it. How much water? She shrugged. How much cornmeal? "I don't know how much to make for ten," she said, looking vague. How long? "About an hour."

Papa Franco arrived first, followed punctually by Maria Stella and her family. Today she had outdone herself: green chandelier earrings, a flamboyant green cocktail ring, and a sparkly necklace matching a turquoise and green silk scarf that set off her luxuriant dark hair. We sat comfortably around an aggregated table, joined seamlessly by a pale beige tablecloth. In Italy, entertaining friends was about food, not staging your table to look like a fancy restaurant's. Instead of a centrepiece of fresh flowers, there was a big pickle jar filled with salt, a litre bottle of extra-virgin olive oil, plastic bottles of flat and sparkling mineral water, and *grissini* in their original cellophane packaging. Maria Rosa plunked the pots and pans directly on the table, without trivets. We used the same plates for different courses.

The antipasto of *peperoni al tonno* would have been more than sufficient for lunch in Toronto. In Repergo, we were just getting started. Maria Stella had brought two bottles of wine. With the antipasto, we drank a lemony Sardinian white, Vermentino di Sardegna 2014. Then we opened a popular red called Cannonau di Sardegna, made from Grenache grapes aged two years in oak. With the molten polenta, Maria Rosa passed a cheese platter containing a blue-veined Gorgonzola *dolce*, a fontina, a fresh *toma*, and a *stracchino*, a creamy, rindless cow's milk cheese from Piemonte that is eaten very young. The same cheese platter would have cost a hundred dollars in Canada. In Italy it wasn't cheap either, but food, not centrepieces, mattered. Everyone cut generous slabs to melt over their polenta. For good measure, we also passed around grated Parmesan, straight out of a bag from the supermarket. Just as there was no cult of pasta, there was no cult of freshly grated cheese. Pre-grated was fine, as long as it was genuine Parmigiano-Reggiano from Emilia-Romagna. Just as a good meal had reminded Marie-Catherine of her simple childhood lunches at the tenant farmer's house, Nonno recalled how hungry Italians had been during the war. "We would have half of a fried anchovy each, just for the flavour," he said.

After we started our third bottle of wine, a Montesanto Chianti, Fiorenzo began to perform tricks. He could close his right eye without moving any other muscle on his face (which is much harder than it sounds). Chiara loudly mocked him and waved her arms. Maria Rosa rolled her eyes. Only Sam was appreciative. It must be a guy thing. Not to be outdone, my son showed off his own trick of folding the tip of his tongue into a flower.

We passed a bowl of oranges, kiwis, and bananas. Maria Stella had brought two golden trays of Piemontese desserts from her favourite *pasticceria*. Wrapped like jewels in pale grey tissue paper and tied with grosgrain ribbon, the trays contained one hundred and ten exquisitely made miniature *bignole*. (Yes, I counted them and calculated we each could have twelve pieces — that's what happens when you grow up in a house with four siblings.) *Bignole* were bite-sized *choux* pastries stuffed with cream and custard, reminiscent in taste and elegance of the wheel-shaped *Paris-Brest* dessert at Kéti's one-month celebration. Indeed, *choux* pastry had been invented in France in 1540 by a Tuscan chef named Pantarelli, who accompanied Catherine di' Medici to Paris. In the eighteenth century, the House of Savoy subsequently urged Piemontese confectioners to experiment with *choux* techniques and even established a university in Piemonte for the art of *pasticceria*. And while the rest of Europe heavily taxed sugar and cocoa, they kept prices here low.

Although we were sated from polenta, we attacked the *bignole*. Made with butter, full-fat cream, and not too much sugar, they were irresistible. There were miniature *cannoli* filled with Marsala-laced *zabaglione*; crème caramels encased in white chocolate; *diplomatico*, a kind of *mille feuille* layered with mascarpone and fresh ricotta; mini *choux* puffs with hand-piped liqueur-lashed cream; teensy tiramisu; tartlets; baba au rhum with real rum; tiny brioche sandwiches of chocolate cream; and petite Mont Blancs with candied chestnuts (much superior to the one I had at Sophie Pic's).

We opened our fourth bottle of wine, a sparkling dessert Moscato. Luigina arrived, ebulliently unselfconscious despite not having been invited to lunch. She brought a plate of homemade *torcet* (dialect for *torcetti*), which were baked rings of yeast, flour, butter, and sugar. "The poor man's *bignole*," said Franco.

Franco, Luigina, and Nonno cheerfully chatted about all the people they knew who had died recently, and all those in the process of dying. At three, no one made a move to leave for Mass. An hour later we were still eating *bignole*. Luigina looked at me and then asked the room in general, "What's that Japanese food called?"

"Sushi," said Bruno.

"*Ecco!* [That's it!]" said Luigina, shuddering at the thought of raw fish. Everyone nodded in agreement because, of course, unlike raw pork sausage, raw tuna was abominable.

At 4:35, it was time to clear the dessert plates and make espresso. We used Maria Rosa's biggest *moka*, a dented six-cup pot, which we stretched to get seven cups. Italian Food Rule: *do not start drinking coffee until you've finished the entire meal (chocolate doesn't count)*. Fiorenzo got out his special stash of Gianduiotto, hazelnut chocolates shaped like an elongated pyramid. While we munched them, Chiara asked Sam about Chinese writing. He sketched a few ideograms to show how abstract ideas such as the numbers 1, 2, and 3 were depicted: 一, 二, and 三. I wrote the Chinese characters for sun, 日, and moon, 月. Side by side, they formed a new character, 明,

which meant bright. Pronounced *ming*, it was Sam's Chinese name and, I realized, also Chiara's name, which meant "bright" in Italian. When the character "ming" was used with the character 白 (white), it created a compound word, 明白, bright-white, which meant "to understand."

Maria Stella's family eventually left. Sam and I helped clean up. When Maria Rosa was leaning over the sink, her T-shirt crept up her back, exposing a bit of skin to the draft. Chiara pulled it back down, affectionately patting her mother's lower back. I envied the mother-daughter relationship. Sam would never dream of fixing any wardrobe malfunction of mine, and it would make me feel odd if he did—Oedipus and all that.

By the time we'd put the kitchen in order, it was six, raining hard, and quite dark. Nonno was nodding off in a corner, waking momentarily whenever he had to sneeze. It was time to make our farewells. We were sad to leave Maria Rosa and her family, but we had to press on. The next morning Sam and I were driving to Bologna and Florence, where Norman would meet us for a brief vacation. Nonno woke up in time to say a formal goodbye. "*Buon viaggio e arrivederci.*" Good voyage and goodbye.

Maria Rosa pressed a bag of ladyfingers on us in case we needed an emergency snack on our five-minute walk home. "Come for dinner," she said. "Just minestrone." I tried to say no. We had just eaten for five hours straight. How could we possibly eat again in two hours? Besides, I knew Fiorenzo wanted to watch a soccer game. I told Maria Rosa that we had to pack. She looked so upset I thought she was about to burst into tears. I'm embarrassed to admit this, but the prospect of a bowl of homemade minestrone sounded delicious, even if I wasn't the least bit hungry. Sam was enthusiastic. "Okay then, we'll bring pasta and some *ragù*," I said.

Two hours later, Sam and I hustled back down the hill. Emptying our cupboards, we brought over tomato sauce and artisanal *maltagliati*, literally "poorly cut noodles," originally named for the ragged edges left after trimming fresh pasta. Nonno didn't seem at all surprised to see us. The table was miraculously square again, now set for six with a fresh tablecloth. Besides "just minestrone," there was a platter of *tomini*, luscious rounds of fresh white cheese bathed in an extra-virgin olive oil and scattered with herbs, sliced garlic, and chili peppers. We ate the cheese with foot-long *grissini* and a green salad with quartered ripe tomatoes bursting with flavour and oven-roasted, dark purple olives so juicy that I momentarily mistook them for grapes.

The minestrone was the best antidote to our over-the-top lunch. Maria Rosa had sautéed some diced zucchini, onion, and potato in olive oil. Then she added a small cube of frozen vegetables especially for minestrone and sold in supermarkets that included white romano beans, carrots, celery, water, and arborio rice. Now why couldn't we get that at home?

The soccer game had started. Fiorenzo turned on the television, the only time I saw anyone eat while watching TV. His team, Juventus, was playing another of its historic rivals, this time the team from Milan. His eyes were glued to the set. He stopped talking. His breathing became shallow. He didn't even notice when I cleared his pasta bowl. The game ended with a 0–0 tie, which I gather was another bad result for Juventus.

In addition to "just minestrone" and our *maltagliati* pasta, Maria Rosa served *involtini di pollo,* chicken breasts stuffed with prosciutto. For dessert, we peeled and ate sweet, juicy oranges and tangerines from Sicily — and picked at the *bignole* left from lunch.

We washed the dishes, again, and said our goodbyes, again. Maria Rosa's eyes filled with tears. I cried a little, too. Sam and Chiara looked solemn. Fiorenzo looked upset. He pulled a piece of paper from his pocket. "Google Translate," he said, handing it to me. It read: "I thank the fate that he has made to meet were intense days and eventful one Jan good luck, good luck Sam goodbye … maybe in a future time!!!!!!"

As we left, Maria Rosa dabbed at her eyes. "Breakfast!" she said. We started to laugh, but she wasn't kidding. She also made us take home some pastries from lunch.

CHAPTER TWENTY-THREE

The Battle of Bologna

The three-hour drive to Bologna took us through the heart of Emilia-Romagna, home of Parma ham, Modena balsamic vinegar, and Parmesan cheese. Maria Rosa recommended lunching at the Autogrill, a chain of cafeterias at gas stations along the efficient Italian autoroute. Sam and I were dubious, but she had never steered us wrong. The Autogrill we stopped at had wall-to-wall windows. The chairs weren't bolted to the floor. It did not sell fries. "Look, fresh buffalo mozzarella and tomatoes!" said Sam. Autogrill also offered a selection of grill-ready panini, plates of good cheese and *salumi*, grilled eggplant and zucchini, even fresh fruit, and slices of sponge cake with wild strawberries. Less appetizing were two steam-table dishes, sautéed fish and a grilled pork chop with bacon and sage.

Suddenly I noticed a server in a corner. "Omigod," I said to Sam. "She's making risotto." In a shallow pan, as big as a bicycle wheel, the cook stirred sausage, diced pumpkin, and raw rice in olive oil. Then she added a ladle of hot liquid from a simmering pot, adding more each time it dried out. Ten minutes later, she plated it and called out to a man waiting at a nearby table. Pumpkin risotto cooked to order at a highway rest stop? Sam and I grabbed a tray. We would have ordered two portions, but the pasta of the day, also cooked to order, was *fiocchi*, frilly little beggar pouches of golden yellow pasta stuffed with spinach and fresh ricotta. She plunged the pouches into boiling water and scooped them out two minutes later with a spider, just as Gigi had used, finishing them in a pan of butter and fresh sage. They looked like a plate of daffodils. The risotto and pasta each cost 7.5 euros or $11.25, including tax.

The Autogrill was Italy's best-kept culinary secret, "the noble workhorses across all of Italy," Gabrielle Hamilton, American chef-owner of New York's Prune restaurant, told *Saveur* magazine. When they first opened in the 1980s, they were popular even among Italians who weren't travelling anywhere but dropped in for Sunday lunch. Italy had five hundred Autogrills across the country, every thirty to fifty kilometres along the Autostrada. As Sam and I savoured our risotto and *fiocchi*, all around us, Italians were talking, relaxing, eating, and talking some more. No one was wolfing down their food or getting take-out to eat in their cars. Everyone was drinking mineral water, a good thing, considering where we were. Chilled splits of Prosecco and lunch-sized bottles of wine, however, cost only one euro more than bottled water.

Like any highway rest stop, the Autogrill sold chewing gum, chocolates, and potato chips. But it also sold cookbooks, wine, dried pasta, extra-virgin olive oil, whole salami, entire legs of prosciutto (bone-in), and twenty-kilogram wheels of Parmesan. You could pick up a package of the uncooked pasta of the day—the same plump little golden *fiocchi* we'd had—which meant you could stop for lunch at the Autogrill, pick up your groceries, and put on a pot of water to boil for dinner once you got home. "It's like the railway stations in Japan," said Sam, recalling the elegant bento-box lunches of sushi and sashimi sold on train platforms in Kyoto and Hiroshima.

The excellence of a country's food shouldn't be measured by its Michelin-starred restaurants but by how it feeds the masses on the move. North American airports offered a travesty of junk food, as did China's. It wasn't always thus in the People's Republic. On a three-hour flight during the Cultural Revolution, my plane landed at a mid-point airport for refuelling—and not just for the aircraft. We passengers trooped across the hot tarmac into a one-room terminal where everyone enjoyed a hot lunch of stir-fried dishes and steamed rice. Then we all got back on the plane and resumed our flight.

Bologna's nickname was *La Grassa*, the Fat One. We planned to decompress here and in Florence before starting the final leg of our journey in China. We dropped off our rental car and headed to our Airbnb apartment, conveniently located across the street from the main train station, according to the website map.

It wasn't. We humped our luggage up and down the traffic-clogged Via dell'Indipendenza. Sam and I always travelled light, but we were now weighed down with an embarrassment of gifts, including nineteen bottles of food and drink. We trudged wearily back and forth, at one point retracing our steps almost to our starting point. Eventually we found our one-bedroom apartment, across from Mercato delle Erbe, a market that dated to the Middle Ages. With time to spare before Norman arrived from Toronto, we checked out the best fruit and vegetable stalls, planning the magnificent meals we would cook for him.

The next day while Norman, still jet-lagged and battling a cold, rested at the apartment, Sam and I headed to the market. It was about to close for the lunch break so we split up, racing from vendor to vendor, eagerly buying everything we needed to show off our new skills. The butcher selling *cavallo* was afraid I didn't understand what I was buying. A 1928 consumer protection law prohibited the sale of horse beside other meat, originally intended to prevent fraud back in the day when horseflesh was cheaper than beef. Now horsemeat was more expensive than beef, and Italians were its biggest consumers in the European Union. "*Sì, cavallo*," I told the butcher. When he still looked worried, I pantomimed riding a horse. He beamed and wrapped up a beautiful fillet for me.

Back in the apartment, Sam and I cooked up a storm: Gragnano pasta with artisanal tomato sauce, a green salad, grilled calf's liver, and *filetto di cavallo*. By then thoroughly indoctrinated by Italian Food Rules, we began arguing over the order of the courses. I thought pasta first, followed by the meats. Sam thought meat, pasta, meat. After some sharp words, we came to a mutual understanding — or so we both thought.

While I was relegated to washing salad, Sam began cooking *everything* at once. Before I knew it, the pasta had hit the boiling water, the horsemeat was sizzling, and the calf's liver had already been seared on one side. I became irrationally angry. I wanted Norman to experience a real Italian progression of our meal, like Maria Rosa had taught us: *antipasti* of olives and cheese, pasta, and only then *il secondo* of two meats — followed by salad and fresh fruit. Sam thought mixing the two meats was a sacrilege. I yelled at Sam. He yelled right back.

"I've been cooking *everything*," he snapped. "You didn't do anything."

"*I* washed the fucking lettuce," I said.

Parenting Food Rule: *Do not use the f-word when speaking to your child about salad.*

Sam began slamming pots around. "Don't throw things, Sam," said Norman mildly, rousing himself from his jet-lag stupor. My husband, an only child, was unused to the rock 'em, sock 'em uproar of internecine warfare. Sam flung the pot of pasta onto the dining table. Then he stomped out of the kitchen, a rather ineffective move because there was nowhere to stomp. (I *told* him to fold up the sofa bed that morning.) Sam stomped anyway, overturning a flimsy folding chair. Then he stormed out of the apartment, slamming the door so hard I'm amazed plaster didn't rain down from the ceiling. A beat later I realized the only key to the apartment was in his pocket. We were trapped. Now I got *really* mad.

"You go out," said my jet-lagged, hungry husband, trying to calm me down. "I'll stay in. I'm sick anyway."

"Let's eat," I snapped.

We righted the chairs and sat down to eat in silence. I ate everything in the correct Italian order, and I was still unhappy. The real lesson Maria Rosa had imparted to me, and which I had promptly forgotten within twenty-four hours of leaving Repergo, was this: *when you cook for a family, you can break the rules.*

Norman set aside a plate of food for Sam. That made me even madder because it underlined his absence. Sam had missed out on the seared *filetto di cavallo*, darkly crusted on the outside, garnet-rare on the inside, as lean and tender as venison. He hadn't tasted the calf's liver, cooked rare, melt-in-the-mouth tender, the kind we could never get back home. And he didn't get to try the Gragnano pasta, perfectly *al dente*, thanks to his precision cooking.

When I describe how good the food tasted, I do not mean I enjoyed it. Mostly I was so upset that the food tasted like ashes. Most Important Italian Food Rule of All: *never fight before a great meal.*

I was helping Norman wash the dishes when I suddenly heard the key turn in the lock. Sam let himself back in and flopped onto the (still unmade) sofa bed. His face was red with Asian Flush Syndrome. I marched over and stood over him. Unable to restrain myself, I barked, "Where were you?"

"I went to have a beer," he muttered. He closed his eyes.

Norman, the more rational parent, said quietly, "We saved you some food, Sam. It was very good."

"I ate something outside," Sam said, rolling onto his face.

Like Mount Vesuvius, I erupted. How could he eat something on the street when we had such good food at home? I started whacking Sam on his arm. My son responded like a millennial: he pulled out his cellphone and began filming. "I am *so* going to put this on the internet," he said.

Blind with rage, I began kicking Sam, with my bare feet, at a rather awkward upward angle. (Who knew it was so hard to kick someone lying on a sofa bed?) To his credit, Sam—who maintains that I was wearing shoes at the time, and that he only threatened to film me and put it on the internet *after* I started kicking him—didn't hit me back or kick me, so I must have raised him right. Of course, had he kicked *me* that would have been elder abuse.

At this point, Norman got upset with both of us. Have I mentioned he's conflict-averse? Sam and I suddenly felt bad about making Norman feel bad. I stopped kicking him. Sam stopped trying to film me and instead took a drunken nap. Norman and I retrieved the key and went sightseeing at the University of Bologna medical school's free museum of eighteenth-century wax moulds of syphilitic genitalia.

Looking back, I realize Sam and I had both been at the breaking point. Why else would we have had a knock-down, drag-out fight over something as trivial as the proper order of the courses in an Italian meal? We rushed straight from Marie-Catherine in France to Maria Rosa in Italy, all the while straining to be on our best behaviour as kitchen guests. We navigated other cultures, in other languages. My brain became so overwhelmed I sometimes blanked out on *English* words. During his years away at university, Sam had grown into an independent young man, used to making his own decisions about how to spend his day, which normally did not include hanging with me. At twenty-two, he had a biological imperative to sleep in as late as possible. Yet he had gotten up early day after day. And late at night when he wanted to chill, he would help me check my notes and chew over the significance of what had happened that day. My anger abated as I thought about all this. Much later, I phoned Sam, who was then living in China. What did he remember about our fight? How had he felt at the time? (This was the annoying part about having a journalist-mother.) He was remarkably restrained, even kind, as he recalled the fight from his point of view. "I just wanted to leave," he said calmly. "I didn't want to be around you at that time because you were being unpleasant." At first, he had only planned to walk around the block. But he kept walking. Eventually he found a deserted bar with only four small tables and no stools at the bar, where he stood. Iron Maiden blasted on the stereo as the bartenders prepared for the night's business. With Sam's first beer the bartender gave him a big bowl of salted potato chips, on the house. Somewhere between the free chips and the music, Sam began enjoying himself. He was hungry, but he was too ashamed to face me and Norman, so he ordered another beer, hoping to get more chips. This time the bartender shaved thin slices of *porchetta* and offered them to him with some bread—no charge.

I felt bad, again, remembering how I had kicked him. For weeks, he had helped me take photos so I'd remember the details of what we cooked, had schlepped the suitcases, and been bottle washer-in-chief. The saying goes: if you want to know what a girl will look like when she's older, look at her mother. No one ever says that about mothers and sons. Yet in some ways, Sam *was* like me. When he got mad, he, too, exploded. One summer when he missed a bus to his cooking job at a golf club and knew he would be late, he rushed home to get enough cash for a taxi. When he realized the taxi fare would almost wipe out his entire day's pay, he hurled a hockey puck onto the kitchen floor (the Canadian male's equivalent of kicking your second-born child on a sofa bed). The vulcanized-rubber disk ricocheted off our oak floor and smashed into the dishwasher, leaving it looking like it had been in a fender-bender with an SUV. Like me, Sam didn't stay angry. After he got home, he remorsefully tried to hammer out the dent. When that didn't work, he searched in vain online for a replacement part. He consulted an autobody shop, to no avail. When I noticed the dent, Sam was contrite and embarrassed, the way I will be when everyone finds out I am such a kickass mom.

Our fight in Bologna was a milestone of sorts. We grew even closer that day. To fight like that with someone you love presumes a bedrock of trust. Sam and I both knew that we could scream and hurl pots because, when we eventually stopped, not only would everything be all right, our bond would be stronger than ever. The only casualty was Norman. After the fight, he changed his mind about meeting up with us in China. "The two of you fighting, you hitting Sam, and he going out and getting drunk—who needs that?"

Don't tell Norman, but Sam and I were secretly relieved, although Sam did feel bad that Norman, who was excited about catching up with old friends in China, was going to forego that opportunity because we'd been so unpleasant. We knew that after Shanghai we would be even more exhausted. We didn't want a third person intruding, someone who hadn't shared our trials and tribulations, who didn't get our shorthand jokes.

Fathers didn't understand mothers and sons, just as mothers didn't understand fathers and daughters. Sam and I both understood the significance of the Battle of Bologna. We had let off steam, and now we were over it.

After that, we never even had a whisper of an argument on our trip. After that, we got along just fine.

China

CHAPTER TWENTY-FOUR

Hilly

I bought bargain-priced Aeroflot tickets from Bologna to Moscow to Shanghai. What was I thinking—especially after all the years I'd flown as a foreign correspondent on creaky second-hand Tupolevs in China? Six months earlier, a Russian airliner had been shot out of the sky over the Sinai desert, killing everyone aboard. Our plane was a modern Airbus A320, but the washrooms stank even before takeoff, my blanket, in a sealed bag, came festooned with two long frizzy blond hairs, and the seats couldn't recline.

Given that Aeroflot was the cheapest way to fly from Italy to China, it was no surprise the plane was packed with Chinese migrants. Sam began chatting in Mandarin to the young man beside him. (Okay, I *asked* Sam to talk to him.) He was wearing Chinese-made jeans and a Chinese-made leather jacket, was surnamed Zhou, and was from a village in Zhejiang, the same province as the owner of the Chinese restaurant in Asti. Unlike her, he hadn't put down any roots. One of eight workers in a Chinese-owned garment shop in Prato, he'd been in Italy eighteen months but had never once eaten Italian food or spoken to an Italian. He'd heard they had many dialects, "like us," but had been "only with Chinese people." Everything, including his meals and the dormitory he had shared with co-workers, had been arranged by the factory boss, a fellow villager. Now on his first trip home, he was unsure if he would return to Italy. And then he went to sleep.

During our five-hour layover in Moscow, Sam and I wandered through a maze of identical duty-free shops. I felt a spasm of sympathy for Edward Snowden, the American whistleblower who spent a month in limbo here. The next leg was on Shanghai Airlines, which had a reassuring safety record—zero accidents in its thirty-year history. The blankets were clean, the seats eased backward, *and* four out of five seats were empty. But instead of a welcome-aboard spiel from the flight attendants, we got a stern recorded message about not fighting over space in the overhead bins. "Otherwise," said the faceless voice over the intercom, "you will be detained."

My friend Hilly had arranged for a taxi driver she knew to pick us up from Shanghai's Pudong International Airport because, she said, it wouldn't be safe to queue for a taxi. To Chinese, the world is a dangerous place. Food, water, air, even random taxi drivers at the airport—*everything* is unsafe. To a manic degree, this echoed Federica's scrubbing her lemons with steel wool or Maria Rosa's insistence on buying her meat from L'Isola della Carne, where she could see the cows grazing out back on good Reperghese grass.

Hilly's taxi paranoia reminded me of her strange behaviour during my previous visit, eight years earlier. Whenever I returned from an errand, she would urge me to change into my pyjamas—even if it was the middle of the afternoon and I wasn't at all sleepy. Gradually I realized she didn't want my street clothes touching her sofa because she was worried about germs infecting her four-year-old son when he watched television. Hilly wasn't unusual. Scarlet, my roommate from Peking University, had a second washing machine exclusively for her grandson's clothing because she didn't want the rest of the family's garments to contaminate his.

This pervasive fear of an unsafe world led people to place an outsized importance on personal relationships, or *guanxi* (关系). Pronounced GWAN-see, it meant "connections." Confucius had stressed the importance of a network of mutually beneficial relationships. In modern China, *guanxi* was the social lubricant that encompassed distant family members, schoolmates, work colleagues—and all *their* friends and contacts. It included everyone, to varying degrees of intensity, from one's ancestral village, county, or even province, which is why the migrant worker on the flight to Moscow said he obtained his job after one phone call to the factory boss, a fellow villager.

Social networking groups like Facebook and LinkedIn were pale imitations of *guanxi*. You can "friend" someone on Facebook in a nanosecond. *Guanxi* was lifelong and reciprocal. Twelve years earlier, I had profiled Hilly and her husband, Allan, in Toronto when they were newly arrived immigrants from China. They both spoke English. He had an engineering degree from China and an MBA from Australia. They had savings of $100,000. Their plan: have a child, apply for Canadian citizenship, and get a job with a Canadian multinational company that would eventually transfer Allan back to China as an expatriate businessman, with all the perks and high salary that entailed. But after Hilly gave birth, on schedule, to a healthy boy they named Dickie, Allan was unable to find work. After the series was published and I no longer needed to be a neutral observer, I helped them out with contacts and job-hunting advice. In desperation, their money running out, Allan sent my profile of him to a Canadian corporation. It interviewed him, hired him, and a few years later, duly transferred him to China. Later, when I was suffering through my depression, they invited me to stay with them in Shanghai.

Hilly explained she used this specific taxi driver because their *guanxi* meant he would reliably show up whenever she pre-booked a taxi to or from the airport. *He* could avoid the hours-long taxi queue at the airport, and *we* wouldn't get cheated. Plus, he knew exactly where to drop us *and* he called Hilly's cellphone en route to let her know we would be arriving shortly. In short, it was a win-win-win situation.

She lived in Pudong (pronounced poo-doong), which meant east bank of the Pu River, short for the Huangpu, a tributary of the Yangtze, Asia's longest river. The Pu divided old and new Shanghai but in 1973 during my first visit to the city, no one had talked about Pudong or Puxi (which meant west bank of the Pu River). Shanghai was Shanghai, a city that wasn't even very old by Chinese standards. One hundred and fifty years earlier, it had been a marshy fishing village nicknamed Muddy Flats.

The fishing village became a bustling port in the nineteenth century as Chinese tea, cotton, silk, and porcelain became fashionable in Europe. Trade went in one direction only—China, which disdained foreign goods, accepted payment only in silver bullion. Searching for an irresistible export to remedy its crippling trade imbalance, the British settled on opium, a drug China banned back in 1729. In 1839, after an imperial Mandarin defiantly confiscated and burned a thousand tons of opium, Britain declared war and decisively defeated China. The peace accord signed after the first Opium War (yes, there were two) forced open five "treaty ports," including Shanghai. Britain and other powers also carved out "concessions" in Shanghai, entire neighbourhoods where they imposed their own laws, courts, and police. It was as if Colombia had fought a war with the US over the right to sell cocaine to the American people and, victorious, governed swaths of five key US cities.

In Shanghai, the Western powers built imposing towers along the waterfront, known as the Bund. With foreigners in charge, China's most cosmopolitan city infamously banned dogs and Chinese from one of its parks. The sign at the Huangpu Gardens at the northern tip of the Bund didn't literally say "no dogs or Chinese," but a 1917 plaque noted these two rules: "The Gardens are reserved for the Foreign Community," and "Dogs and bicycles are not admitted."

Not surprisingly, Shanghai was the birthplace of Chinese capitalism *and* Chinese communism. Taking advantage of the protection afforded by extraterritoriality, Mao Zedong and a small group of radicals met in the French Concession in 1921 to found the Chinese Communist Party in Puxi, the old Shanghai.

Pudong, where Hilly lived, was originally the site of warehouses for ocean-going cargo. In Mao's time, rice-paddy fields replaced the warehouses. In the 1990s, seemingly overnight, the paddy fields were paved over for luxury developments and office towers. Shanghai became Manhattan, London, and Paris rolled into one, a seething, pulsating, polluted, gaudy monster of a metropolis. Above ground, impressive eight-lane elevated highways beribboned it. Below ground, it was threaded with subway lines. And the Shanghainese began to acquire pet dogs — many, many dogs — which they took to whatever park they pleased.

Hilly lived in an upscale real estate development called Benevolence Town. Her two-thousand-square-foot flat, on the twelfth floor of Building Eighteen, had four bedrooms, two bathrooms, and a large balcony. She rarely used the latter because of Shanghai's severe pollution. Like all Chinese cities, it issued hourly air-quality index bulletins. One in five days was polluted. Fine particulate matter, called $PM_{2.5}$, was especially hazardous to health. In Shanghai $PM_{2.5}$ averaged fifty micrograms per cubic metre, 43 percent higher than the upper safety limit set by the World Health Organization.

China was the world's biggest emitter of greenhouse gases, followed by the US. After Donald Trump's election as president, China urged all countries to abide by their climate commitments. Although it burned as much coal as the rest of the world combined, it had pledged that by 2030 at least 20 percent of its energy would come from hydropower, nuclear power, and wind and solar sources. Meanwhile, the pollution level had reached a crisis in Shanghai. During a "red alert," the most urgent warning, the school Hilly's son attended cancelled all outdoor activities. A vice principal stood guard at the front door to make sure no one left it open. On the worst days, when the $PM_{2.5}$ air-quality index exceeded a stunning

300, Shanghai authorities advised the elderly to remain indoors. It closed Pudong International Airport because pilots couldn't see the runways.

Shanghai's smog looked like grey shadows, its brightest lights a watery yellow. On "orange alert" days, the second most urgent warning, Hilly and her maid cautiously opened the kitchen and bathroom windows for a few minutes to air out the apartment. Then residents would power-walk around the walled compound, like prisoners on exercise break. To avoid breathing outdoor air, people would drive even very short distances, one or two blocks. Sam thought it funny when Hilly pulled into her underground garage—and *then* opened her SUV windows. She thought the air was better in the garage than outside. Sadly, she was probably right.

Benevolence Town, built by Singapore money, was a gated community. It had indoor and outdoor swimming pools, playgrounds, basketball and tennis courts, a golf driving range, squash and badminton courts, ping-pong tables, a gym and a sauna, a spa and a beauty parlour, and a clubhouse amid manicured gardens. I kept getting lost, and not just because of the smog. The thirty identical towers were marked with stainless-steel sculptures that had a bland sameness to them, as if someone had mass-commissioned the pieces. The complex of four thousand apartments, some with as many as eight bedrooms, housed many times the combined populations of Allex and Repergo. But unlike in Repergo, where if you coughed the person ahead of you would turn around to say hello, at Hilly's compound you never greeted anyone. The only neighbour I ever saw her acknowledge was the other family on her floor. And she didn't even like them because they had once borrowed her son's bicycle and failed to return it.

Hilly had just dropped Dickie at his private school, a branch of an elite British institution. She was free until mid-afternoon, when she had to pick him up and drive him home. She was a helicopter parent, or perhaps a tiger mom, always driving him from activity to activity, forever nagging him to eat more, fretting aloud that his heavy book bag would damage his spine, even though, at eleven years old, he was taller than she was.

A slim woman with cranberry-red glasses and glossy hair that fell past her shoulders, Hilly suffered from chronic depression. Erratic and highly strung, some days she tackled her errands with a frenetic energy that soon left her exhausted and unable to function. She was in her late forties, with a degree in piano. She had previously owned a successful business in Pakistan, where she had met Allan. Reinvented as a Canadian citizen, he was now a senior executive whose perks included free housing and $50,000 in annual fees for their son's private school. Allan had just been promoted, again, to a rank that entitled him to a company car, chauffeur, and even better housing in Shanghai, one of the hottest real estate markets in the world. Because his rental allowance had also doubled, to nearly $11,000 a month, Hilly was preoccupied with deciding between a two-storey penthouse apartment across from Dickie's school or a stand-alone three-storey house with a garden.

The promotion was a big moment, but Hilly never seemed satisfied. Exquisitely sensitive to status and money, every time her husband made it up another rung of the corporate ladder, Hilly wished aloud it had been several rungs higher. Perhaps that was because she didn't work and instead devoted herself to keeping up with the other moms at Dickie's school. She often dropped by their homes but never invited them to her apartment, which she was keenly aware was the least expensive housing in her social circle. When the family finally moved to their next, even more luxurious place, she said, she planned to finally invite the other mothers over.

Her current apartment had hardwood floors, granite counters, and walk-in showers, but Hilly felt insecure about everything, even the food in her fridge. She drove an imported SUV, but one morning when we passed a young woman driving a Rolls Royce, she sighed that her own car was too ordinary. "We have several Rolls Royces in my building's underground parking lot." Only then I began noticing the BMWs, Mercedes-Benzes, Porsches, and Teslas. As part of Shanghai's nouveau riche, Hilly's yardstick for what was good depended on price. One morning, she showed me the French butter she had purchased. She wanted my opinion. It was Beurre d'Isigny, an excellent brand. But it had been mixed, yuck, with vegetable oil, apparently to make it spreadable. "I bought it by price," she told me regretfully. "I thought that was good."

Oddly, she didn't care at all about her cramped kitchen, which appeared to have been designed not for the woman of the house but the maid. It lacked counter space and adequate cupboards. There was no room for a table. It didn't even have a dishwasher. No matter. Hilly rarely made a meal. She had never once used her oven. She normally went into the kitchen only to give orders to her maid.

Originally Hilly arranged for us to cook with the maid of one of her richest friends. But when the lady of the house got pregnant and backed out, Hilly urged Sam and me to cook with her instead. I knew my friend wasn't the least bit interested in cooking, so when I demurred, Hilly found not one but three families.

"They are very, very rich," she said happily. "They are all excellent chefs."

But wouldn't we be cooking with their maids?

"None of their maids can cook," she said dismissively.

For the first couple of days, we stayed with Hilly to get over our jet lag. Sam and I slept in the maid's room. I got the narrow bed, and Sam was on the floor, a few inches away. I envisioned intimate late-night chats, but we were both so tired we fell straight asleep at night. I think I snored.

During our brief stay, Hilly lost no time imposing a Shanghai-style makeover on us. Since Deng Xiaoping's get-rich revolution, seven hundred million Chinese had escaped extreme poverty in a single generation. With memories of deprivation still painfully fresh, no one wanted to look poor. The popularity of knock-off Chanel bags and fake Rolex watches were sartorial shorthand for *I'm rich!*

Sam and I had shown up on Hilly's doorstep looking un-rich. My carry-on wardrobe was rumpled, my hair scraggly, my skin un-exfoliated. (That's a joke. I have never exfoliated, which has always sounded to me like some form of ISIS torture.) Sam not only had a self-inflicted haircut, but to avoid hassles at airport security he hadn't packed a razor. After weeks on the road, he had sprouted a scruffy goatee and a Fu Manchu moustache. His facial hair occasionally startled me—what had happened to my little boy? Hilly pushed him into a bathroom, ordering him to use her husband's razor. She appraised his stained, dented, mustard-coloured shoes, which were cast-offs from a university classmate. "You can't go to people's houses with those shoes," she said. "They will think you're poor. You must buy new shoes. And you *both* need haircuts. You both look awful."

The famously inscrutable Chinese were shockingly blunt when it came to commenting on physical appearance. Hilly was especially harsh because the way we looked reflected on *her*. She was using precious *guanxi* to persuade her rich friends to take us into their homes. If we looked poor, she would lose face. Thanks to the same *guanxi*, Hilly's hair salon took us immediately. It was a hole in the wall with mismatched towels, piles of unswept hair, and hairdressers who chain-smoked. While Hilly spent lavishly on clothes, purses, and shoes, she cheaped out on hairdressers. After all, who would know where you got your hair cut? Sam and I both got fabulous haircuts for next to nothing in no time at all.

"I don't really want new shoes," Sam whispered to me, as Hilly parked her gleaming SUV at a cavernous underground bazaar. I shot him a look that said: *What do you want me to do about it?* At Hilly's urging, Sam reluctantly tried on some fake Adidas. He settled on the cheapest shoes in the store, a pair of black mesh slip-ons. Before he could start bargaining, Hilly had shoved the money into the sales clerk's hands. "My gift to you!" she told Sam.

Among the new rich, the unthinkable had happened: Chinese food had lost its lustre. Instead, foreign food, especially Italian, Japanese, and, surprisingly, Irish, had become fashionable. To thank the boss for his recent promotion, for instance, Allan invited him to dinner at an Italian restaurant in the old French Concession (yes, where Mao founded the Chinese Communist Party). Curious, I went online to check out the restaurant. An Italian owned Bella Napoli, and he happened to be looking for a cook. "Hey, Sam," I half-joked. "You could get a job here!" Hilly looked slightly green. She tried to smile, but couldn't.

A day later, she told me — mother to mother — I was making a big mistake. "Jan, why do you want Sam to be a cook?" she scolded. Marie-Catherine and Maria Rosa had applauded my son's ambition. Hilly dismissed that as insanity, and said I would ruin Sam's life if I let him become a cook. To prove her point, she pulled out her cellphone and searched an app called Love the Big Chef. "Look how cheap it is to hire a cook!" she cried. For as little as one hundred yuan (twenty dollars Canadian), you could hire a chef to come to your home to cook four dishes, a soup, and rice. (The ingredients were extra.)

In France and Italy, every woman we cooked with had a full-time job or, in Marie-Catherine's case, had just retired. Hilly was a full-time housewife with a full-time maid. That gave her abundant time to plot out her one and only child's life. To thwart Dickie's addiction to computer games and mould him into a high-earning adult, she crammed every waking moment with tennis lessons, debating, art classes, and saxophone lessons. University was six years away, but Hilly obsessed about getting him into a famous school to, she believed, guarantee he would end up with a lucrative job. I was also guilty of overscheduling Ben and Sam, but at least some activities had been team sports. None of Dickie's activities involved learning to relate to others, what psychologists would call improving EQ, or emotional intelligence. At Hilly's complex, Sam was frustrated no one ever played pickup games of basketball or soccer.

As a philosophy major, my son was used to sardonic comments about his career prospects. No one, however, had been quite so blunt about his impending lifelong penury as Hilly. How could I explain to her, who had scrabbled so hard to get ahead in life, that I believed happiness lay in pursuing work you loved? I had the luxury of growing up in a developed democracy where the gap between rich and poor wasn't as stark as in China. I also had my own role models, parents who loved their own work — restaurants and nursing—and had not looked askance when I dreamed of becoming a journalist. My first boss, Fox Butterfield, the first *New York Times* correspondent in Beijing, has pointed out that the traditional greeting in China—"Have you eaten yet?"—was essentially materialistic. In a society that suffered millennia of famine, the question delineated rich from poor. In the West, you counted heads. In China, food was so important you counted *mouths*. The Chinese word for population was *ren kou* (人口), literally "people-mouths." And yet the chef's status was in free fall. In a society that valued only money, a chef had become a servant, a skill devalued to a twenty-dollar dinner. Cooking for a living was servitude, not much different from shining shoes on a sidewalk.

CHAPTER TWENTY-FIVE

Shanghaied

Hilly wanted us to cook spaghetti for Dickie, just the way we had learned in Italy. "What else should we have with the spaghetti?" she asked. "Mashed potatoes? Dickie loves mashed potatoes." Spaghetti with mashed potatoes broke some Italian Food Rule, but Sam helpfully suggested a *primo* of pasta, followed by a *secondo* of steak, mashed potatoes, and caesar salad. Hilly took us to a grocery store that sold imported food, just outside the guarded gates of Benevolent Town. (We still drove.) The store stocked fresh rosemary, lemons, romaine lettuce, Australian steaks, French butter and cream, Swiss cheese, strawberries, and Italian wines, including Barolo, which cost ten times as much as in Italy. Once home, Hilly immediately lost interest. She wandered off, suggesting we teach her maid how to cook spaghetti so she could make it for Dickie after we were gone.

The maid, who had moved into the study so we could have her bedroom, worked six days a week. She cleaned, cooked, did the laundry, and handled all Sherpa duties. Whenever we bought groceries, for instance, Hilly would summon her by cellphone to the underground garage to carry our bulging bags into the elevator. During the day, like the servants in *Downton Abbey*, the maid never sat down, and she tried to make herself invisible. In nineteenth-century England, at least the architecture had been conducive. Grand homes had back staircases leading to attic dormitories; I once visited an estate in Ireland that had tunnels so servants could approach the manor house without marring his lordship's view. But in a modern Shanghai condo, Chinese servants were unavoidably visible (as they were all over the city).

Indeed, 40 percent of Shanghai's population was migrant, part of the largest demographic shift in world history. Some two hundred and fifty million peasants had flooded into China's urban areas, ten million into Shanghai alone. This same demographic shift had also enabled more people — seven hundred million — to lift themselves out of poverty than any time before in world history. This was China's industrial revolution, like that other Industrial Revolution, except compressed into a few decades. In 1851, one-third of young women in London aged fifteen to twenty-five were servants and another third were prostitutes, according to Bill Bryson, author of *At Home: A Short History of Private Life*. In China, they were called *wai di ren* (外地人)—"outsiders." Hilly's maid wasn't undocumented like Davit and Rüska in France, or in mortal peril like the woman surnamed Levi hiding in Nonno's attic. But she was an outsider in her own land, trapped on the margins of society, with only a precarious right of abode in urban China.

Her name was Peace. She was thirty-seven, with a husband and two children—a daughter, thirteen, and a son, ten. Because she lived in a rural area *and* her first child had been a girl, she was permitted to have a second child. (China's one-child policy varied widely in implementation in recent years.) To work in Shanghai, she had left her family behind in Gansu province, some 1,700 kilometres away. She saw them only twice a year, during Chinese New Year and in summer when Hilly and her family travelled abroad on vacation.

Each morning, Peace got up at six a.m. to prepare breakfast—boiled eggs, fried eggs, toast, hot milk, fried peanuts, peeled sliced cucumbers, oatmeal boiled with milk, and a traditional flapjack called Old Mother-in-Law Pancake. "You're so lucky to have a maid make you breakfast," I told Dickie.

"Why?" he said, looking at me blankly. "Who makes breakfast in Canada?"

At dinner, Peace ate with the family because the condo had no room for a second table. She set the expensive dishes—fish, chicken, and pork—in front of Allan and Dickie, and took a spot at the far end of the table. She ate only from the closest dish, usually cheap vegetables, until the family had eaten its fill and Allan passed her the meat and fish. On Sunday, her only day off, Peace stayed with her sister-in-law, who had her own apartment. She was a maid, too, and had also left her children behind in Gansu. As Peace departed on Saturday night, when she was no longer dressed in a worn apron and her hair wasn't yanked back in a maid's ponytail, I noticed that she was in fact quite pretty, with shiny black hair and even white teeth. It struck me that looking too attractive on the job wasn't helpful for a maid's job security.

Peace never spoke unless spoken to, and then it was usually to clarify her orders. I disrupted the status quo after lunch one day by asking about her children. She told me she missed them badly. Two summers ago, she rented a no-frills one-bedroom apartment and brought them to Shanghai for a holiday. "This year I bought a designer coat for my daughter for 300 yuan. It was half price," she said. I asked the brand, and Peace started to tell me when Hilly interrupted.

"That's *not* a designer," said Hilly.

"Well, in China," Peace said uncertainly, "it counts as a designer."

"No, it's *not* a brand," Hilly said firmly.

The migrants came from China's poorest provinces, speaking mutually unintelligible dialects, taking the jobs the Shanghainese disdained. They swept floors, made beds, washed toilets, pulled weeds, cut grass, trimmed shrubs, walked dogs, watched children, hauled trash, scrubbed dishes, washed windows, cooked in restaurants and homes, worked on factory assembly lines, offered massages and pedicures and haircuts, bussed tables, delivered parcels, paved roads, and built the city's gleaming skyscrapers. Some amassed enough savings to open small businesses such as florists, convenience stores, and tailor shops.

Shanghai's newest arrivals had ruddy faces and work-roughened hands. Their children wore traditional split-crotch pants instead of expensive diapers. Like migrants everywhere, they were blamed for rising crime, unemployment, and a general decline in civilized behaviour. In 1879, during the Gilded Age, *The Gentlemen's Book of Etiquette* attempted to sand the rough edges off German and Irish migrants flocking to Boston and New York by explaining how to drink soup, chew politely, and help one's self to the sugar bowl. In 2006, the Shanghai government published a similar etiquette handbook called *How to be a Lovely Shanghainese*, according to author Rob Schmitz. Instructions included "How to Eat Western Food" and "How to Cut Your Hair."

One day, on Shanghai's gleaming, ultra-modern subway, Hilly and I happened to sit beside a migrant mother with a toddler in split-crotch pants. Suddenly she set her child on the floor. A large yellow puddle formed, ebbing and flowing as the subway car lurched. At the next stop, two unwitting passengers stepped in the urine. I nudged Hilly.

"You can't let your child pee on the subway," she scolded the mother. "You should put a diaper on her."

"She doesn't like diapers," the mother said, looking embarrassed. Hilly later told me she'd once seen a toddler poop on the subway. The mother thoughtfully set down a piece of newspaper.

Hilly was also from another province, as were many of the mothers at Dickie's school, but they would never dream of describing themselves as *wai di ren*. Only *poor* people were migrants. Anyone with money was … Chinese. The average migrant worker in Shanghai — hairdressers, waiters, and factory workers — earned 3,000 yuan a month ($600), plus meals and a dormitory bed. As housing prices soared, it became clear that they could never afford to buy housing in Shanghai. Many saved their money, with the goal of building a new home back in their village. Others became alienated or depressed. Suicide was not uncommon. Some young women became mistresses, in return for a property deed.

Migrants had no right to stay permanently in cities. Ever since the Xia dynasty, circa 2000 BCE, every citizen was required to have a *hukou* (户口), an ancient system of household registration that shackled them to a specific village, town, or city. Over the millennia, the system had been used for taxation, conscription, and political control. During Mao's Great Leap Forward, an urban *hukou* had made the difference between life and death. During a famine from 1959 to 1961, known as the Three Years of Natural Disasters, thirty million Chinese peasants starved to death after authorities transferred desperately needed grain from rural areas to the cities.

To satisfy the low-wage labour needs of China's industrial revolution, *hukou* restrictions were loosened. Still, migrants could be expelled at any time. For almost any bureaucratic procedure — a marriage licence or a passport — they had to return to their villages. Their children couldn't attend municipal elementary schools, so migrants were forced to establish their own schools. When their children finished primary school, they had to return to their villages because they could only take the highly competitive university entrance exams in the high school of their *hukou*. In Canada, at least, newcomers were promised eventual citizenship and equality. In China, the *hukou* system created a permanent apartheid.

Peace got room and board and earned nearly 70 percent more than the average migrant plus a bonus at Chinese New Year. The higher wages seemed to include what I'd call a servility surcharge. Although we had taken her bedroom, Peace never betrayed resentment, even when Sam and I sheepishly gave her our dirty clothes to wash. Maids in China were called "amah" or *ayi* (阿姨), pronounced like the letters I-E. They called their master *xian sheng* (先生), literally "born first," originally meaning a superior in the Confucian hierarchy, but the modern equivalent of "sir." They called their mistresses *tai-tai* (太太), which meant "greatest-greatest," the modern equivalent of "madam." Before the Communist revolution, *tai-tai* was the title of the alpha female in a household that typically included a concubine, or two or three. After the Communist victory in 1949, *tai-tai* and *xian sheng* had been discarded as reactionary, replaced by the gender-neutral "comrade." Now the archaic titles had been dusted off. In the West, calling someone "sir" or "madam" wasn't overly obsequious, but in China it reeked of bootlicking. And in fact, Peace didn't merely polish the family's shoes, she also cleaned the soles—and arranged them in perfect rows.

Sam told Peace that *spaghetti bolognese* was like Sichuan *dan dan* noodles —both were boiled wheat noodles with a sauce of seasoned ground meat. As she watched, he fine-diced celery, carrot, onions, and garlic, and showed her how to sweat the vegetables over low heat before adding ground beef and a splash of milk. For the mashed potatoes, he told her to boil them first then mash them with butter and a whole head of roasted garlic. It fell to me to teach her caesar salad. As I blended an anchovy with mustard and lemon juice, I prattled on, rather uselessly, that "Caesar was a leader of ancient Rome."

"Oh, he invented caesar salad?" she asked.

"Actually, caesar salad was invented in Mexico."

Peace looked confused.

Sam didn't think to ask how Hilly, Allan, and Dickie wanted their meat cooked. He aimed for medium rare, but the steaks turned out rare. Allan and Dickie loved theirs. Not Hilly. The bright red blood pooling on her plate grossed her out. Every country had great food that disgusted someone else—bunny rabbit in France, raw pork sausage in Italy, sanguinary steaks in China.

Over dinner, the subject of marriage came up. I mentioned that I had warned Sam to be careful. In Canada, he was just another guy with dim career prospects, but in China, he was someone with a foreign passport and a pulse. "Sam, you're going to have lots of girlfriends in China," Allan joked. "They think you're rich." Sam burst out laughing, and whipped out his stunningly ugly wallet, which he'd made from olive-coloured duct tape. Allan recoiled as if Sam had pulled out a dead rodent, ran into his bedroom, and fetched a new expensive leather billfold. "For you, Sam," he said.

The next day we would start our cooking adventure. As we helped Peace clear the dishes, Hilly described her three friends, ranked by real estate values. Family Number One rented a gorgeous penthouse. Family Number Two owned a monster house with a garden inside a gated community. Family Number Three lived in a house, also in a gated compound, but a semi-detached house, and their garden was tiny compared to Family Number Two's.

"I told them you are a famous author and that your book is called *Cooking with Sam*," Hilly said. "I told them Sam was a wonderful cook and that he would be their private Western chef."

I choked. Sam looked horrified.

"Now why would you say *that*?" asked Allan, whom I'd copied on all my emails to Hilly. "That makes no sense. Why would she write a book about *that*? They came here to learn *Chinese* cooking. Sam is not going to make your friends *Western* food."

Hilly got mad at Allan. She snapped, "If they're going to someone's home, *bai chi, bai zhu* (白吃, 白住; live for free, eat for free), why would anyone say yes unless they got something out of it?" Hilly had finally said out loud what Sam and I had been wondering the whole trip. Why indeed *were* these rich Shanghainese allowing us into their homes? Marie-Catherine and Maria Rosa had extended hospitality out of national pride and, yes, *guanxi*. But Shanghai's me-first materialism changed the equation. Hilly had dismissed my offer to compensate her friends as ludicrous for anyone paying $50,000 per child in private-school fees. But how had she gotten my project so wrong? Hilly suffered from clinical depression, which I knew from personal experience could distort memory and warp perceptions. It was possible she genuinely believed I had emailed her a book title like that. (I hadn't.) Or perhaps she had figured dangling a Hollywood-style private chef was the only way to sell us to her wealthy, status-conscious friends. Either way, Sam had just been Shanghaied.

That night, in the privacy of our shared bedroom, we chewed over the problem. If we didn't want to get tossed out, I said, we had to go along with Hilly's condition. "But we're supposed to learn *Chinese* food," said Sam, distressed. He knew how to cook lots of Western dishes, but he wasn't quite ready to bill himself as a personal chef. In the end, my son agreed our only option was to ingratiate ourselves with these rich Shanghai folks by making, say, macaroni and cheese. That night, I hardly slept. I saw my book project disintegrating. Who would want to read about Sam cooking Western food in China?

The next morning my son slept in and missed breakfast. He made his go-to snack, a fried egg with leftover rice. Peace, who was hovering in the kitchen, taught him how to make egg-drop soup out of nothing. In other words, *cucina povera*, Shanghai style.

SAM'S FRIED EGG ON RICE

1 serving	leftover rice
1 tbsp.	peanut or canola oil
1	egg
½ inch	scallion (green part), finely minced
¼ tsp.	light soy sauce*
2 drops	sesame oil (optional)

Microwave cooked rice in the same bowl you will eat it in. Over high heat, fry egg in oil until white is crispy, but yellow is still runny. Slip fried egg onto hot rice. Sprinkle with scallion, soy sauce, and sesame oil.

*This is not a low-sodium version. Light soy is *sheng chou* (生抽) – different from "dark soy," which is *lao chou* (老抽) and is used sparingly in cooking, never for eating directly.

PEACE'S TOMATO EGG-DROP SOUP

1	ripe tomato, cut in 6–8 wedges
1 tbsp.	peanut or canola oil
¼ tsp.	salt
1	egg, beaten
½ inch	scallion (green part), finely minced
a few drops sesame oil	
1 cup	water

Stir-fry tomato in oil in wok over medium heat for 1 minute. Add salt and 1 cup of water. When it comes to a boil, gently stir in the egg, and immediately turn off heat. Sprinkle with minced scallion. Add a few drops of sesame oil and serve.

CHAPTER TWENTY-SIX

The Penthouse

Our new host was willowy and unusually tall for a Chinese woman. At fifty-one, Anthea had ivory skin, artfully plucked brows, even white teeth, and high cheekbones. Her dark hair tumbled past her shoulders. She looked elegant, even while padding around her penthouse in hot-pink silk embroidered slippers. Forceful and sophisticated, she was someone I could imagine sipping a glass of Barolo at the Four Seasons Hotel in Florence, a place she had recently stayed.

As Hilly had promised, Anthea's five-thousand-square foot, five-bedroom, two-storey penthouse was spectacular. Floor-to-ceiling windows in the living room overlooked that rarest of Shanghai luxuries, an unobstructed view of green space—a quadruple soccer field for the British-run school that Dickie and Anthea's daughter, Joy, attended. Beyond that was a Tesla car dealership and a Starbucks where Anthea and Hilly got together with the other mothers for morning coffee. In the distance, when pollution was only moderately dangerous, you could discern Shanghai's skyline, which included some of the most architecturally daring skyscrapers in the world. The pollution was unfortunate because the penthouse had three terraces. It wasn't healthy to sit outside, but Anthea used the terraces to grow pots of hibiscus, daisies, petunias, geraniums, rosemary, camellias, carnations, azaleas, and fuchsia.

The penthouse was tastefully decorated with Chinese antiques and art. A square marble table so heavy it took ten men to move dominated her formal dining room. In the living room, the sofas were piled with embroidered silk cushions. A massive jardinière held a dozen cascading white orchids. Hand-knotted silk rugs covered dark hardwood floors. On one wall I spotted a watercolour by the late Qi Baishi, one of China's most famous scroll painters of the twentieth century, which Anthea had bought at auction. Pleased that I had noticed the Qi, she took me upstairs to show me two other original works, one by Li Kuchan and the other by Lin

Fengmian. It was like living in a home with a Monet, a Degas, and a Picasso. Qi Baishi's annual auction sales had recently topped $60 million a year, third only to Picasso and Andy Warhol. Li Kuchan's paintings were in New York's Metropolitan Museum of Art. And in 2011, Christie's sold a Lin Fengmian landscape for $3 million.

Anthea was open about how much rent she paid — $106,000 a year. Her niece, who worked in a bank, and the maid occupied two bedrooms on the main floor. Upstairs, Sam got her son's bedroom because he was living in Beijing; I got Anthea's daughter's bedroom. Like Philomène, Joy, who was twelve, was thrilled for the chance to share her mom's bed. Anthea would have bought the penthouse outright, she told me, but the Chinese corporation that owned it figured it was too good an investment to divest just yet. Real estate prices had jumped 50 percent in the past year alone. Although she was a renter, Anthea had installed a white gourmet kitchen at great expense. There was a breakfast bar, garburator, dishwasher, microwave, gourmet stove, two-door Whirlpool refrigerator, and a full-height wine cooler. Like Gigi in Asti, Anthea had even calibrated the granite counters for her unusual height.

Anthea was from Taizhou, a city legendary for the beauty of its women. Just as Allex had been on the medieval salt route in France, Taizhou, at the confluence of the Grand Canal and the Yangtze River, had been a centre of the salt trade during the Tang dynasty (618-907 CE). Anthea was born there in 1965, in the last decade of Chairman Mao's draconian rule. Her father was chief engineer of the Taizhou shipyard. Her mother worked in the yard's machinery department. Despite his rank, her father earned little more than an ordinary worker. They lived in cramped state-owned housing, with dreary whitewashed walls and bare concrete floors and, like everyone else, without a washing machine or a refrigerator. Her mother left a cooked lunch for Anthea and her sister in a wooden cupboard, screened to keep out flies.

During the Cultural Revolution of 1966 to 1976, she had been too young to join the forced exodus of seventeen million urban youth to rural China. Throughout her childhood, however, food was strictly rationed. She ate meat and fish only once or twice a week. Mao's death in 1976 ended the madness. Anthea was eleven, just in time for her to resume her education. After she graduated in mechanical design from Nanjing University, she set her sights on a girlfriend's nerdy older brother. Luke was a graduate in finance from Peking University, with an MBA from Qinghua

University—the Chinese equivalent of someone with business degrees from Harvard and MIT.

Their first child, a boy, should have been their only child, as per China's one-child policy. But around the millennium, Anthea and Luke moved to New Zealand, with the goal of obtaining foreign citizenship. She enrolled in a university program in design and architecture. She also had her IUD removed. She figured China's draconian one-child law would no longer apply to her once she became a New Zealand citizen. And Joy, born in 2003, was automatically a New Zealander by birth. They took out New Zealand citizenship for their son, too. Years later, when he applied for admission to prestigious Peking University, he did so as a foreign student, sidestepping the highly competitive entrance exams for Chinese citizens.

Anthea's husband, however, retained his Chinese citizenship (China didn't permit dual citizenship). When he later opened a textile factory in their hometown, he received the preferential treatment Chinese citizens enjoyed, not just for corporate taxes but also for less onerous regulations. In 2005, after five years in New Zealand, the family returned to China. Anthea stayed in Shanghai with the children while Luke commuted from Taizhou, now a city of four million people, just three hours from Shanghai by super-highway. Riding the wave of China's red-hot growth, his privately held company expanded into real estate, trade, and investments. Anthea never spoke about the company, but a little digging online revealed that it had fifteen hundred employees and annual revenues of half a billion yuan (a hundred million dollars). Anthea had vaulted from famished child to trophy wife. Now she was a *tai-tai* who filled her days with kaffeeklatsches and art lessons.

After the penthouse tour, she left us alone with the maid, who would take us grocery shopping. Anthea said she would show up later to demonstrate how to cook dinner. "The important dishes I do," she said. "Our old amah can't cook."

"*Of course* I can cook," Orchid later told us. At forty-seven, she was several years younger than *Tai-Tai*, but looked ten years older. Hard labour had aged her. She was barely five feet tall, with sallow skin and a flat nose. Her hair was pulled back into a utilitarian ponytail, the same no-nonsense hairdo that maids around the world adopt to keep their hair from falling in the toilet as they scrub it. Her figure was lumpy, but that might have been because of her baggy brown sweater and pants. Her hands were knobby, her knuckles red and swollen. She had the watchful and alert air of a peasant woman. In the kitchen, she was hesitant and polite with me, obviously confused about who we were and why we were going shopping with her to the market.

Like Peace, Orchid did not speak unless spoken to. I asked where she was from. "Sichuan," she said. Spicy Sichuan food was one of China's great regional cuisines. Excited, I asked if she knew how to make *Hui Guo Rou* (回锅肉), Back to the Wok Pork Belly, a dish so famous that, like *cassoulet*, it had its own Wikipedia page. It's often called Twice-cooked Pork, but Back to the Wok is a better translation: you simmer a chunk of pork belly to denature the fat; slice it thin; stir-fry it with green chilies and any crunchy green vegetable; make a sauce of rice wine, soy sauce, *dou ban jiang* (豆瓣酱, fiery chili soybean paste), *tian mian jiang* (甜面酱, sweet fermented flour paste), and the Chinese *soffritto*—ginger, garlic, and scallions. Of course, I didn't recite the recipe to Orchid. I just wanted to know if she could make it. She looked at me as though I was a simpleton. "I'm *from* Sichuan," she repeated.

As we headed out the penthouse door, Orchid vanished then reappeared through a side door. I realized we'd just had a *Downton Abbey* moment. Orchid was not allowed to use the front door, even when going out with us. Ditto for when she walked the family dog. I couldn't suppress the thought: *no dogs or Chinese allowed.*

Outside a friendly man greeted us. *How much friendlier than Hilly's compound!* I thought. *Why, it's just like Repergo.* But then he opened the doors to a dark blue van, and I realized he was Anthea's chauffeur. In the privacy of the van, Driver Zhang and Orchid became loquacious. They told me they each had had only one child, as per China's one-child policy. "In those years, we were only allowed one child. Starting this year, people are allowed a second child, but I'm too old," she said, referring to a recent policy change. She smiled, but it was the grimace Chinese made when they feel bad. She said her son was twenty-five, and a graduate student in computer engineering in Xi'an, the city of terracotta-warrior fame. Despite the apartheid-like *hukou* system, social mobility was fluid—a maid's son would soon be a high-tech engineer.

Driver Zhang parked outside a wet market called Fragrant Hills. At the entrance were a cobbler, a seamstress, and an umbrella repairman. Otherwise it resembled markets in Italy and France. Certain stalls specialized in eggs—hen eggs, pickled eggs, "thousand-year-old" jellied eggs, salted duck eggs, fresh duck eggs, and tiny quail eggs. There were tubs of live freshwater carp and slithery eels, baskets of grey-green crabs immobilized by straitjackets of straw, mounds of artisanal tofu, and all manner of fresh pasta. The vegetables looked like they had been just picked—green bok choy, dark brown water chestnuts, feathery Chinese celery, zucchini and cucumbers with yellow blossoms still attached, winter *and* spring bamboo shoots, the first peas of spring, and pale button mushrooms. When I sighed over the freshness of everything, Driver Zhang snorted. "Fresh? It's not fresh. It's been sitting here half a day."

Orchid and the driver shopped in tandem, barely speaking, each enthusiastically poking and inspecting the goods. She bought a kilo of river snails, a bunch of fresh Chinese chives and a bag full of crisp greens for stir-frying. The driver checked out a stall selling premium Beijing Black pork, a cross-breed of a Berkshire with a common Chinese pig. The vendor, a young man in a bright yellow jacket, claimed his meat was free-range, organic, and raised in the mountains. It cost five times as much as ordinary pork, but *Tai-Tai* would eat nothing else. The vendor displayed a few pieces in anatomically correct position, front trotters on one side, tail on the other. Unlike in Italy, no glass protector prevented shoppers from touching the meat. With his bare hands, the driver picked up a chunk and threw it back down. "Too fatty," Driver Zhang said contemptuously. That was merely a bargaining stance. In the end, he bought half a kilo of pork with the prized skin still attached.

Back in the kitchen, Orchid donned velveteen sleeve protectors and a blue-checked apron. Without even pausing for a sip of water, she set to work. She soaked the river snails in a basin of cold water to rid them of grit, like Mirella had done with the pasta clams in Repergo (but without adding salt). Then she rehydrated dried bamboo shoots for a duck that Anthea had bought that morning from an itinerant poultry dealer. She had called his cellphone, and he met her on a corner with a selection of live birds, transported in cages on the back of his motorcycle.

Short-sighted, Orchid squinted as she checked the freshly slaughtered duck. For half an hour, she plucked pinfeathers and washed it under running water. She cut off the pope's nose and threw out one damaged claw. She removed the tongue (a delicacy), discarded the green membrane from the giblet, and pulled out the liver. By the time she finished, the duck weighed less than a kilo. Despite the awkwardly high countertop, she expertly chopped the duck into bite-sized pieces, bones and all. Then she blanched the pieces in a Le Creuset oval casserole (a pretty shade of aqua marketed as "Caribbean" that retailed for $350). With a start, I realized Orchid was using French-made pots in China, while Mirella and Maria Stella had used Chinese-made woks in Italy. And just as Bernadette had dumped out *her* first Le Creuset casserole of water when she made *blanquette de veau*, Orchid also threw out her first Le Creuset pot of water. Refilling the casserole with fresh water filtered through a Brita pitcher, she brought the duck back to a simmer. An hour later, she added the rehydrated bamboo shoots, ginger, scallions tied in a knot, and rice wine.

ORCHID'S SIMMERED DUCK SOUP WITH DRIED BAMBOO
Serves 4 with a couple of vegetable dishes and steamed rice.

Time; 3 hours, mostly unattended.

1	duck, hacked into bite-sized pieces (or leave whole and carve later)
10	pieces dried bamboo, rehydrated and rinsed
3	slices ginger, peeled
3	scallions, left whole
3 tbsp.	Chinese cooking wine (料酒)
salt to taste	

In a medium-large pot, cover duck with water, bring to a rolling boil, then simmer on low for 1 hour. (Orchid changes the water; I say don't bother.) Add drained bamboo, ginger, scallions, and cooking wine. Simmer for another 2 hours. Before serving, add salt to taste and remove spent scallions. If you didn't chop it before cooking, now carve duck into bite-sized pieces. Serve in a tureen or straight out of the pot.

Our next dish, stir-fried snails with chives, was Anthea's daughter's favourite, the Chinese equivalent to *escargots à la bourguignonne*. Orchid blanched the snails in a wok of water. Then she gave us each a darning needle to pick out the flesh. Pushing away the grey sequin-like cap at the opening of each proto-conch shell, we dug around until we could extract the meat, a grey-and-tan squiggle the thickness of a pencil eraser. "We only want the top half," Orchid instructed authoritatively. "The bottoms are the intestines." Someone should tell the French they've been eating *escargot* guts since 10,000 BCE.

For ten minutes, Sam and I poked out snail squiggles as fast as we could. Orchid beat us five to one. After thirty minutes of intense work, the three of us extracted one heaping cup of snail flesh. Compared to French and Italian dishes, Chinese food was crazy-making. Imagine a French chef plucking out snail meat for hours so diners could scarf down entire mouthfuls. Nope, you got half a dozen *escargots* drenched in garlic butter and parsley and the work of teasing them out was up to you.

Orchid glanced at the clock and dashed out to walk the dog, a purebred miniature poodle. Opal had been an expensive bribe to persuade a reluctant Joy to move into the penthouse. Mostly, the dog was ignored, tied up under a dark staircase, with a bowl of water and a litter box lined with a disposable pet diaper. The thrice-daily task of walking Opal fell to the maid.

When Orchid returned, she diced potatoes, carrots, and mushrooms for a stir-fry with imported giant shrimp, an uninspired combination (but nobody asked me, just like nobody asked Orchid, who I'm sure could have turned it into a whiz-bang Sichuan dish). Sam watched as she bashed a chunk of juicy ginger with the flat of her giant cleaver then coarsely chopped it with the *blunt* edge of the blade and finally minced it with the sharp edge. Presto! Ginger paste in a few seconds.

"You don't have to peel the ginger if the skin is thin and clean enough," Sam explained. "That's what they do in Chinatown." How did Sam know that? None of the seven restaurants he'd worked in served Chinese food. But I didn't have time to ask because Orchid was washing the Beijing Black pork, understandable after the driver poked the meat with his bare hands. Using a cleaver, virtually the only knife a Chinese chef used, Orchid scraped the remaining bristles and trimmed the fat, which she would later render into oil.

Joy popped into the kitchen just after five but left almost immediately. Like Cristina in Asti, she wasn't the slightest bit interested in cooking. Then Anthea appeared in the kitchen, the way I imagined Martha Stewart swept into her television studio at the last minute to film a cooking segment. Orchid, who'd been outside gathering laundry, darted back inside in a wordless panic. Apparently, she was Anthea's off-camera assistant, preparing the *mise en place* so the celebrity chef could demonstrate her art.

"Where's the ginger?" Anthea snapped. "Oh, here it is." She frowned. "Don't make a paste of it. Just slice it," she scolded. "My daughter doesn't like ginger."

Orchid's face instantly assumed a stupid affect. Her shoulders curved into a hunch of self-abnegation. As she moved around the kitchen, she executed a kind of pretend-fast walk, like a choo-choo train. If you looked carefully, however, she was moving at normal speed. Her new gait was a Stepin Fetchit manoeuvre, a tactical hop-to-it performance to placate an irritable slave master.

Anthea reached into her fridge for a big jar of rendered leaf lard, the visceral fat surrounding a pig's kidneys and loins. "When I was young, we were very poor, but we had lard. Just a small teaspoon and we could down two bowls of rice. It's so *xiang*." That was the Chinese word for "fragrant," coined centuries before a Japanese scientist discovered umami. "Leaf lard has a high smoke point," she added, scooping a spoonful into the hot wok. Before tossing the Chinese chives into the hot wok, she sprinkled salt on them. "The chives cook too quickly—no time to reach for the salt." She mounded the wilted chives onto a plate and then stir-fried the snails, adding rice wine, dark soy for colour, a pinch of sugar, three garlic cloves cut into chunks, half a red chili pepper, and a generous shake of white pepper as fine as dust.

"Because snails come from the river, they're *liang* (涼, chilly) for the stomach," she explained, invoking the concepts of hot and cold in traditional Chinese medicine. "The white pepper's heat counteracts the cold of the snails." She held the finished plate straight out to her left, like a surgeon thrusting contaminated instruments at the operating-room nurse. The problem was Orchid was on her right, at the sink, didn't notice, and failed to snap to attention. Anthea looked around and put down the plate in disgust.

"Before I got married, I watched my mother cook. After I got married, I kept cooking," she said. Like Dominique Grimaud in France, Anthea made her own charcuterie. At the coldest time of the year—Chinese New Year—she made air-dried sausage and cured pork belly. The meats were now dangling from butcher's string in the cool air above her kitchen balcony.

Her next dish was jumbo shrimp. But where was the wok? Orchid was still at the sink, washing it. "You're so slow," she scolded her amah. Orchid grimaced, a rictus of pain. Snorting with impatience, Anthea grabbed a clean wok. She stir-fried some broccoli and cauliflower. "It needs colour!" she suddenly shouted. "Where's the carrot?" Orchid rushed to the refrigerator, found one, peeled it lickety-split, and chopped it into small cubes. If there was an Olympic contest for speed-dicing, the maid would have won it.

"Oh," said Anthea with annoyance. "You should have cut it into matchsticks."

Orchid's shoulders slumped deeper. It felt like we were with Gordon Ramsay, filming *Hell's Kitchen*. Like a celebrity chef on television, Shanghai's new rich flaunted their power by shouting at servants. Wielding a pair of extra-long red silicone cooking chopsticks, Anthea tossed the diced carrots into a bit of hot peanut oil. "When carrots hit oil, their flavour and nutrition come out," she said. "Amah can't get the flavour out."

Next Anthea stir-fried gluten, or *mian jin* (面筋; *seitan* in Japanese). Often used as a meat substitute in Buddhist vegetarian cuisine, it resembled pale knots of tofu. She seasoned it with light soy, sesame oil, chicken stock, a pinch of sugar, three drops of aromatic Zhenjiang rice vinegar, a sprinkle of salt, and a condiment new to me, *hua jiao you* (花椒油). Translated as "oil of Sichuan peppercorn," a few drops added a frisson of numbing spice to an otherwise bland dish. Incidentally, in all my years in China, I never encountered anyone allergic to gluten, peanuts, fish, or shellfish. And now I understand why — new research in the West has found that early exposure to common allergens, such as peanuts, dramatically lowers a child's chance of becoming allergic. In my experience, Chinese babies were fed *everything* adults ate.

Anthea stir-fried the Beijing Black pork with slivers of fresh celery. As in Italy, we were making too much food — six dishes, including the simmered whole duck. "Normally we always make four dishes," she said. "Amah eats the leftovers for lunch." At dinner, Orchid ate alone in the kitchen while Anthea, Joy, Sam, and I moved into the formal dining room. The square marble table was big enough for twelve, so we awkwardly grouped ourselves around one corner, spinning the dishes on a large glass turntable. To celebrate our arrival, Anthea opened a bottle of a Deetlefs 2009, a spicy South African Shiraz. Over dinner, she confided why she kept

Orchid on, despite her supposed incompetence as a cook. "It's because of her sweet personality and because she's honest. If they're too smart, you have lots of problems." Hmm. From what I observed, Orchid was so smart she had to act dumb. So far, we had dodged the personal-chef bullet. After dinner, Sam broached the subject.

"Do you want me to cook Western food for you?" he asked politely.

"Yes," Anthea said instantly. "You can make breakfast for Joy."

I heard my son politely inquire what the twelve-year-old wanted. Bacon and eggs? Apple pancakes? Anthea said that Joy had developed Type I juvenile diabetes when she was seven. She could have bacon and eggs but only ordinary pancakes. Her breakfast had to be ready at seven a.m.

"Okay," said Sam agreeably, masking his horror at rising before the crack of noon.

Anthea warmed to Sam. "I really want to learn how to make bread. When I make it, it always turns out hard. I want bread like *this*." She spread her arms wide. I panicked. That sure looked like a baguette to me. Even Julia Child didn't know how to make a baguette, which is why she didn't include it in volume one of *Mastering the Art of French Cooking*. Judith Jones, her New York editor, pressured Child to include a chapter on bread in volume two. Her French co-author, Simone Beck, was passionately opposed, arguing that no sane Frenchwoman baked her own bread. When Child acceded to the editor's demand, Beck refused to participate—at all. "Two years and some 284 pounds of flour later, we had tried out all the home-style recipes for French bread we could find, we had two professional French textbooks on baking, we had learned many things about yeast and doughs, yet our best effort, which was a type of peasant sourdough loaf, still had little to do with real French bread," Child recalled in her memoir, *My Life in France*. By "we," she meant her husband, Paul Child.

Finally Child and her husband flew from Boston to Paris for a master tutorial with a French baker at the Paris École Française de Meunerie—French School of the Flour Trade (of course there was one). The expert painstakingly explained the process. It was, Child wrote, "entirely different from anything we had heard of, read of, or seen." She returned to Boston and many failures later finally nailed a formula that worked with American flour. The recipe in *Mastering the Art of French Cooking, Volume II*, took twenty-one pages and thirty-four drawings. To create the requisite burst of steam, Paul lined the oven floor of their Garland range with red quarry tiles, placed a pan of water on the bottom and then dropped in a red-hot brick. The first bricks they used were tiles made of asbestos cement, which was only just beginning to be recognized as a carcinogen. In subsequent editions Child quietly deleted asbestos tiles from the recipe.

Baking had never been part of the Chinese vernacular, and most people didn't even have ovens. Hilly, who had a Western-style kitchen in her condo, used hers for storing pots. Scarcity shaped Chinese cuisine. Widespread deforestation and population pressures created fuel shortages as far back as the Ming dynasty (1368-1644). To extract every bit of energy from one burner, the Chinese steamed bread (and those awful cornmeal pyramids) in stacked bamboo baskets. Stir-frying, relying on bursts of intense heat, also conserved energy. And to cook faster, all ingredients, especially cheap, tough cuts of meat, were cut into tiny pieces. Combined with vegetables and lots of rice or noodles, one small chunk of meat could satisfy an entire whole family—the way it did in Italy.

Luckily for us, Anthea didn't want to make a baguette. She yearned for white sandwich bread. "Soft, fluffy, with holes in it," she said dreamily. Sam didn't know how to make sandwich bread, either, but I heard him say confidently, "Okay. Do you have flour? Yeast?" Anthea pulled us into her kitchen, where Orchid was finishing up the dishes. He found imported General Mills Gold Medal All Purpose Flour and two types of yeast, Chinese instant and Japanese. Anthea even had a bread machine.

"I'll be right back," said Sam, racing upstairs. I followed him.

"I didn't know you could bake bread."

"Well, I can, sort of, but it's not my specialty at all," he said, opening his laptop. He knew how to make focaccia and pizza dough. "Who makes *sandwich* bread?" he muttered in despair as he clicked through a dozen online bread recipes. "It's like somebody asking you how to make *ketchup*. No matter what you do, it's going to taste like shit. Just buy Heinz." His mood darkened. The instant yeast was problematic. Also, Sam didn't like using all-purpose flour.

"When it fails," I said helpfully, "blame the humidity."

Sam went back downstairs to tell Anthea we needed active dry yeast and bread-specific flour. "No problem. Let's go," she said, grabbing her designer purse and pale blue cashmere coat.

"She's crazier than you are," Sam whispered. "Make bread? *Tonight?*"

As we hurried out the door, she speed-dialed the chauffeur on her cellphone. It was nearly ten, but apparently he was on call 24/7. As we stood outside in the dark waiting, she muttered impatiently, "Where is he?" (I'm guessing he was in bed.) The driver soon appeared, looking none too happy. The store, which specialized in imported foods, was about to close. We found organic bread flour, but no active dry yeast. Suddenly, Sam spotted a whole-grain mix for a bread machine. "Let's use the bread machine tonight. And tomorrow we'll use the organic flour and make a loaf from scratch," he told Anthea. I held my breath. She reluctantly agreed.

At eleven, Sam got the dough into the bread machine. It would take three hours to rise and bake, which meant he had to get up at two to extract the bread from the hot machine and rouse himself again at six thirty to start Joy's breakfast. (A friend in Fredericton, a master baker, wondered why we didn't just set the timer on the bread machine so it would be ready in the morning. Good question. I have no idea.) At the time, unaware of such nifty things as timers on bread machines, I considered intervening. I wasn't worried about child exploitation. I was afraid of Bologna Take Two: Sam ripping off his apron and stomping into the Shanghai night. "I'll take out the bread," Anthea volunteered. "I have to get up at two every night anyway to test my daughter's blood sugar." My impression of her suddenly softened. I had caricatured her in my mind as a spoiled *tai-tai*, and perhaps she was, but she was also a devoted mother.

The next morning, I witnessed a miracle: clear blue skies over Shanghai. The yellow-grey miasma of pollution had finally dissipated, blown out to sea. Another miracle: at seven a.m. Sam was up, the bacon was sizzling, the eggs were frying, and the non-apple pancakes were ready to go. The bread machine had turned out a decent whole-wheat loaf. Joy ate silently, standing at the kitchen bar. Anthea, willowy in slim-cut capris, ate only eggs on a bed of mesclun, sprinkled with soy sauce. So much for Chinese Food Rule: *never put soy sauce on your salad*.

Orchid told Sam to make a pancake-bacon sandwich for Anthea's niece, a twenty-something who ate on the subway on her way to work. The niece had ducked out of dinner the previous night, and that morning she rushed by as Orchid wordlessly handed her the foil-wrapped packet. The doorbell buzzed. It was the chauffeur, letting Joy know he had arrived to drive her one and a half blocks to school. No one invited him in.

The vaunted Chinese family was looking a lot like an American family. The niece didn't speak to anyone in the morning. Joy's father was absent half the week. And I discerned no warmth between Orchid and Joy, even though the maid had arrived when Joy was six, half her lifetime ago. In *The Help*, Kathryn Stockett's best-selling novel set in Jackson, Mississippi, in 1962, the black maids and white children developed close bonds. In China, it was merely a servant-master relationship, perhaps because people in Shanghai were one generation removed from poverty. Class distinctions were important, so the driver had to cool his heels outside the front door while the kid finished her bacon and eggs.

Sam and I occupied a confusing grey zone. Anthea was mostly gracious and hospitable because we were, sort of, guests. But at other moments our status was close to migrants. For instance, I'd brought New Brunswick teabags with me for my morning cuppa and, unsure of where to keep them in her pristine kitchen, left them in a clear baggie on a side table in the hall. "What's this?" Anthea instantly demanded, poking at my teabags with irritation. I apologized. From then on, I kept them in my suitcase. Please note we're talking about *tea — in China*. In Sam's case, he *was* a servant, a private Western chef making a child's breakfast.

After dropping Joy at school, the driver returned to drive Anthea to her regular kaffeeklatsch with the other *tai-tais* at the Starbucks one block away. Sam finished washing the dishes with Orchid. It was 8:15. He went back to bed.

CHAPTER TWENTY-SEVEN

Maid in China

When Anthea wasn't around, Orchid unhunched her shoulders, wiped the ingratiating grin from her face, and stopped hustling around the kitchen. She liked Sam because he admired her cooking techniques. He was also respectful. After meals, he helped her wash the dishes and scrub the pots.

Just as the migrant worker had found a job in Prato, Italy, a fellow villager had passed on the message that maid jobs were plentiful in Shanghai, and, six years earlier, she had made the long journey, signed up with an agency, and interviewed with Anthea, who was specifically looking for someone who had never worked anywhere else. "I didn't want someone coming with habits from another family," said *Tai-Tai*, who previously had done her own housework. The pay should have been at least 5,000 yuan a month ($1,000). Anthea, however, would pay only 4,000, reasoning that was plenty for a household of three: herself, her daughter, and her niece. (She didn't include her husband, who was home only three nights a week.) "Amah doesn't cook," she added. "She just prepares the food and cleans the house. And she gets lots of days off because the school has holidays. We pay her during the holidays."

From my experience working undercover as a maid for a month, there was no question the job was a killer because it was so much more than weekly vacuuming. Orchid's workday began at six when she had to take Opal out for a walk. Then she made breakfast for the family. She also made artisanal school lunches for Joy, and we're not talking ham sandwiches. She handwashed the crystal wineglasses we'd drunk from the night before. She made the beds. She opened the curtains and aired out the house. Every day, without exception, she cleaned the huge penthouse from top to bottom— mopping floors, washing four bathrooms, polishing sinks, wiping baseboards, and dusting furniture, lamps, tchotchkes, and each step of the stairs—all to exacting standards no sane person would bother with if they had to do it themselves. Like Bernadette, who *did* clean her own house, *Tai-Tai* was *une maniaque*.

Orchid shopped for most of the groceries. She prepped the meals, which, as all sous chefs know, is more work than the actual cooking. She washed the dishes and did the laundry. She also boiled and cooled *all the drinking and cooking water* for the household. Like Hilly's maid, she wiped the soles of our shoes. After dinner, she cleaned the kitchen, which included mopping the floor. At night, she wasn't off duty until nine or ten p.m., after she closed the blackout shades in the skylights in our bedrooms, removed the many decorative bed cushions, and turned down the sheets. All that was missing was the hotel chocolate on the pillow. She did, however, prepare bowls of fresh fruit, plucking each grape from its stem to save us the bother.

Orchid wasn't allowed to sit on the living-room sofa. That meant she was also barred from watching the television. In his book *At Home*, Bill Bryson described how servants in nineteenth-century England had nowhere to sit during their workday, either. They put in long hours and faced never-ending chores: polishing boots, trimming lamp wicks, lighting fires, and emptying chamber pots. But the hardest part of the job was mind reading. Bosses barked orders without explanation. Class stratification meant the rich did not talk to the help.

A few years after taking the job, Orchid had screwed up her courage to ask for the going rate. Anthea responded with a humiliating one-hundred-yuan monthly increase, the equivalent of sixty-five cents more a day. Orchid quit. The agency sent a replacement who didn't work out. Anthea hired her old maid back at, yes, 5,000 yuan a month. And this time, Orchid demanded and got a television set in her bedroom.

Like Peace, Orchid always vanished on her day off. She had nowhere to go, but that apparently was better than her spacious bedroom in the penthouse. Once upon a time she did get breaks during the school vacations Anthea had mentioned. But now, the acquisition of a family pet meant when the family travelled abroad, Orchid was tethered to the dog. Sichuan was two thousand kilometres from Shanghai. Was she able to get back regularly to visit her husband? Orchid rolled her eyes. "He's worthless," she said, spitting out the word. At any rate, she added, she only got one week's vacation a year. *One week?* I was stunned. How could she even get to Sichuan and back in that time? She gave me a sharp look. "Just one week."

Anthea's husband, Luke, returned every Friday afternoon by chauffeured car and left every Monday morning the same way. The four nights a week he was in Taizhou, he lived in a flat next to his office where he kept a private chef and, the other moms whispered, a mistress. A 2013 study by People's University in Beijing found that a stunning 95 percent of "corrupt" officials kept mistresses. Corrupt or otherwise, many rich businessmen kept mistresses and didn't go to much trouble to conceal them. China was, after all, the country that invented concubines.

Richard Ling, a Canadian lawyer friend who had been living in Shanghai for several years, invited us to dinner at Crystal Jade Garden in the old French Quarter. He regaled us with the abundant Chinese slang for kept women: *xiao san (*小三, Little Third), meaning the third person in the marriage, and *er nai (*二奶, Second Set of Breasts). When a man had multiple mistresses, additional ones might be called *san nai* (三奶, Third Set of Breasts) or even *si nai* (四奶, Fourth Set of Breasts). I thought Richard was pulling my leg. He summoned over the female maître d' and a waitress, partly to tease Sam about dating them (and them about dating Sam). Amid giggles, they confirmed the nicknames. Like bird watching, once someone had pointed out what to look for, it was easy to spot second sets of breasts (or maybe third). At a nearby table, the young woman was glammed up while her date was dressed carelessly. She placed the choicest morsels on his plate, clung to his every word and, when he deigned to speak, laughed as if he were the wittiest man imaginable. I watched my son absorb this misogynist paradise. "Hey, Sam," I said. "Do you want to be worshipped?" He glared at me.

Modern Shanghai was like a Jane Austen novel where the heroines were always angling for rich husbands. "A large income is the best recipe for happiness I ever heard of," said Mary Crawford in *Mansfield Park*. Just as in Regency England, no one in China thought it crass, merely sensible. But unlike in Regency England, no one in China thought marriage was a prerequisite to a sexual relationship. Many mistresses were in it for the real estate, Chinese media reported. Shanghai's superheated market had put an ordinary flat beyond the reach of secretaries, teachers, and nurses. As a mistress to a wealthy man, young women could and would demand a condo, with the plan of later marrying someone else and starting a family. Richard cited a Chinese proverb: *xiao pin, bu xiao chang* (笑贫不笑娼; Ridicule poverty, not prostitution). Marriage itself was monetized. On first dates, Chinese women were blunt. *Do you own a house? Where? A car? What model? How much does your job pay?* To meet the parents, the suitor might be expected to fork over half a kilo in weight of one-hundred-yuan notes, the highest denomination of Chinese currency. The equivalent value was $30,000.

For the *tai-tai,* divorce was possible, but it brought economic disaster. Real estate, bank accounts, and other assets were typically registered in the husband's name. Instead a new industry sprang up: "dispelling the mistress." For a hefty fee, a personable young man or woman would be dispatched to befriend the mistress, perhaps by moving into her apartment building or joining her health club. The goal was psychological, to discover her motivation. Money? Love? Sex? And then the dispeller would persuade the mistress that it was in her own interest to leave the *tai-tai*'s husband, usually by helping to find her a good job in another city — or a newer, richer lover.

Anthea invited us to go with her to return a kettle. That sounded unpromising, but I had learned to always say yes. As the chauffeur headed downtown toward the city's newest, most luxurious mall, Anthea explained she had been undercharged for a Le Creuset kettle. If she didn't return it, or pay the difference, the sales clerk would have to pay.

As she strode past the Cartier, Louis Vuitton, Dior, and Gucci boutiques, Anthea looked like a fashion model. Her ice-blue cashmere coat emphasized her height and slimness. In a country where so many people were short because of malnutrition, she *looked* rich, even though she had grown up poor. I felt that even more when we found the clerk, a young migrant woman who stood less than five feet tall.

She effusively thanked Anthea for her kindness in preventing her pay being docked. In gratitude, she proffered the only thing she could afford that a rich *tai-tai* might like: a Starbucks latte. Anthea, of course, had just come back from her three-hour kaffeeklatsch *at* Starbucks. She waved it off. The clerk turned to me. "Amah! You drink this." Sam chortled so loudly people turned their heads. Mustering all my dignity, I graciously accepted the latte. I even shared it with Sam.

Anthea had an oil-painting class one morning, so we watched Orchid make a lunch for Joy. The school had a large cafeteria with a salad bar, pizza station, and sandwich grill, but like many of her classmates, Joy preferred hot lunches prepared by her maid and delivered by her chauffeur. This one included handmade egg-crepe dumplings, a dish in which the main ingredient seemed to be slave labour. Just like Maria Rosa had done when making *frittatini*, Orchid washed and blanched two pounds of fresh spinach, squeezed out the excess water, and chopped it finely. "You can use Chinese celery or cabbage if you want," she explained, as she minced fresh shiitake mushrooms and a half kilo of lean pork, impressing Sam with her knife skills. After mixing the spinach, mushrooms, and pork together, she added soy sauce, sesame oil, and a pinch of salt. So far this had taken forty-five minutes.

The next step was making the dumpling skin. Orchid beat several eggs. Using a large non-stick pan, she made lacy, almost transparent egg crepes, which she cut into rectangles and stuffed with the spinach-mushroom-pork mixture. "It's the same fold as the *tortelloni* in Italy," Sam observed. Next Orchid poached the dumplings in a savoury broth spiked with marinated shrimp and packed the dumplings in a leak-proof container. She added fruit to the lunch bag and, for good measure, a few pieces of salmon sashimi. The doorbell rang. Like a military operation, the chauffeur had arrived to deliver the hot lunch to Joy. Total elapsed time for one kid's lunch: one hour and fifteen minutes.

When Anthea returned from her art class, Sam taught her to make focaccia from scratch. Without measuring, he combined salt, sugar, yeast, flour and water, and began kneading it. There was no warm place to let it rise so, somewhat nervously, he turned the oven on as low as possible and stuck the dough inside. After it rose, he punched it down so it could rise a second time. Anthea belatedly suggested adding a paste of sweet osmanthus, made from the fragrant yellow flowers of the cassia tree. Sam tried to work some into the dough, but to his annoyance he ended up squishing out the air. He reshaped his now deflated loaf into a rectangle. It was a success—a golden crusty Italian focaccia, scented with Chinese osmanthus paste.

Anthea instructed Orchid to wash the bok choy from their farm. Their farm? That's when I learned that Luke operated an organic farm next to his factory. The staff grew vegetables and fruit and raised sheep, pigs, ducks, and free-range chickens. Each Friday, before driving him to Shanghai, his chauffeur would fill the trunk with fresh eggs, bok choy, cilantro, spring onions, and corn. The farm also supplied the factory canteen, which provided a hot lunch for the fifteen hundred workers at his textile factory. In a country where famine still haunted recent memory, a company lunch was an important perk. Anthea's niece received subsidized lunches at her bank, and Hilly's husband had recently persuaded his CEO to offer all employees a free lunch.

"Joy shouldn't eat anything with hormones. My husband loves her so much. He wants her to be healthy," Anthea said. She was an extreme version of Marie-Catherine, Maria Rosa, and Federica. They all preferred growing their own food, but Anthea was deeply paranoid about food safety. Like many Chinese, she felt nothing was safe in the food chain after recent scandals — melamine in baby formula, rat meat sold as lamb, exploding watermelons dosed with a growth chemical, and forty-year-old frozen chicken wings. Each week, at great expense, Anthea imported two litres of fresh milk from New Zealand. Perhaps food hazards were an inherent part of an industrial revolution. In England in Samuel Pepys's era, vinegar was sharpened with sulphuric acid, sugar stretched with plaster of Paris, and bread adulterated with bone ash and chalk, according to Bill Bryson.

In Shanghai the water itself was a menace. Three years earlier, officials had found sixteen thousand bloated pig carcasses floating down the Pu River, which supplied much of the city's tap water. For all its shiny expressways and modernistic subway system, the Shanghai government had abdicated a fundamental responsibility: providing clean drinking water. Although Anthea paid thousands of dollars in rent, she had to implement her own in-house, five-step system of water purification. She installed a filter at the intake pipe to the penthouse and a second filter at the kitchen sink. From this tap, Orchid constantly filled pitchers equipped with Brita filters. The maid then boiled the triple-filtered water, cooled it, and stored it for drinking, cooking, and making tea.

As we were preparing dinner that night, we suddenly we ran out of cool boiled water. Anthea, who wanted to poach vegetables, was furious. "Amah! Why is there no water?" Orchid looked panic-stricken, and rushed around filling a kettle. "There's no time!" Anthea snapped, angrily opening three bottles of mineral water to cook the vegetables. Sam and I exchanged guilty looks. We had been thirstily drinking amounts of water in quantities that had made us objects of amusement in France and Italy.

At dinner, we sampled Anthea's home-cured pork belly and sausages, which she had made with soy sauce, sun-dried baby shrimp, salt, and sugar. The sausages were rich and deeply flavoured, with little cubes of translucent pork fat. The preserved pork belly was as good as the finest acorn-fed Bellota ham from Spain.

After dinner, Anthea still wanted Sam to make fluffy white bread. He looked desperate. Suddenly I remembered a *New York Times* recipe for fail-proof crusty bread that famously required *no kneading*. Sitting side by side with Anthea on her velvet sofa, I searched the internet on my laptop. Although the Great Firewall of China blocked Google, Instagram, Facebook, Twitter, Bloomberg, Reuters, and the *New York Times*, like so many Chinese, including Communist Party members, I bypassed the censors by paying a low monthly fee to subscribe to a Virtual Private Network. The VPN made it appear like I was signing on somewhere outside of China. But the weak Wi-Fi signal in Anthea's penthouse meant we could access only the printed recipe but not the how-to video. Using the *Times* recipe, Sam made his third loaf of bread. It was a disaster, a leaden beige lump that failed to rise. He was mortified. "It smells good," Orchid said kindly.

"I'm going to try one more time tomorrow," Sam vowed.

CHAPTER TWENTY-EIGHT

The Help

The next morning Orchid awoke with a bad cold. Sam and I were in the kitchen getting breakfast ready when Anthea shouted, "Amah, mop the floor! Look how dirty it is!" To me (and Sam) the floor didn't *look* dirty. But Orchid dutifully grabbed the mop and began swabbing as fast as she could. It was like watching an ugly stepsister bully Cinderella (except Anthea was quite beautiful).

Whenever *Tai-Tai* wanted Orchid, she hollered from any part of the penthouse, and Orchid fake-hurried over. My lawyer friend, Richard Ling, said *tai-tais* shouted at their maids to demonstrate who was boss. "It's almost as if they're thinking: I'm rich, and if I don't abuse you, I'm not rich enough. It's not that I *need* to be nasty—I'm nasty because I *can* [be]." In other words, yelling at a maid was a form of conspicuous consumption, the HR equivalent of a designer purse.

Speaking of purses, Richard's theory was that *tai-tais* revenge-shopped. "They're thinking: my husband is spending money on third breasts, so I might as well buy something for myself." Richard suggested yet another reason why *tai-tais* abused the help. Despite all their comforts and prestige and wealth, the women were unhappy. "They are not treated well. They know their husbands are cheating on them." He knew this from his personal experience dealing with the super-rich. He wasn't a wife, just a big-time international lawyer for a top firm. As such, he got calls day or night from his powerful Chinese clients, once at three a.m. on Easter Sunday. "It's dominance," said Richard. "To show they own you. It's the same with the maids."

That morning, when Anthea noticed Orchid sniffling, she asked, not solicitously, "What's wrong? You have a cold?" Orchid nodded. "Take some medicine," Anthea said brusquely. There was no "take it easy" or "go back to bed" or "take the day off." Sam listened to this exchange while he was poaching eggs. The night before, Anthea had approved the breakfast menu for Joy: eggs benedict. At 7:15 a.m., the bacon was crisp, and he had already poached the eggs. He was whisking egg yolks with melted butter and lemon juice for hollandaise when Joy raced into kitchen. To his surprise, she grabbed a hunk of his freshly made focaccia and smeared it with Nutella.

"It's almost ready," Sam told her politely, motioning to the bowl of pale yellow sauce.

"Oh, I'm not eating breakfast. I have to be at school early today," Joy said.

And then she was gone. No apology, nothing.

No one had ever treated Sam quite so cavalierly before. As his mother, I felt sorry for him but also a twinge of *schadenfreude*. When he was Joy's age, I used to get up at four thirty to make *him* breakfast before his early peewee hockey games. To his credit, Sam merely sighed and went back to whisking hollandaise. Anthea had eggs benedict on her regular bed of salad, without toast or bacon. I realized she had an iron discipline about calories, apparently to maintain her willowy figure.

Like servants, Sam and I sat down to eat after Anthea had finished. "Being an amah must suck," he said. "It's not just the hours. That's manageable. It's the way you're treated. No 'thank you.' No acknowledgement of your work. Only criticism." As he headed upstairs to go back to bed, I heard him mutter, "So *this* is what it's like being a movie star's private chef." Mind you, Sam had experienced abusive treatment before. At his first-ever restaurant job, washing dishes in a high-end Toronto restaurant, the chef openly referred to him as "the retard" and screamed at him for sneezing.

Later, after Anthea had gone out, again without saying a word about the arrangements, I asked Orchid what the day's plan was. "I have no plan," she said, without rancour. "Only *Tai-Tai* has a plan. Whatever it is, she'll tell me." If knowledge was power, maids were the most powerless of all. The *tai-tais* never told them when they were going out, or where, or when they would be back, or who was eating dinner at home, or at what time. Partly it was to keep them on their toes, so they could never slack off. But lack of communication also caused logistical problems. One day, for instance, an hour before serving dinner, Orchid discovered that Joy had invited a classmate. Then just as suddenly, she learned that the meal had to start early because a math tutor was coming. The tutor showed up even earlier than announced, so Joy and her friend had to gulp their dinner in five minutes. But then it turned out that the girls weren't hungry anyway because they had snacked on pancakes.

"Nobody tells you anything. Then they yell at you for not reading their minds," said Sam, still smarting from getting up to make eggs benedict for Joy.

This was classic Marxist alienation, not that anybody in Shanghai was reading Marx anymore. Psychologists say lack of control over one's work is a trigger for workplace stress. Orchid had zero control, but she did have one pressure valve. One morning, the miniature poodle escaped from its jail beneath the stairs and, ecstatic about its sudden liberation, was barking and racing madly around the kitchen. When it almost tipped over the garbage can, Orchid aimed a vicious kick. It didn't connect, but I was shocked at the naked hatred on her face. And then I understood. Opal was the only member of the household with lower status than the maid.

I felt the same loss of control over my life when Anthea surprised us with another request. She had consulted with Hilly and the two other *tai-tais* in our project, and they wanted us to make them afternoon tea, with fresh scones, clotted cream, and pastel *macarons*. Call it the *Downton Abbey* effect. When the Chinese premier visited the UK, Prime Minister David Cameron had presented him with an autographed copy of the first season's script from its creator, Julian Fellowes. An estimated 160 million Chinese had been transfixed by the series, but the country's new rich found useful role models in the way this aristocratic family treated its footmen, valets, chauffeurs, cooks, and scullery maids. With over one million millionaires and four hundred billionaires, China was the fastest-growing market in the world for British-style butlers. A school in Chengdu, Sichuan, trained aspirants to wear white gloves, pour wine, and precision-set tables with knives and forks. So this latest *tai-tai* request shouldn't have been a surprise. Still, I felt panicky. I never intended to make Western food in China, any more than I wanted to make Chinese food in France or Italy. I was mad at Hilly — and at myself for foregoing the opportunity to learn that damn brioche from Marie-Catherine's neighbour's husband.

"We can make Chiara's yogourt cake," Sam said nonchalantly. "It's easy to make finger sandwiches. I can cure some gravlax for smoked salmon. We can modify that tuna sauce that Mirella taught us. I'll bake some chocolate chip cookies."

"What about *macarons*?" I had no idea how to make them, except I knew it involved squeezing batter through a piping bag. Have I mentioned I can't bake?

"We'll be fine," Sam said, with a shrug. "I mean, who cares?"

I looked at my son. We were having another role-reversal moment. Surprises and challenges didn't faze him. *He* was bolstering *my* confidence, calming me down.

One morning after Sam went back to bed, I went out shopping with Anthea. I would have dragged him with us had I known she was going to buy a chicken — the kind that didn't come chilled on a foam tray wrapped in plastic. Driver Zhang dropped us near an intersection a couple of blocks from the penthouse, kitty corner from the Tesla dealer we could see from Anthea's terrace. A sunburned man in his thirties was standing next to a motor scooter. Strapped to it was a wide metal cage crammed with live chickens, ducks, pigeons, quail, and partridge. Atop the cage, five more squawking fowl were tethered by their feet, creating the effect of a super-sized brown and gold feather duster.

"I'm making *Bai Qie Ji* (白切鸡, white-cut chicken)," Anthea said.

The man — whom I'll call Birdman — selected an orange-feathered specimen. As he poked and prodded the bird, it frantically flapped its wings. Anthea nodded. Pinning its wings to immobilize it, Birdman weighed it on a portable electronic scale. With a swift half-rotation of his wrists, he wrung the chicken's neck. Using a pair of heavy iron scissors, he snipped its throat. Birdman carefully bled out the chicken, its wings flapping feebly, into a dangling yellow bucket half-filled with fresh blood, feathers, and guts. There was no rotten smell or even a speck of gore on the sidewalk or his camouflage pants. In the wake of an earlier outbreak of avian flu, he and other poultry vendors had to be fastidious. They dodged health inspectors by staying on the move. Regular customers like Anthea kept in touch by cellphone and met at pre-arranged spots.

I'd never seen an animal slaughtered before. Was the *tuade* in France like this —simultaneously gruesome and matter-of-fact? The other birds remained, well, unruffled. That was surprising since, as I learned at the Jeanselmes', chickens are cannibals and, in overcrowded conditions, will peck one another to death. Birdman lifted the lid of an old metal pail wedged on the foot-bed of his scooter. In fact, there were two pails—the bottom one filled with hot charcoal that heated water in the top pail. Using tongs, Birdman plunged the dead chicken into the boiling water for ten seconds. Within two minutes, he had plucked it clean, eviscerated it, and dropped it into a clean plastic bag labelled "Expo 2010 Shanghai."

Back home, Orchid rinsed the still-warm chicken and simmered it in filtered water spiked with rice wine, scallions, and a few slices of ginger. Authentic white-cut chicken should be cooked very briefly—a quick boil, and then an hour or two of steeping in the same pot, lid on, flame turned off. It was a Cantonese classic from Guangzhou, twelve hundred kilometres to the south. Orchid, who was from Sichuan, twelve hundred kilometres northwest of Guangzhou, simmered the chicken for about two *hours*.

Apparently, it was chicken night at Anthea's. She taught us how to make spicy chicken wings, and in return, she wanted Sam to demonstrate an Italian chicken dish. To make the wings, she toasted a spoonful of wrinkled reddish-brown Sichuan peppercorns (花椒) in a bit of oil in a wok. "We want the red ones," she said. Until that moment, I'd only known about brown Sichuan peppercorns. Brown or red, they are like itsy-bitsy hand grenades of tongue-tingling buzz, and are also widely used in Tibetan, Nepali, and Indian cuisine. When the Sichuan peppercorns turned aromatic, Anthea removed them and used the same oil to sauté five slices of ginger, several whole scallions, and five cloves of smashed garlic. "Too little garlic," she snapped. Orchid hopped around, preparing another ten cloves in thirty seconds. Pushing the herbs and spices to one side of the wok, Anthea browned the wings in batches in the fragrant oil. She added cooking wine, light soy (生抽), and dark soy (老抽). I've always disliked dark soy, which is bitter and overpoweringly salty. Anthea was the first cook to explain how to use it. "It doesn't taste good," she agreed. "It's just for colour."

After two minutes, she added chopped fiery green and red chilies. Now she would add a bit of water, right? "Nope." Cornstarch? "I *never* use cornstarch," said Anthea, with contempt. I felt like I was back with Maria Stella, making *spaghetti carbonara* while she yelped, "No garlic!" Anthea's wings were addictively spicy. Sam said it was her best dish.

ANTHEA'S SPICY AND NUMBING CHICKEN WINGS
Serves 2 (or 4, as part of a meal with rice and other dishes).

1 tsp.	Sichuan peppercorns (*hua jiao* [花椒]), red or brown
3 tbsp.	canola oil
5	slices of ginger
5	scallions, washed and left whole
10	cloves garlic, smashed
2 lbs.	chicken wings, separated into drumsticks and wings
¼ cup	rice wine (料酒)
3 tbsp.	light soy (生抽)
½ tsp.	dark soy (老抽)
10	fresh red chilies (Thai), seeded and cut in chunks
10	fresh green chilies (jalapeño or Thai), seeded and cut in chunks

In a wok, toast the peppercorns in a spoonful of oil over medium heat until they are fragrant but not dark. Remove from oil. Turn heat to high. Add remaining oil. Sauté ginger, scallions, and garlic. Push seasonings to one side so they don't burn. Brown the chicken wings in small batches. Add extra oil if necessary. When all the wings are browned, return them to the wok. Add rice wine, light soy, and dark soy. Bring to a simmer, stirring the wings. Add red and green chilies. Stir-fry 2 more minutes. Discard long scallions. Serve with rice.

Sam demonstrated Maria Stella's chicken *scaloppine* with fresh lemon juice. He dusted some chicken cutlets with flour and salt, seared them, poured on a cup of lemon juice, and reduced the sauce until it was syrupy. He dashed out to Anthea's terrace garden for a sprig of fresh rosemary, which he swished in the sauce for the final five minutes to give it an herbaceous tang. I set the square marble dining table for dinner. As we sat down, Anthea suddenly shrieked at Joy, "Don't use those chopsticks!" She pointed to the lime-green pair that I had put at her daughter's spot. They had been the only lime-green ones in the drawer, and I thought they were rather pretty, which is why I gave them to Joy. Startled, I snatched up the offending green chopsticks and rushed back to the kitchen for another pair.

"Those were Amah's chopsticks," Anthea said, more calmly, as I returned.

Amah has her own chopsticks? I knew better than to say that out loud, but later while we were washing the dishes, Orchid explained that she had to use a separate set of chopsticks, dishes, and water glasses. Before I could process that, she added, "The Sunday amah has black chopsticks."

Wait, there's a Sunday amah? I'm sorry to keep writing in the interrogative italic, but I was having conversational whiplash.

On Sunday, Orchid's only day off, another amah came to Anthea's home. The family's inability to do without a servant for one day was startling. The chopstick segregation policy, however, was downright shocking. Suddenly I recalled an incident at Hilly's where, again, I had set the table. As we sat down to eat, she whipped away the bowl in front of Sam and swapped it for another. "Use *this* bowl," she told him, in a slightly embarrassed tone. Sheepishly, she explained the first one was reserved exclusively for Dickie's use. And now an earlier scene at Anthea's made sense. Joy's classmate had come to dinner one night. Again, I had set the table. "Those are *my* chopsticks," Joy said, with a self-conscious laugh, reaching over and switching chopsticks with her startled friend.

For the new rich, servants and outsiders were dangerously germ-ridden. The attitude seemed part of the overall anxiety associated with an industrial revolution. Virginia Woolf, in her diaries, described servants as irritating as "kitchen flies." Bill Bryson wrote that in Edwardian England, "servants ... were constantly accused of being dirty, which was decidedly unfair since a typical servant's day ran from 6:30 in the morning to 10:00 at night." (Not unlike Orchid's.)

Tableware segregation reminded me again of *The Help*, set against a backdrop of Rosa Parks and the assassination of Medgar Evers on the eve of the Civil Rights movement. Tension especially revolved around toilets. "All these houses they're building without maid's quarters? It's just plain dangerous," said one of the white women. "Everybody knows they carry different kinds of diseases than we do." In Shanghai, where everyone was the same race, money was the essential difference between Anthea and Orchid. Both women came of age in the Cultural Revolution, with its draconian system of secret police and everyone earnestly singing songs in praise of Chairman Mao, but now Anthea was lording it over Orchid. However, the real estate bubble could burst at any moment. Fortunes could evaporate. Downward mobility was an omnipresent risk because China's have-nots were not accepting their lot in life. Amah's son was studying computer engineering. Who was to say where he would end up?

Shanghai's luxury condos and monster homes must have taken their architectural templates straight from developed democracies because they were not designed for live-in servants. Peace occupied a normal bedroom at Hilly's and shared a bathroom with Dickie. Orchid occupied a bright main-floor bedroom and used the same luxurious bathroom as Anthea's niece. No one could object to their amahs using the toilets because there were no special amah toilets.

In other ways, life did imitate art. In the segregated South and in Shanghai, the mistresses deemed their servants dirty, diseased untouchables who had to use their own plates. Of course, these same servants prepared the family's food. Likewise no one in Shanghai seemed to understand that if you treated someone badly enough, she could spit in the soup. In the most famous scene in *The Help*, a maid named Minny drops by the house of a hateful white lady who slandered her as a thief, destroying Minny's hopes for future employment. The maid brought her famous chocolate pie, which the white woman interpreted as appeasement. After she ate one delicious slice and started on another, she inquired about the secret ingredient.

Minny snapped, "Eat my shit."

CHAPTER TWENTY-NINE

Smashed Cukes

Orchid was still battling her cold when the chauffeur took us to the wet market to shop for our last supper. "Do you get sick days?" I asked. She rolled her eyes.

We returned with Beijing Black pork, tender green cabbages, bok choy, and slender Chinese celery. As soon as we walked through the door, Anthea insisted we go right back to the market. That was the inefficiency of slavery. Driver Zhang's time, my time, all worthless, and never mind the wasted gasoline. But I kept that thought to myself. At the fish stall, Anthea bought river clams, gigantic bivalves the size of salad plates. The fishwife expertly pried them open, sliced through their adductor muscles, pulled off their frilly gills, and swished them in a bucket of water. At the mushroom stall, Anthea bought fresh shiitake mushrooms. As we were leaving, she whirled around. "Give me some scallions," she said. It was not a request, it was a command, and it meant: give me *free* scallions. The woman obeyed, expressionless, adding a bunch of scallions to the mushrooms. Despite her cashmere coat, her trendy Spanish-made Camper boots, her aqua-blue Le Creuset cookware, Anthea didn't hesitate to chisel a Chinese migrant who made a living selling mushrooms. She did the same at the Beijing Black pork stall. After buying some meat, she used the word "gift" as a verb, as in: "*Gift* me (送我) some leaf lard. *Gift* me (送我) a bit of liver." Perhaps I am being too hard on Anthea. After all, she was one of his steady customers so perhaps she deserved frequent-flier points in fat and offal.

Back home, Anthea demonstrated *Hong Shao Rou* (红烧肉), melt-in-the-mouth soy-braised pork belly. All twenty-three of China's provinces claimed it, in various iterations, as *their* classic dish. Cut into cubes, skin attached, the pork belly was typically braised in light and dark soy, rice wine, ginger, garlic, scallions, star anise, and rock sugar. Anthea cautioned that rock sugar should only be added toward the end, or it would toughen the meat. (I've never found that to be true.)

ANTHEA'S HONG SHAO ROU (红烧肉)
– SOY-BRAISED PORK BELLY

Serves 4 with stir-fried bok choy and steamed rice.

1 lb.	pork belly, skin on, cut into 1-inch cubes
3	scallions, whole
3	slices ginger
¼ cup	cooking rice wine (料酒)
¼ cup.	light soy (生抽)
2 tbsp.	dark soy (老抽)
¼ tsp.	salt
1	whole star anise
3	chunks crystal sugar (or substitute 3 tbsp. white or brown sugar)

Bring ¾ cup of water and all ingredients except sugar to a hard boil. Simmer on low heat for 90 minutes. Add crystal sugar. Simmer another 30 minutes. (I often make it one day early; I remove the pork and chill the sauce separately so I can later discard the fat.)

In Western cooking, the diner does most of the work, sawing away at a steak, digging into a baked potato, even adding salt, pepper, and ketchup, and don't get me started on lobster and *escargots*. In China, all the work is done in the kitchen. For instance, our next dish — *Za Cai* (杂菜), which means mixed vegetables (a better translation is Rainbow Slivers) — required ten ingredients, each shredded by hand, the culinary equivalent of cloisonné, a make-work project for oppressed women and/or slaves. A Moulinex chopper, the go-to gadget in France and Italy, was unacceptably crude because the aesthetics of the dish — perfectly uniform shreds, each with its own texture and colour — required a human hand. Anthea had chosen carrots, ham, dried tofu, cabbage, green and red peppers, yellow egg crepe, translucent mung-bean vermicelli, crunchy wood-ear fungus, and shiitake mushrooms. Orchid had already parboiled some ingredients. Then Anthea absentmindedly plunged some rehydrated mung-bean vermicelli into boiling water, a blunder, like trying to re-boil cooked spaghetti. "Oh, stupid," Anthea said, meaning herself. Orchid tittered in embarrassment mainly because none of us would have dared utter such a thought aloud. *Tai-Tai* sautéed all ten ingredients in a sauce of sugar, chicken stock, dark vinegar, light soy, sesame oil, oil of Sichuan peppercorn, chili-garlic sauce, and chopped cilantro. The result was underwhelming. After all that work, Rainbow Slivers was a muddled dish, tasting mostly of soy sauce.

The bulging grey river clams resembled prehistoric faceless monsters. Anthea cut each in half, and showed me how to squeeze them so that the mud (or something else icky) oozed from their intestines. I felt disgusted, even more so when I thought about how many clams on the half shell I'd eaten in my life. Anthea washed the halved clams six times, and then rubbed them with salt, flour, and oil. "These things I do myself," she said, meaning Orchid was incapable of washing clams. Anthea stir-fried the clams with ginger and scallions in a pressure cooker, and added rice wine and several bottles of filtered water. She screwed on the lid and continued to cook them for half an hour.

The appetizer, smashed cold cucumbers, *liang ban huang gua* (凉拌黄瓜), was one of my favourites. Unlike Rainbow Slivers, it required almost no work. All you had to do was smash the cucumbers with the flat of the cleaver, chop coarsely, and season. Or so I thought. "That's not right!" Anthea yelled at Orchid. *Tai-Tai* impatiently took over the task, cutting away the watery core, a step I've never bothered with. But, I must admit, Anthea's tasted better.

ANTHEA'S SMASHED COLD CUKES
Serves 4 as an appetizer.

4	small Asian cucumbers (or 1 medium seedless English cucumber)
1	clove garlic, finely minced
1 tbsp.	aged black vinegar made from sorghum, preferably from Shanxi (山西老陈醋)
1 tsp.	sesame oil
salt to taste	
10	cilantro leaves (optional)

5   drops oil of Sichuan peppercorn (花椒油)
(optional)

Rinse cucumbers and whack them with the flat of your Chinese cleaver (or any broad knife). If you are finicky, cut away the watery core and discard. Coarsely chop the fragments into bite-sized bits. Just before serving, toss with rest of ingredients.

Anthea finished the pork belly with a small handful of topaz-hued crystals of rock sugar. Orchid gave the pot a stir and added six hand-tied knots of tofu skin, made from the film collected during the boiling of soy milk. (The Chinese waste nothing.) "Amah!" Anthea shouted. "You put the tofu knots in too early." Orchid, who looked strung out from her cold, said nothing.

For once, the niece was going to eat with us. After three hours of cooking, our dinner was ready and cooling on the dining-room table. Just as Maria Stella insisted we wait for her son and her son's partner to arrive before we could eat the *spaghetti carbonara*, Anthea said we had to wait for the chauffeur to bring Joy home from a music-theory tutorial. When she finally arrived, we attacked the now lukewarm dishes: drunken shrimp, smashed cukes, blanched jade-green celery slicked with fragrant sesame oil, sautéed Chinese chives, stir-fried greens, Rainbow Slivers, clam soup with matching pale grey oyster mushrooms, and soy-braised pork belly. The shrimp and pork belly were correctly made, the vegetables perfectly stir-fried. The clam soup was oddly metallic, but perhaps the mud put me off.

By ten we could eat no more. But everyone wanted to sample Sam's fourth attempt at baking bread. This time he worked without a recipe, adding an Italian flourish—*pignoli*—at the end. (Yes, the Chinese ate pine nuts, which they called, yes, pine nuts [松子].) This time Sam's bread was a success. As I cut it into tiny cocktail-party sized squares, Anthea asked, "Do you like cheese?" She returned to the table with a block of aged cheddar, a costly item in China, and a chilled bottle of New Zealand Chardonnay. Anthea was a nice person—if you weren't her maid.

As we relaxed, she said to me, "How do you feel about Sam getting a Chinese girlfriend?" Sam squirmed and blushed. The niece cracked up.

Surmising this was the wrong company in which to talk about predatory Chinese women, I said lamely, "He's too young."

"It's good to practise," Anthea said, with a smile. Somehow that sparked a memory of the time someone had stolen her purse while she was shopping at IKEA.

"Sam, you must be careful no one steals your cellphone."

"Nobody wants my phone," he said, pulling out his broken-down phone, a cast-off from his older brother (or maybe from Norman). When he saw Anthea's horrified face, Sam gleefully showed her his duct-tape wallet, too.

"You'll *never* get a girlfriend!" Anthea said, shaking her head.

Revelling in his inconspicuous consumption, Sam confided to *Tai-Tai* that the shoes he arrived in Shanghai in had been so gross that, to impress her, Hilly had insisted on buying him a new pair. At that, Anthea put down her wineglass and shouted for Orchid. The amah, feverish from her cold, had already retired for the night. When Orchid didn't answer, Anthea shouted again, "Amah!" Orchid hustled to the table a minute later, looking dazed. Soon maid and mistress were trooping to and from a storage room with armloads of clothing and boxes of shoes, all rejects from Anthea's twenty-five-year-old son in Beijing. Sam was thrilled. Everything fit him, including the shoes. He accepted a pair of well-made trousers, a brand-new hoodie, two T-shirts, and a pair of expensive athletic shoes.

"Sam, you're really helping me out. I couldn't get rid of these clothes," Anthea said happily. Orchid looked quite *un*happy, and not just because she'd been hauled out of her sickbed. Had it never occurred to *Tai-Tai* that her maid had a twenty-five-year-old son who just might appreciate some clothes?

The next morning was a Friday. Anthea's husband, Luke, was due home that afternoon. Hilly had obliquely warned us that we were welcome only when Luke was away. She said we weren't supposed to meet him because he didn't like anyone knowing anything about his businesses, or anything else for that matter, and Anthea didn't want us around then, either. By now, I knew, but I wasn't sure if Anthea knew that I knew. This wasn't a topic one could casually broach.

As his return drew near, I felt something change in the household. It was hard to put my finger on it. It was not joyful anticipation. Wives who have been married to the same guy for twenty-five years don't get excited when he shows up after an absence of four days. But there was a flurry of preparation. Like a bride getting ready for her wedding day, Anthea had booked a spa appointment, including a facial, a massage, and a manicure. She was also going to get her hair done. No one had asked Sam to make breakfast on the last day. He was contentedly frying himself some eggs when Joy wandered into the kitchen. Out of politeness—as a Canadian, he can't help himself—he asked if she would like some fried eggs. "Yes," the twelve-year-old muttered, without raising her eyes. Sam slid the perfectly fried eggs onto a plate for her. She ate them. She didn't say thanks.

Sam cracked two more eggs in the pan. He was just about to sit down and eat *them*, with bacon, when Orchid asked if she could grab the eggs for the niece, who was rushing to work. Sam made two more eggs. Anthea usurped those for her usual morning mesclun salad. Sam cooked two more eggs. I was tempted to claim them, as a joke, but I resisted. Finally, he sat down to eat his breakfast. Only Orchid noticed. "You've got a good son," she said. "He's very hard-working."

From Orchid, that was the highest praise.

CHAPTER THIRTY

Peony

Peony was transplanting trees. Not saplings, mind you, fully grown trees. She was moving them from one side of her expansive backyard to the other to make room for several newly acquired trees, including a thirty-five-foot-tall gingko. Of course, *Tai-Tai* wasn't humping the trees herself. A crew of four sunburned peasants in blue overalls had dug holes more than a metre deep on one side of the yard. And now, in a titanic tug-of-war with nature, they were hauling out the existing trees, dragging them sixty feet across the lawn to replant them.

Trees were Shanghai's latest status symbol. Property developers often removed mature trees during construction, stuck them in the ground somewhere else, and later replanted them to boost real estate prices. Given the city's severe pollution, green was the new gold. The rich, who Midas-like once craved anything gilded, now lusted after anything green. Instead of Golden Villas or, say, Golden Land, Anthea's compound was called Green Court. Nearby gated communities were called Green Garden, Emerald Shanghai, Bellewood Villas, Green Villas, Greenhills, Riviera Garden, Oasis Villa, Pasadena Garden, Palm Spring [sic] Garden, Jade Cloud Villas, and Green Land (not to be confused with Among the Clouds Green Land Villas).

Our new *tai-tai* lived in a gated community called Willowbrook at the Green Hills. Peony, forty-nine, was a slender Chinese woman with a taste for diamonds and cashmere. She and her British husband, Paul, fifty, and their two children lived not far from Anthea's penthouse in a three-storey, six-thousand-square-foot house. They had bought the empty shell in 2009 for several million dollars. Now it had five bedrooms, five bathrooms, hardwood floors, big windows, and an all-white gourmet kitchen, and was worth $10 million (which explained why Chinese mainlanders thought real estate was such a bargain in North America).

British design and architecture magazines cluttered her coffee table.

Peony hadn't finished her renovations—she planned to redo the basement and add a second kitchen, like an Italian *cantina*. In the meantime, she was re-landscaping her large backyard, which had real grass, blooming tulips, and flowering trees, including pomegranate, cherry, orange, and chestnut. In an overcrowded city, it was the ultimate status symbol.

That first afternoon, Peony and I watched the transplanting frenzy from the raised terrace. The full-grown gingko was too heavy for the crew, so the boss, a thirtysomething man in a well-cut tan suede jacket, had summoned a fifty-ton crane. It couldn't access the backyard, and instead had parked out front, blocking the street and preventing at least one of Peony's neighbours from getting out of his driveway. The crane operator blindly hoisted the gingko up over the rooftop, where it swung and swivelled like a car being offloaded from a ship. As Peony gleefully filmed the action on her iPhone 6, the gingko whacked the terrace balustrade and nearly smashed a kitchen window. We hurried to a safer spot on the side of the house while the crew shouted warnings to the crane operator, who couldn't hear over the din of his motor. The boss ran back and forth between crane operator and the crew, bawling orders. A cellphone call might have been just the thing, but no one asked my advice.

Peony kept filming and laughing. Finally, the boss ordered the crane operator to extend the boom to its full length. One leg of the outrigger jack lifted dangerously off the ground, like a dog peeing in a bush. With the crane about to topple, the operator refused to extend the arm any further. He released the gingko about five feet above the ground, where it crash-landed two feet shy of the pit, snapping several lovely branches.

"Tomorrow," the foreman promised Peony, "we'll send ten men to put the tree in the hole."

Earlier, the household had been chaos. Suzy, nine, was late for her gymnastics class. "She'll eat in the car," her father, Paul, hastily instructed the maid in fluent Chinese. "Make her some of Grandma's won ton soup." The maid boiled the frozen won ton, prepared a broth out of nothing but soy sauce, salt, and powdered chicken essence, and handed the child a brimming porcelain bowl as she climbed into the back of her chauffeured van.

Sam and I, along for the ride, hungrily eyed the won ton. We hoped we would make that for lunch, but when we got home, Paul didn't seem interested in eating. His son, Pete, eleven, had disappeared into the basement to play video games. The maid had returned to her household chores. And

Peony had scheduled her regular weekly three-hour massage in her dedicated third-floor therapy room, equipped with a massage table, fluffy towels, heat pads, and scented oils. The masseuse, a stylish young woman with a designer purse, arrived each week by motorcycle. "The massage is really good," said Peony, in perfect English. "Would you like to try it? You can't have anything less than two hours. Otherwise, it isn't worth it." With no glimmer of hope for lunch, I opted for a two-hour massage, the longest and most painful of my life. The next day, I had bruises all over my neck and calves. How *Tai-Tai* endured three hours was baffling, but she said it had transformed her life and she never missed a session.

Peony, who was Chinese, ran her own import company. Paul was the chief representative for a British manufacturer in China. Their children, Suzy and Pete, attended different private schools, for a total tuition bill of $100,000 a year. The family vacationed in France and Italy and went on weekend ski trips to Japan. Recently they had bought a large flat in Kensington, one of London's most expensive neighbourhoods.

Like Anthea, Peony's childhood had been marked by deprivation. She grew up in Puxi, in the heart of old Shanghai. In those days, to conserve fuel, the government prohibited indoor heating anywhere south of the Yangtze River, including Shanghai. "We had no heat, no food. In the winter, it was -3°C in our apartment," she recalled. Mao's fanatic Red Guards beat and tormented her father, a schoolteacher. "My father always said, 'If Mao could have died ten years earlier, it would have been so much better.'" Instead, Chairman Mao unleashed the Cultural Revolution in 1966, which only ended with his death, in 1976. In those days of food rationing, Peony remembered, during International Children's Day one year, the teacher had distributed pieces of cake. Peony dropped hers by accident. "It was so hard," she recalled, "it didn't break."

Speaking of food, that day it seemed like we were never going to have lunch. Peony was on a diet, but not like Maria Stella, whose idea of dieting was to eat *bagna càuda,* pasta, and *carne cruda*—and then skip dessert. Peony didn't eat lunch, period. She told me she hadn't eaten rice in ten days. Paul was also trying to lose weight and had sworn off alcohol for three months. They both looked fine to me, but my svelte standards were low and involved elasticized pant waists. Okay, if I stared hard at Peony, I might discern a tiny tummy, but most women I knew would have killed for her slender figure.

Sam and I exchanged worried glances. We'd come all the way to China to cook, but people had become so rich they were afraid to eat. Anthea ate her poached eggs on mesclun. Peony was skipping entire meals. China had gone from famine to fasting in a single generation. To put the dieting in context, Anthea and Peony grew up in the aftermath of the Three Years of Natural Disasters, the worst famine in Chinese history.

Mao's Great Leap Forward in 1958 sowed the seeds of disaster. He tried to jump-start an industrial revolution with backyard steel furnaces and, as part of his grand plan, ordered the peasants to melt down their woks for steel. Each family also had to turn over their rice, cooking oil, firewood, livestock, poultry—even their rice bowls and kitchen tables. Eliminating family meals—the glue of the traditional unit—was part of Mao's scheme to catapult China into the future. "Families are the product of the last stage of primitive communism," he said in a 1959 speech. "And every last trace of them will be eliminated in the future."

Soon 90 percent of rural families were eating in mess halls. Everyone eyed how much their neighbours ate of the collective supplies, and gorged—the first all-you-can-eat Chinese buffets in China. (Dad's were the first outside of China.) Food was wasted. The kitchens soon ran out of rice. Meanwhile, to boost agricultural output, Mao collectivized the land, too. The next three years, the harvest failed. Authorities blamed the weather, but other factors were sagging morale, toxic overdoses of fertilizer, and unscientifically dense planting of crops. When people began dying of starvation, there were no riots because few understood how widespread the problem was. Armed guards prevented peasants from leaving the villages to beg in the cities, and outbound letters were censored. The world did not learn about the famine until the 1990s.

It was no accident that the amahs we met came from the provinces that had suffered the highest death tolls: Peace was from Gansu, Orchid from Sichuan, and Peony's maid, Little Chen, from Jiangsu. Like Sam and me, she was caught unawares her first day of work that rich people had stopped eating. "I kept waiting and waiting for lunch. I didn't realize they didn't eat," Little Chen said, adding that she had nearly fainted from hunger. After that, she learned to bring her lunch, which she ate surreptitiously when no one else was around. Unlike Peace and Orchid, she did not live in. She typically worked twelve hours a day, six days a week, and did not leave until she was dismissed, usually after she had washed the supper dishes.

"There's never a moment's rest here," said Little Chen, who was thirty-two and had thick, glossy hair pulled back in a ponytail. She had started working here a month earlier, one year after she'd given birth to a daughter, her second child. That first month, she had lost more than ten pounds from running up and down four flights of stairs. Peony's house was the biggest she had ever cleaned. She earned 6,600 yuan ($1,300) a month, one-third more than Anthea paid Orchid, and substantially more than a factory job. To put it in perspective, Little Chen's salary put her squarely in China's new urban middle class, according to a Goldman Sachs report. "This job pays more, and there are no night shifts. At night, I have to look after my baby daughter," she said. Unlike Anthea and Peony, who both had second children with impunity, Little Chen had been punished for violating the one-child policy. "I paid the ten-thousand-yuan fine," she said unhappily.

Working for Peony was stressful, Little Chen said, because *Tai-Tai* was so demanding. "In a factory, there are standards. You meet them, you're fine. Here there are no standards. You don't know if you're doing okay. You don't want to *fan cuo wu* (犯错误)." *Fan cuo wu* meant "make a mistake," but no English translation could do it justice. It wasn't used to indicate a wrong turn on your way to the store. In Maoist China, *fan cuo wu* meant serious, career-destroying, quasi-criminal, fatal mistakes of political judgment. So I was surprised that, throughout our stay, Little Chen muttered incessantly about *fan cuo wu*. When I needed a vase for a bouquet of orange ranunculi and yellow freesias I'd bought as a hostess gift, Little Chen blanched. She had no idea what vase to use. As I blithely opened kitchen cupboards hunting for a container, she looked so terrified that I stopped. "I'm afraid of *fan cuo wu*," she said miserably. China's nouveau riche had usurped the fear factor previously monopolized by the Communist Party. *Fan cuo wu*, once used to castigate Mao's enemies, was now invoked when discussing a flower vase.

When Peony sent Little Chen to buy milk, she took a cellphone photo of the brand Peony preferred. And when Little Chen was sent to buy bread flour (Sam was again baking up a storm), she texted back photos of the various labels so Peony could choose which to buy. "I don't want to *fan cuo wu*," she explained. Another day, Little Chen sought my advice. "Should I dump these flowers? I don't want to *fan cuo wu*." The bouquet in question was withered and yellow, with slimy green stems. Fear of *fan cuo wu* was contagious. I suggested we all wait until *Tai-Tai* got home.

Little Chen had made a conscious decision to endure her nitpicking employer for the extra pay. During her decade of working as a maid in Shanghai, she saved enough to buy a house back in her hometown. When her son, now ten, reached high-school age, she would move the family back so that he could take the college entrance exams from the village school, the one to which his *hukou*, or residence permit, was tied. Many other migrants had left their offspring back in the village — sixty million children, or one in every five — to be cared for by grandparents or other relatives. Despite the logistics and the cost, Little Chen was determined her family would stay together.

Peony's and Little Chen's respective housing was a Dickensian tale of two cities. Willowbrook at the Green Hills was a gated enclosure of faux Tudor, Georgian, Tuscan, Spanish, and Provençal monster homes. To impart a European flavour, the streets were paved with cobblestones, which Peony complained broke the spike heels of her friends' $800 Jimmy Choo shoes.

Perhaps because of her childhood memories of freezing in old Shanghai, Peony had installed radiant heating under all the hardwood floors. She liked to walk around barefoot in winter, even though the electricity bill was outrageous. Her living room was filled with over-stuffed sofas, Chinese antiques, and silk curtains that puddled onto the floor. There were giant vases of fresh-cut lilies and branches of cherry blossoms. Her all-white kitchen had granite countertops, a pro-style stove, a top-of-the-line silent dishwasher, and, like Mirella's, a professional meat slicer.

On each end of her work island were thirty-litre, stainless-steel, hip-high, touch-free Brabantia garbage cans, just like the one Marie-Catherine had in Allex. I'm sure Marie-Catherine never paid this much in France — Brabantia was made in the Netherlands — but online the garbage bins cost $500 each. When Peony expressed her desire for one (or two), Paul had objected. She nagged him until one day he made the mistake of saying, "Fine. If you see someone else bringing one back, okay." Peony spotted someone schlepping a Brabantia through the Shanghai airport, so she, too, brought back two garbage cans from Europe, each packed in its own large suitcase.

Like Bernadette, Peony was a control freak. Come to think of it, they would have made quite a pair: maniac *tai-tai* and *maniaque* housekeeper. Peony also kept four dishtowels, each with a separate and specific function.

Starting from the left, the first one was for drying hands and ... after that, I lost track. Scared to *fan cuo wu*, I simply stopped using the dishtowels altogether, especially after I saw Peony scold Little Chen for incorrectly hanging them up. The amah had hung the towel by a corner. "Look at this! The towel is dragging on the floor," Peony upbraided her. "You must tuck the towels in from the *mid*-section."

Little Chen had lodgings in a shantytown called Three Bridges, a ten-minute scooter ride away. She rented two shabby rooms in separate tumbledown buildings for a monthly total of 1,000 yuan, or one-sixth her pay. Neither room had a toilet, bath, or kitchen. She and her husband, who worked at a security-and-monitoring company, lived in one room with their baby daughter. Their nine-year-old son and the grandmother occupied the other. The village of Three Bridges had an air of impermanence, as though it would be bulldozed at any minute for a shiny new expressway. And indeed, it *was* slated for demolition.

Hilly had warned me that Peony's maid couldn't cook, but of course Little Chen knew how to cook. In fact, her husband, who had previously worked as a chef in a Shanghai restaurant, relegated the cooking at home to her. Thrilled, I asked if she knew how to prepare Lion's Head Meatballs, a Jiangsu specialty named for their resemblance to the curly manes on the mythical Chinese lion statues outside the Forbidden City.

"Of course, I can make it," said Little Chen, rattling off the recipe. "You take a chunk of pork belly and chop it up. Add ginger, scallions, an egg, and a bit of cornstarch."

"And cooking wine and soy sauce?" I asked, showing off.

"No! No cooking wine or soy sauce!" said Little Chen. "Then you shape them into meatballs and fry in oil or poach in water. Very simple."

Sam and I hoped we might make Lion's Head Meatballs for lunch, but Little Chen didn't dare do anything without explicit orders from Peony. And *Tai-Tai* was incommunicado, having her three-hour massage upstairs. Eventually Paul took pity on us and suggested lunch at his favourite Irish pub. Sam and I hid our disappointment. We hadn't come all the way to China for plates of bangers and mash. Later, Peony told us she wanted us to cook Western food for the family, as per Hilly's misguided arrangements. For the afternoon tea Sam and I were supposedly making, she was already flying in almond flour and silicone *macaron* moulds from the US. The items would arrive any day.

When Suzy returned home from her gymnastics class, Sam taught her how to bake meringues and make Bernadette's mayonnaise. But he was uncertain what to prep for dinner. "What should I do?" he asked. I shrugged. Like Little Chen, I decided passivity was the safest approach.

At dinnertime, Peony made a weird mishmash of dishes: a Japanese chicken curry from a pre-packaged sauce, oven-broiled mackerel, a salad, and unadorned, sliced avocado. Paul grilled thin-cut pork chops on the terrace barbecue. Little Chen stir-fried bok choy with fresh winter bamboo shoots, the tastiest dish by far. As we ate, Peony regaled Paul with the tale of the giant gingko tree. I mentioned that for my birthday gift the previous year, Ben and Sam had dug out a dead six-foot evergreen on our front lawn.

"Did you have a chainsaw?" Paul asked.

"We broke two shovels," Sam said, with a snort. "The wire basket was still around the roots. It took us three hours."

Peony smugly noted their neighbour across the street had paid US $10,000 for a cherry tree.

"Wait—how much did we pay?" said Paul, looking alarmed. Peony assured him she had paid a fraction of that amount for their cherry tree. He relaxed.

For dessert, Peony set out some gigantic hothouse strawberries. She herself refused to eat even one. "My diet," she explained. Later I looked it up: one strawberry was six calories. Little Chen had eaten her dinner in an adjacent room. As she came into the dining room to clear the table, she noticed an unopened bottle of French red wine on the floor. "What should I do with this?" she asked.

"That wine is horrible," Peony snapped. "Throw it out."

"If you want it, take it," Paul said, kindly.

Little Chen smiled shyly and picked up the bottle. I imagined her showing her husband. *Hey, look at this. Those weird millionaires didn't want this bottle of French wine.*

Without explicit permission, however, Little Chen could not take anything, even from the trash. It would have been construed as theft. When I asked Hilly why she hadn't hired a live-out maid, given the lack of privacy and that the pay was no different. "A live-in maid," Hilly said, "won't steal your meat and cooking oil."

Peony had put us in a huge room on the top floor with a queen-sized bed and a bunk bed. We had our own luxurious bathroom with a glassed-in shower, soaking tub, and heated towel racks. Sam, however, was less than thrilled to share a room with me. "Why can't Peony let me sleep in her massage room?" he groused.

Secretly I was happy for the intimacy. With the end of the trip in sight, I felt time was running out. Soon Sam would disentangle himself from me and fly away. Sharing a room meant we could talk late into the night, and we did. We discussed the food and how the amah was treated. We mulled over the paradox of how, when you get rich enough to eat anything you wanted, you stopped eating.

Sam noticed that Little Chen tried to do everything for him. "When I wanted to wash my hands in the sink, she pushed the spout toward me. And before I could reach for the tap, she turned it on." He said he enjoyed hanging out with Suzy and teaching her how to separate eggs for meringues. Then, sounding surprisingly like a parent, he added he was afraid that she and her brother would never learn how to take care of themselves, to cook, do their laundry, and make their own beds. He thought it was bad for kids to be raised with servants. "Do you realize what's happening? *The driver carries their shit into the house.*"

Indeed, the kids always hopped out of the van and walked into the house empty-handed. The chauffeur followed, carrying their backpacks, an obsequious smile pasted on his face. When Suzy was performing at an after-school concert, Little Chen got a text message from Peony. Her nine-year-old daughter had forgotten her dress shoes, socks, *and* choir folder. The amah rushed around hunting for the shoes, which she polished until they shone. Unsure whether Suzy needed ankle socks or knee socks, she set out a pair of each. The chauffeur picked up the shoes and socks. He had also received a text from Peony, instructing him to drop off her daughter's music folder. The driver, who could read neither music nor English, asked me to vet the loose-leaf binder. It was the choir music. "Oh, thank you, thank you," he breathed, looking relieved. As he hurried off to deliver the shoes, socks, and music, his third trip to school that day, Little Chen screamed.

"Wait, Driver Huang!"

The driver came back to the front door. "What?"

"Does she need water to drink?"

And after all that fuss, neither of Suzy's parents went to the concert.

CHAPTER THIRTY-ONE

Pearls and Scallion Pancakes

I'd planned to get up the next morning to watch the spectacle of ten peasants humping a giant gingko tree across the lawn. But the gardeners had been as silent as mice, and I awoke to find it duly planted. Peony had bought snacks of Shanghai street food for breakfast. Sitting on the sunny terrace, we ate deep-fried crullers and steamed buns stuffed with pork and chopped greens. Peony ate almost nothing. At one point, she stood up and shouted at the migrant workers painting her neighbour's fence. "The smell of your paint is ruining our breakfast. You must stop working while we eat," she told them. They instantly acquiesced.

After, Peony invited us to go with her to a flower market across the river, in old Shanghai. She said she was also planning to visit her father, who was in the hospital. I was taken aback. She hadn't mentioned her father even once. I couldn't help comparing her to Marie-Catherine, who had made sure at least someone looked in on Mamie every day. It was the chauffeur's day off, so Peony drove. Weirdly she instructed Sam and me to sit in the back, which didn't stop her from pleasantly chatting with us. She told me her Buick van cost $103,000 — more than twice the sticker price because China taxed imported vehicles heavily. The Shanghai licence plates cost an additional $15,000, but she felt lucky to have paid it because the all-powerful municipal government had started limiting plates to reduce traffic congestion. (Unlike, say, New York City, Shanghai issued its own licence plates.) Now you had to buy monthly lottery tickets and pray your number came up. Until you got licence plates, of course, you couldn't put your car on the road. Hilly, for instance, had blundered by purchasing cheaper ones from a nearby province. The municipal government subsequently imposed zone restrictions on non-Shanghai plates, which meant she could no longer drive on expressways, including to the airport.

The flower market was packed. Peony settled on one vendor where she bargained hard for four gigantic hanging baskets of petunias and dozens of pots of ranunculi, which the migrant gardeners would later plant in a single afternoon. Prices weren't posted, so after negotiating a good deal, Peony asked for some freebies from the vendor, who threw in several pots of vivid pink gerbera daisies.

"Do you like pearls?" she asked as we drove away from the flower market. She took us to a multi-storey building that consisted almost entirely of small jewellery shops. She was ostensibly looking for outsized South Sea pearl earrings for her British sister-in-law — at $1,000 per pearl — but Peony tried on some jade and pearl necklaces for herself. The shopkeeper, sensing a rich *tai-tai,* urged her to consider some antique brooches inlaid with turquoise kingfisher feathers. When I mentioned I'd seen similar pieces in museums, the shopkeeper nodded eagerly, "They're from the Imperial Palace." Peony was tempted. Then I spotted two identical "antique" brooches and whispered that they were fakes.

Tai-Tai next showed me her favourite cashmere sweater shop, where the prices were as high as in Paris. Sam, who had trailed us from store to store, was tired of cooling his heels outside. "I'll never understand shopping," he hissed to me, when Peony was out of earshot. "I don't see how that was enjoyable at all. I spent six hours walking in a fucking circle."

It wasn't *quite* six hours, but it was nearly two p.m., and Sam was getting *hangry.* Unfortunately, Peony drove to yet another shop, one that specialized in bespoke cashmere sweaters. She asked Sam to remain in the van so she wouldn't get a parking ticket while she picked up several custom-made jewel-coloured sweaters for Paul. She also wanted to commission a slinky black cashmere dress for herself, based on a photograph torn from a fashion magazine. Suddenly I understood why Peony had been dieting. A clingy knit dress looked good only if you were bone-skinny. Otherwise it would expose every bump and bulge. Of course, my solution was simple: don't buy a slinky cashmere dress (and save $500).

The shopkeeper, an older woman with dyed coal-black hair and red enamelled talons, discussed the proper yarn weight so the dress would drape *just so.* Now even I was getting a touch *hangry.* Outside, Sam glared at me from the van. I found a fruit store and bought a couple of bananas. Fearing I might *fan cuo wu,* I first checked with Peony that it was okay for Sam to eat in the van. He looked so pathetically grateful I felt guilty.

Peony arrived at the van a moment later, laden with parcels. "I'm so sorry. I didn't know you were hungry," she said apologetically. "Do you want to grab a snack before we head home? There's a famous *xiao long bao* place around the corner." I was confused. I thought we were supposed to visit her father in the hospital. "Oh, I completely forgot," said Peony. "Okay, we can stop at the *xiao long bao* place and pick up something for my parents."

Xiao long bao or little-basket buns got their name from the bamboo baskets in which they were steamed. No one made them at home because they were so challenging to make. Done properly, each bite-sized bun should look like the onion dome on a Russian orthodox church. You had to twist a paper-thin circle of dough around a tiny raw meatball *and a spoonful of broth.* The trade secret was that the broth had to be made well in advance, chilled into gelatin, and cut into tiny cubes. Eating *xiao long bao* also required advanced chopstick skills — gently lifting each drooping bun without piercing the delicate wrapping and losing the broth.

The restaurant, called Wealthy Springtime Little-Basket Buns, was a hole in the wall with rough wooden tables, a blackboard menu, and laughably cheap prices. We had to crowd around the cashier, thrusting bills at her to place our order. After we paid up front, we had to find a seat by hovering over a diner who looked about to finish. Peony insisted on treating us — and ordering. Sam and I were too faint with hunger to fight her. She bought us each two *liang* plus an extra three *liang* to take out to her parents. A remnant of food rationing, one *liang* was equivalent to one ounce, the weight of flour used to make five bite-sized buns. Most restaurants in China had abandoned this system, so Sam didn't realize Peony had ordered him just ten bites of food when he could have easily eaten fifty. We scarfed down our respective two ounces. As we hurried out, Sam looked hungrily at the steaming bowls on other diners' tables. Peony, naturally, didn't eat a bite.

On the drive to the hospital, she told me her father had been hospital-ized for a month for dangerously high blood pressure. I asked if his med-ical bills were high. "I don't know," she said, genuinely puzzled. It was a good thing we were sitting in the back seat because Sam shot me a mean-ingful look. Clearly, *she* wasn't paying. I knew that Peony's parents only visited the grandchildren when she and Paul were travelling. I also knew that whenever she went shopping with her mother, they invariably had a fight and ended up going their separate ways. Perhaps her mother wasn't a fan of bespoke cashmere. Or perhaps China's get-rich-quick fever was erod-ing family ties. A few years earlier Beijing had passed an "Elderly Rights

Law" ordering adult children to visit their aging parents, but it was widely ridiculed on Chinese social media because it had no enforcement mechanism. The lack of filial piety was glaring in the nation that invented it. I thought of Maria Rosa, who had moved nine years earlier to care for Nonno, and Marie-Catherine, who put a baby monitor in Mamie's room in case she needed anything at night.

Shanghai had luxurious private hospitals, but Peony's father was in a shabby state institution. He was one of six patients in a room that afforded zero privacy. Her mother was there — the one who made frozen won tons for Suzy. Peony handed her parents the take-out container containing three ounces of little-basket buns. "Too much for us," her father said politely, insisting she take back one *liang*. At seventy-seven, the former schoolteacher was distinguished looking, with neatly combed grey hair and a quiet voice. We had stayed less than ten minutes when Peony signalled it was time to leave. Her father put his coat on over his hospital-issue striped blue flannel pyjamas. He tied his street shoes. Her mother also put on a coat. Peony explained that her father had to use the washroom, but the one in the hospital was so filthy he wanted to use his own bathroom at home. I assumed we would drive them home, but suddenly we were in the hall without them. Peony said her parents had declined her offer of a lift. "He wants to take the bus. He says he needs the exercise," she said. Sam gave me another black look.

At the elevator, I was surprised to see a sign with instructions.

Don't charge into the elevator.

Let people out first.

Don't lean on the door.

Wasn't using an elevator self-evident? "It's because of all these *wai di* people," Peony said, her voice vibrating with venom. As the only native-born Shanghainese among our three *tai-tais*, Peony was the most ferociously anti-migrant. "Shanghai is a mess because of them. It's so nice at Chinese New Year when they all go home."

China's nouveaux riches had themselves grown up poor, hungry, and oppressed, which may explain why they segregated chopsticks, why they barked at their maids, why they had such an undeveloped rich-people's culture. They reminded me of Edna St. Vincent Millay, the American poet and feminist, who also grew up poor, and wrote, "The only people I really hate are servants. They are not really human beings at all."

On the drive home, Peony spotted some migrants on motorbikes. She aggressively bore down on them in her van. Granted, they *were* going the wrong way on a one-way street. When other migrants crossed an intersection against a red light, Peony confessed she wanted to run them over. I felt like I was in the Deep South with a crazy white supremacist who'd just spotted a couple of African-American jaywalkers.

Or maybe Peony was merely *hangry*.

Sam kept baking loaves of bread. Each time, Peony sent Little Chen to the store for different flour. "But which flour?" Amah asked nervously.

"*Bread* flour," Peony snapped, as if she were talking to a mentally disabled person.

One evening Paul hauled out a mix for multigrain bread he'd bought online from IKEA. Sam baked it into a dense, dark loaf. We soon had bread coming out of our ears. But — phew! — we were off the hook for afternoon tea. What with the oil-painting classes, massages, spa appointments, and kaffeeklatsches at Starbucks — the *tai-tais* had been unable to find a common time.

Although I yearned to cook Lion's Head Meatballs with Little Chen, Peony nixed it. "Our new amah can't cook," she said dismissively, "so I will show you the specialties." On our last day she taught us how to make one of my favourite snacks, a traditional Shanghai specialty called *Cong You Bing* (葱油饼). Scallion Pancakes were a crispy pan-fried bread, studded with chopped scallions and crunchy salt.

Barefoot on her radiant-heated floors, Peony was wearing slim black slacks, a grey cashmere sweater, and diamond earrings. She looked glamorous, even when she wrapped a pale blue reindeer-print apron around her slim waist. She got out a bag of all-purpose flour. She said the ratio was critical of boiling water (70 percent) to room-temperature water (30 percent). She added the blended water to the flour, mixing it with chopsticks until the dough was shaggy, and began working it with her fingers until it was smooth. "If it's too wet, add flour," she instructed. "The dough should be fairly wet and sticky." Once she was satisfied with the dough, she tipped it onto the granite counter to rest, flipping the mixing bowl over to cover it. Little Chen quickly minced two thick bunches of scallions.

After thirty minutes, the dough looked shaggy again. Peony began kneading it, adding fistfuls of flour until it was soft. Pinching off a chunk of dough, she rolled it into a translucent disk, scattered salt and minced scallions on top, and fried up a sample. Naturally, her diet precluded even taste tests, so the task fell to me. "Too salty," I blurted, a nanosecond before I remembered who had seasoned it. Peony sought a second opinion. "Amah, what do you think?"

The maid took a bite. She looked up at the ceiling, as if thinking deeply. "It's ... not bad," she said. Peony smiled.

"Little Chen," I said, "you should be in the diplomatic corps."

PEONY'S SCALLION PANCAKES (葱油饼)
Makes 10–12 pancakes.

2 cups	all-purpose flour, plus more for kneading
1 cup	water (5 ½ oz. boiling, 2 ½ oz. tepid)
2 bunches	scallions, finely chopped
3 tsp.	salt (or to taste)
	canola oil

Gradually add water (in the proper heat ratio) to the flour. Mix with chopsticks until shaggy. Then mix with your hands. The dough should be wet and sticky. If it's too wet, add flour; too dry, add tepid water. Flip the mixing bowl over the dough and let rest at room temperature for half an hour.

Sprinkle flour over a clean surface. Grab a chunk of dough that fits comfortably in your palm, roll it out, adding flour when necessary to avoid sticking. Rotate the pancake as you roll it so you get a thin circle the size of a salad plate.

Lightly oil a separate area of your counter. Roll out the circle of dough a bit more over the oiled surface, until the pancake is almost translucent. If it sticks, add a little more oil. Sprinkle on ¼ tsp. salt and 2 tbsp. of scallions. Roll the circle up like a cigar, join both ends like a bagel, and then flatten gently. With the rolling pin, flatten the pancake into a ½-inch thick circle – this will distribute the scallions evenly throughout the pancake.

Repeat with the remaining dough, separating each finished pancake from the others with plastic wrap. Pancakes may be frozen at this stage. They will thaw in a few minutes at room temperature.

To eat immediately, heat ½ tsp. of oil in a non-stick pan. When hot but not smoking, fry pancakes, one at a time, until crispy and golden. Cut in wedges and serve with oolong or jasmine tea.

The next dish, which I've dubbed Eight Treasure Spice 'n Dice, was like Anthea's ten-ingredient Rainbow Slivers, another make-work project for slaves. This time, however, we were making it with only six ingredients: pork, potato, carrot, tofu, bamboo shoots, and *jiao bai* (茭白, known as Manchurian wild bamboo shoots). Peony was going to stir-fry it with chili sauce, a bit of sugar, and *an entire jar* of Lee Kum Kee brand sweet fermented flour paste (*tian mian jiang* [甜面酱]), which is often confused with hoisin sauce. It was one of Paul's favourite dishes, but I thought it tasted like dreck. The whole jar of sauce brought back bad memories of Federica's mother's *insalata russa*.

Because of a miscommunication, Little Chen had *fan cuo wu*—slivering the chicken instead of cubing it. "Oh, no!" Peony shrieked, as though this were the Apocalypse. "You were supposed to *dice* it. Now we have to buy more meat." As Sam and I hustled out the door with Little Chen for the emergency diced-meat run, we felt like prisoners on a day pass. The fifteen-minute walk to the store was a rare chance for her to vent. It turned out she had carefully analyzed Shanghai's hierarchy of oppression.

"Foreigners are polite and respectful. Chinese families are much worse than working for foreigners. Among the Chinese, the worst are the Shanghainese. They're so *tiao* (挑)." *Tiao* meant nitpicky. Little Chen suddenly stopped walking. "Why are foreigners better?" she asked. She meant Westerners, like Canadians and Americans and Europeans. I remembered Paul and the jettisoned French wine. I noticed that he often set a place for Little Chen at the family table, even though she always ate alone in the piano room. As we hurried along the sidewalk, I recalled the way Marie-Catherine treated Bernadette. "Perhaps people from democracies are nicer because we believe in human rights," I told the maid. "We believe in equality." Little Chen looked baffled. I dropped the subject.

At the meat store, the butcher chatted amiably with Sam. "You want to work here?" he said. "I can teach you everything." Sam was thrilled and seriously considered accepting the offer until he remembered he was going to north China to study Mandarin.

When we arrived home, Little Chen messed up again. Another *fan cuo wu*. And another. This time she properly cubed the meat, but for a second dish she sliced the pork into thin pieces. That was all wrong in Peony's eyes. She wanted the meat cut in *si* (丝), matchsticks, about an inch long. "Everything is *yi ta hu tu* (一塌糊涂)," Peony continued angrily. It was a phrase that meant "collapsed and confused," but I prefer the technical translation: a fucking mess. For good measure, she got mad at Little Chen even for the way she was drying the dishes. "You're just like my mother!" Peony snapped.

There was a pause. Then both women burst out laughing. (In fairness, Peony scolded her kids and yelled at her husband, too. "She's impossible," Paul would say, fondly.)

Suddenly Peony spied some uneven cubes of raw potato. "What is this?" she said, rounding on Little Chen again, in a tone that meant, *Are you seriously thinking I'm going to cook with these raggedy-ass potatoes?* In *Heat*, Bill Buford recounts the trauma of working in Mario Batali's flagship New York restaurant. "The nightmare was fine dice, which meant cutting every bit of the carrot into identical one-millimeter-square cubes." When the chef dumped his first efforts into the garbage, Buford felt like weeping. "It took me three days before I could tell anyone about the experience."

Little Chen had also badly diced the smoked tofu, which further enraged *Tai-Tai*. "I don't understand how you can cut it so unevenly," Peony shouted. "We can't eat *this*." She shoved the bowl of aesthetically challenged tofu cubes at Little Chen and ordered her to pick out all the uneven bits. The amah flushed, ducked her head and, before my eyes, morphed into a stupid person. Just like Orchid had, Little Chen hunched her shoulders and began shuffling around the kitchen with that toy-train walk. Incensed, Peony grabbed a fresh chunk of smoked tofu, trimmed the uneven edges, and then cut them into perfect cubes. Later, out of earshot of *Tai-Tai*, Little Chen, like Buford, was near tears.

"Of course, if you *trim* the edges, you'll get perfect cubes," she vented. "But if *I* had done that, I would have been cursed out for wasting food."

Alice, a businesswoman friend of Peony's from Hong Kong, joined us for dinner. As we ate scallion pancakes and Eight Treasure Spice 'n Dice, they compared notes about their maids. Household help, it turned out, was paid more in Shanghai than in Hong Kong. Peony and Alice clucked their tongues about the headache a mutual acquaintance was having. She had recently bought a house in Los Angeles and was having trouble finding a live-in maid.

"You can get someone to come in once a week to clean," I said helpfully. Peony and Alice looked horrified.

"How is that possible?" said Peony. "I need someone here every day."

CHAPTER THIRTY-TWO

Plum and Building-the-Army

Unlike Anthea and Peony, who were tall and willowy, Plum was petite and curvaceous. And unlike them, she didn't flaunt designer brands. Disconcertingly, however, she wore false eyelashes day and night, which the beauty salon painstakingly glued in place, lash by lash, every month. Furthermore, unlike the other *tai-tais*, Plum didn't expect Sam to be her private Hollywood-style chef. By now, however, he was resigned to his role. Upon arrival, he politely asked whether she wanted him to bake bread. She did, but she baked with him. One night they produced a soft white loaf from, amazingly, leftover rice.

At forty-seven, Plum had a sunny personality and a silvery laugh. Alone among the *tai-tais*, she had the courtesy to explain our book project to her maid, Little Wang. "Home cooking is so *ordinary*," said the amah, reddening. "It's just our village food. It's very *chou* (丑)." By *chou*, literally "ugly," she meant the kind of food she cooked was unexceptional and unworthy of special attention, in short, *cucina povera*. Little Wang *was* proud of her home cooking—she was merely displaying standard Chinese modesty. Praise a child and the Chinese parent will say, *Oh no, he's stupid.* Or they used to, until the 1980s when China turned into a nation of crazed helicopter parents and spoiled onlys. While the other two *tai-tais* trashed their maids' cooking, Plum implicitly endorsed her amah's skills by including her in our project.

Little Wang turned out to be an excellent cook, with a discerning palate and asbestos hands. Like a true chef, she could lift a scalding dish right out of a pot. She was, however, illiterate. Peace, Orchid, and Little Chen had primary school educations and could read and write. Little Wang had never gone to school. Plum had tried to teach her to read, starting with the simplest ideograms, including Chinese numbers like 一, 二, and 三. But the maid's self-confidence was so low she had convinced herself she could never learn, and it became a self-fulfilling prophecy. Illiteracy was the defining feature of her life, the bane of her existence, the crater of her self-worth. Little Wang would end practically every conversation with Sam and me by smiling sadly, pointing at herself, and saying, "*Wo bu shi zi* (我不识字, I am illiterate)."

From our first day, Plum left us alone with Little Wang. She and Sam quickly formed a mutual admiration society. He applauded her knife skills as she chopped the fresh goose into bite-sized pieces. She gave him a thumb's up as he shredded carrots. "Knife skills are very important in Chinese cooking," she said. Sam beamed. Little Wang addressed him as *xiao huo zi* (小伙子), which was a friendly way of calling him "young man."

She showed him how to blanch pieces of goose in a pot of boiling water, the way Bernadette had blanched the veal for *blanquette de veau*. "Now we stir-fry some ginger and sear the goose," she said, heating canola oil in a wok. She added rice wine, one tablespoon of dark soy, three-quarters of a cup of light soy, a chunk of crystallized sugar the size of an ice cube, and one cup of water. Then she threw in a little cheesecloth bag that she had sewn herself for a *bouquet garni*: six star anise, six cloves, some Chinese cinnamon bark (桂皮), and a few peeled cloves of garlic. "Let it simmer for a couple of hours," she instructed Sam.

Little Wang had started working at Plum's the previous year, after her former employer relocated to Hong Kong. Most *tai-tais* would have rejected an illiterate maid. "Her illiteracy is a problem," Plum acknowledged. "However, Little Wang has a pleasant nature." The maid was two years younger than Plum, but whereas *Tai-Tai* looked soignée, Little Wang looked frumpy in black stretch pants and a green apron. Her heavy silky hair was tied back in a careless knot. Her cheeks were often flushed from the heat of the stove.

Little Wang couldn't read shopping lists, so Plum had already bought the groceries for dinner. Besides the freshly killed goose were two fish couriered from a fisherman in south China, twelve hundred kilometres away. That's right, Plum flew in seafood from a personal supplier, someone she trusted wouldn't inject the fish with something weird to make them plumper. Like all the *tai-tais,* she worried about adulterated food. In this way, she was like Maria Rosa, who insisted on buying her meat where she could watch the cows, or François, who raised his own laying hens. Previously, when Plum lived in Peony's compound and her backyard was so big no one noticed the coop, she had also raised her own chickens. After she moved to her current home, with its smaller yard, the neighbours objected. When Shanghai went through a bird flu scare, the compound's security guards finally insisted she destroy her flock.

The air-couriered fish were ten inches long, silvery with lemon-yellow bellies. They were called *chan*, which I had no idea how to write in Chinese characters (and obviously, neither did Little Wang). She scraped the scales using a scissor blade. Sam grabbed another pair of scissors and cleaned the other fish. Together, they cut out the gills and gutted the fish. Rubbing salt on the inside, she explained, "gets rid of the *xing* (腥, fishiness)." She showed him how to stuff the fish with ginger, scallions, and peeled cloves of garlic. To my surprise, she sprinkled some sugar on the fish, which, she said, also got rid of *xing*.

"You're so tall and so pretty," she suddenly said to Sam, who blushed. In Chinese, "pretty" can be used for both males and females. We had trouble deciphering what Little Wang was saying because she never attended school and thus never learned to speak Mandarin, the dialect chosen by the Communist Party as China's national language. Instead she spoke a regional dialect of Anhui province, which wasn't even close to Mandarin. Sam, who had sharper ears than I, noted that she pronounced *ji* as *jer*, *fan* as *huan*, *bai* as *bei*, and *nian* as *li*. The phrase "You're welcome," *bu yong xie* in Mandarin, came out as *bu ying sher* in her dialect.

We managed because cooking was more like show than tell. Together we prepared several more dishes: bok choy, beef with oyster sauce, broccolini with thinly sliced daikon radish, blanched bean sprouts with a sauce of fermented red bean curd called *fu ru* (腐乳, which, if you closed your eyes, tasted a bit like young Gorgonzola *dolce*). We also made stir-fried emerald-green *dou miao* (豆苗), pea sprouts that were the tendrils of snow-pea vines and were one of the more expensive Chinese vegetables, at least in Canada. But Little Wang was dismissive. "We never eat this at home in the village. It grows like a weed."

Plum dropped by the kitchen as Little Wang was trying to balance the plate of fish over *two chopsticks* in a wok. "Amah, I think you should use the steamer," Plum said quietly.

"This is fine," Little Wang insisted. Right on cue, the dish fell into the wok. Little Wang sheepishly fetched a bamboo steamer. Yet Plum didn't yell at Amah. She didn't even say, "I told you so." Sam gave me a look that said: *Wow, Plum is so nice.*

Plum's ancestors, like mine, hailed from Guangdong, the southern coastal Chinese province, where we preferred our seafood lightly cooked. Chinese like Little Wang from landlocked provinces like Anhui prudently cooked their fish to death. Plum had instructed Little Wang to steam the silvery fish for "ten minutes, twelve max." Little Wang steamed the fish for twenty minutes, until they burst their silvery skins. When Plum found out, she...laughed.

Just before we served dinner, we all tasted the simmering goose. "I'm sure it's terrible," Little Wang said modestly, in advance. Plum tasted a spoonful. We all waited in suspense. *Tai-Tai* smiled. "It's ready. It's great." And it was, tender and rich, its meat dark and tasting of game.

Plum lived with her husband and two children in a gated community called Among the Clouds Green Land Villas. Her house was not quite as grand as Peony's, although she had paid about the same, $3 million. But because she bought it a few years after Peony, soaring real estate prices meant that instead of a stand-alone villa on a large lot, $3 million only got a semi-detached home and a tiny yard. Seven years later, that same crazy real estate market had nearly doubled the value of Plum's house, to $5.5 million, an increase of almost $1,000 a *day*. Low to no taxes made it an even more attractive investment.

Little wonder the Shanghainese were crazed about real estate. At Hilly's compound, half a dozen young men in business suits loitered at the gate, seven days a week, thrusting sales brochures at the rare person who happened to emerge on foot. I once accepted a flyer out of curiosity. The cheapest condo — nine hundred square feet, two bedrooms, two baths — cost $1.7 million.

"Shanghai is having a collective anxiety attack over real estate," said Deborah, a Canadian lawyer I met for coffee at Starbucks with Hilly. "You go to a meeting and that's all everyone talks about." Deborah said no one was euphoric when their property increased in value — it only made them anxious. She herself was having seller's remorse. Fearing the property bubble would burst, she had sold her home the previous year. They'd made money on the sale, but her husband was depressed they hadn't made *more*. Now she was renting and glumly watching prices continue to climb. "*Nobody's happy in China*," she said. "If you're poor, you're angry. If you're rich, you worry that the government will take your money away, or that you can't take your money out. Foreign-capital controls are getting stricter."

On this visit, I had difficulty accessing foreign funds. Although China had all the trappings of a modern economy, the ATMs kept rejecting my various bank cards, a disconcerting change from a decade earlier when they'd worked seamlessly. My Visa and Mastercard were often rejected, too, except at hotels or foreign-owned stores. Transferring money overseas was politically sensitive as critics raised questions about the source of the elite's wealth. "They don't believe they will hold on to power long enough — sooner or later they will collapse, so they transfer out their money," Luo Yu, a former colonel in the Chinese People's Liberation Army, told the *New York Times*. He knew what he was talking about. His father was a former chief of staff in the military and his younger brother was a business partner with a founder of Anbang Insurance Group, best known for buying the Waldorf Astoria hotel in New York.

To combat illicit transfers (and rampant counterfeiting), the government capped the highest-denomination banknote at one hundred yuan, now worth twenty dollars. Although many Chinese used e-transfers on their cellphones to pay for everything from coffee to taxi rides, China remained a cash economy. One Saturday morning, when Sam tried to open a bank account in anticipation of his language studies, we had to wait a long time even though the branch was virtually empty. A clerk apologetically explained that the only other customer was making a large cash deposit — with shopping bags stuffed with hundred-yuan bills.

The widening gap between rich and poor was starkest in Shanghai. Every upscale compound was gated, with checkpoints monitored by migrant guards at each entrance. Nevertheless, residents at Among the Clouds Green Land Villas had suffered break-ins, which worried Hilly, who was considering moving there. The compound's design motif was Spanish. Landscapers planted mature palm trees on every block, but that winter a severe frost had killed half of them, making it look like a hurricane had torn through the compounds. Plum's four-level hacienda-style home had white stucco walls, a stone chimney, curved archways, and Spanish terracotta roof tiles. Like Peony, she had five bedrooms plus a study. She put me in a second-floor bedroom and thoughtfully gave Sam his own room in the basement. Her kitchen had white Corian countertops, a centre island, a Bosch two-door fridge and dishwasher, a GE hood fan, and a Panasonic microwave. The built-in cooktop had only three burners, widely spaced to handle big woks. Two were super burners, with concentric double rings of fire, essential for high-temperature cooking. The shortage of burners, however, meant that Sam and I were constantly jockeying for space with Little Wang.

The purchase price had included the previous owner's living-room furniture. Plum told me she couldn't pass up the convenience of having a furnished living room. The white silk Louis XVI settees looked like super-sized, cartoonish copies on steroids of the worn antiques at Marie-Catherine's farmhouse in Allex. We rarely sat in the living room, where the walls were so thin you could hear the neighbour's child in the semi next door playing Beethoven's *Für Elise* on the piano, again and again. Plum had a piano, too. In fact, all the *tai-tais* except Anthea had one. The piano, once perceived as an instrument of the bourgeoisie, was *de rigueur* now that so many had *become* the bourgeoisie. Chinese parents saw it as a way for their offspring to get ahead in a ferociously competitive world. It didn't hurt that eighty-eight, the number of piano keys, was a pun on getting rich. Some forty million Chinese children were learning to play, compared with six million American kids. Steinway & Sons, whose concert grands sold for US $200,000 and up, was planning a sixty-thousand-square-foot headquarters in Shanghai, complete with recital hall.

The next morning, I met Plum's husband, Building-the-Army—yes, that was his name, a reflection of Maoist-era communist optimism. He was tall and distinguished looking, with trimmed, greying hair. He was dressed for work in immaculate dark trousers and a white shirt. Born in 1968, he was fifteen years younger than my classmates at Peking University, but he felt like a kindred spirit. Over breakfast, we exchanged Cultural Revolution war stories. I told him I had headed to China when I was nineteen, not speaking any Chinese, and had ended up at Peking University where the curriculum included toiling in the wheat fields and working at a machine-tool factory. I told him I nearly got expelled for having an innocent relationship with a young Swedish diplomat. "You should write a book," said Building-the-Army.

A powerful real estate executive, he was CEO of a firm that managed a multi-billion-dollar portfolio on behalf of a foreign government, which I'll call The Country That Can't Be Named. Until a few years ago, his perks had included free rent, which was why he and Plum had deferred becoming homeowners. An ongoing perk was $100,000 in annual tuition for their two teens, who attended the same British-run private school as the other *tai-tais'* children. His chauffeur would soon pick him up, but he helped Plum make breakfast for their slumbering kids. He poured glasses of milk. He stirred the oatmeal. He even apologized to me for missing the previous night's dinner because he had business visitors from The Country That Can't Be Named. Regretfully, he added, he would be tied up with dinner meetings all week. Then he told me he had joined the Chinese Communist Party at eighteen, an unusually young age.

"Everyone was left-wing then," he said, smiling slightly.

Suddenly, everything made sense. He was a *Communist*. And that was why he was helping his wife make breakfast, even though he earned mega-yuan and she was a stay-at-home mom. Building-the-Army had internalized Chairman Mao's teaching that "women hold up half of heaven." Plum, on the same wavelength, was trying to eradicate illiteracy, one amah at a time. That was why she didn't abuse Little Wang. And that was why they politely accepted — and ate — the bruised apples Little Wang's husband brought home from his job at a supermarket. Like me, Building-the-Army and Plum once believed in Maoism. Now the idealism and fervour were gone, but they retained a core decency. Like Marie-Catherine, they treated migrants with dignity and respect.

Building-the-Army and Plum met in the late 1980s at Qinghua University, China's MIT. His parents were officials in the ministry of forestry in Shandong province. Her parents were from Guangdong province and Shanghai, but lived in Beijing. He had been accepted by Qinghua University to study civil engineering. She was one of only five female students in the entire engineering department. At the time a mere 3 percent of Chinese youth were accepted into university. Only a tiny fraction of *that* elite was accepted into the Chinese Communist Party.

For Plum and Building-the-Army to have hooked up, she was likely a party member, too, although she never told me (there was no taboo about asking what something cost, but there *was* a taboo about asking about party membership). When I was at Peking University, party members typically dated other party members. The one time I saw a party member date a non-party member, it ended badly. My class president, who was both a People's Liberation Army officer and a party member, promised a coquettish classmate he would get her into the party if she had sex with him. She did. And because China of the 1970s was puritanical and sex was a big deal, she assumed, rather naively, he would marry her. When she discovered he was already engaged to the daughter of his military commander back in the provinces, she angrily reported him to the authorities. She got a black mark in her dossier; he was expelled from university.

As China became capitalist, Building-the-Army adjusted and prospered. He graduated ahead of Plum, who was double-majoring in low-temperature engineering and economics, adding an extra year of study. Meanwhile the Chinese government sent him to oversee its engineering projects in The Country That Can't Be Named, an outsized responsibility for a young graduate. Plum followed him eighteen months later. Their first child, Amanda, was born in 1998. They decided not to take out citizenship for her from The Country That Can't Be Named because that would have been politically incorrect behaviour for a party member. Three years later, when Plum wanted to flout the one-child policy and have a second child, Building-the-Army again feared political problems. In taking the oath to become a Communist, he'd sworn to "carry out the party's decisions, strictly observe party discipline."

In 2002 Chinese authorities, impressed with his excellent work, sent him all expenses paid to Harvard Business School. Plum and Amanda joined him in Boston, where they lived frugally on their savings. On a freewheeling campus where people said and did whatever they felt like, Plum and Building-the-Army began once again to contemplate the impossible—a second child. They spied a loophole: Building-the-Army was on leave from his Chinese company and was technically a student, not an employee, so no one was monitoring his birth quota. Amanda was five when Plum gave birth to Fred, who automatically became an American citizen. That provided an additional loophole: the Chinese government couldn't very well penalize the parents of an American citizen for having him.

With money now impossibly tight, Plum took the two children back to China to await Building-the-Army's graduation. They spotted another loophole. If he quit his company upon graduation, his only obligation would be to repay his tuition. That provided another layer of protection against punishment for having a second child. Becoming a free agent also turned out to be a smart gamble. After he earned his Harvard MBA, The Country That Can't Be Named hired him to manage their bazillion-dollar real estate investments in Greater China, namely Taiwan, Hong Kong, and mainland China.

Despite his high-powered job, Building-the-Army's values hadn't changed, and neither had Plum's, which was remarkable considering their environment. The couple did practice a moderate form of tableware segregation, reserving special tea mugs for their children. (Building-the-Army looked slightly embarrassed when I started to use one, and he had to tell me.) But he wouldn't drop off the two teenagers at school—the company had a strict rule against using the chauffeur for family business.

As his kids stumbled sleepily into the kitchen, he served them oatmeal and quietly asked about their upcoming day. Amanda had an art exhibition at school. He told her he was very sorry—his work schedule that day was so packed he wasn't sure he could make it. He checked on his son's math marks. Fred merely grunted. The following week, Building-the-Army had high-level meetings in The Country That Can't Be Named. Because it coincided with their school's spring break, he was going to fly his family with him. Plum wanted to continue on to Europe alone with the children for a brief vacation, but a suicide bombing at the Brussels airport the previous evening—thirty-four dead and more than one hundred and eighty injured—gave her pause.

You could tell that Building-the-Army's daughter, who was tall like him, idolized him. Amanda, eighteen, was in her final year of high school. She had recently applied to Harvard, her dad's alma mater, but to her intense disappointment she had been passed over without even an interview. (Hilly, ever the strategist, opined that Amanda's parents had made a mistake. They *should* have taken out citizenship for her in The Country That Can't Be Named. "There are way too many mainland Chinese applying to Ivy League schools.")

Building-the-Army loaded the dishwasher even though it was Little Wang's job. As I helped him, I mentioned I was surprised the amah was totally illiterate. "It's a problem," he agreed. "But my wife wanted to hire her." I confessed I could hardly understand a word she said. Building-the-Army nodded. "Me, too," he said.

Then his chauffeur arrived to drive him to his office in one of the gleaming skyscrapers in Lujiazui, Shanghai's newest financial district.

CHAPTER THIRTY-THREE

Taste Essence

Some mothers take their sons to natural history museums. I thought Sam should witness a chicken slaughter. One morning with him in tow, I found Birdman in front of the post office, kitty corner from the Tesla dealership. He was wearing the same military camouflage pants, standing beside his battered poultry-shop-on-wheels. Birdman remembered I had come with Anthea. He even remembered how much she had spent on her last chicken (fifty-four yuan). When I asked for a slightly larger bird, he picked out one with russet-brown feathers and weighed it.

"Seventy-two yuan," he said. I nodded. While Sam watched goggled-eyed, Birdman swiftly snipped the chicken's throat, bled it out in two minutes, and plunged it in scalding water. As he plucked it clean, I asked where he sourced his chickens. His buyer went from farm to farm, he said, choosing the best birds, and then they met on the outskirts of Shanghai. As Sam snapped photos on his cellphone, Birdman slit the belly open and pulled out most but not all of the intestines. He cut open the giblet, scraping out some greenish pebbles. He didn't spill a drop of gore on the ground. Sam and I were fascinated to see dozens of kumquat-coloured embryonic eggs clustered at the base of the backbone. Only one had a shell, white, the size of an elliptical ping-pong ball. The other eggs were mere yolks, tiny as grapes and peas. I couldn't solve the age-old question of which came first, the chicken or the egg, but I could finally say that when it came to eggs, the yolks came first.

Back home Little Wang praised the chicken. "This is just like the kind we have at home in the countryside," she said. "We always eat free-range chickens. The intestines are the most delicious. Their eggs are extremely nutritious. My grandfather ate one of these eggs raw every day. He died at age ninety-seven." She rinsed the chicken, telling us the comb and feet were also good to eat. Then she sliced open the bit of intestine that Birdman hadn't discarded, cleaned it, and boiled it briefly, along with the ping-pong-sized egg. The cooked intestines were wrinkled and dun brown, delicately chewy, and tasting pleasantly of chicken. The tiny boiled egg was meltingly tender, its yolk like velvet.

The surprisingly large chicken liver, seared in a hot cast-iron pan, tasted like *foie gras*, without a trace of bitterness. As we munched on guts, embryonic eggs, and liver, Little Wang told us about her life. Sometimes she had to say something two or three times before we understood her dialect, but everyone persevered. She would talk, I would repeat in Mandarin what I thought she had said, and if I was right, she would nod. If I was wrong, she would try again, until Sam and I understood.

Little Wang was born in 1971 in Anhui, China's Appalachia where, a decade earlier, hundreds of thousands of peasants had starved to death during the Three Years of Natural Disasters. In the 1990s, Little Wang and her husband joined the flood of internal migrants flocking to Shanghai. They tried to start a business peddling tofu because she knew how to make it in a dozen iterations—smoked, dried, fresh, soft, dense, and liquid. The venture failed. He found a job working nights in the shipping and receiving department of Metro, a German-owned supermarket down the road. She went out to work as an amah. "I am illiterate," she said, for the umpteenth time. "This is the only work I could find."

One of Mao's earliest campaigns, after seizing power in 1949, was to eradicate illiteracy. But when he died in 1976, Little Wang was only five years old. And his successor, Deng Xiaoping, invoking capitalist principles, ruled that even the poorest peasants had to start paying school fees. Little Wang's father elected to educate his two sons but not his three daughters. In all my years of living and working in China, I'd only met elderly people who couldn't read or write. For Sam, hanging out with Little Wang was an eye opener. His whole life, he'd heard the mantra that education was important, without ever really understanding why. Now he saw that Little Wang couldn't read labels on bottles, couldn't discern whether a product was for eating or cleaning, couldn't follow a to-do list. And never mind those text messages saying the kid needed her dress shoes for a concert (which was probably a good thing).

Little Wang earned 72,000 yuan ($14,400) a year, more than Orchid but less than Little Chen. Little Wang's husband earned about the same at his supermarket job, which also came with a pension. Like Little Chen, their salaries vaulted them into the burgeoning middle class. As China became the world's second-largest economy, authorities worried about dissent. To prevent unrest, they kept prices artificially low for electricity, water, and mass transit, including taxis. The real basis of stability, however, was upward mobility for people on the bottom rung. A higher standard of living was important, but more crucially, the goal of those like Little Wang was to change the lives of their only children. Orchid, for instance, was so proud that her son had attended university and would soon earn a good living as a computer engineer. Little Chen planned to move back to her village when it came time for *her* son to enter high school, so he could later take the national entrance exams for university. Little Wang, whose own father had refused to educate her, made sure *her* only child graduated from university. She and her husband spent 8 percent of their combined income renting a tiny flat, a ten-minute scooter commute away. The rest they invested in their son. After he graduated from university in finance, they gave him half a million yuan ($100,000) in seed money to start a business, the equivalent of about seven years of wages for her. They also bought him a three-storey house in their village, a prerequisite for marriage. "When I got married, my father didn't give my sisters or me even a penny," she said, her smile not quite concealing her bitterness. She added, "He was a gambler, drinker, and smoker."

Like practically every single person in China, Little Wang had a cellphone. (Among 1.4 billion people, China had 1.3 billion cellphones.) While she couldn't text her son, she often called him. At twenty-five, he, too, had left Anhui province, and he'd opened a business in Zhejiang, the same home province of the Bologna garment worker and the Asti restaurateur. "He's very successful. He has ten people working for him. He just bought a car for 300,000 yuan ($60,000)," she said, reflecting the uninhibited materialism of a proud Chinese mother. "He even hires someone to cook for him." Next, he was thinking of opening an artisanal tofu business in Japan. He already had a passport. "He learned the techniques from my father and grandfather. He's trying to learn more before he leaves. He reads every night until four a.m." Every mother was proud of her son. But for an illiterate mother like Little Wang, nothing made her prouder than being able to say her son stayed up all night reading.

I told Little Wang that if I were a maid and Sam were a successful entrepreneur, I'd make him hire me to cook. Sam laughed nervously. Little Wang shook her head. "Oh, I'm illiterate. He would lose face in front of his workers." For good measure, she repeated, "I'm illiterate." But her relative wealth meant that Little Wang was a big shot whenever she returned to her village for a wedding or funeral or to celebrate a cousin building a new house or a nephew getting into university. "We go to a restaurant. Nobody cooks at home any more. We invite a table of ten, and spend 2,000 yuan just for food. But we bring our own napkins and liquor," she said, "When we go home, we don't want to work."

She worked very hard the rest of the time. Six days a week, she arrived at Plum's at eight a.m. For twelve hours, she scrubbed, vacuumed, and dusted. She made the beds, did the laundry and ironing, and did all the prep work for meals. In the evening, her tasks included drawing the dining-room curtains closed, cleaning the kitchen, and washing the dishes. She was thorough and meticulous, but every task seemed to take her forever. "She tries hard, but she moves slowly," Plum said.

Often, she was still folding laundry at nine p.m., long after dinner was over. Yet she was anxious to get home because her husband always waited for her to make him dinner. And he couldn't fall asleep unless she was beside him, even though he had to get up for his two a.m. shift at the grocery store. On Sundays, her only day off from Plum's, Little Wang cleaned two other houses. "My son doesn't want me to work. But I'm from the countryside. We're used to hard labour. I've worked ever since I was little." The amah who replaced Orchid on Sundays also worked the other six days a week with another family. My friend Richard Ling, who lived a bachelor's life in the former French Concession, told me his maid came in at seven a.m. seven days a week to make him breakfast: oatmeal with milk, boiled eggs, handmade won tons. Every night, she came back to make him dinner. In between, she cleaned other people's houses.

Seeing how hard these women worked, it seemed entirely possible China might one day rule the world. The only break for migrants came at Chinese New Year. Then, two hundred and seventy-five million workers crammed onto planes, trains, and buses to return to their ancestral villages.

Little Wang was in a black hole of indecision. When I presented her with my purchase from Birdman, she hesitated to make white-cut chicken. Being from Anhui province in central China, she was unsure about Cantonese food, like Maria Rosa would be if asked to make an Umbrian specialty. Reading a cookbook was not possible either. Nor did Little Wang have any faith that I knew what *I* was doing. She had Anthea's maid on speed-dial, however. She phoned Orchid several times for advice, but never got through.

Suddenly Little Wang's cellphone rang. It was Anthea calling back. Little Wang, looking like she was going to have a heart attack, had an animated, confusing, five-minute conversation. After hanging up, she reported Anthea had said to cook the chicken for *two and a half hours*. I said that was ridiculous (to Little Wang, not to Anthea — I'm not that brave). Still, the maid held back. When we were one hour from supper, exasperated, I threw the chicken into a pot of water with scallions, chunks of ginger, a splash of Chinese rice wine, and — Little Wang's idea — six cloves of peeled garlic. We argued about whether to add salt at the beginning. I said yes — otherwise it would taste flat. Little Wang said no — it would toughen the bird. Little Wang won.

My grandmother, who was born near Guangzhou in the late 1880s and ran a meat-and-potatoes restaurant in small-town Canada, passed on the classic recipe for white-cut chicken to her Canadian-born daughter, my mother. Mom taught *me* to bring an uncooked chicken to room temperature, sprinkle it inside and out with salt, and then simmer it briefly in a pot with water barely covering the breastbone. Unlike Orchid, Mom added nothing else. A couple of hours of resting later, the meat was succulent and moist. The broth could be served with the meal, or saved for another day. The classic condiment was a chimichurri-like dipping sauce of minced, gently cooked ginger and wilted scallions. White-cut chicken should really be called red cut because the litmus test was blood in the bone. If the marrow wasn't red when you hacked it into pieces, you had overcooked the bird. It repelled me, but my husband loved it and called it "Cantonese done." To avoid the yuck factor and bone splinters, I usually carved my *Bai Qie Ji* like a roast turkey.

In Shanghai, behind my bravado, I had my own doubts about making white-cut chicken because I'd never poached a freshly killed free-range bird, and we were running out of time. I simmered the chicken for twenty minutes, let it sit for a while, and then took it out. But when the juices did not run clear, I put it back in for another ten minutes. It was ready — chewy with an intensely chickeny in flavour. The broth, however, was insipid. Sam came to the rescue. He stripped two drumsticks of meat, hacked the bones to expose the bloody marrow, and threw them back into the pot. (Unlike me, he had a chef's indifference to yuck.) I added salt and my late mother's secret flavour booster, a spoonful of sugar. But the broth still needed a kick.

"Where's your MSG?" I asked Little Wang.

Embarrassed, she told me they didn't have any. Now that I thought about it, none of the other *tai-tais* had stocked monosodium glutamate, not Hilly, not Anthea, not Peony. How could Chinese people *not* use MSG? I had to remind myself that before I went to live and work in China, I had never cooked with MSG either. In the West, it was blamed for "Chinese Restaurant Syndrome." The hysteria began in 1968 when a Chinese-American physician in Maryland named Robert Ho Man Kwok wrote a letter—not a research paper, mind you, but a *letter*—to the prestigious *New England Journal of Medicine* to report that after eating at Chinese restaurants, he suffered "numbness at the back of the neck," "general weakness," and "palpitations." After the letter was published, others spoke of headaches and tightness at the temples. Researchers began injecting MSG into mice, which showed signs of brain lesions. A subsequent double-blind study, however, showed little correlation. But by then no one noticed.

To be honest, Kwok may have had a point. After the gold mines tapped out and the trans-national railroads were completed, Chinese migrants who were unable to find jobs opened mom-and-pop eateries. Their food was not authentic, only what they assumed the locals would like, a genre that came to be known as "Chinese-American" food. Not being actual cooks, they used copious amounts of monosodium glutamate to rescue dishes such as chop suey—which did not exist in China.

Too much sodium would certainly make you thirsty, but too much MSG wouldn't harm you. In 1987, after extensive research, the World Health Organization placed the additive in the safest category of edible ingredients, alongside salt and vinegar. The US Food and Drug Administration joined other government agencies in Australia, Britain, and Japan in deeming MSG safe. In 2000 researchers at the University of Miami discovered glutamate receptors on the tongue. In 2009 Russian scientists in Saint Petersburg discovered glutamate receptors in the stomach lining.

"Chinese Restaurant Syndrome" had been thoroughly debunked. I now roll my eyes and grow uncooperative when Canadian friends ask me to transmit their no-MSG request to Chinese waiters, who of course speak fluent English. Aside from my friends' presumption that I alone can communicate with the waiter, I resent the innuendo that only Chinese food uses MSG. In fact it is in everything from Goldfish crackers to seasoned fries to ranch dressing to the hydrolyzed vegetable protein in fast food.

Moreover, MSG naturally occurs in many foods, including tomatoes, Parmesan, caramelized onions, asparagus, shiitake mushrooms, and the browned crust on roasted meats. Breast milk has it, too, which means humans are programmed from birth to love it.

Its discovery can be traced to 1908, when a Japanese chemistry professor was eating a bowl of his favourite seaweed soup. Kikunae Ikeda wondered what gave the vegetarian broth such a meaty flavour and, in a Eureka moment, realized he had discovered a fifth taste, after sweet, sour, salty, and bitter. He called it umami, after *umai*, the Japanese word for "delicious," and hypothesized that dried kelp (*kombu* in Japanese) was responsible for the flavour. Ikeda dropped his other work in physical chemistry and, after days of tediously cooking and evaporating kelp, isolated brown crystals of glutamic acid. Its molecular formula, $C_5H_9NO_4$, turned out to be identical to the glutamate that the human body produced on its own, which plays a crucial role in learning and memory. Two years later Ikeda patented a process for mass-producing MSG from wheat and soybeans. He named the sparkly white crystals *Ajinomoto* (taste essence).

When Japan invaded Manchuria in 1931, patriotic Chinese scientists independently created their own version of MSG, called *wei jing* (味精) which, like Ajinomoto, also meant "taste essence." Chinese food scientists endorsed it, claiming it even improved mental alertness and prevented childhood constipation. As Beijing bureau chief for my newspaper in the 1980s, I discovered that all my friends in China used MSG. So did Master Mu, my Chinese chef. Eventually I began using a pinch or two when I cooked, with no ill effects, and I could also reduce the salt in the dish. The average North American adult currently consumes a half-gram of the additive daily, the average Chinese several grams daily. To paraphrase *Vogue* food writer Jeffrey Steingarten: if MSG is so bad for you, why doesn't everyone in China have a headache?

MSG has made a comeback in the West. When a new upscale chain called Umami Burger opened in New York in 2013, the lines were three hours long. Of course, umami *was* MSG. As one biochemistry professor put it, "Glutamate is glutamate is glutamate." So it was ironic that the *tai-tais,* who met at Starbucks several times a week and embraced all the latest Western trends, boycotted MSG. They had heard about the hysteria and were concerned about the safety of their food. Like some of my Canadian friends, the *tai-tais* had no idea they were decades behind the times.

JAN'S EASY WHITE-CUT CHICKEN (白切鸡)
Serves 4–6, with steamed rice and stir-fried vegetables.

FOR THE CHICKEN:

1	whole chicken (2–3 lbs)
1	bunch scallions (2 stalks left whole for poaching, the rest minced for the sauce [see below])
5	thick slices ginger
¼ cup	cooking rice wine (料酒)
1½ tbsp.	salt
½ tsp.	MSG (divided between cooking the chicken and later seasoning the broth)

FOR THE DIPPING SAUCE:

2 inches	ginger, peeled and finely minced
¼ cup	canola oil
1 tsp.	salt
	remaining scallions, minced

Put chicken in a pot, breast side up, with all the ingredients except MSG. Add water until it barely covers the breastbone. Bring to a boil, then cover and simmer for 25–30 minutes (add 5 minutes if chicken came straight out of the fridge). Turn off heat. Add ¼ tsp. MSG. Leave covered and untouched for 2–3 hours.

To serve, carve into bite-sized pieces, or you can pull it apart like pulled pork. The chicken should be warm but not too hot to handle. Don't discard the skin, which is delicious. You can cut off the wings and drumsticks to eat with your fingers.

For the dipping sauce, soften the minced ginger in oil over low heat. When fragrant, turn off heat, immediately add salt and stir in minced scallions, which should wilt from the residual heat. Pass the bowl of scallion-ginger sauce with the chicken.

Use the broth as a soup base another day, skimming off excess fat. Add ¼ teaspoon MSG to improve the soup's taste essence.

Too soon, we had to leave Plum's house. Spring break was starting, and they were about to leave for a vacation. For our farewell meal, Sam proposed another steak dinner, which Plum agreed to with alacrity. We went shopping at Metro, the same place where Little Wong's husband worked in shipping and receiving. Sam and I bought romaine lettuce, spinach, thin-skinned potatoes, and imported Australian steaks. Plum bought pork ribs, bok choy, fresh shiitake mushrooms, and spring bamboo shoots. That confused me. Were we making steak or Chinese food?

"Both," she said, laughing.

Just like Hilly (and Mirella and Maria Rosa), she assumed the steak, salad, mashed potatoes, and spinach au gratin would be four dishes within a multi-course meal. After all, Plum always ate family style from large platters in the centre of the table, like, come to think of it, the French and Italians. She left only vague instructions for dinner at seven, which made Little Wang anxious. She had a deadline but no information about what to prepare. Sam felt her pain.

"An amah job requirement is that you have to be an astrologist," he said, "because you never know who's coming to dinner or what you're supposed to cook."

I had been working for days like an amah, too, always on my feet, never clear about the marching orders. As far as I knew, to go with Sam's steak dinner, we were making pork-rib soup with spring bamboo shoots and thick-cut Chinese prosciutto, stir-fried greens with shiitake mushrooms, and spectacular five-inch-long shrimp, which Building-the-Army obtained through his office. That's right, powerful Chinese businessmen used their clout to obtain humongous shrimp.

Sam began peeling potatoes. Then he boiled them. Little Wang searched through every cupboard and drawer for a potato masher, in vain. "Is there a garlic press?" Sam asked. No garlic press, either. Little Wang found a mortar and pestle as big as a cantaloupe. Sam grimaced and instead minced the garlic as finely as possible. To purée the potatoes he used the back of a spoon to force them through a cheap plastic colander.

"Lots of mash is falling out the sides," I pointed out helpfully.

"I know," he hissed, teeth gritted. "What do you want me to do?"

Sam, too, was showing the strain of living for weeks in strangers' homes. He was tired of baking endless loaves of bread. He was sick of cooking

Western food for indifferent offspring. But he only showed his impatience with me. Toward Plum and Little Wang, he was unfailingly respectful.

Tai-Tai dropped by the kitchen briefly then disappeared again. The three of us debated whether or not she had told us to make a Japanese beef curry. Sam said no. I said yes. Little Wang ruled down the middle—we would make the curry once we had further instructions from *Tai-Tai*.

For dessert, Sam prepared a fruit platter. Ever since Sam and Ben were little, my husband, a software engineer who hated cooking, had prepared geometrically enticing platters of cut-up fruit. Now Sam sliced tangerines into vivid pinwheels. He washed some perfect hothouse strawberries. He used up those bruised apples from Little Wang's husband, lopping off the unsightly bits. As he arranged everything stunningly on a platter, I realized he had absorbed one of his father's parenting skills. If I squinted hard, I could even see him making fruit plates for his own kids one day. Of course, Sam first had to get a girlfriend, and that would never happen because of his duct-tape wallet.

The house was so huge we were never sure who was home. The teens typically went straight to their rooms after school. *Tai-Tai* was nowhere to be seen. Despite the late hour, Little Wang still thought we should wait for a green light for the beef curry. At 6:50 p.m., Sam made an executive decision. He knew it was Plum's son's favourite dish and thought we'd be better off making it than not making it. He began searing cubes of beef. Unfortunately, the directions on the curry sauce were in microscopic Japanese.

"Do we put in a whole package?" he asked Little Wang. She furrowed her brow and shrugged helplessly.

"Let's put in half a package," I suggested. "If it's not enough, we can add more later."

Sam also reheated the mashed potatoes and began frying up the stack of expensive imported Australian steaks. Plum suddenly materialized. She expertly sautéed the giant shrimp with sugar, rice wine, and light soy. Like Anthea and Peony, she abruptly called for chopped scallions and ginger, but not in an angry way. Somehow the amah managed to produce both in under one minute, and Plum tossed the seasonings in with the shrimp. The beef curry was still tough, but it was almost an hour past dinner time. We called everyone to the table. Everyone ignored us. Even Plum had disappeared. Sam was upset—the steak and potatoes were cooling on the huge Lazy Susan on their circular dining table. "They're all deaf," joked Little Wang.

Plum reappeared. Eventually the teenagers showed up, too. Sam had once again forgotten to ask each person's preference for doneness. He had cooked the steaks medium rare, but Fred wanted his meat medium, Plum medium-well, and Amanda insisted on dry brown meat. All three recoiled at the blood pooling on their plates. So much for the stereotype that Chinese eat icky, weird, disgusting things.

Sam headed wordlessly back to the kitchen to redo the steaks. When he returned, the table was still laden with food. Fred, thirteen, wouldn't touch the chicken, pork-rib soup, giant shrimp, stir-fried vegetables, or even his favourite, that damn beef curry. He ate only the steak and the mashed potatoes. It turned out he was a Chinese version of an Italian *teledipendente*. While he was playing video games in the basement, he'd scarfed down two family-sized bags of potato chips.

CHAPTER THIRTY-FOUR

Love the Big Chef

Sam and I moved back briefly to Hilly's, but voted not to cook for at least a day. Instead, we decided to return to Wealthy Springtime Little-Basket Buns, this time *without* someone on a diet. Like at Eataly, we had to put in our order directly with the cashier. Unlike at Eataly, we had to contend with a mob of hungry customers. The restaurant was as packed as a busy Paris bistro, with diners crammed together cheek by jowl. Three young women agreed to let us share their small table, where two of them were devouring bowls of scallion-oil noodles (*cong you mian* [葱油面]). Did they recommend this Sichuan street-food classic? They did. I rushed back to the cashier and added the item to our order.

An older man enjoying little-basket buns at the next table overheard that we were from Canada. He told us — and all within earshot — that his son lived there. Then, since we were in Shanghai and everyone was crazed about real estate, he said his son had just bought a home in Brampton, Ontario. "Only 3.5 million yuan!" he said, sounding amazed. He showed everyone a photo on his cellphone of a modern two-storey suburban brick home with a double garage. The diners studied the picture with interest and marvelled at the bargain price. To put it in perspective, our noodles cost the equivalent of $1.50 and the house $700,000. "So cheap!" the father said, as if not quite believing his son's luck. "You'd never get anything for that price in Shanghai."

I had ordered half a dozen bamboo steamers of little-basket buns so Sam could finally eat his fill. I'd also ordered a plate of *zao liu yu pian* (糟熘鱼片), sliced grouper poached in a golden sauce of fermented rice. The sauce was impeccable, with just the right balance of winey sweetness, but the chef had sliced the fish crosswise, right through the bones, so that each mouthful was like eating a pin cushion.

The scallion-oil noodles, however, were a revelation. They arrived bathed in an intense sauce of light and dark soy, spiked with sugar, slicked with pungent scallion oil, and topped with a tangle of charred scallions. Inch-long chunks of scallions, braised over low heat until they caramelized, flavoured the oil. This was Chinese *cucina povera*. Scallion-oil noodles were kissing cousins to *spaghetti aglio e olio*. Instead of scallions, the Italians used garlic and dried chili flakes to flavour the oil. To moisten the noodles, they splashed in hot pasta water while the Chinese added soy sauce. Marco Polo would have approved.

Sated, we headed to the Jewish Refugees Museum on the site of the former Ohel Moshe Synagogue. Norman's ancestors were Jews from Minsk. In 1916, his seven-year-old mother escaped czarist pogroms and landed at Ellis Island, where the health inspector calmed her fears by first giving her doll a physical. Although we had raised our boys in a firmly secular culture, I wanted Sam to understand his heritage. I also wanted him to know that the Chinese had something in common with Marie-Catherine, that they hadn't always been so hard-hearted toward migrants. During World War II, while Mamie was helping Resistance fighters and Nonno was bringing food up to the attic for a Jewish mother in Repergo, Shanghai was one of the few spots in the world that hadn't required passports or entry visas. As a free port, it became a haven for more than twenty thousand Jews fleeing the Holocaust, at least until the Japanese marched into Shanghai and forced the Jews into a ghetto. Most survived the war, partly because the Japanese ignored Hitler's suggestions to build gas chambers or hand them over.

During the war, Sir Victor Sassoon, a British Baghdadi Jew whose family made a fortune in the opium trade, donated immense sums to help the refugees pouring into Shanghai. As one of the world's original globalized entrepreneurs, he had business interests in India, China, and the Persian Gulf. Sam and I headed to the Cathay, the landmark ten-storey art deco hotel Sassoon built on the Bund in 1929. Whenever he was in Shanghai, Sassoon occupied its penthouse. His friends who'd stayed there included George Bernard Shaw; Charlie Chaplin, who danced to the hotel's jazz band with Paulette Goddard; and Noel Coward, who dashed off the first draft of *Private Lives* there while convalescing from influenza.

The Cathay fell on hard times in 1941 when the Japanese army occupied the hotel. In 1949, the victorious Communists renamed it the Peace Hotel. And during the Cultural Revolution, Madame Mao and her Gang of Four made it their Shanghai headquarters. The hotel had been recently renovated and was now called the Fairmont Peace. As a surefire tourist magnet, a rotating troupe of ostentatiously elderly musicians reprised the jazz band's 1930s hits, even in the daytime, while the hotel served afternoon tea for two for $120 ($150 if you added two flutes of champagne). That was equivalent to a hundred bowls of scallion-oil noodles. I suddenly understood why the *tai-tais* had been so fixated on Sam and me making them a proper afternoon tea.

"You want afternoon tea?" I asked Sam.

"Nah," he said. Like street urchins, we pressed our noses up again the latticed glass doors, and listened to the muffled sound of the band playing "The Way You Look Tonight." Outside, we strolled along the Bund, arm in arm. Sam much preferred walking unhindered, but he didn't protest when I wanted to be close. When he was thirteen and I was in the depths of my clinical depression, he occasionally consented to go with me for pointless walks around our Toronto neighbourhood. He even allowed me to clutch his arm, despite the serious risk of being spotted by a classmate. One classmate's mother *had* seen us. "You're so lucky!" she had said. "My son would never walk like that with me."

I was no longer depressed, of course, but I was sad that our culinary adventure was ending very soon. Looking back, it was remarkable he'd agreed to join me. On that hockey trip to Scandinavia nine years earlier, Sam had been trying to bond with his new teammates. I was severely depressed, narcissistically needy, and perpetually on the verge of tears, with the self-esteem of a tapeworm. Photos from the trip show me leaning in to Sam, my arms clamped around his shoulders. Never wanting to be alone, even for a moment, I would ask him to sit with me at every meal. "Can I *please* just eat with my team?" he begged. He consented to eat breakfast every day with me, but not lunch.

The night before we flew home, he wanted to play ping-pong in the hotel game room with his teammates. I refused. I couldn't face the evening alone. He pleaded. We had a fight. Sam could have stomped out, but he knew I was depressed. Instead we both cried ourselves to sleep, side by side, in twin beds at the Stockholm airport hotel. "I just wanted to hang out with them," he later told me. "Even someone's little sister, who was *nine*, was allowed to stay up."

That workplace-related depression, which lasted two years, put our mother-son relationship to the hardest test. But it also bound us more tightly. What Sam had done for me on that trip had been the reverse of his childhood plea, "Carry!" When *I* had desperately needed a "carry," Sam stepped up, even though he was only thirteen years old. As we navigated the crowds along the Bund, we gazed at the view across the river to Puxi, where Hilly and all her *tai-tai* friends lived. The new Shanghai seemed otherworldly, with its post-modern skyscrapers—daring ziggurats, twisting swizzle sticks, towers tilting backward like runway fashion models. Somewhere a set of bells tolled on the quarter hour. With a start, I realized they were chiming "The East is Red," the de facto anthem of the Cultural Revolution. I used to hum that old Maoist ditty while my classmates and I toiled in the rice-paddy fields. Unable to resist, I began to sing softly, in Chinese. Sam looked like he wanted to sink into the ground. But he didn't. He kept holding my arm.

For our last dinner in Shanghai, Hilly agreed to order a chef online. Love the Big Chef—www.idachu.com — billed itself as offering "homemade meals." It operated in Beijing, Shanghai, Shenzhen, and Guangzhou, China's four richest cities. For the equivalent of twenty dollars, the chef would cook us dinner in our own home. "That's why Sam shouldn't be a cook," Hilly said again. The price, which did not include groceries, was the same for four, five, or six dishes. Clients had the option of buying the ingredients themselves or reimbursing the chef. Worried about food safety, Hilly ruled that we'd buy everything ourselves.

Like a dating site, each chef's listing included a photo, customer comments, and a brief description of his specialties. (Yes, they were all male.) Love the Big Chef had more than three thousand chefs on call. Some were said to be adept at creating delicate flavours for the elderly and the infirm. Others specialized in Sichuan, Hunan, Fujian, or other provincial cuisines. We picked Chef Xu Zhaoyou because he specialized in Sichuan food, and, well, he looked nice. We ordered five dishes: *Hong Shao Rou* (红烧肉, soy-braised pork belly), *Song Shu Yu* (松鼠鱼, sweet-and-sour squirrel fish), *La Zi Ji* (辣子鸡, firecracker chicken), *Yu Xiang Rou Si* (鱼香肉丝, fish fragrance pork), and *Gong Bao* chicken (宫保鸡丁, kung pao chicken with peanuts).

Chef Xu (pronounced Hsu) arrived promptly at our specified time of 4:15 p.m. Before entering Hilly's apartment, he pulled paper booties over his shoes. Then he donned a clean white chef's jacket and toque. He scrubbed his hands as thoroughly as if he were preparing for surgery. Hilly soon lost interest and left the kitchen. Chef Xu, who hadn't expected an audience, looked less than thrilled when the rest of us lingered to watch.

"Knife? Wok?" he asked brusquely, like a surgeon at the operating table.

Peace scurried to supply him. "Don't you carry your own knife?" I asked, pen poised. I thought every self-respecting chef carried a personal knife kit. Chef Xu looked at me as though I were an idiot.

"I took the subway," he said. "They won't let you take a knife on the subway."

I'd forgotten. In China, which stringently controlled access to firearms, cleaver-wielding teams of terrorists and mentally ill individuals had carried out mass slashings in the past decade in Nanping, Fujian province; Leizhou, Guangdong province; Hanzhong, Shaanxi province; Kunming, Yunnan province; the northwest "autonomous region" of Xinjiang; and other places. In 2010 the Shanghai subway system installed airport-style security checks at entrances. Bags and purses were inspected. Firecrackers, paint, phosphorus, and knives were forbidden.

Chef Xu was thirty-six and a migrant from Anhui, the same landlocked province as Little Wang. Unlike Little Wang, he could read and write. He also spoke Mandarin, sort of. Whatever we couldn't understand, Peace filled us in, even though she was from Gansu, another province that wasn't even geographically proximate. The chef told us his day job was cooking in a company cafeteria. Once he'd served the employees lunch, he was free to moonlight and did, several times a week for Love the Big Chef. After this gig, he said, he would hurry home to make dinner for his wife.

At the last minute, Hilly had nixed the soy-braised pork belly, deeming it too fatty. Sam and I were disappointed when Chef Xu said it was one of his specialties. He set to work on the four surviving dishes. Squirrel fish, which had nothing to do with squirrels, was a whole fish that, once filleted, scored, and deep-fried, supposedly resembled a squirrel. Considering the rodent had been hunted to near extinction in China, how would anyone here know what a squirrel looked like?

Sam watched in awe as Chef Xu swiftly filleted a Mandarin fish. He reserved the bony skeleton with its tail intact, then crosshatched the two fillets, dipped them in cooking wine, cornstarch, and salt, and deep-fried them and the skeleton in a wok of hot oil. In a separate wok, he prepared the sweet-and-sour sauce: sugar, water, salt, white vinegar, cornstarch and

… Heinz ketchup, which Hilly had on hand. In the wok where he had just fried the fish, he deep-fried cubed carrots and chunks of scallions for thirty seconds as a garnish. He finished by tucking the crispy skeleton between the two golden fillets and pouring the shiny red sauce over everything. Okay, if I squinted hard, it resembled a Chinese squirrel drowning in sweet-and-sour sauce.

Originally grumpy and brusque, Chef Xu warmed up under Sam's undisguised admiration. He told the chef that he, too, wanted to be a cook but wasn't sure about culinary school. The chef smiled and said he had trained in Shanghai restaurants. "I never went to cooking school," he added. "It's not practical. You really need experience."

Firecracker chicken resembled a pile of spent firecrackers, at least more than squirrel fish looked like a squirrel. The dish contained a terrifying volume of dried red chilies, outnumbering each morsel of chicken ten to one. However, the chilies merely lent heat to the oil and weren't eaten because, frankly, they were indigestible. Although I'd had firecracker chicken many times, I'd never realized the dish was made from chopped-up chicken wings. Chef Xu hacked the wings in thirds and marinated the pieces in shredded ginger and rice wine.

"Light soy sauce?" he asked Peace. The amah shook her head. He grunted with displeasure as he poured a bit of dark soy onto the wings. (As Anthea had explained, it should be used only for colouring, never flavouring.) Next the chef asked for white pepper, which the Chinese used in everything from congee to hot and sour soup. Hilly had only black, which is rarely used in Chinese food. Chef Xu sighed and shook his head.

He stir-fried minced ginger, sliced garlic, chopped scallions, and a *cupful* of dried red chili peppers that Peace had scissored into half-inch pieces. Dipping the chunks of wing in a mixture of cornstarch and egg white, he deep-fried them in a second wok. Then he drained the wings and tossed them in the first wok with the hot chilies and ginger.

For kung pao chicken, another of my favourite Sichuan dishes, he diced some chicken breasts, and sprinkled on some cooking wine. "Where's the MSG?" he said, turning to Peace. "We don't have any in this house," she replied, looking embarrassed. I waited for an explosion, but Chef Xu stayed calm. Perhaps he often cooked in homes where people had ketchup but no light soy, where no one knew how to cook, which, come to think of it, made sense.

"What about bicarbonate of soda?" he asked. Peace searched through the cupboards. No bicarbonate of soda, either. Chef Xu sighed and reached for an emergency stash he kept in his backpack.

"This tenderizes the meat," he told Sam.

"Green peas?" he asked. Peace shook her head apologetically.

"Not even *frozen* green peas?" he said, almost pleading. Peace checked the freezer. There were none.

"Do you have *dou ban jiang* (豆瓣酱)?" he asked, referring to the spicy, salty fermented soy bean paste. Peace said that *Tai-Tai* only had Korean-style soy bean paste on hand.

"That's the wrong kind," Chef Xu snapped. "You really should have bought *Chinese* soy bean paste."

Peace and I exchanged worried looks. Chef continued working. He chopped up eight cloves of garlic. Then he put down his knife and stared, for some reason, at *me*.

"That's why people usually tell *me* to buy the groceries. Then I get everything that I need."

He soldiered on, tasting the raw, yes, *raw*, chicken for seasoning. He parboiled the meat then quickly stir-fried it with oil, garlic, ginger, lots of sugar, salt, and soy. To substitute for the missing soy bean paste, he dejectedly splashed in some dark vinegar.

Fish fragrance pork, the final dish, had no fish in it. Unlike *vitello tonnato*, which combined meat and fish, this was cooked *in the style* a fish is prepared in Sichuan, with the same bamboo shoots and pickled red chilies. For this dish, Chef Xu boiled a fresh bamboo shoot, which looked like an ivory tusk, for ten minutes. As quick as a Moulinex, he slivered it and cut some pork filet and carrot into matching shreds, which he stir-fried with the bamboo, adding soy and chili. As Chef Xu cooked, he tasted continually, using a spoon that he meticulously washed each time under the tap. Like the prophylactic booties he wore over his shoes, he was clearly trying to assuage the fears of a Chinese clientele paranoid about tuberculosis, hepatitis, and, possibly, bubonic plague.

When Chef Xu finished, Hilly urged him to eat with us, but everyone knew she was merely being polite. He left exactly three hours after he arrived. As we gathered around the table, I mentioned that he had tasted every dish. Hilly made a face. I assured her he had washed his spoon every single time. She still looked upset. But she was *horrified* when I told her he had tenderized the meat with baking soda. (In fact, Chef Xu was correct. I later researched baking soda, and learned that briefly soaking meat in a solution of baking soda raises the pH on the meat's surface, which prevents the proteins from bonding excessively and keeps the meat tender and moist, according to *Cook's Illustrated*, my favourite technical cooking magazine.)

Dickie wolfed down the squirrel fish. We shared the skeleton, which was as crispy as potato chips. The spicy wings were addictive. The fish fragrance pork tasted too much like the kung pao chicken, which itself was soggy and overly sweet. But I couldn't really fault Chef Xu. We didn't have half the ingredients he needed. And he was from Anhui, which was fifteen hundred kilometres from Sichuan province. I only wish Orchid had had a chance to show us the real thing.

At least I now knew the secret of tenderizing meat.

FIRECRACKER CHICKEN (JAN'S EASY VERSION)
Marinating time: 30 minutes.
Serves 4 as a main course.
Serve with rice and stir-fried vegetables.

3 lbs.	chicken wings, tips removed

FOR THE MARINADE:

¼ cup	rice wine (料酒)
¼ cup	light soy (生抽)
1 tbsp.	dark soy (老抽)
1 tsp.	finely ground white pepper

FOR THE CHICKEN:

3	eggs, whites only
2 tbsp.	cornstarch
Enough canola oil to fill the wok ⅓ full for deep-frying	
1	inch ginger, peeled and shredded
2	cloves garlic, sliced thin
5	scallions, chopped in ½-inch segments
1 cup	dried red chilies, scissored in half
salt to taste	

If you want to do it Chef Xu's way, chop each wing into thirds. My easy way: leave the wings whole. Marinate wings in rice wine, light and dark soy, and white pepper for 30 minutes.

In a shallow bowl, mix egg whites and cornstarch until smooth. Fill a wok ⅓ full of canola oil. Heat until oil shimmers. Dip wings into egg-white mixture, then deep-fry wings, adjusting heat higher if it doesn't sizzle. Remove using a spider and drain on paper towels. Let hot oil cool 10 minutes then carefully pour out all but about 2 tbsp. (Save or discard the frying oil – it's up to you.)

In the same wok, reheat remaining oil over high heat and stir-fry ginger, garlic, scallions, salt, and chilies for 1 minute. Add the fried wings, and stir-fry until they're hot again. Serve immediately.

CHAPTER THIRTY-FIVE

Farewell

After Shanghai, Sam and I took a few days off before heading north to Beijing to find him a place to continue his Mandarin studies. Ever since the Battle of Bologna, I was wary about how we decompressed during sudden down time. Another problem—we had accumulated too much stuff.

"Why are you carrying it all?" Hilly laughed. "You can courier it to Beijing. It's very cheap. They come right to the house. They'll even pack it for you."

One hour after she phoned the courier company, a scrawny, hyperactive migrant worker was at the door. I had piled our gifts, including Anthea's cast-offs, on the floor. The courier whipped out a bag made from recycled plastic threads, stuffed our goods inside, and taped it snugly closed. Next-day delivery for door-to-door air freight cost less than a Starbucks grande latte—including the free bag, packing help, and complimentary duct tape.

I now understood why, seemingly overnight, brick-and-mortar stores in China had become ghost towns. With delivery so cheap, online sales were soaring. Sales for Alibaba Group, the world's most popular online shopping site, exceeded those of eBay and Amazon.com combined. Alibaba's founder, Jack Ma, a former English teacher, was China's richest man, with a net worth of $34 billion. Inside Hilly's compound, couriers on electric scooters zoomed around the footpaths with towers of boxes stacked behind them. When we were at Anthea's penthouse, an online shipment of four big cartons arrived filled with paper towels, dish detergent, laundry soap, plastic wrap, baggies, garbage bags, tissues, toothpaste, dried noodles, soy sauce, and dark vinegar. She had also ordered furniture online, including her daughter's brass bed and the big glass Lazy Susan on her marble table. Hilly bought her clothes and shoes online, and Peony shopped for kitchen gadgets.

Because we were leaving very early the next morning, Hilly again booked her favourite taxi driver. *Guanxi* would ensure he delivered us safely to the airport instead of, I suppose, kidnapping us. That morning, Sam and I jumped into the waiting taxi at the foot of Hilly's building. We were halfway to the airport when I got a frantic call from her.

"Where are you?" she screamed.

"In the taxi, on the way to the airport," I said.

"You're in the *wrong* taxi. Turn around right away. *My* taxi driver is waiting for you."

Sam and I had gotten into a taxi meant for another woman, who was also going to the airport. She and Hilly's favourite taxi driver were both waiting impatiently outside Hilly's building. Everyone was angry, including the driver of the taxi we were in.

"You have to pay me for wasted gas," he yelled. "If you don't, I'm going to dump you on the highway right now."

I handed over fifty yuan. He screeched into Hilly's compound, the other woman jumped in, and we threw our suitcases into the other cab and went back the way we came. We had just wasted forty minutes and were in serious jeopardy of missing our non-refundable flight.

Hilly's taxi driver drove as fast as he dared. He glanced at me in his rear-view mirror. "Why didn't you just continue to the airport?" he said. "I could have driven the other woman."

I looked at Sam. *Guanxi*.

We did catch our plane — after a breathless foot race through Pudong International Airport, so sprawling it processed double the entire population of Canada through its terminals every year. Three hours later, we were in Guilin, in southwest China.

"Hey, Mom," he said, when we had a chance to regroup, "you know I've learned more on this trip than a whole year at university." Kids usually don't bother to tell you things like that. I thought of all the things I hadn't told my own parents. And now they were gone.

We were in good spirits, even though we were sharing a room. I woke up early. Sam stayed up late. One night, the glare from his laptop screen kept me awake. He was watching cooking videos on YouTube.

"Sam, it's twelve thirty," I said. "We've got to go to bed."

"Okay, I just want to learn how to make octopus." Our relationship had changed. I was no longer telling him what to do. Well, not *all* the time.

We hoped to take a raft from a nearby village down the Li River to view the otherworldly limestone karst mountains. But how to find the village with the rafts? The easiest way was by booking a tour. The next morning, as our sightseeing bus headed through the countryside, the guide suddenly announced an unscheduled and unwelcome stop at a jade factory. We were herded, along with the other tourists, all local Chinese, into a meeting room. A shy young woman in a cheap polyester uniform recited a speech by rote: *the factory was marvellous; the jade deals were amazing.* Next, we endured a ten-minute promotional video. Then another young woman breathlessly announced that the general manager himself would grace us with his presence. The manager wanted to inspect the quality of work of the first young woman, who apparently was on probation. Now *that* was interesting (at least, more interesting than the video).

The new hire begged us to help her out so she wouldn't lose her job. Then the general manager strode in. He dressed like a Chinese Elvis, with a velvet maroon blazer printed with a pattern of golden Chinese palaces which impressively matched the print of his maroon silk shirt. His Hermès belt buckle was an unsubtle four-inch-high *H.* I couldn't tell if it was a knock-off, but his necklace appeared to be solid gold beads the size of pearl onions.

Introducing himself as General Manager Li, he said he would conduct a quality-control survey by voice vote. The young recruit stood beside him, looking frightened and unhappy. Trying to be supportive, our tour group shouted affirmatively to every question.

"Did she smile enough?" *Yes!*

"Did she display the video correctly?" *Yes!*

"Were her facts all correct?" *Yes!*

We figured the young woman had the job in the bag. But General Manager Li wasn't finished. He launched into a long, rambling speech about himself—his career, his vast experience, his time in the south. He then began describing the fabulous jade items for sale. His voice rose until he was almost shouting, an oratorical climax that was apparently our cue to break into enthusiastic applause.

I'd had enough. We'd been in the meeting room for half an hour. I wanted to get to those bamboo rafts. Ostentatiously I raised my wrist, tapped my watch face, and glared at General Manager Li.

"What's your problem?" he demanded, rounding on me.

I gulped. I hadn't expected to be singled out. "We're here to sightsee, not shop," I managed to say.

"No one is forcing you to stay!" General Manager Li shouted. Livid, he stalked over to the door, opened it, and closed it again. "See?" he said sarcastically. "The door is not locked!"

"Okay!" my son said, very loudly. "Let's go."

We stood up to leave. To my surprise, the entire busload of Chinese tourists rose in unison and followed us out. No one bought a single piece of jade. Everyone grinned at me. Several gave me a thumbs-up. One young woman grabbed my arm to congratulate me. I felt like Norma Rae. The best part was that Sam had supported me instead of cringing in embarrassment. It was nice to have an ally. My son had courage. No matter what life threw his way, I thought he would be okay. But I felt a tug of sadness, too. Sam had grown up.

After another flight, we arrived in Chengdu, foodie capital of Sichuan province. We climbed part way up Emei, one of China's four sacred Buddhist mountains. We visited a panda research station. We listened to the metallic twang of traditional ear-cleaners at work in a city park as we sipped freshly picked green tea. But our real goal in coming here was to taste Sichuan cuisine *in situ*. In its most authentic form, it should isolate three addictive sensations, *ma* (麻, numbing), *la* (辣, spicy), and *tang* (烫, burning). In the 1990s, for a magazine story, I enrolled as the first student at the first post-Maoist-era cooking school in Chengdu. I learned to make authentic kung pao chicken, ma po tofu (麻婆豆腐), and *dan dan* noodles (担担面). In the dead of winter, the chef and I worked alone in an unheated amphitheatre, the kind I imagined was used in the nineteenth century to teach medical students how to dissect a corpse.

On several previous reporting trips to Sichuan, I'd found I could drop into any hole in the wall and find classic cuisine. But now it seemed that globalization had transformed Chengdu. As we roamed the downtown core, our eyes peeled for a good restaurant, we encountered burger joints, fried chicken outlets, and pizzerias but only one eatery serving Sichuan food. It was mediocre. Farther afield, we found Mongolian hotpot and Cantonese restaurants but again, no authentic Sichuan ones. In four days of hunting, we found only one that served a respectable kung pao and two others that served a decent ma po tofu, but none that could prepare both dishes properly. KFC had cannibalized Sichuan cuisine. When I last checked Trip Advisor's list of top ten restaurants in Chengdu, seven served *foreign* food: a pizzeria, a Mexican-American fish-and-chips joint, two burger outlets, an Irish pub, a sandwich shop, and a hotel sushi bar.

The week flashed by. I could see Sam getting happier and happier. I was getting sadder and sadder. "Sam, there's only ten days left," I said, with a tiny wail. He tried to look distressed but failed. Some people can't wait for their offspring to leave home. I admit to being thrilled when my boys no longer used diapers, when Norman and I no longer had to hire babysitters, when we could go out without a stroller, toys, and emergency juice boxes. But now that Sam was grown up and moving on with his life, I wanted to slow time down. On the other side of the world, Ben had become a vegetarian-almost-vegan (even though he confessed to me he still liked the taste of meat). As an omnivorous mother, it seemed like another step in the inevitable separation process. As for Sam, soon we would no longer eat every meal together, sit side by side on a bus or plane, or share a room. That was how it should be, but it didn't mean I had to like it. I felt lost in a fog of separation anxiety.

At least I had had this journey with him.

Peking University was the most prestigious university in China. However, I didn't want Sam to study at my alma mater, or even in Beijing. The Chinese capital had too many foreigners, too many bars, too much pollution. The nearby city of Tianjin was thirty-three minutes away by bullet train. Like every major Chinese city, it was polluted, but at least it was on the coast. And I liked Tianjiners, who were known throughout China as stolid, honest types. My aunt, the one who had made me spring rolls during the Cultural Revolution, was now in her nineties, but she still lived there with her adult children. Sam would know someone in case of an emergency.

What's more, Ben Mok, a McGill classmate of mine living in Beijing, had run the Tianjin office of a major multinational corporation for years and had deep *guanxi* in the city. His company once donated scholarships to Tianjin's acclaimed Nankai University, and Ben now agreed to help me arrange for Sam to study there. That same *guanxi* required that Ben personally take us to Nankai. One day after we arrived in Beijing, we headed to Tianjin in his chauffeur-driven Mercedes-Benz SUV.

Guanxi also prescribed that the former president of Nankai University, a distinguished-looking white-haired scholar in his seventies, greet us on the front steps outside the administration building. Over steaming cups of jasmine tea, the former president asked Sam when he wanted to start. "Right now?" Sam asked. The spring term was already in full swing, but thanks to *guanxi*, that would not be a problem. A senior university administrator showed us around a dormitory. Again thanks to *guanxi*, a room was available that very minute. Then the former president and his wife invited us to a twelve-course banquet in a private reception room.

"She's even more powerful than her husband," Ben whispered to me. "She's a big shot in the Ministry of Education."

In China, debts were repaid and favours incurred, always over a meal. The former president asked Sam for his cellphone number so they could stay in touch. When Sam pulled out his crappy old phone, the official's wife said, "Would you like a brand-new iPhone? I bought it for our grandson, but he already had a cellphone."

That afternoon, I had barely glimpsed Sam's new dorm room when Ben checked his watch. "We have to go!" he said. "Now!" It was after four p.m. I didn't know that traffic restrictions on his Beijing licence plates meant that we had to clear Tianjin's city limits by five. Otherwise, we would be forced to pull over by the side of the expressway until seven p.m.

But I hadn't yet inspected the showers. I hadn't thumped Sam's mattress. I hadn't even seen the cafeteria where he would eat his meals. I needed more *time*. I'd known for weeks that this day was coming. But splitting up like this, with Ben hustling me into his car, felt like ripping a Band-Aid off a wound. Or snipping the apron strings.

I gave Sam a long, long hug. He tried to look sad, but he couldn't hide his excitement at, well, finally getting rid of his mom. I had a sudden flashback to my boys' first days at junior kindergarten. His older brother, Ben, had clung to my ankles and sobbed his heart out. Sam had trotted off, without a backward glance.

This time, Sam, obeying the rules of Chinese etiquette, politely followed us outside the building to formally see us off. He did not object when I hugged him again. For one last time, I recreated the Chinese character 好 for "good"—a woman 女 nuzzling a son 子.

My son stood in front of his dormitory building. As our car pulled away, he waved, a little ironic flick of the wrist. And he smiled.

Bye, Sam.

Afterword

François made it safely to Iraqi Kurdistan and back.

After I returned to Canada, I contacted the public relations agent representing the star of *Heartland*, who kindly sent Pierre-Marie some autographed photos of his favourite actress. Four months later, Marie-Catherine emailed to say that Pierre-Marie had consented to a fifteen-day tryout at Le Béal. He took the *Heartland* photos with him, calling it the best present he had ever received, and left home in high spirits. The stint went well, but he remained unenthusiastic about moving there permanently.

Philomène learned to make pizza at her special-needs school and brought a sample home for her parents to taste. She proposed opening a pizzeria in Allex with Sam.

Davit had gone to Paris to present his file to the French Office for the Protection of Refugees and the Stateless People.

With Marie-Catherine's help, Pierre-Marie managed to track down his birth mother. "Part of your dream has come true! I am your biological mother," she wrote back, adding that she was still together with his biological father, and that they had had a daughter. Then she rejected him for the second time. "The solution for us was to turn the page.... We have decided not to meet you again."

Six months after we left Allex, Mamie died in her sleep at home in the farmhouse.

In Italy, two men in suits talked their way into the house when Nonno was home alone. They managed to steal several hundred euros. Luckily Nonno was unhurt. The Multipla was still chugging along, although it, too, had suffered the indignity of a break-in.

In Shanghai, Hilly and her family moved into a six-bedroom penthouse apartment in the same compound as Anthea. The new chauffeur drove Dickie one block to school. The family also acquired a dog, which Peace looked after whenever they went on vacation.

After seven months of study in Tianjin, Sam passed the second-highest level of national Mandarin exams. His goal was to pass the highest level, learn how to barbeque lamb in Mongolia, and then find a job cooking in Beijing.

Back in Toronto, Norman and I installed security cameras on the advice of police. After we suffered a third vandalism attack—white paint splashed on the front door and the family van—my brother was arrested based on the video footage, and ordered to stay away from me, pay reparations, submit to anger-management counselling, and perform community service.

Acknowledgements

I'm one of those reporters who walk around with a pen and notebook in hand. So I must thank above all the people who unreservedly opened their homes and hearts to me. In France: Marie-Catherine Jeanselme, François Jeanselme, and their children Pierre-Marie and Philomène; Bernadette Seguin; Davit and Rüska; Odette Cleysac; and Dominique Grimaud. In Italy: Maria Rosa Beccaris, Fiorenzo Cavagnino, and their daughter, Chiara; Nonno and Papa Franco; Mirella and Beppe Massasso, their son Alessandro, and her mother, Luigina; Federica Battilla and Luigi Campini, and her mother, Maria; Antonella Bossotto, Gigi Epifani, and their son, Matteo; Maria Stella Puddu, her husband Bruno, their daughter Cristina, their son, Matteo, his partner, Giulia, and *her* parents, Maria Lucia and Beppe. In China: Hilly, Allan and Dickie, and their maid, Peace; Anthea and her maid, Orchid; Peony, Paul, and their maid, Little Chen; and Plum and Building-the-Army and their maid, Little Wang.

I'm grateful to my son, Ben, who introduced me to the Jeanselmes; to Ashley Prime and Silvia Ardizzone, who introduced me to Maria Rosa; and to Hilly, who introduced me to her *tai-tai* friends. I would like to thank St. Thomas University for a research grant and Dr. Michael Dawson, Associate Vice-President, Research, for his advice and support.

Thanks are due to my long-time agent, John Pearce, and to Karen Pinchin, the acquisitions editor at Goose Lane Editions. At Goose Lane, thank you also to Susanne Alexander, Kathleen Peacock, and Martin Ainsley. Thank you especially to Jill Ainsley (yes, she's related to Martin), who did a masterful job of editing the manuscript. Jess Shulman (no, she's not related to Norman — see below) copy-edited the book with rigour and sensitivity and saved me from an astounding number of errors. Paula Sarson expertly proofread the book and caught — and fixed — more mistakes. Julie Scriver and Jaye Haworth designed the evocative cover. Angela Williams wrestled the index into submission. Silvia and Maria Rosa verified the Italian words and phrases, and caught even more errors. Robert MacPherson and Fabienne Horton, both press officers at the United

Nations, scrutinized the French words and phrases. My husband, Norman Shulman, double-checked the Chinese characters and translations.

A huge thank you to Norman, who has always been supportive whenever I get crazy ideas—like taking our son to three countries and embedding with locals to learn home cooking. But the biggest thank you of all is to Sam. You took a chance on me, and said yes. While we were cooking, I often took so many notes I had no chance to stir the pot. You handled that, and all the dirty dishes. You wondered aloud at unusual techniques. You observed. You helped me fill in the gaps at night when I wearily reviewed the day's cooking. Thank you for keeping a minimalist diary to reinforce my notes. Thank you for taking endless cellphone photos, which provided a visual record that was indispensable during the writing of this book.

All mistakes are mine, not Sam's. Of course, I'm sure I'll blame him for them later.

Index

W

X

Y

Z

Jan Wong is a prize-winning journalist,
bestselling author, and professor of journalism
at St. Thomas University. A third-generation
Canadian, she is the eldest daughter of a
prominent Montreal restaurateur.